NOT AT HOME

Edited and Introduced by
Christopher Reed

NOT AT HOME

The Suppression of Domesticity in Modern Art and Architecture

With 91 illustrations

THAMES AND HUDSON

Acknowledgments

Many of the essays in this volume are expanded versions of panel presentations on the topic of "Domesticity and Modernism," delivered at the annual convention of the College Art Association in 1993. Thanks are due to this organization's staff and panel selection chairs for making this kind of collaborative project possible. A Mellon Fellowship in the Humanities from the University of Pennsylvania made possible the timely completion of this book. Sharon Haar took time from her busy schedule to provide on-going help and advice with the sections of the book dealing with architecture. The greatest debt of thanks, however, is to the contributors, whose hard work is evident in the essays, and to the families of the contributors, who facilitated that work in a thousand invisible ways. No-one has done more to teach me about the meaning(s) of home than my parents and my domestic partner, Christopher Castiglia. It is to them—along with the parents, spouses, partners, children, housemates, and other family members of all of the contributors—that this work is properly dedicated.

British Library Cataloguing-in-Publication Data
A catalogue record for this book is available from the British Library

ISBN 0–500–01692–5

Printed and bound in Slovenia by Mladinska Knjiga

Contents

Introduction

CHRISTOPHER REED

ALTHOUGH often taken for granted, the idea of domesticity is an invention of the modern age. According to the cultural historian Walter Benjamin, it was in the early 1800s that, "for the first time the living space became distinguished from the space of work."[1] If we isolate the values that comprise the notion of domesticity – separation from the work-place, privacy, comfort, focus on the family – we find that each has been identified by historians as a defining feature of the modern age. Domesticity, in sum, is a specifically modern phenomenon, a product of the confluence of capitalist economics, breakthroughs in technology, and Enlightenment notions of individuality.

When we think of modern art, however, we do not generally think of domestic imagery or objects for the home, for in the arts the linkage of domesticity and modernism has been obscured by another conceptual invention of the nineteenth century: the idea of the "avant-garde." As its military-derived name suggests, the avant-garde (literally "advance guard") imagined itself away from home, marching toward glory on the battlefields of culture.[2] While, in fact, most makers of buildings, furniture, sculpture, and paintings supplied the rapidly expanding market for domestic structures and decoration, these workers and their products did not meet avant-garde definitions of "architecture" and "art". From the Victorian drawing-room with its étagères full of trinkets to the twentieth-century tract house with its mass-produced paintings, the home has been positioned as the antipode to high art. Ultimately, in the eyes of the avant-garde, being undomestic came to serve as a guarantee of being art.

This book has a dual purpose: to analyze, in some historical detail, the antagonism of twentieth-century art and architecture toward the values associated with domesticity, and to explore alternatives to this trend. All but two of the essays appearing here were specially commissioned for this volume; each offers a detailed scholarly appraisal of some aspect of the relationship between domesticity and modernism. As a preliminary to these case studies, this introduction surveys the last century, documenting the growing divergence of domesticity and modernism, despite – or because of – their intertwined roots in turn-of-the-century culture.

The tendency for avant-garde artists and architects, along with their promoters, to assert their accomplishments through contrast with domesticity has characterized modernism at least since Charles Baudelaire's famous defense of Impressionism, "The Painter of Modern Life." Begun in 1859, this essay cast the modernist painter as a *flâneur*, "a man of the crowd," who curses the hours he must spend indoors, when he could be out recording "the landscapes of the great city."[3] It is significant that, despite the many Impressionist paintings with domestic subjects, the movement is best known for its treatment of landscapes and city scenes, supposedly rendered on the spot by artists far from home and studio. As Griselda Pollock points out in reference to the work of women Impressionists, "spaces of femininity" (which she catalogs as dining-rooms, drawing-rooms, bedrooms, balconies, terraces, and private gardens – in short, the spaces of domesticity) were made subordinate to the theaters, nightclubs, cafés, and brothels that constituted the urban pictorial realm of the male Impressionists. Pollock argues that even when men turned to domestic subjects, their images "are painted from a totally different perspective." The men, she says, present the home as spectacle to be witnessed by an audience of outsiders, rather than "with a sureness of knowledge of the daily routine and rituals" that characterizes the women for whom the domestic sphere was home-turf.[4] In this book, Susan Sidlauskas analyzes the way anxiety and alienation are staged in the composition of interiors by a number of male painters of the Impressionist era, while Linda Docherty describes the mixed success of two American Impressionists who attempted to bring together the spaces of parlor and studio.

Perhaps because most architects' careers begin with domestic commissions, modernist architects have insisted even more vehemently than modernist painters on their antipathy to the home. The historic rise and fall of domestic values is the subject of architect Witold Rybczynski's influential book, *Home: A Short History of an Idea*. He traces the phenomenon of domesticity from a faint presence in the Middle Ages, through a florescence in seventeenth-century Holland that lasted through the nineteenth century, and finally to a crisis at the dawn of the twentieth century when the "distinctly unhomey" International Style aesthetic of what critics called the "cold storage warehouse cube" came to dominate the most prestigious ranks of architecture and design.[5]

Rybczynski cites the Viennese architect Adolf Loos as a pioneer in the "process of stripping away, which is so characteristic of modern interiors." In a now-famous 1908 manifesto, Loos equated ornament with crime, arguing that the tendency to decorate manifested the same impulses as graffiti and tattooing, and that all were symptoms of degeneration, inappropriate to a forward-looking modernism. In fact, despite their stripped-down exteriors, the insides of Loos's houses were often sumptuous displays of materials and craft. Nevertheless, recent feminist analysis has assessed Loos's domestic interiors in much the same terms that Pollock used to describe interior scenes by male Impressionists. Beatriz Colomina argues that, for Loos, domesticity is not so much lived as staged. Insisting on the architect's status as an artist, Loos wrote in 1898, "The artist, the *architect*, first senses the effect that he intends to realize . . . He senses the effect that he wishes to exert upon the spectator . . ., homeyness if it is a residence." And "homeyness" was not always the drama that Loos's houses were intended to stage. His 1903 review of interior designs by a competing architect mocked their studied tastefulness by imagining them as settings for "birth and death, the screams of pain for an aborted son, the death rattle of a dying mother, the last thoughts of a young woman who wishes to die . . ." One of Loos's domestic designs was a house he proposed for Josephine Baker in Paris, in which the dancer's residence was imagined as a kind of perpetual nightclub, where visitors arrived under a two-story indoor pool lined with glass windows affording views of the swimmers. It was, Colomina notes, "a house that excludes family life."[6]

The anti-domestic tenor of avant-garde architectural theory is nowhere more evident than in the career of modernism's most influential architect, Charles-Edouard Jeanneret, known as Le Corbusier. As important as his buildings were his writings, which first appeared in the 1920s in *L'Esprit Nouveau* (*The New Spirit*), an avant-garde French journal of which he was an editor (and where Loos's "Ornament and Crime" appeared in translation in 1920). Anthologized in 1923 and quickly translated under the title *Towards a New Architecture*, Le Corbusier's essays made him the pre-eminent early spokesman for modernist design. In these texts, Le Corbusier inveighed against the "sentimental hysteria" surrounding the "cult of the house," and proclaimed his determination to create instead, "a machine for living in." His heroes were engineers, "healthy and virile, active and useful, balanced and happy in their work," as well as "big business men, bankers, and merchants" who work in a world where "economic law reigns supreme, and mathematical exactness is joined to daring and imagination." His enemies were conventional architects, trained in schools like "hot-houses where blue hortensias and green chrysanthemums are forced, and where unclean orchids are cultivated." According to Le Corbusier, the old-fashioned houses produced by such architects "ruin our health and our *morale*," threatening the heroism of their male inhabitants:

> One can see these same business men, bankers and merchants away from their businesses in their own homes, where everything seems to contradict their real existence – rooms too small, a conglomeration of useless and disparate objects, and a sickening spirit reigning over so many shams . . . and absurd bric-à-brac. Our industrial friends seem sheepish and shrivelled like tigers in a cage . . . We claim in the name of the steamship, of the airplane, and of the motor-car, the right to health, logic, daring, harmony, perfection.

Le Corbusier's own architectural style – industrial elements assembled with a mathematical precision drawn from Classical ideas of proportion – aimed to create a new "spirit of living in mass-production houses" appropriate to his vision of the modern age.[7]

As Benjamin points out, the steel and glass aesthetic he identified with Loos and Le Corbusier stakes its claim to modernity on its antagonism to the conventional function of the home as a refuge of privacy and an assertion of individual – or family – identity. Contrasting to the modernist "glass houses" the homes of the 1880s, Benjamin notes the way the inhabitant left his trace [*Spur*] in every spot [*Fleck*] of the traditional home. The German nouns here evoke physical tracks or stains, an implication that jars purposefully with Benjamin's catalog of the middle-class furnishings that exemplify his thesis: "the knick-knacks on the shelves, the antimacassars on the armchairs, the filmy curtains at the windows, the screen before the fireplace." These things, he says, are so intimately identified with the bourgeois house dweller that the breakage of any household furnishing could occasion highly theatrical tantrums, "the reaction," he said, "of someone who felt 'the trace of his earthly days' being obscured." Benjamin's blurring of the boundaries between the house and its inhabitant echoes the strategies of the Surrealists, who at mid-century countered modernism's rationalistic faith in reason and technology with their vision of the uncanny, in German the *unheimlich* or, literally, the unhomey. (This notion of the house as a space physically embodied is explored in this book in essays by Susan Sidlauskas and Anthony Vidler.) The Surrealist vision of the house made "unhomey" by a superabundance of connotations contrasts sharply with what Benjamin identifies as the ethos of modernist design. "Glass is such a hard and flat material that nothing settles on it . . . It is above all the enemy of secrets. It is the enemy of possessions," Benjamin says. The accomplishment of the new glass and steel rooms, then, is that, "it is difficult to leave a trace."[8]

The writings of Loos, Le Corbusier, and Benjamin may seem melodramatic in their vision of modernist architecture transcendent over conventional forms of domestic design characterized by degeneration, dirt, and disease. Such ideas were, nevertheless, highly influential in avant-garde thinking. When modernist architecture was presented to the American public by the Museum of Modern Art, the catalog followed Loos in describing "the avoidance of applied decoration" as one of the newly christened International Style's three basic principles. The domestic applications of the new style were reserved for a final chapter in the MoMA catalog, which cited two obstacles to be overcome: "local traditions" of domestic life, which are "in America . . . further complicated by an excessive sentimentality about the 'homes' of the past."[9] Underlying such statements are the avant-garde imperatives to be both elite and progressive. The domestic realm, seen as simultaneously popular and old-fashioned, became a perfect foil for architects aspiring to avant-garde status.

The same tendencies characterized the promotion of modernist painting in the first decades of this century. The introduction to a pioneering multi-volume study of the development of modern art by the German critic Julius Meier-Graefe in 1904 attributed the "retrogression" of popular painting to a decline in church patronage and a concomitant rise in art made for houses, where the chief criterion of value is "comfort". "In these days, the pure work of art has been brought into immediate contact with everyday life; an attempt has been made . . . to make it the medium of the aesthetic inspiration of the house," Meier-Graefe complained:

> Art under such conditions ceases to be divine; she is no longer the enchantress . . . but rather a gentle little housewife, who surrounds us with tender attentions, and eagerly produces the sort of things that will distract tired people after a day's work.[10]

Ten years later in 1914, Wyndham Lewis, the leader of London's Futurist-derived Vorticist movement, echoed Meier-Graefe as he anticipated Le Corbusier in his description of the "modern city man," who "in his office . . . is probably a very fine fellow – very alert, combative, and capable of straight, hard thinking," but in his "villa in the suburbs" is reduced to "an invalid bag of mediocre nerves, a silly child." Promoting his hard-edged abstract pictures, Lewis insisted, "The best type of artist would rather give expression to the more energetic part of that City man's life – do pictures to put in his office, where he is most alive – than manufacture sentimental and lazy images . . . for his wretched vegetable home existence."[11]

Given the anti-domestic attitudes of European modernists, it is somewhat ironic that after World War II, when a new generation of American modernists sought to distinguish itself from their forefathers, what they condemned was the domesticity of modern European art. The Abstract Expressionist painter Robert Motherwell, citing the vast size of his canvases, proclaimed, "The large format, at one blow, destroyed the century-long tendency of the French to domesticize modern painting, to make it intimate." His contemporaries, Adolph Gottlieb and Mark Rothko, announced to the *New York Times* that their art "must insult anyone who is spiritually attuned to interior decoration; pictures for the home; pictures for over the mantel."[12]

So common was this kind of rhetoric that by 1957 Clement Greenberg could describe "decoration" as "the specter that haunts modernist painting." This idea of a ghost from the past, repeatedly repressed but returning, offers a striking image of modernism's relation to the decorative and the domestic – related terms that, as in Gottlieb and Rothko's manifesto, were merged in avant-garde indictments. The spectral power of the decorative derived from its importance in modernism's founding years. The anti-domestic rhetoric of someone like Baudelaire, for example, was countered at the time by critics who identified modernism with the decorative and the look of the bourgeois home. Gauguin's painting, for instance, was celebrated by the avant-garde French painter and critic, Maurice Denis, for its "decorative deformations," which shocked audiences trained in the minute realism of academic art. Like Loos, who was his contemporary, Denis associated decoration with primitive impulses, but he praised Gauguin's self-conscious return to "the first principles that he called *the eternal laws of beauty*." Promoting Gauguin, he asserted:

> Here we are dealing with a decorator . . .! The man who decorated the living room of the inn [he stayed in] as well as his gourd and clogs! The man who, in Tahiti, in spite of worries, illness and poverty, cared about nothing so much as the decoration of his hut.[13]

Turning to the next generation of modernists, Joyce Robinson's article in this volume examines the impact of ideas about decoration and design on the early career of Henri Matisse.

Even more than in France, Anglo-American modernism found its roots inextricably entwined in notions of the decorative, which were central to both Aestheticism and the Arts and Crafts Movement, the twin strands of the anglophone avant-garde in the Victorian era. Both movements focused on the decorative arts, making the look of daily life their central concern. In John Ruskin's influential essays, readers were exhorted to "look around this English room of yours, about which you have been proud so often . . . Examine again all those accurate mouldings, and perfect polishings, and unerring adjustments of the seasoned wood and tempered steel." Denouncing the mind-numbing labor behind such productions, Ruskin reproved his audience, saying, "these perfectnesses are signs of a slavery in our England a thousand times more bitter and more degrading than that of the scourged African, or helot Greek." Just as, for Ruskin, the look of the home was a vital index of the moral health of the nation, so too a reassertion of domestic values was the road to reform. He argued that virtue lay "not [in] Rationalism and commercial competition," but in "household wisdom" and "the incidents of gentle actual life," which he saw enacted in "primitive" Italian painters such as Giotto. "If we do our duty," Ruskin exhorted his readers, we can "enter upon a period of our world's history in which domestic life aided by the arts of peace will slowly, but at last entirely, supersede public life and the arts of war."[14]

Ruskin's vision was profoundly influential. His example was invoked and his words were echoed by Aesthetes and Arts and Crafts activists alike. In the lectures he gave across America, Oscar Wilde cited his tutelage with Ruskin, and he described his Aesthetic ideal with the Ruskinian phrase,

"We want to see that you have nothing in your houses that has not been a joy to the man who made it, and is not a joy to those that use it."[15] More than anyone else, however, it was William Morris, the pre-eminent Arts and Crafts entrepreneur, who embodied the domestic focus of English modernism. Abandoning a brief career as a painter, he founded the enormously influential guild that made simplified quasi-medieval furnishings and fabrics staples of "artistic" home design by the turn of the century. At the same time, Morris's prolific writings kept Ruskin's domestic model of social reform constantly in the public eye: "My extravagant hope is that people will some day learn something of art, and so long for more, and will find, as I have, that there is no getting it save by the general acknowledgement of the right of every man to have fit work to do in a beautiful home," Morris said.[16] This was the essence of the Arts and Crafts ideal, which made the home, and the arts associated with domesticity, a primary arena of engagement.

Writings by Ruskin, Wilde, Morris, and their followers – along with illustrations of architecture and design animated by their principles – flooded art magazines and interior design journals around the world, offering a model of aesthetic and social reform based on domestic principles to a wide public increasingly troubled by the consequences of the Industrial Revolution. In this book, Michelle Facos's essay on Carl Larsson's Villa Hyttnäs bears witness to a primary Swedish manifestation of this domestic impulse within modernism, while my essay on the Bloomsbury group examines its lingering legacy in England. In France and Belgium, the movement known as Art Nouveau was grounded on the theories of Ruskin and Morris. In Germany and Austria, associations of modernist painters and sculptors devoted themselves to design and the decorative arts, promoting the ideal interior as a *Gesamtkunstwerk*, or "total work of art," where a single aesthetic consciousness determined the look of everything from the paintings on the wall to the clothes worn by the inhabitants.[17]

The influence of English modernism was, perhaps, most deeply marked in the USA, where it merged with an indigenous philosophical tradition that celebrated the home and its arts. In the 1850s Ralph Waldo Emerson and Henry David Thoreau, like their English counterparts, advocated social reforms indexed and inspired by an ideal of wholesome domesticity. "One of the most beautiful buildings in this country is a logger's hut in the woods," wrote Thoreau, "and equally beautiful will be the citizen's suburban box, when the life of the indweller shall be as simple and as agreeable to the imagination." And Emerson, claiming to discover in the artistic masterpieces of Europe the same "familiar and sincere" virtues he had left at home, concluded, "I now require this of all pictures, that they domesticate me, not that they dazzle me." In this book, Michael Clapper's essay on Victorian chromolithographs attests to the importance Victorian America put on the home as a repository of moral values. By the turn of the century, across North America, workshops for the production of handmade (or handmade-looking) "art" furniture and pottery were supplying an enormous market for domestic goods, based on European models, but responding to such indigenous ideals.[18]

Despite – or, again, because of – its ubiquity, this early trend toward a highly domestic modernism was not sustained as a viable avant-garde strategy long into the twentieth century, however. Where the avant-garde defined itself as an elite, at once aggressive and progressive, versions of modernism founded in the home were quickly popularized and feminized, and the Arts and Crafts nostalgia for medieval simplicity came to seem simply old-fashioned in contrast to the extravagant primitivism of a Gauguin or a Picasso. The feminist art historian Norma Broude has documented this shift in the career of the German painter Wassily Kandinsky, who abandoned his early work in Munich craft guilds for a rigorous focus on abstract painting.[19] Jenny Anger's essay in this volume analyzes a parallel shift in a turn-of-the-century German critic's abandonment of a decorative ideal of modernism that came to seem tainted with connotations of women's work and popular success.

Perhaps the most dramatic renunciation of early modernism's domestic roots came in the episode described in this book in David Van Zanten's essay on Frank Lloyd Wright. Wright's anguish over the competing claims of his domestically focused Arts and Crafts practice and the anti-domestic imperatives of high modernism make his biography an index to the era. After his abandonment of his studio, school, and family in 1909, Wright for the remainder of his long life felt the need to counterbalance his domestic designs with both a torrent of theoretical writings on technology and a series of high-tech designs such as the Price Tower in Oklahoma and the Guggenheim Museum in New York, both of which have been likened to spaceships.[20] Wright's career, in this context, can be seen as the constant struggle of an ambitious and talented modernist against the label of the "merely" domestic.

The kind of revisions Wright made in his own career, art historians and critics have imposed on other early modernists tainted with the stigma of domestic accomplishment. Ruskin and Morris's shared abhorrence of machine-made ornament has been translated by historians into a Loos-like rejection of all decoration, in an effort to position them as the progenitors of a modernist architecture they would have despised.[21] Similarly, Matisse's decorative works were severed from his career as a painter by critics like Clement Greenberg, who attempted to prove "[h]ow little a decorator Matisse is by instinct":

> His paper cut-outs, his ventures into applied art, and most of what I have seen

> of his tapestry designs, book decorations, and even murals seem to me the feeblest of the things he has done. He is an easel painter from first to last.[22]

For Greenberg, and his contemporary Harold Rosenberg, the domestic was the antithesis of art. One of Greenberg's best-known essays defines the avant-garde through its opposition to "kitsch," a term identified with the knick-knacks of the middle class home, and defined explicitly by Greenberg to include "popular, commercial art" and "chromeotypes." Imputations of domesticity could be inherently damning, as when Greenberg attributed to some of Motherwell's paintings an "archness like that of the interior decorator who stakes everything on a happy placing," or when he dismissed de Chirico's late work with the phrase, "It was not even easel painting; it was elementary interior decoration." In an important theoretical statement, which he titled "The Crisis of the Easel Picture," Greenberg cited the "fatal" influence of "all-over" abstract art, which, because "it comes very close to decoration – to the kind seen in wallpaper patterns that can be repeated indefinitely," now "infects" painting as a whole. For Greenberg, the only value of decoration was to destroy itself by becoming "vehement," "turbid," and "violent". Part of the "mission" of modernist painting, he said, was "to find ways of using the decorative against itself." Likewise, Rosenberg in a well-known essay argued that abstract "action paintings" became simply "apocalyptic wall paper" if, in his words, artists shirked "the Open Road of risk that leads to the farther side of the object and the outer spaces of the consciousness."[23]

If Rosenberg's rhetoric evokes, as he intended it to, the extravagant impulses of Walt Whitman, it also looks forward from Whitman to the wanderings of Jack Kerouac in *On the Road*, and, of course, it harkens back to a topos, current at least since Odysseus, in which the domestic figures as the opposite of the heroic. In this view, home is a place you leave behind at the start of something significant – hence Greenberg's anxiety to claim about the sedentary Cézanne, his "was a more heroic artist's life than Gauguin's or Van Gogh's, for all its material ease."[24] This has been the standard of modern art: a heroic odyssey on the high seas of consciousness, with no time to spare for the mundane details of home life and housekeeping.

This book brings modernism's domestic "specter" into focus. It is a project justified by both psychoanalytic and linguistic theories, which emphasize the conceptual importance of what is apparently "othered": the repressed always returns, and definitions of necessity perpetuate both terms of the difference that creates meaning (the meaning of "up," for example, relies on its opposite to be understood as "not down"). Michel Foucault has explicated the historical implications of this apparent paradox, in which power depends on its "points of resistance," which "play the role of adversary, target, support, or handle in power relationships."[25] What Foucault found to be true for the histories of sexuality, criminality, and sanity, is exemplified as well in the history of modernist art, architecture, and design. The domestic, perpetually invoked in order to be denied, remains throughout the course of modernism a crucial site of anxiety and subversion.

For all the authors, issues of sex (in its broadest sense) are central, for it is primarily in the home that we are constructed as sexual and gendered beings. If the domestic is the main arena for the enforcement of conventional divisions of masculinity and femininity (along with their complement, heterosexuality), however, the modern home has also been a staging ground for rebellion against these norms. This complexity structures many of the essays in this volume, which detail the way attachment to the domestic realm has offered particular artists or groups the potential to evade aesthetic and social conventions associated with high art and high culture, only to find their accomplishment recontained (in the example of the Bloomsbury group) or expanded beyond their control (as, for instance, with Paul Poiret). This dilemma was clearly most acute for women, who were associated with the domestic sphere. For the most part excluded from masculine realms of creativity, women were assigned the role of consumer, commonly as decorators of their own homes and, for the wealthy, as patrons of the arts. Essays by Lisa Tiersten and Alice Friedman explore the poles of exhilaration and frustration attending these roles in turn-of-the-century France and mid-century America.

Looking at the modern era through the lens of domesticity, however, underlines a point feminists have been making for some time now: sexuality and gender are not just women's issues. Rhetorics of masculinity and femininity work powerfully to structure the experience of both sexes, perhaps most acutely in professions associated with art and interior design, which have historically been feminized, though most of their practitioners are men. Anxieties over threatened masculinity can be detected behind the vehemence of the anti-domestic pronouncements quoted in this introduction. Linda Docherty's essay on two turn-of-the-century American painters of domestic scenes, Nancy Troy's analysis of art marketing in pre-war Paris, Jenny Anger's piece on German art theory in the same period, Cécile Whiting's chapter on the display of Pop art, and Christine Poggi's study of Vito Acconci – all describe the inherently contradictory position of men eager to exploit elements of feminine culture while anxious to preserve their masculine status. For gay men, transgressing gender boundaries through engagment with the domestic became both tantalizing and terrifying. Essays by Lisa Wainwright and Kenneth Silver explore the articulation of gay identity through domestic imagery in a range of twentieth-century art.

Today the domestic is returning to a position of cultural prominence, impelling us to look back over the mainstream of modernism in an effort to trace its domestic subcurrents. This book brings together scholars engaged in the preliminary stages of that effort. For now, it is too early to tell what the new focus on domesticity will portend for the arts, or for society at large. Anthony Vidler's "Homes for Cyborgs," in this volume, concludes with an analysis of recent work and critical theory that challenges nostalgic visions of the home by reasserting the Surrealist challenge to the boundaries between art and architecture, machine and human, house and inhabitant. In the final chapter, I collaborate with an architect to offer a broad – and broadly polemical – outline of the place(s) of domesticity in an era that calls itself postmodern. Ultimately, however, the future of domesticity will not be just the work just of professionals, be they scholars, artists, and/or designers. It will be enacted, rather, in the "off-hours" of everyone. This book, then, is dedicated to its readers in the hope that it will occasion moments of self-consciousness, creativity, and pleasure in our inevitably constant fashioning of home life.

1

The Chic Interior and the Feminine Modern: Home Decorating as High Art in Turn-of-the-Century Paris

LISA TIERSTEN

All the arts are chic . . . Don't ask me why.
Etincelle, *Carnet d'un mondain*, 1882[1]

1. Introduction: The Housewife as Modern Artist

"Nowadays everyone is more or less an artist," observed the popular writer Emile Bayard in a guide to good taste published in France in 1908.[2] In Bayard's view, and that of decorative arts reformers, fashion journalists, and advertisers of the era, the bourgeois home had become the epicenter of a new aesthetic democracy in early twentieth-century France. Home decorating, they argued, provided women both with new opportunities for artistic self-expression and a crucial role in defining a modern aesthetic for the bourgeois Republic. Portraying the housewife as a modern artist of the domestic interior, turn-of-the-century taste professionals entered into a broader debate about the nature of women's artistry, the meaning of modernism, and the gendered boundaries of bourgeois cultural authority.

The *fin-de-siècle* preoccupation with aesthetic matters emerged as the bourgeoisie lay claim to a degree of cultural authority commensurate with its already considerable economic and political power. To fashion itself as a taste elite, however, the bourgeoisie needed both to contest the aesthetic power of the aristocracy and to overcome its own traditional reputation for bad taste, an image incarnated in Molière's bourgeois gentleman. In contrast to Molière's laughable patriarch, the French housewife of the turn of the century was cast as an aesthetic arbiter, particularly within the home, and charged with the task of redeeming bourgeois taste.

Women's new aesthetic authority was also rooted in a broader transformation of their domestic role, a consequence of the gendered separation of the public and private spheres prescribed by the nineteenth-century bourgeois social order. Whereas the bourgeois home of 1850 tended to serve as a showplace of male class and occupational status, the late nineteenth-century interior emerged as a separate sphere of feminine aesthetic self-expression and identity formation. The ascription of new aesthetic expertise to women by the popular literature on decorating served to professionalize the role of housewife, helping to solidify the boundaries between private and public and to assert the particular cultural authority of the domestic realm. At the same time, the increasingly divergent worlds of bourgeois workplace and home were far from completely separate spheres, either in practice or prescription: as the decorated interior became an arena for the construction of feminine identities, it also became a forum for the articulation of bourgeois class identity. As the guardians of aesthetic value, bourgeois women were to forge a distinctively modern and middle-class taste code and, equally important, to police the cultural borders of the bourgeoisie.

While the representation of the bourgeois housewife as an artist and the elevation of the decorative arts to the stature of the fine arts was a way to challenge the aesthetic authority of the aristocracy and to consolidate a new bourgeois cultural identity, the ethos of modernism helped to articulate this new identity and, within it, a particular role for the housewife. First, modernism rejected the traditional artistic sources of history and myth, and established the everyday, including the domestic interior, as both a site of aesthetic experience and an object of aesthetic scrutiny. Second, modernism enshrined individual subjectivity. By transforming taste from a property associated with particular objects (and a particular caste) to one possessed by particular persons, modernism attributed beauty to the eye of the beholder and permitted the bourgeoise to overcome her reputation for vulgarity. In the face of the aristocratic complacency that blamed the middle-class woman – in particular, her penchant for cheap bibelots and eclectic clutter – for the erosion of French aesthetic standards, modernism offered bourgeois women both cultural legitimacy and personal aesthetic authority: an opportunity to be elegant on their own terms. Thus, the "everyone" of Bayard's comment followed from the modernist conception of art as rooted in the individual's private experience and from the related notions that every experience could be approached aesthetically, and that anyone could assume the role of artist. Finally, by characterizing the artistic process as one of sensory receptivity, modernists redefined creativity as a reactive, essentially *passive* trait. In so doing, they undermined the nineteenth-century construction of men as active creators and women as passive appreciators of art. Bourgeois decoration not only broadened the definition of the artist to include "everyone," but incorporated as core elements what were considered to be "feminine" traits: passivity, domesticity, affinity with nature, and a sensate, as opposed to strictly rational orientation.

By privatizing and feminizing art, modernists not only challenged the authority of traditional aesthetic codes, but transformed the very grammar of decorating. Just as high modernism defined itself in opposition to neoclassical art forms and to the notion of absolute beauty associated with the nobility, bourgeois wives were instructed to dismiss the advice of the traditional authorities on decorating, and to assiduously avoid the neoclassical values of symmetry and uniformity. Rather than discard the aristocratic heritage entirely, however, bourgeois women were to reinterpret the past in personal terms by pillaging, appropriating, and merging a variety of noble styles. Far from elaborating a new unitary aesthetic code, then, modernist-inspired bourgeois decoration privileged the expression of individual sensibility over conformity to a particular style. Eclecticism, or the ability to absorb and recontextualize elements of the past, stood as the signifier of individual sensibility and, at the same time, of bourgeois modernity.

2. Art and Comfort: Interior Decorating as Bourgeois Ritual

In a lecture on the history of French furniture delivered to workers of the trade in 1886, M. Fresson, a high-ranking official of the furniture-makers' syndical association, characterized home decorating as a uniquely bourgeois activity. According to Fresson, the roots of bourgeois decorating lay in economic constraints: since the middle-class housewife rarely inherited an ancestral home full of heirlooms, she was forced to create her milieu by artful consumption and had become devoted to the cult of the bibelot. For the taste reformer Marius Vachon, home decorating was as much a modern phenomenon as a middle-class one. He traced the emergence of smaller, use-oriented furniture in the bourgeois home to the fashion cycles characteristic of bourgeois consumerism: whereas the eighteenth-century noblewoman had stored a permanent wardrobe in magnificent, oversized chests, the nineteenth-century bourgeoise discarded her wardrobe so often that she had no use for furniture on such a monumental scale. The bourgeois housewife also preferred small, simple pieces which were easy to maintain, he argued, because so many *fin-de-siècle* bourgeois families had to manage without a maid, and because such pieces were more easily transported during their frequent moves. According to both Fresson and Vachon, the middle-class family's lack of economic and psychic investment in its possessions encouraged housewives to refurnish regularly and gave them unprecedented license for freedom of expression.[3]

In linking home decorating to bourgeois modernity, commentators signaled a broader shift in the concept of the home. The French importation of the English word "le *home*," evoking the Arts and Crafts conception of the home as a place of beauty and comfort, offered one sign of this transformation. In contrast to the noble conception of the home as a public theater for the display of the family's caste status, bourgeois housewives were taught to consider home decorating as a mode of personal expression and a means of creating an aesthetically-pleasing, but also a comfortable

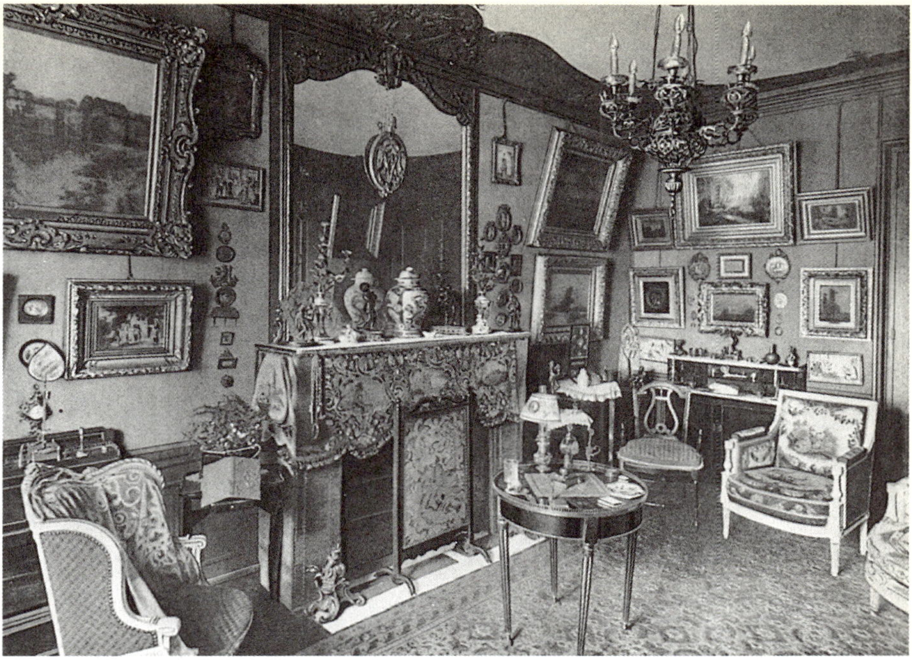

1 *Anon,* Petit Salon de Madame B., *1903*

and intimate space for the family's domestic life. The public character of the aristocratic *hôtel* had demanded the skills of the professional decorator; but as the private arena of family life, the bourgeois home could *only* be properly decorated by the lady of the house. Thus the decorating handbook author Henri de Noussane insisted on the private and individualized nature of bourgeois decor, in contrast to that of the aristocrat: "An apartment must bear the character of the people who inhabit it, it must carry their stamp. There is no other way to really be at home. To live differently, one must live . . . in an aristocratic town house."[4]

Beginning in the mid-1880s, decorating handbooks flooded the market, announcing that women who could not afford to hire professionals could now decorate their homes themselves and feel proud of, rather than embarrassed by, the "intimate look" of their salons. In fact, the stigma which had been attached to doing one's own decoration was now reversed, and women who hired professionals were portrayed in the prescriptive literature as lacking both artistic ability and domestic sentiment, while the bourgeois housewife was celebrated as an aesthetic paragon and a moral exemplar. The handbooks and women's journals contended that it was not only psychologically unhealthy to live in an environment designed by a total stranger, but that the moral sanctity of the home was compromised by the intrusion of outsiders. The modern interiors created by the bourgeois

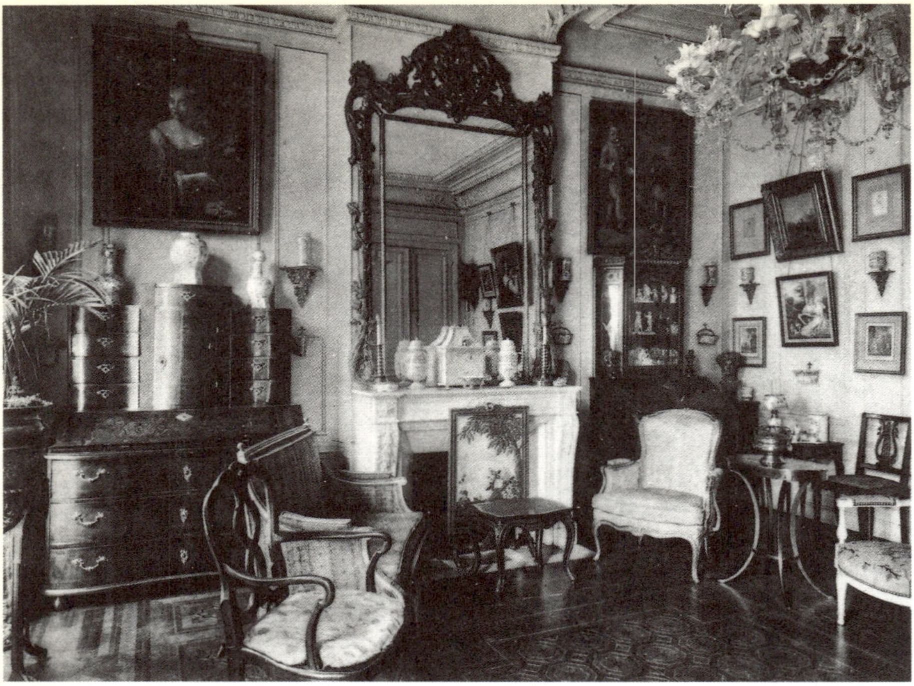

2 Le Salon. *La maison de Mlle Mimaut, 1901–10*

housewife were said to be more attractive, more intimate, more comfortable, and more economical than the sterile, overpriced designs of the professional, and she herself was enriched by the opportunities afforded her to cultivate her aesthetic sensibility and foster her originality. The popular journalist Uzanne even claimed of the chic bourgeoise that her unerring eye for simple elegance had changed the very course of modern art.[5]

Attitudes toward the bourgeois housewife's new aesthetic authority varied tremendously. For critics of bourgeois philistinism, both modernists like Baudelaire and Flaubert and antimodernists such as Maurice Barrès, the conflation of art and decorating in the women's press and advice literature of the late nineteenth century meant that, as decor was elevated, art was proportionately diminished in status. These critics objected strenuously to the cult of the bibelot as symptomatic of the middle-class debasement of art to the level of mere ornament; for them, the bibelot's vulgarity derived from a combination of shoddy craftsmanship, cloying sentiment, uninspired imitation, and, in spite of all this, the presumption of artistic value. The problem, they suggested, was less the bourgeois preference for the bibelot over the true work of art than the inability to distinguish between the two. Thus the traditionally bad taste of the bourgeoisie had become exponentially worse since the burgeoning of a consumer economy and, with it, the proliferation of tasteless objects.

By contrast, proponents of the aestheticization of the home, whether from the camp of the decorative arts movement or that of the marketplace, promoted the blurring of the borders between art and decor and the creation of a modern domestic aesthetic. The taste educator Marius Vachon told his students that taste was nothing more than "the ability to experience artistic pleasure," and referred to interior decorating as "that other form of creation." Similarly, the critic Jules Claretie likened the modern *Parisienne* to the bibelot, as opposed to the "marble statuette" evoked by other (perhaps aristocratic) genres of womanhood, and insisted that the bibelot was more beautiful than the conventional artwork. Emphasizing the democratic cachet of bourgeois chic, the journalist Etincelle compared it to a parvenu with whom the most exalted aristocrats sought to consort. Conflating taste with the individual, these metaphors – of the *Parisienne* as bibelot and of chic as the sought-after parvenu – rooted aesthetic sensibility in the unique individual, rather than in a historical lineage on the aristocratic model. In the same way, Vachon's equation of art with taste and, above all, with the *experience of pleasure*, reveals that, in the lexicon of the decorative arts, "art" and "decor" as well as "creativity" and "taste" were becoming increasingly interchangeable terms. Writers for the popular press, advertisers, and art educators and reformers welcomed the breakdown of distinctions between art object and commodity, artist and amateur, and art object and woman as signs of the explosion of art into all aspects of life, rather than the pollution of authenticity by artifice.[6]

Domestic decoration was also represented by taste reformers as a linchpin of the bourgeois Republic. Simplicity of style was considered a mark of modernity, a reaction against the baroque indulgences of the past, and an aesthetic reflection of the new self-discipline and energy of the democratic Republic. A publicity piece for the Grands Magasins Dufayel celebrated the trend toward homespun, cozy interiors not only as an aesthetic development, but as the moral triumph of bourgeois domesticity over aristocratic values:

> Life was once full of pomp, a constant parade. We were the slaves of our armchairs, our rugs, our credenzas . . . What we value today in our furniture and our bibelots is no longer absolute authenticity (which is so difficult to achieve) . . . what is important is that our guest be won over the moment he crosses the threshold of our home, that the harmony of the room pervades his spirit and makes him declare: "I feel at home here!"

Exalting hospitality and coziness over "absolute authenticity" – a codeword for the hand-crafted, expensive *objet d'art* – the advertisement suggested that tasteful consumption and decorating were a means of constructing a bourgeois style of living available to the humblest housewife. The quality of the objects themselves did not matter so much as their

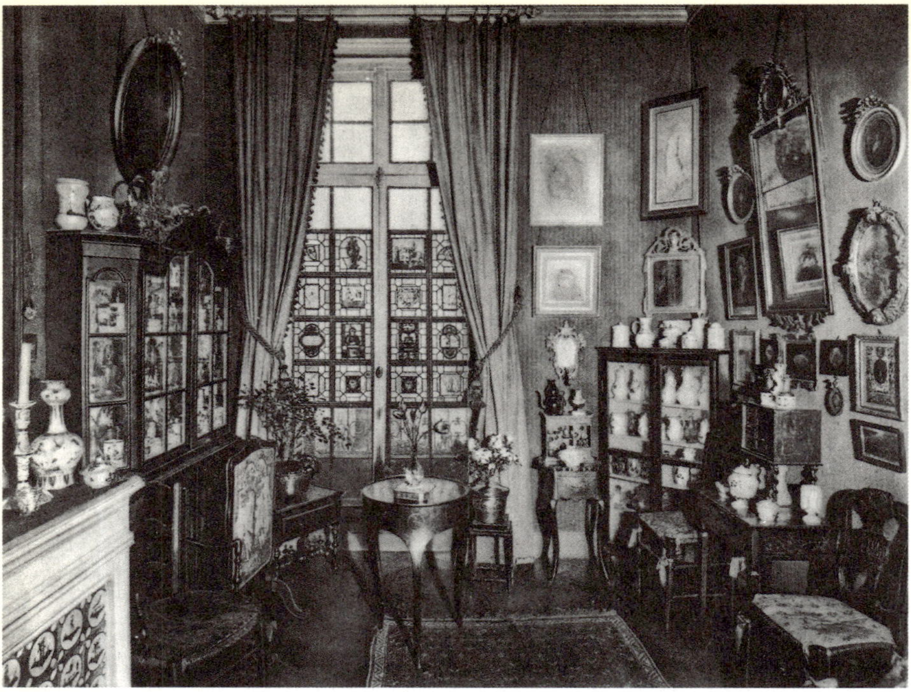

3 Le salon bleu vu de l'entrée. *La maison de Mlle Mimaut, c. 1905*

disposition and arrangement, the aesthetic composition which revealed the originality and artistic vision of the lady of the house. As the actress Marguerite Carre put it, a woman's "chic" was the unique imprint of her sensibility, the equivalent of the artist's signature.[7]

Linking aesthetic practice to female citizenship, taste experts portrayed the housewife-artist as the guardian of the nation's artistic prestige and, consequently, of a key aspect of its economic and political power. In an advertisement of 1904 for a sale on silks, the Pygmalion department store lavishly thanked its customers for their loyalty to French workers: "Ladies, we give you our deepest gratitude. It is you, sovereign *Parisiennes* . . . with your taste for beauty and refined luxury, who have combined the useful with the beautiful and performed a true act of patriotism in supporting a national industry . . ." This vision of consumer nationalism went beyond the purchase of French over German or English products, to the cultivation of a distinctly personal style: one's duty to the bourgeois Republic lay in self-expression, as if the style of the nation were the aggregate of every individual Frenchwoman's unique style. As the author of a housekeeping handbook of 1890 pointedly reminded readers: "You are too good Frenchwomen to believe that you can fulfill your duty by giving a lot of money and carte blanche to a decorator."[8]

The architects of domestic taste reform recognized, however, that bad taste still lingered in certain bourgeois milieux. The advent of mass production, it was said, encouraged an unfortunate propensity toward conformity which violated every rule of taste. Thus a furniture catalogue for the Galeries Lafayette affected outrage at the idea of women buying mass-produced furniture: it was a "monstrous crime" for Madame X, a brunette with a tragic expression, to have furniture identical to Madame Y, a tall, dreamy, indolent redhead. Even so, according to the advertising copy, a woman who would faint at the sight of someone wearing an article of clothing identical to one of her own often thought nothing of decorating her home according to a standardized design:

> What, the same armchairs for every woman? The same bibelots on the same tables? The same curtains? Rugs and wallpaper of identical color? You stop at nothing to be original in your toilette and you are right to do so; your hats are yours and yours alone . . . You can be sure that the decor you live in is every bit as important.

Similarly, Uzanne insisted that, although only a modicum of aesthetic ability and domestic feeling could transform a shabby garret into an artwork, the parvenu wife of the doctor, lawyer, or dentist too often ignored the modern decorating rules of simplicity, harmony, proportion, and individuality, and crowded her home with gaudy, interchangeable bibelots. The woman of taste, he claimed, could not tolerate opulence, particularly at the expense of self-expression:

> Excessive luxury . . . is unbearable for a sensitive soul who understands the delicacy and discretion of taste . . . such an individual will reveal her taste and yet spend hardly any money in doing so . . . it will be felt in the harmony and the balance of proportion in everything and everywhere . . . in that special sensation of a harmonious whole . . . as measured as a masterpiece.

The message was that the objects of a woman's choosing were extensions of her inner being, and that without the note of individuality, a room risked "banality." As these examples show, even in denunciations of bourgeois ostentation and vulgarity, the conflation of individuality with art was repeatedly emphasized.[9]

Individuality and modernity were to be achieved, according to the handbooks, through aesthetic eclecticism. According to the decorating expert Henri de Noussane, modern decoration was an exercise in pastiche: "The salon of the bourgeois home and apartment should be furnished in a modern style. Understand well what we mean by modern: it signifies a mélange of styles." The etiquette expert Emmeline Raymond offered the same advice as a dictum: "'the more *modern* the salon, the more that decoration which is truly modern must be kept out of it. It should contain furnish-

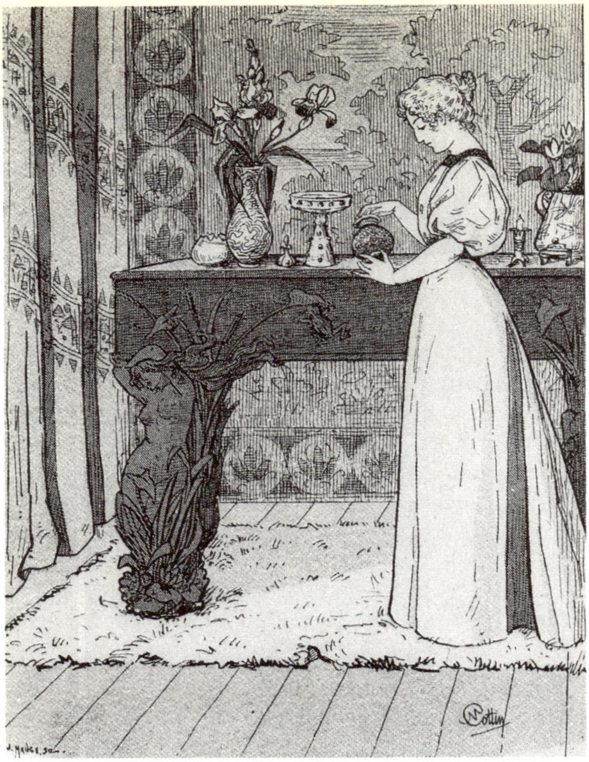

4 *M. Cottin,* Les petits riens, *in Henri de Noussane Le goût dans l'ameublement (Paris, 1896)*

ings of every possible style . . .'" The eclectic method was portrayed particularly as a way to subvert the rules of neoclassical decorating: as the editors of the decorating journal *L'Intérieur* solemnly intoned: "One may formulate this rule: there is no, and there must not be any, general, uniform, or absolute style: each interior and . . . each room must have its own style." Similarly, Etincelle celebrated the eclectic's irreverence toward the aesthetic past:

> The ancient, the exotic, the cosmopolitan make of her furniture an original and brilliant mélange, which, as the opposite of Greek tragedy, respects neither the unity of time nor place. With the taste with which she is . . . gifted, she reunites all the disparate elements in a single marvelous symphony.[10]

As an eclectic aesthetic, chic turned the standard criticism of the bourgeoise's style – that, lacking any taste of her own, she plundered the fashions of different epochs, and threw them together in outlandish or hackneyed combinations – into a prime asset. Just as the Impressionists imagined that the act of painting imposed an ordering subjectivity on the chaotic sensory barrage of urban life, the chic bourgeoise sought wholeness and harmony through a coherent eclecticism, a kind of systematic clutter. The journalist Roger-Milès described modern chic as a form of artistic appropriation, a kind of rational eclecticism based on the intelligent juxtaposition of motifs and styles of different epochs: "Eclecticism is the rule of the day, but a rational eclecticism, one which adopts only that which it understands, and which refuses to copy blindly."[11]

The rational eclecticism promoted by Roger-Milès and other advocates of chic decor refigured creativity as a kind of original imitation; thus fashion journalists and interior decorating experts alike encouraged women to borrow motifs from other periods and people, but to use these in a fresh and original way that revealed their personal sensibility. Eclecticism blended into exoticism, as the mixture of foreign motifs became as popular as historical montage. According to Etincelle, the home of the chic *Parisienne* was decorated with Japanese bibelots, Chinese fabrics, Venetian crystal, German porcelain, Spanish chests, Flemish paintings, Dutch linens, Genoan lace, and English silver. In a magazine article of 1890, Blanche de Regnault waxed enthusiastic about the popularity of *japonisme* in contemporary furnishing, offering advice on the artful disposition of fans and screens *à la japonais*. Art Nouveau, the apotheosis of chic at the turn of the century, combined gothic, Japanese, and organic motifs in a contemporary synthesis. The predilection for exotica and eclecticism in bourgeois furnishing evokes the converging influence of Japanese woodblocks, Dutch interiors, and Velázquez in Impressionist painting.[12]

Although they lavished praise on the woman of ingenuity who integrated apparently clashing items, decorating manuals and magazines warned against being arbitrarily eclectic. Since the goal was to express oneself through forms already used, one ran the risk of losing one's identity or of generating sheer chaos. Thus an object which appeared beautiful in one setting could become ugly "in bad company," as Blanche de Regnault put it. Whereas a rose in a crystal vase would do nicely next to an antique bronze, the same bronze set beside "a badly painted vase, mounted on a false bronze base" would cause her to suffer a crisis of nerves. What held true for the individual pertained to the era. In his lecture to the furniture-makers' organization, Fresson declared that the exaggerated eclecticism of the present day evoked the sensation of living amid the debris of the past, "as if the end of the world were near." Yet, he insisted, it was both possible and desirable to elevate eclecticism from this kind of chaos to an exercise in rational choice and aesthetic development by learning to successfully appropriate pieces of the past to forge a new, distinctively modern aesthetic vision. To this end, Fresson urged both artisans and consumers to seek an aesthetic education so they could emulate the successes of the past but avoid its mistakes. Just as, in Fresson's view, the artisans and industrialists of the late nineteenth century were to work toward defining the style of the epoch, so the decorating experts of the period taught the chic woman to pursue a signature style: for both producers and consumers, assimilating the aesthetic legacy of the past, as opposed to slavishly imitating it, was a recipe for being modern.[13]

3. Conclusion: The Bourgeoise as Modernist Manqué

The construction of the housewife-as-artist in the discourse on decorating may be characterized as an essentially modernist undertaking. In contrast to the traditional feminine role of refined appreciator of and midwife to the arts, the bourgeois woman of taste of the late nineteenth century was portrayed as a modern artist, herself a creator. In the modernist spirit, decorating was perceived as a form of self-expression, an exercise in the cultivation and expression of one's particular artistic individuality. Accordingly, the style and decor of a room were to aim toward the creation of an aesthetic harmony and unity out of disparate elements, rather than conformity to a set standard.

Although the Impressionist art of the 1870s was intended by its practitioners and seen by the bourgeois public to be deliberately anti-bourgeois, modernist aesthetics were gradually assimilated by bourgeois culture over the course of the next twenty years. The immense popularity of Impressionist art among the middle-class public of the 1890s, in contrast to Impressionism's negative reception by the same public twenty years earlier, is one index of the influence of modernism on bourgeois aesthetics; another is the adaptation of a modernist rhetoric of self-expression by the fashion magazines, home decorating manuals, and advertising of the late nineteenth century. By the turn of that century, the notion of an "art of everyday life" was as much a guide to chic for an emergent middle-class elite as it was a slogan of the avant-garde.

Anticipating the way Art Deco clothing of the 1920s mimicked the Cubist geometric perspective, and the advertising of the 1930s adopted Surrealist iconography, decorative arts reformers and journalists of the ladies' press of the 1890s introduced modernist aesthetic values into home decorating by establishing parity between art and decor. The numerous decorating handbooks of the period disseminated the views of these writers among bourgeois housewives, expounding rules of design which echoed the tenets of modernism: self-expression, truth to materials, harmony of color, and the construction of an aesthetic unity. Decorative arts reformers such as Vachon taught women that "a piece of furniture is just as valuable as a painting," and that the decorator's tasks of juxtaposition and arrangement were as creative as any aspect of artistic production. They instructed bourgeois women to think of decorating as a form of painting and to compose a room as they would a canvas, paying scrupulous attention to the distribution of color and light, and the organization of lines and angles.[14]

A paradigm of modernism that was feminine and domestic was thus elaborated in these handbooks. This paradigm differed in important ways from canonical modernism, but was nonetheless fundamentally related to it, in ideological and, to a lesser extent, in stylistic terms. As ethos, to be modern was to be individual. As method, the feminine modern was based primarily on techniques of imitation, appropriation, and pastiche of a variety of historical and modern stylistic motifs; yet, even in its reliance on the past, it was oriented psychically and aesthetically toward the present and future. Bourgeois historicism may be seen as a response to a sense of aesthetic weightlessness; decor played the role not so much of creating a past or emulating the culture of the aristocracy, but rather of forging a particular bourgeois aesthetic out of disparate elements. The historicism of the *fin-de-siècle* bourgeois salon commodified the past: it invoked an attitude toward history not unlike that of the consumer toward the goods in a department store, and far removed from that of the spectator toward the objects in a museum.

Art historians have tended to overlook the evidence of the feminine modern, taking modernists too much at their word by conceiving of the clinical eye of the male *flâneur* as the heart of the modernist project. In fact, the perceived polarity between masculine high modernism and feminine decorative domestic culture concealed an underlying intimacy between the two aesthetics. Although there existed no direct female analogue to the male *flâneur*, modernism did engender the creation of a feminine point of view, one which was situated in the bourgeois interior rather than in the street. This aesthetic at first competed with the dominant male forms (a conflict manifest in the opposition between modernist painting and the decorative arts movement of the 1880s and 1890s), but by the time of the post-war Art Deco movement came to complement the modernist mainstream. Conversely, the Impressionists' belief in the sensory basis of aesthetics implied that women's supposedly sensate natures were intrinsically aesthetic and imbued the domestic ideals of comfort and intimacy with aesthetic purpose and meaning. For the decorating expert Emile Cardon, for example, the aesthetic knowledge required by the painter was the same as that required of the housewife-decorator; the only difference between the two was that women who attained this knowledge came to it by instinct, and not by a rational learning process: "woman, no matter how incomplete her artistic education, has an innate feeling for artistic things, and the most fine and delicate taste; she lacks the science of art, but she guesses; she doesn't know, she feels."[15] By emphasizing the decorative, defining creativity as reactive rather than active, and aestheticizing the everyday, modernism unintentionally mobilized what were regarded as elements of feminine subjectivity.

However, early modernists themselves ardently disavowed these "feminine" elements. By maintaining a rigid distinction between high art and decorative art, between the male and female spheres of artistic practice, modernists sought to protect art from its appropriation by amateurs and – as in the case of many other male occupations – to professionalize in order to prevent the entry of women (among others) into the discipline. More importantly, the decorative art commentators and journalists who codified the feminine modern themselves drew on a number of fundamental high-modernist assumptions. Thus, even within the popular discourse of decorating, basic distinctions were implicitly preserved between the feminine modern and the high modern. Although they characterized the bourgeois woman as an artist, decorative arts reformers themselves ultimately permitted the male modernist to retain a virtual monopoly in the production of high art. Even though they celebrated the housewife, rather than the male professional, as the creator of the domestic interior, they relegated her to a lower sphere in the aesthetic hierarchy.

The confining of women to a lesser aesthetic role was accomplished in several ways. First, the power ceded women was more or less limited to the spheres of the home and of consumption. To that extent, decorative arts reformers and capitalists formed an unintended, and at times uneasy, alliance in mediating modernism to bourgeois women. Decorative arts reformers were concerned with the preservation of the crafts and with standards of decorative beauty in the age of mechanized production; capitalists wished to promote consumption by elevating it from a household routine into an artistic and personal ritual. In a sense, decorative arts reformers and journalists for the ladies' press inhabited a middle ground between the commercial marketplace and the world of high art: they accepted the machine age and the cultural power of the bourgeoisie – in short, modernity – and sought to create an aesthetic out of these building blocks. But as much as they sought to educate the housewife's aesthetic instinct toward this end, they clearly limited her purview to shopping for the home and arranging its objects.

Second, the subordination of the feminine modern was accomplished by positing a feminine intimacy with objects so great that the bourgeois woman herself became a part of the decor. The decorating guides conveyed two conflicting messages to women: that they were artists, yet that they were themselves objects of art. Decorating handbooks and magazine columns so emphasized the need for aesthetic harmony and unity between the woman and her home that the *body* of the bourgeois housewife became an integral part of the interior, a decorative object to be harmonized with the other objects of the home. "Use your rugs and curtains to dress your-

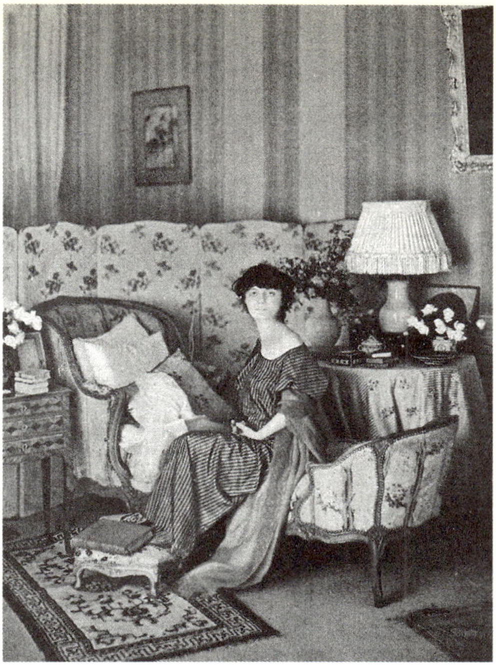

5 *Comtesse de Nouilles at Home, 1913*

self," suggested one journalist. Bourgeois wives were not to select the fabrics in vogue, but to pick those which best blended with their hair-color and skin tone; blondes were said to be best set off by rooms with accents of sea-green, sky-blue, or cherry-red, while brunettes were supposedly flattered by backgrounds of olive, gold, or deep blue. As the journalist Marcelle Tinayre put it, "Our home . . . is the extension . . . of our personality. Our furniture, our bibelots, chosen by us, reveal our secret tastes, our ideas, our conceptions of happiness and beauty. When an unknown visitor awaits us alone in our salon, he first meets our objects, the witnesses and confidants of our lives."[16]

Tinayre portrayed the bourgeois woman as a dedicated consumer who gathered objects for the purpose of her private delectation. Her remarks pointed toward a broader distinction drawn between masculine and feminine modes of display. Men were said to exhibit objects in both public and private venues for the spectatorial pleasure of others; women, by contrast, did not so much display objects as surround themselves with them. Men collected objects as evidence of their erudition and taste, or of their economic and social power, but these objects remained separate from the man himself. By contrast, the objects in a woman's home played a synecdochal rather than a symbolic role in relation to her identity; a room decorated by the bourgeois housewife was ultimately not so much her creation as an extension of her very being. In this intimate, organic relationship posited between woman and thing, women became the objects, more than the subjects, of modern art.

Finally, the domain of the feminine modern was limited to the extent that women were taught to express themselves artistically, but not that they were "original," in the way that male artists were said to be. As an eclectic style, the bourgeois decorative did in fact place new emphasis on the choice and, especially, the juxtaposition of objects, and exert new "creative" demands on the housewife. However, despite the glorification of the chic woman's creativity, the concept of originality implicit in chic was considerably more limited than that of artistic modernism. In contrast to the supposed freedom of the modernist artist, the chic woman was confined to skillful variation within a more or less rigidly-defined code, her originality measured by her talent for the composition of already existing objects and styles. Henri de Noussane hinted broadly at the distinction between feminine decoration and masculine art-making:

> I don't ask you to *create* a style. Just arrange the furniture . . . to your own taste, aided by your imagination . . . You have old furniture, some imitations of ancient pieces, some modern trinkets, a portrait by Largillière, a landscape by Corot: be inventive in the play of the rugs and wall-hangings, and in harmonizing the disparate elements to make an elegant unity. You will thus be able to add a personal note . . . to this composite mélange.

According to the journalist Louise de Salles, the bourgeois woman knew "how to be original within the limits of the permissible."[17]

Despite the rhetoric of individuality used to figure the bourgeois woman, she was construed as a talented imitator as much as an inventor, an *objet d'art* as much as an artist. Although the fashion journalists, decorating experts, and advertisers of the late nineteenth century depicted decorating as a form of self-expression, they also drew upon broad cultural assumptions about femininity which were ultimately incompatible with their conception of art; while they ceded new aesthetic power to the bourgeoise, they simultaneously undermined and restricted that power by reinscribing the feminine and decorative modern within the hierarchy elaborated by canonical modernism, promoting the aesthetic development of bourgeois women not only to help them become artists, but also to make them into good wives and smart shoppers. Like the modern artist, the chic woman's originality was said to lie in truth to a personal vision; her best means of realizing that vision, however, was to hone her skills as a consumer. For the modernist artist, on the other hand, the culture of domesticity expanded the purview of art, yielding the rich interior vision and decorative complexity of early twentieth-century painting.

2

The Chromo and the Art Museum: Popular and Elite Art Institutions in Late Nineteenth-Century America

MICHAEL CLAPPER

THE development of modernism in the late nineteenth century depended on the emergence of a distinct alternative set of artistic values and practices, a "popular" art that by opposition helped define the "elite" art of modernism. This process of classification was set in motion by social, economic, and technological changes which fall under the broad heading of industrialization. It was in response to the challenges and opportunities raised by industrialization that two new kinds of institutions appeared in the USA: the chromolithograph industry, which included not only factories but also distribution channels to thousands of middle-class homes, the main places where chromolithographs were viewed; and the metropolitan art museum. These two institutions were both concerned to maximize the benefits of machine production with an eye toward international industrial competitiveness, and to educate the aesthetic sensibility of a broad public. But despite their similar purposes, the chromolithograph industry was intimately related to the home, while art museums were public places. One of the defining attributes and virtues of the home, according to proponents of domesticity, was that it was not public and thus could remain free of the gritty material concerns and selfish ambitions that governed the realm of commerce. Viewers for chromolithographs and museum visitors occupied significantly different positions relative to the important divide between private and public.

The common concerns and the eventual divergence in the aims and practices of the chromolithograph industry and art museums reveal much about how and why various kinds of visual art became differentiated. Home and museum were ideologically-charged environments where the definition and uses of art, and especially its bearing on the social and psychological turbulences involved in industrialization, were contested and reshaped. By the early twentieth century museums had gained the power to define "high" art, and art in the home was consigned to other classifications – decoration, crafts, entertainment, kitsch, etc. – and accorded much lower status.

Antebellum Art Institutions

In the early nineteenth century, there was a permeable boundary between "popular" art and "elite" art in the USA. Cultural nationalism and the professional interests of artists fueled schemes for the encouragement of art, but broad public interest, financial means, and institutional infrastructure were lacking. Most early art institutions foundered amid unresolved questions of purpose, constituency, and means of support. Those institutions that were successful, such as the Boston Museum and Charles Willson Peale's Museum in Philadelphia, sought to appeal to a broad audience with eclectic displays that were entertaining as well as educational. Not only did these museums mix what we might call "popular" and "elite" imagery, but art, natural science, and theater mingled freely.

The most successful antebellum institution devoted specifically to the fine arts was the American Art-Union of New York. This organization collected a $5 membership fee and used the money to purchase artworks from American artists. The Art-Union gallery displayed these works free of charge, sent an engraving of one work to all members, and dispersed its collection to members by lottery once a year. At its peak in 1849 the Art-Union had 18,960 members and bought and distributed over 1000 works by American artists to private domestic spaces across the country.[1] The Art-Union was a success (until the lotteries were ruled illegal in the early 1850s) because it provided an institutional form for the widespread support and distribution of art. Uniting the cultural cachet of art with the financial self-interest of a large constituency (many of whom failed to send in their memberships until just before the annual distributions) proved indispensable to the Art-Union's success. Once the annual lotteries were proscribed, the Art-Union tried in vain to find a workable substitute, and soon afterwards collapsed.[2]

In the 1850s, with the economy booming but unstable, tension between material and aesthetic concerns became severe. The strain is clear in the leading art magazine of the time, *The Crayon*, published in New York City from 1855 to 1861. Editors W. J. Stillman and J. Durand, firm believers in the aesthetic doctrines of John Ruskin, set as their goal "the education of our countrymen to the perception and enjoyment of Beauty." They thought it fitting that the launch of their magazine coincided with an extreme downturn in the business cycles, a moment, as they put it, "when trade has shown its hollowness, and money-pride its brittleness." Stillman and Durand proposed that "Beauty is the antidote to those wearing, consuming cares of the material life."[3] Ironically this call for attention to Beauty and rejection of avarice came from the heart of a metropolis thriving on the new industrial capitalism, but then it was precisely the new and increasing stresses of modern urban commercial life that, the editors

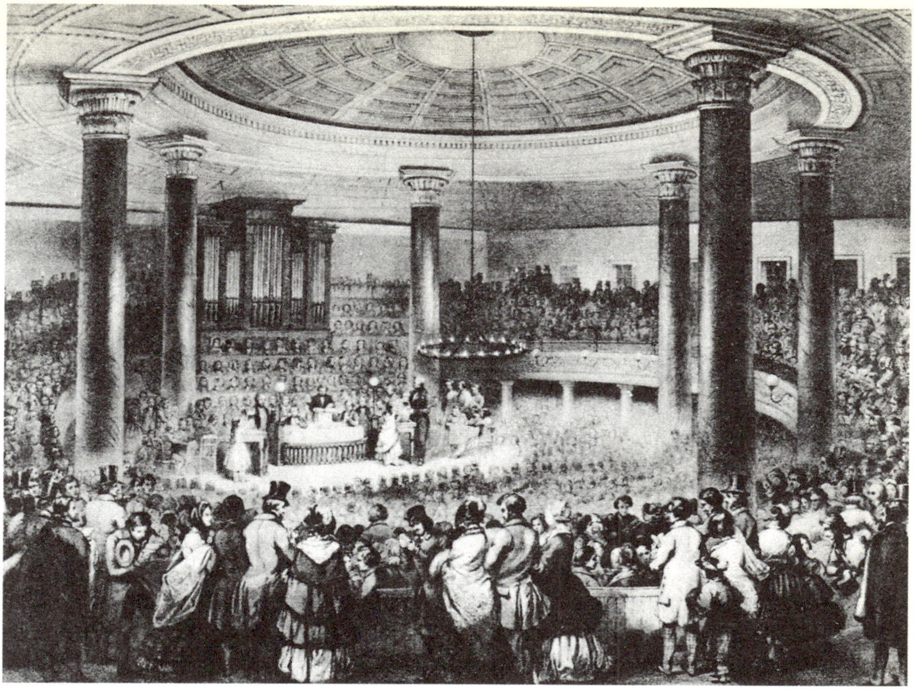

6 1847 Annual Distribution of the American Art-Union, at the Tabernacle, Broadway, New York City

argued, made the need for psychic renewal through art so urgent. Stillman himself fell victim to the exacting demands of commercial survival – by 1856 his physical health had so deteriorated that he was forced to give up his intense involvement with *The Crayon*. Durand became sole editor, and began leavening the journal with comic stories and general interest pieces in place of the serious, high-minded essays Stillman had written. The broader readership's desire for lighter fare won out over Stillman's desire to promote loftier aesthetics. Using art as an "antidote" to materialism remained an unrealized potential.

The Debate over Chromos as Domestic Art

The Civil War ended in triumph for a way of life characterized by the industrial capitalism and urban centers of the victorious North. Trends towards urbanization, corporatization, social mobility, and accumulation of wealth accelerated; the perceived need for art as a balm for the social and psychic upheavals brought on by industrialization became even greater. The problem of how art could be brought to a wide audience remained.

Two institutions arose that offered solutions: the chromolithograph industry and metropolitan art museums. Chromolithography, which had

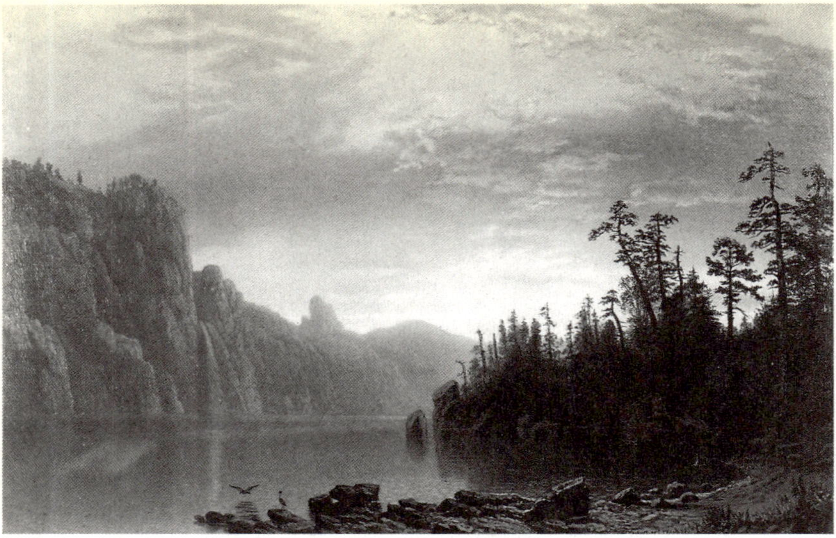

7 Sunset (California Scenery) *William Haring after Albert Bierstadt. Chromolithograph, 1868*

been a minor, underdeveloped technique used mostly for commercial printing, became in the 1870s a hugely popular medium for the manufacture of high quality reproductions of oil paintings. A single image sometimes sold thousands of copies.[4] In the same decade, the art museums in New York, Boston, and Philadelphia were founded or underwent major reconstruction and expansion.

Chromolithographs, or "chromos", became tremendously popular as art for middle-class homes, beginning in the late 1860s. Louis Prang, an innovative leader in using chromolithography to reproduce oil paintings, argued that chromos made works of art widely available, thus improving public taste, providing uplift and gratification, and promising both immediate and growing support for art. As early as 1867, *The Nation* reported of L. Prang & Co., "Hundreds, and in some cases thousands, of their chromos . . . have been sold in all parts of the United States." By 1879 a *New York Times* article titled "Art in the House" declared, "The fact is quite clear that art is not only making its mark upon the walls outside, but is getting into the house. This movement is very general . . ."[5]

As the editors of *The Crayon* had done, post-Civil War observers linked burgeoning interest in art to psychological distress brought on by modern industrial development. Regarding the causes of the need for and popularity of household art, the author of "Art in the House" suggested that:

> Sober thinking has rebelled against the dissecting-knife of science, and cried out for the artist's pencil and chisel to save nature and life from being murdered in the rage for cutting everything up.

It was not only science which was discomfiting people, according to this author, it was "the monotony of machinery and the routine of mechanism" as well, from which there was a need to be "delivered by the living hand of art."

The popularity of art in the home was part of a more general interest in personalization and sentimentalization of domestic spaces and objects, a trend in which women's decisions about their homes carried significent cultural implications. Sentimental fiction of the 1850s is the best-known manifestation.[6] For both sentimental fiction and household art, women were the main audience. In the case of art, however, women were also responsible for choosing what others would see. Homemakers looked to an aestheticized home environment to promote the emotional well-being of their families. The notion of household art as spiritual retreat from a harsh outside world is clearly at issue when the author of "Art in the House" asks, "May not art in every good house have its sanctuary, however modest, where memory shall be refreshed and faith and hope can be fed . . . a little chapel of thought and prayer?" Providing a healthful environment for growing children and world-weary husbands was the main charge of women in the "domestic sphere" given over to them, and art could make a major contribution. The Beecher sisters, authors of the influential domestic advice manual *The American Woman's Home* (1869), joined many other prominent supporters of chromos, declaring that judicious decorating of a home with art "contributes much to the education of the entire household in refinement, intellectual development, and moral sensibility."[7] Chromolithograph publishers contributed to this educational mission by producing art instruction manuals, images intended for copying, and children's books, as well as fine art chromos. If art had been conceived of simply as decoration, it would not have become such a source of cultural activity and controversy. Freighted with the tasks of moral, intellectual, and cultural edification, as well as adornment, art of the middle-class home became an important ideological battleground.

A large part of the hope for art in domestic settings to serve significant cultural functions lay in chromolithography, which, as one commentator observed:

> . . . promise[d] to diffuse not a love of art merely among the people at large, but to disseminate the choicest masterpieces of art itself. It is art republicanized and naturalized in America.[8]

Several forces are invoked here, including a growing artistic nationalism and pride, and a democratization of the increasingly elite realm of high art. Aesthetic appreciation, cultural refinement, democracy, and national identity are conjoined and encouraged by the diffusion of art through chromos.

But not all observers were enthusiastic. The conservative weekly *The Nation* published three articles railing against chromos, the last in 1870:

> the chromo-lithographic imitation of oil-painting is a type of everything in bad art that is most disgusting to the artist and to the cultivated . . . At bottom of this disgust we shall find the sensation of sham, of a swindle which disappoints even while it deceives.

Here the author condemned chromos as neither original works of art, nor adequate facsimiles of original works. Anxiety over the deceptiveness of chromos had characterized *The Nation*'s concerns since its earliest article on chromos in 1867:

> One thing only, quite unnecessary and quite inexcusable, throws discredit on the whole matter and makes the pictures merely merchandise; some of the pictures are made to look like oil-paintings on canvas, by printing them all over with indented lines to imitate the effect of the threads of the canvas, and by giving them a varnished surface.

The fact that chromos were mechanically reproduced counted decisively against them in the eyes of many critics, one of whom counseled prospective art buyers of limited means to buy engravings: "These are much more desirable than chromo-lithographs . . . [which] are too mechanical to be artistic . . ." *The Nation* declared that "The touch of the master's hand on the canvas can never be reproduced by the press."[9]

Because of the range of its attacks, *The Nation* provides a concise encyclopedia of the sometimes contradictory arguments leveled against chromos. One common complaint is that the chromo, in fooling the ignorant, debases the public's already questionable taste. In this view, the better chromos are technically, the worse they are morally, because they mislead one (if naïve) into believing that one has gotten art, when really one has gotten only a "sham". Pronouncing that "a color reproduction must be perfect or it is nothing," *The Nation* admonished that a true art lover would have to get rid of all chromos before being able to make any progress in the study and appreciation of art.[10] Chromos were caught in the bind that the more they imitated paintings, the more clearly they appeared as fakes. Another major strand in the invective is the poisonous influence of the profit motive. Castigating the images for not being art, *The Nation* downgrades them severely to "merely merchandise." The author's underlying concern is a desire to keep art and common commerce separate. He reminds us that "The chromo-manufacturer is not called upon by his profession of making as much money as he can to elevate the taste of the public."[11] The distinctions between original artwork and reproduction, and between art and commerce, were becoming uncomfortably blurred in the late nineteenth century. The problem for contemporary critics was to make a credible, principled case for welcoming some innovations and rejecting others. The heated debate over chromolithographs indicates that they occupied a vital piece of terrain in a struggle for cultural power centered in the "domestic sphere" of the ideal middle-class home.

The Nation was not the only defender of high culture to speak against chromos. Prang struggled to get good reviews from Clarence Cook, art critic for the *New York Daily Tribune*. Prang sent copies of new chromos to Cook, as well as to other culturally prominent individuals, hoping to gain their approval and support. Many of the positive letters Prang received he excerpted in his promotional journal, *Prang's Chromo*. Though he sometimes lauded Prang for his efforts, Cook was constantly on guard against inferior work or overstated claims. On one occasion he advised:

> Mr Prang would do the general public a much greater service than he is doing at present, if he would devise some way of employing the excellent invention of chromo-lithography that would give us an individual and independent result. A clever imitation is nothing but an imitation, after all. It can teach nobody anything, nor benefit anybody; and, as every art has its own particular application and field of work, we hinder progress by every effort to wrest it to the cheap imitation of the results of some other art.[12]

Like *The Nation*, Cook insisted on the purity and integrity of each artistic medium in the name of "progress" in art and taste. *The Nation* proclaimed that, "the absurdity of the chromo-picture lies in this, that it uses oil-painting to imitate oil-painting." This line of argument would be developed further in the writings of modernist critics such as Clement Greenberg, who was also concerned to guard the sanctity of high art from debasing incursions by popular culture.[13]

This threat to the emerging distinction between art and popular culture is precisely what is at issue in bringing art into the home. As the art journal *The Aldine* observed in 1869:

> If chromo-lithography is not an art, it is in one sense better, since it goes where pure Art cannot go, [into] . . . popular aesthetic culture . . . Mr Prang has made possession [of art] an easy sequence of desire. For ten dollars the working man may glorify his house with one of Correggio's masterpieces . . . delight his eyes and his soul with the harmonious richness of Bierstadt's "Sunset in California;" [fig. 2] he may warm his patriotism and feed his ambition by contemplating "The Boyhood of Lincoln;" or he may renew his youth in gazing on the inimitable portrait of Whittier's "Barefoot Boy."[14]

This passage celebrates just the developments that Cook and *The Nation* feared. Even the "working man" may own and appreciate art, and easily. The distinction between chromos and art is undermined (though not entirely collapsed – *The Aldine* acknowledges that chromos are not "pure

Art"), for chromos serve the functions of art within the home. Home decoration, simple pleasure in pretty colors, nationalism, and sentimental reverie all are rolled into one messy, unintellectualized bundle and presented to a broad public. This was a serious challenge to the authority of an elite which had defined itself largely in terms of greater cultural (and implicitly moral) refinement.

In the process of debate over the cultural worth of chromos, opponents and supporters heightened the distinction between popular and elite culture and associated homes with popular culture, and thus with images that were less highly valued if they were conceded to be art at all. What was at stake was the cultural authority to define and control the power of art in a rapidly changing society. The separation between the private "domestic sphere" of the home and an aggressive, masculinized public sphere of industrial labor and capitalism was the core of the doctrine of domesticity. Hostile critics argued that chromos allowed mechanization and commercialization to contaminate art in domestic environments which should have been places of retreat or escape from these forces, while also allowing mechanical, commercial products to make a claim (a false claim, as they saw it) to the status of art. In conceding that perhaps chromos were not really art, chromo advocates like the writer for *The Aldine* permitted their adversaries to assign chromos to an inferior position.

The larger interests connected to chromos were discussed only indirectly. *The Nation's* deep-seated fears were voiced in an 1874 article discussing a love-affair scandal currently in the news. Though chromolithographs are never mentioned, the article is entitled "Chromo-civilization". The author contends that many of those who have rapidly ascended in the social hierarchy falsely believe that they are properly cultured and informed, and thus see fit to speak and act on the major issues of the day without concern for or deference to the opinions of the established authorities. The idea that the formative role played by art, and indeed the very definition of what was art, should be given over to the "domestic sphere" of middle-class women was intolerable. After stressing the need for self-discipline, and the formation of ideals "through labor and self-denial," and noting that "a good deal of it [character building] was obtained from the old Calvinistic theology," *The Nation* proceeds:

> If all this be true, the mischievous effects of the pseudo-culture of which we have spoken above may be readily estimated. A society of ignoramuses who know they are ignoramuses, might lead a tolerably happy and useful existence, but a society of ignoramuses each of whom thinks he is a Solon, would be an approach to Bedlam let loose, and something analogous to this may really be seen to-day in some parts of this country. A large body of persons has arisen, under the influence of the common-schools, magazines, newspapers, and the

> rapid acquisition of wealth, who are not only engaged in enjoying themselves after their fashion, but who firmly believe that they have reached, in the matter of social, mental, and moral culture, all that is attainable or desirable by anybody, and who therefore tackle all the problems of the day – men's, women's and children's rights and duties, marriage, education, suffrage, life, death, and immortality – with supreme indifference to what anybody else thinks or has ever thought . . . The result is a kind of mental and moral chaos, in which many of the fundamental rules of living . . . seem in imminent risk of disappearing totally.[15]

Here *The Nation*'s basic concerns surface. The author implicitly identifies himself as a member of a small, powerful minority which has traditionally exercised social and cultural hegemony. This elite was being threatened by a flourishing middle class, a *nouveau riche* bourgeoisie, and the increased demands of women. The threat took the form of members of these newly empowered groups questioning the legitimacy of the power of the old elite, questioning as well the tenets of social ordering which this elite endorsed. Thus, many of the "fundamental rules of living" were indeed being challenged. Among these were power relations between the sexes, the power of the father in the family, the proper form of marriage, socialization practices, and women's participation in politics – such is the net content of the author's own list, to which he frivolously appends "life, death, and immortality." This nervous camouflage gives some indication of how grave and far-reaching the issues at hand felt to him. And symbolizing and summing up all the perils was the chromo.

Chromo Industry and Museums: Concerns, Differences, Divergence

At the same time that chromos were giving thousands of people the opportunity to bring artworks into their homes, plans were underway in a number of cities to give the public another way to view and learn from art. Metropolitan fine art museums were established in New York, Boston, and Philadelphia in the 1870s. Over the next two decades smaller cities and those to the west followed this lead. These new art museums were distinct from previous museums both in what they contained and in how they were run. The new museums' collections might well include antiquities, decorative arts, and plaster casts and other reproductions along with paintings, sculptures, and prints, but they had no scientific curiosities or live entertainment. Metropolitan art museums could afford to concentrate exclusively on the fine arts because they did not depend primarily on admission fees for revenue, and thus did not require the appeal of spectacle. Instead of being private (if perhaps civic-minded) enterprises, as previous museums had been, the new museums were organized as public not-for-profit corporations ultimately governed by a board of trustees. Such an arrangement was in line with national trends towards incorporation and consolidation of businesses.[16] Trustees were often themselves prominent businessmen. Museum boards insisted on strict and cautious financial management, but had to rely for funding on large donations they and their associates made, combined with money solicited from the public at large on the ground that museums were public educational institutions which could benefit everyone. Despite successful fundraising, careful management, restrained activities, and heavy reliance on volunteered expertise and service, museums frequently ran deficits and had little or no money available for acquisitions in the 1870s and 1880s.

The simultaneous development and shared concerns of the chromolithograph industry and metropolitan art museums suggest that despite the lack of much direct interaction between them they were products of the same social forces in a nascent modernist era. The complicated relationship between these new institutions implies complex negotiations of categories such as public and private as the boundaries between high art and popular culture were formed. Chromolithograph companies were private in the sense that they were individual for-profit ventures, whereas museums claimed to serve the public good. But while the chromolithograph industry included all purchasers in its broad "public", museums were public only in the sense of being freely available to those who had the leisure to visit. The point is not that there were no significant differences between the chromolithograph industry and art museums, but that their differences do not take the form of categorical oppositions.

These two institutions were the dual response in art to issues raised by industrialization, issues that bound the chromolithograph industry and museums together and distinguished them from existing art institutions such as academies and clubs, which were primarily concerned with developing training and patronage in the fine arts for a small group of specialists. Indeed, the chromolithograph industry and metropolitan art museums were strikingly similar in their concern to combine art and industry for the spiritual and material benefit of the country. Charles C. Perkins, a prime motivating force behind the foundation of the Museum of Fine Arts in Boston, mirrored the sentiments of supporters of chromos when he called for increased support of the visual arts because of "their elevating effect upon us as a nation, and because through them we may give a hitherto unknown value to our industrial products."[17] In the case of chromos, industry fostered art; in the case of museums, art was to foster industry.

Industry and commerce both gave rise to the need for the popularization of art and, through the chromolithograph industry and art museums, facilitated that popularization. For the chromolithograph industry, machine production allowed art images to be multiplied and the cost per image to be reduced enough that middle-class families could own them. Thus mechanical reproduction made affordable what were originally costly hand-crafted images. In metropolitan art museums, art was to have an "elevating effect," in Perkins's words, as well as a tangible monetary benefit through imparting design skills to American workers. For both the chromolithograph industry and metropolitan art museums, mechanization allowed for humanization of what was perceived to be an overly mechanized world of daily experience.

Walter Smith, an art educator and an important voice in favor of museums, looked forward in 1873 to the imminent realization of the goals that *The Crayon* had articulated in the 1850s:

> The time has come, which has been so long looked for, when this country, prosperous, and developing beyond all precedent, has sought in art the enjoyment and refinement which trade and commerce alone cannot give.[18]

The material prosperity that grew from industrialization was to make possible artistic cultivation. But for Smith, art had another purpose besides fostering "enjoyment and refinement". He cautioned that:

> A museum, however rich in its contents, and perfect in its arrangements for exhibition, is but a show, unless it combines with its wealth of art the active educational agencies in the classroom which are to translate this wealth into currency.[19]

Smith's metaphor is somewhat muddled because supporters looked to museums for both the spiritual and the material benefits of aesthetic refinement. Museums were meant to generate "currency" both metaphorically and literally. Those in charge of museums would later deem it necessary to efface or to conceal connections between art and industrial commerce, but early advocates saw the potential industrial applications of artistic knowledge and skills as a crucial argument in favor of establishing museums.

Given that the chromolithograph industry and art museums shared concerns about making effective use of the potentials of industry and about having a salubrious humanizing effect on a broad audience, one must look at other attitudes embodied in the two institutions to mark their important differences. The chromolithograph industry interpreted refinement as gratification through edifying or heart-warming images. Museums stood for a more austere and practical refinement – the acquisition of visual, manual, and mental skills through diligent study. Ironically, whereas the chromolithograph industry embraced technology, reveled in the present (while still relying on traditional styles and themes for its images), and was sanguine about the future, the technical skills promoted by museums

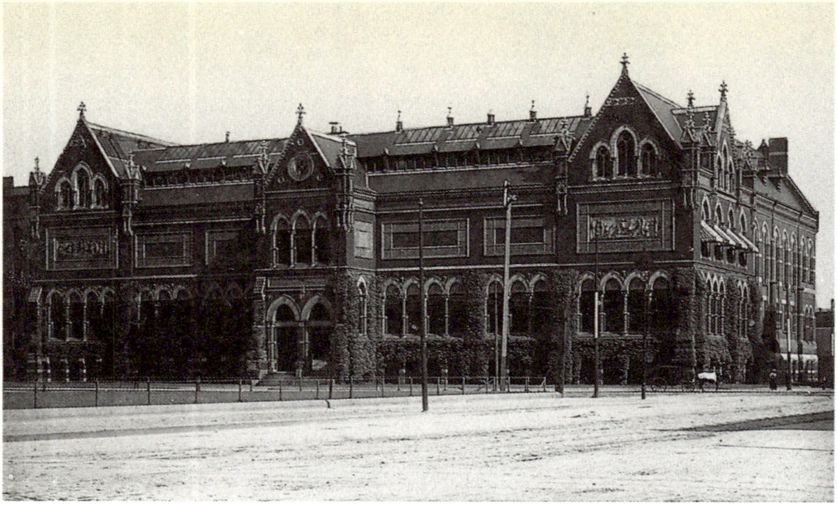

8 *Museum of Fine Arts, Boston. Copley Square building, as expanded 1879 (demolished)*

sought to cope with industrialization by looking to the past for models. These differences grew from a fundamental divergence in attitude that became more clear as the two institutions matured. The basic question was how to face industrialization, the modernization of industry and commerce. The chromolithograph industry looked forward, foreshadowing the development and proliferation of mass culture. Art museums looked back, evolving from educational resources to the shrines to the past condemned by Progressive era muckrakers.

As they developed, the chromolithograph industry and museums moved away from each other and from their initial shared concerns. Popularizing art was a major goal of both institutions at the outset, and educating a broad public was the way to achieve meaningful popularization. The chromo industry moved away from this goal in the direction of supplying novelties and "fancy goods" to consumers and eye-catching advertisements to business customers. The chromolithograph industry's reliance on support from a large market meant focusing on satisfying (rather than reforming) popular tastes. Art museums developed an emphasis on displaying masterworks and laid less stress on practical design education. As available resources increased, museums chose to replace casts and copies with originals, rather than to expand educational programs.

The early twentieth century saw the construction of a number of new museum buildings. These were not the practical, contemporary designs approved by museum founders, but the imposing neoclassical, palace- or temple-like structures most commonly associated with museums today.

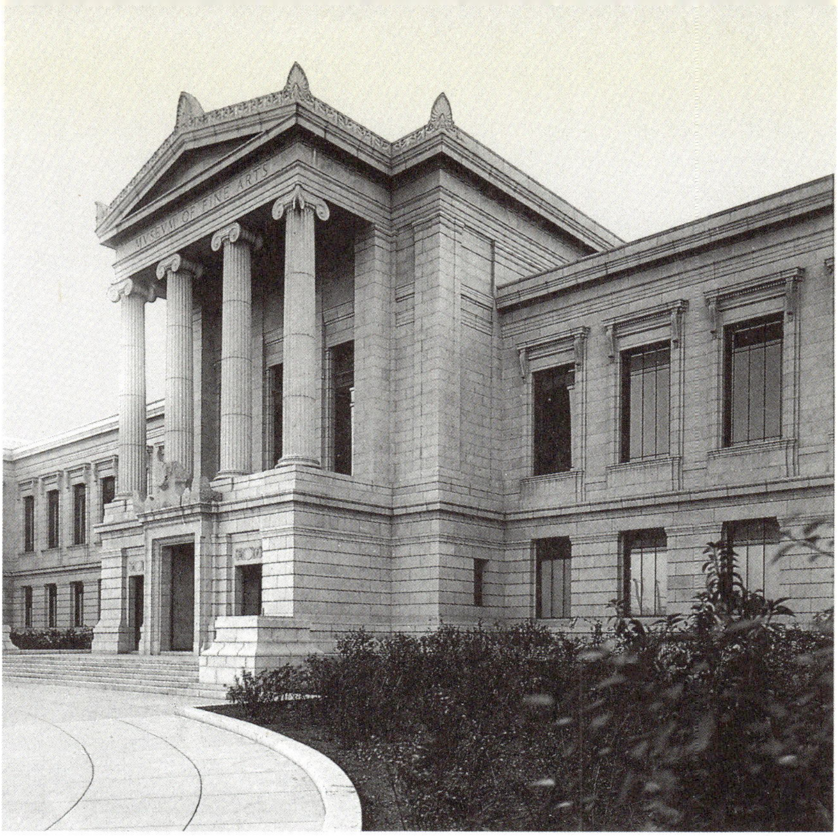

9 Museum of Fine Arts, Boston. Main Entrance of the Huntingdon Avenue building, opened 1909

The first building of the Museum of Fine Arts Boston, opened in 1876 and expanded in 1879, exemplifies the defining features of early metropolitan art museums. The use of architectural terra-cotta placed this building at the forefront of building technology in the USA, and more importantly allied the museum explicitly with the ideal of an integrated arts and design program serving manufacturing industry. The model of Britain's South Kensington Museum (now the Victoria and Albert), established in the wake of the 1851 Great Exhibition to improve the country's manufactures, was thus invoked not only in the stated objectives of the Boston museum founders, but in the building itself.[20] Museum buildings of the early twentieth century, by contrast, usually avoided references to modern industry and instead invoked the weighty precedents of Greek temples, Roman civic architecture, and Renaissance palaces, thereby laying claim to the cultural heritage of the Western tradition and definitively announcing their separation from the concerns and vicissitudes of contemporary life.[21] This architectural change denoted a change in function. Twentieth-century museums fulfilled Walter Smith's hope that industrial wealth would make the refining influences of art publicly available, but disregarded his admonition that active educational programs would be necessary to reap the practical benefits of the collections. Museums abandoned their mission of education in practical art skills and became primarily places for awed contemplation by a select group of cultural initiates.

Domesticity and Modernism

Art museums eventually institutionalized art as anti-domestic. Architecturally, homes could not rival the grandeur of museums. The expenditure of money and energy on museum buildings was an overwhelming demonstration of their cultural authority. The separation of everyday experience and material exigencies from the aesthetic experience offered in museums disallowed integration of art and pragmatic concerns. Museums modified their initial idea that art could teach skills and/or morals, in favour of the modernist notion of art as a vehicle of individualism and subjective experience.[22] This change in museums' focus separated them further from domestic ideals of parental instruction and family members' subordination of personal desires to the good of the family unit. At the same time, contemporary observers remarked that high culture as a whole was taking on a feminine aspect, though women still had very limited presence in institutional hierarchies.[23] This perceived "feminization" of culture linked museums and the social function of art within them to notions of the civilizing role of women in homes.

The fact that chromos, as well as other objects and images, were in homes became evidence that they were not art; museum collections and displays came to define what was. Only certain types of objects, usually tremendously expensive, were admissible for museum display (in contrast with art museums' earlier policy of displaying casts, photographs, and other reproductions for their educational value). These were displayed removed from contexts of making, use, or social function within particular cultures, indicating that the objects were for the purpose of aesthetic appreciation only. Such display was neither feasible nor desirable in most homes. The popularity from the early twentieth century onwards of period rooms in museums suggests visitors' interest in understanding art as related to domestic life, but in art museums, as opposed to historical museums, these rooms were still much more for aesthetic contemplation than for gaining an understanding of the reasons for which the objects were created. Still, "great art" was rarely relegated to period rooms, and art museum displays simulating domestic environments were (and are) usually segregated from displays of individual works and located as detours from the main routes suggested by museum floor plans.

That museums shifted their emphasis from providing the means for practical art education to enshrining masterpieces was an important part of the basis for the institutionalization of modernism (firmly established in the USA with the foundation of the Museum of Modern Art in 1929 and the Whitney Museum of American Art in 1930) as a series of images encapsulating the achievements, anxieties and potentials of their era. Industrialization threatened the very notion of what it meant to be human, as is clear as early as *The Crayon*'s worries in the 1850s. In holding fast to the conviction that "original" artworks, unique creations of extraordinarily sensitive, skillful, and/or perceptive individuals, were of paramount importance, modernist artists were profoundly anti-modern. They responded to the increasing mechanization and bureaucratization of modern life by seeking an alternate reality in the individual and collective psyche. If order, stability, and a wholly positive sense of progress were impossible to maintain in the world of lived experience, perhaps they could be established in the ideal world of an increasingly formalist artistic practice.

This strategy of creating a private, inward-looking world of art as a refuge from and antidote to the impersonal hurly-burly of competition in an industrialized economy is very much like the construction of a "domestic sphere" in the mid-nineteenth century, though the masculine gendering and heroic avant-garde posture of much modernist art make it resistant to this association. Modernist art historically has been accessible only to a well-informed few capable of grasping its formal and theoretical complexities. Another sort of art, more widely comprehensible and often mass reproduced (and therefore called "popular" art), has been necessary to the self definition of artistic modernism. The main institutional precursors of these two sorts of art, the chromolithograph industry and metropolitan art museums, were created as two answers to the question of how art and industry could best work together to promote material and emotional well-being. Subsequent divergence of aims and attitudes need not blind us to the fact that much art, both "popular" and "elite", has continued to respond to this question.

3

Model-Families: The Domesticated Studio Pictures of William Merritt Chase and Edmund C. Tarbell[1]

LINDA J. DOCHERTY

WHEN the American painter-critic Samuel Greene Wheeler Benjamin claimed that the artist's studio was "the one place on earth where the dominion of the ever busy and tidy housewife cannot hold sway"[2] his vehemence betrayed anxiety about feminine intrusion into masculine territory. If the male painter's studio constituted a private workplace where he could develop his aesthetic vision in freedom and disorder, it also, in the late nineteenth century, functioned as a public showplace for the tangible products of his labor. Although brokered by men, the marriage of art and capitalism depended for its success on women, who became regular visitors to the artist's workplace in this period. Their attraction to the studios – where collections of pictures, props, and bric-à-brac resembled department store displays – supported criticism of such spaces as self-indulgent and even seductive. At the same time, the more traditional equation of the female sex with spiritual values glossed the commercial function of these cultural emporia.[3] Even more significant than the literal presence of women in the studios was their pictorial omnipresence. While resisting domination by "the ever busy and tidy housewife," male painters self-consciously deployed domestic subject matter to distinguish their artistic enterprise from the crass materialism of the age. Through pictorial colonization of the female sphere they laid imperialistic claim to the most favorable and desirable aspects of modern American life.

A distinctive product of this campaign was what I call "domesticated studio pictures," images in which the lines between home and workplace, so firmly drawn by urban capitalism, were purposefully blurred. Such paintings simultaneously celebrated the virtues and/or pleasures of domesticity and alluded to the process of artistic production. By conflating their professional activity with the sacralized realm of the home, artists might ascribe a spiritual character to art while displaying (and, with luck, increasing) their material success. A comparison of works by William Merritt Chase and Edmund C. Tarbell will demonstrate, however, that the gambit was not a sure one. To succeed, the male painter had to lower barricades

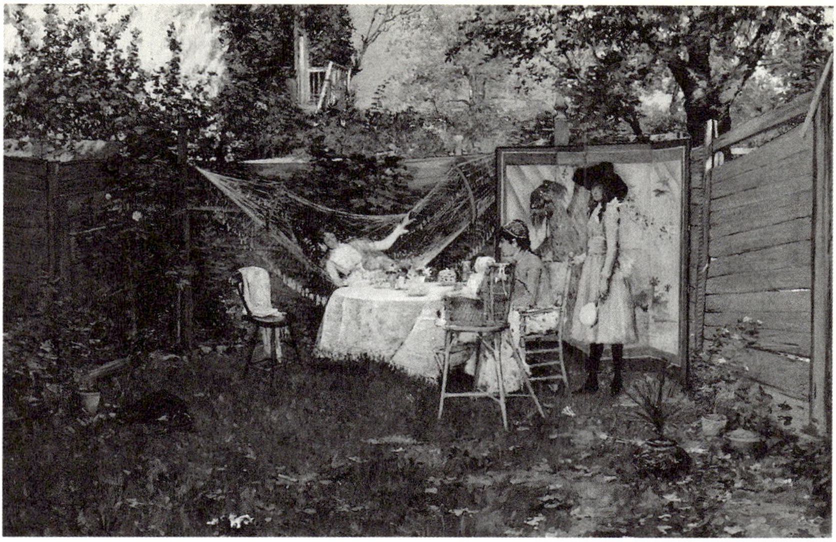

10 *William Merritt Chase,* The Open-Air Breakfast, *c. 1888*

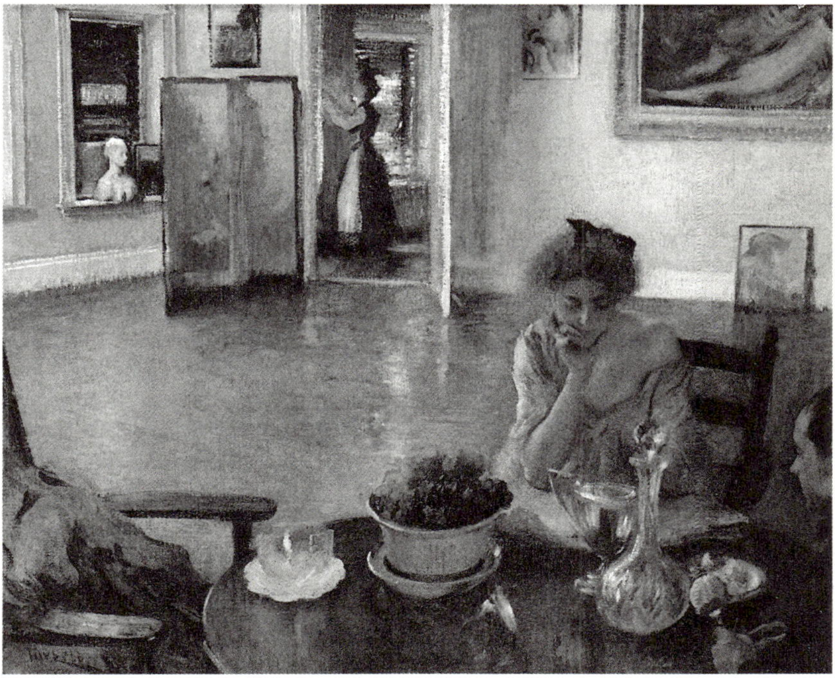

11 *Edmund C. Tarbell,* The Breakfast Room, *1903*

between his studio space and the domestic sphere without being subsumed by it either personally or artistically.

10, 11 Chase's *The Open-Air Breakfast* of 1888 and Tarbell's *The Breakfast Room* of 1903 constitute early experiments with the domesticated studio theme. Both works combine studio props with what appear to be ordinary episodes in the lives of upper-middle-class Americans. Chase's picture is set in the backyard of his Brooklyn home. The artist's wife, Alice, presides over the breakfast table with their first child, Alice Dieudonnée, beside her in a high chair. Alice's oldest sister, Virginia Gerson, lounges in a hammock, and the two women are absorbed in conversation. Surrounding this image of home life, we see signs of studio life: a plant in a decorative pot, a piece of fabric draped over a chair, and an oriental screen. In front of the screen, wearing a tall hat and holding a fan or mirror, Chase's sister Hattie alludes specifically to the aestheticism of Whistler; her white dress against the white background of the screen recalls *Symphony in White, No. 1: The White Girl* (National Gallery of Art, Washington DC), and the vignette as a whole resembles *La Princess du pays de la porcelaine* (Freer Gallery of Art, Washington DC).[4] The natural illusion of Chase's artful composition hinges on the figure of Alice, who bridges the boundary between studio arrangement and family group. In her dual capacity as model and wife, she appears simultaneously framed by art and immersed in life.

While Chase's painting documents his home and family, Tarbell constructed his first domesticated studio pictures entirely within the workplace. Painted on Dartmouth Street in Boston's exclusive Back Bay, *The Breakfast Room* features not the artist's wife, Emeline, but Mary Sullivan, a paid model.[5] As in Chase's painting, a central female figure is surrounded by studio props: still life objects, again a screen, works of art in various media. Though the woman's dishabille marks her as a model rather than the lady of a house, the servant in the background and the man who shares the table with her make the setting seem, to quote one contemporary reviewer, "a breakfast-room of the well-bred."[6] Domestic content is implicit in Tarbell's image, yet here it is the man (artist) and not the woman (model) who occupies the border between pictorial construction and lived experience. The lone male figure projects beyond the picture space and metaphorically into real life. The females, by contrast, both living and artificial, are all circumscribed by frames.

While these pictures bespeak different visions of art and domesticity, they exemplify the desire of male painters to colonize spaces specifically characterized as feminine. In the rigidly compartmentalized interiors of nineteenth-century homes, these areas included the drawing-room, boudoir, and breakfast or morning room. Unlike the boudoir, which was reserved exclusively for women, the breakfast room was accessible to family members and visitors of both sexes.[7] Chase's garden breakfast conveys a sense of sociability noticeably lacking in Tarbell's interior, yet both works imply female acceptance of the male artist's encroachment into their domestic realm. Surrounded by references to art and its creation, the women in these images pursue their morning activities unperturbed.

The blurring of boundaries between art and life that characterizes domesticated studio pictures had precedents in French Impressionism. Edouard Manet, the father of the modern movement, created similar ambiguities in *Le Déjeuner sur l'herbe* (Musée d'Orsay, Paris) by combining studio props and an outdoor setting, old master composition and individual technique, nude female model and men in contemporary dress. When first shown publicly at the 1863 Salon des Refusés, this assaultive (and still controversial) image elicited admiration, ridicule, and confusion from contemporary viewers. Ambitious young French painters – the future Impressionists – saw Manet's work as a challenge to academic and, by association, aristocratic hegemony.

Impressionist painters in America followed Manet's lead in form but not in content. In a nation where art was governed by capitalism more than by inheritance, a second generation of admirers used his radical pictorial strategies for frankly bourgeois ends. While the French *flâneur* had collapsed distinctions between the artistic process and the public spaces of Second Empire Paris, Chase and Tarbell conflated the painter's workplace and the private sphere of home and family. Rather than challenging the established social order by identifying with its marginal aspects, they strove to attain a prominent place within it by equating their work and themselves with its highest ideals.

The different political aims of Manet and the American Impressionists are exemplified by their treatment of the female model. In Manet's *Déjeuner* the unabashed nakedness and confrontational gaze of Victorine Meurent raised a spectre of the Parisian demimonde that gave the picture revolutionary power. More interested in sales than in subversion, Chase and Tarbell eschewed blatant references to sex. In *The Open-Air Breakfast*, Alice Chase transcends objectification as an object of desire in her role as wife and mother. And even in *The Breakfast Room*, where the still life of decanter and sugar bowl constitutes an unmistakable sexual metaphor, Mary Sullivan's pensive pose and downcast eyes gainsay the intimation of physical union between the figures.

In their preference for domestic subject matter and decorous treatment, Chase and Tarbell have more in common with Mary Cassatt and Berthe Morisot than with their male counterparts overseas. Griselda Pollock has shown that the difference between masculine and feminine space in the late nineteenth century did not correspond neatly to public and private, but was complicated by issues of class intersection and female sexuality. On her map of urban life, ladies occupy the drawing-room, bedroom, veranda, garden, theater (loge) and park, while fallen women are found in the theater (backstage), cafés, folies, and brothels (subjects painted exclusively by men). According to Pollock, Cassatt and Morisot confined their art to the spaces of ladies not only because they were familiar to them personally, but also because of the risks involved in venturing too far into public life. She explains,

> To enter such spaces as the masked ball or the café-concert constituted a serious threat to a bourgeois woman's reputation and therefore her femininity. The guarded respectability of the lady could be soiled by mere visual contact for seeing was bound up with knowing.[8]

Although knowledge of public spaces posed no threat to the masculinity of American Impressionists, domesticated studio pictures exemplify a growing tendency to avoid the urban scene that had fascinated their French predecessors. For modernist painters with genteel pretensions, Chase and Tarbell included, turn-of-the-century cities possessed problematic connotations of industry, immigration, and increasing social strife. Home, on the other hand, had long been viewed as a refuge from worldly concerns. The domestic sphere, traditionally construed as women's sphere, represented a stable universe where morality was inculcated and preserved.[9] As the United States moved from a producer to a consumer economy, the home also became a stage for conspicuous display of goods and idleness, a phenomenon analyzed in Thorstein Veblen's *Theory of the Leisure Class* (1899). According to historian Warren Susman, America evolved during this period from a culture of character to a culture of personality.[10] While character was rooted in hard work and self-denial, personality expressed itself in pleasure and self-fulfillment. In the culture of personality, images of beautiful women in aesthetic interiors became a source of delight for its own sake.[11]

In late-nineteenth-century painting, women were almost systematically disempowered by domestic iconography and decorative style.[12] While idyllic representations of home and family touted the advantages of separate spheres, didactic allegories composed of symbolic figures in shallow spaces further separated women from the real world of political agency. Like other male artists of this period, Chase and Tarbell tended to confine their female models iconographically and formally and to portray women as beautiful, cultured, maternal, industrious, modest, passive, sensual, or some combination of these traits. In *The Open-Air Breakfast*, Chase conceals Alice behind their baby daughter, while in *The Breakfast Room*, Tarbell exposes Mary Sullivan as a sexual object. Neither of these works presents a progressive view of women, yet the contrast they exemplify between individualization of family member and sexualization of hired model is worthy of note. Both Chase and Tarbell used their wives and daughters as models for their paintings, and both developed their visions of domesticity in relationship to these women. The relative success of their domesticated studio pictures paralleled the degree to which each artist's home and family exemplified patriarchal norms of American culture.

When William Merritt Chase married Alice Gerson in 1886, he surprised friends and acquaintances who regarded him as "a bachelor of the most confirmed type." The couple's first meeting, six years earlier, followed the painter's return to the United States from Munich, his critical triumph at the first Society of American Artists exhibition, and his establishment of a lavishly decorated studio in New York's famous Tenth Street Studio Building. Alice was the youngest daughter of Julius Gerson, a cultured and modestly wealthy New York widower who actively supported artists and writers. She and her sisters, Virginia and Minnie, often modeled for young painters who could not afford to pay professionals. When Chase met the Gerson family, he was thirty-one and Alice was fourteen; he was immediately attracted to her beauty and that same night asked her to pose for him. A newspaper account of their wedding described Alice as "a handsome and spirited brunette of a good family" and confirmed the artist's initial impression that she was eminently "paintable."[13] For thirty years of marriage she modeled for her husband as both volunteer and conscript, and according to Chase's early biographer, Katharine Metcalf Roof, "in every way contrived to create in his home the atmosphere of art."[14]

Throughout the 1880s Chase enjoyed celebrity as a leader of the modern movement in America. His reputation was enhanced by association with rebellious organizations – the Art Students League (where he taught painting) and the Society of American Artists (of which he was repeatedly elected president) – and, above all, by the Tenth Street studio. This sumptuously furnished workplace, which epitomized postbellum cosmopolitanism and aestheticism, proclaimed to all New York the dignity of the artist and the rarefied atmosphere he required.[15] Although Chase's devotion to art was unquestioned and his technical skill unrivalled, his work was often criticized as superficial. In 1889 Kenyon Cox wrote in his defense,

> Of all our artists Mr Chase is most distinctively and emphatically a *painter*, marked for such both by his powers and by his limitations. His is not so much the art of the brain that thinks or of the imagination that conceives as of the eye that sees and the hand that records.[16]

Cox had high praise for Chase's paintings of Brooklyn parks and docks, which signalled a shift from realism and aestheticism to Impressionism and demonstrated the picturesque quality of modern American subjects. The fact that Alice and baby Cosy figured in many of these works may have prompted Chase to link his studio practice with his new domestic life.

The domesticated studio theme, which Chase first explored in Brooklyn, reached its climax in the following decade at Shinnecock, Long Island. From 1891 to 1902, the artist summered with his wife and children on the dunes near Southampton, while he directed America's first important school for plein-air painting.[17] Many of the couple's nine children were born in these years and one, their first son, William Merritt, Jr, died in infancy. In 1892 Chase moved his growing family into a large Dutch Colonial house designed by Stanford White that typified the "cottages" of the area's fashionable summer residents. The painter's studio occupied the west side of the building and was connected to the living quarters by a short flight of stairs.

An 1893 article on Chase at Shinnecock by John Gilmer Speed presented his professional activity as a form of recreation. Published in *Harper's New Monthly Magazine* and titled "An Artist's Summer Vacation," it located the artist (as opposed to the merchant, lawyer, judge, and physician) in "that class to whom their work is their life and the giving up of the one means the giving up of the savor of the other." Based on observations of Chase made during the previous season, Speed portrayed him as ever busy painting ("four pictures made in two weeks") and teaching ("nearly a hundred" pupils "of all degrees of proficiency"), but never fatigued. He concluded,

> The work that most men do is full of weariness, and they tug on their loads as a horse against his collar when climbing a hill. Such men have reason to envy those whose callings make their work so great a pleasure that vacation-time entails only a change of scene with the continuation of the occupation in a new field.[18]

Speed's equation of labor with leisure in his description of Chase at Shinnecock was supported by a photograph of the artist in his summer studio. Surrounded by paintings, sculptures, textiles, and props, he sits casually on a long bench and contemplates an open portfolio. Compositionally and iconographically, this image resembles an early oil of the Tenth Street studio (The Brooklyn Museum, New York) in which an unidentified female visitor is absorbed in a large volume of pictures. Chase appears in the photograph not as a producer of art, but as a consumer, a role more frequently ascribed to women in this period than to men. On the floor to his right, a painting of Alice meditating in the Shinnecock studio with a portfolio in her lap (Arthur Altschul Collection) reinforces the feminine connotations of the scene.

A propensity to reverse conventional gender roles characterizes Chase's domesticated studio pictures. In *The Hall at Shinnecock*, from the summer of 1892, the painter moved his studio, quite literally, into the domestic sphere.[19] This large pastel on canvas depicts a quiet moment of leisure, in which Alice watches Koto, the Chases' second daughter, unfold a Japanese

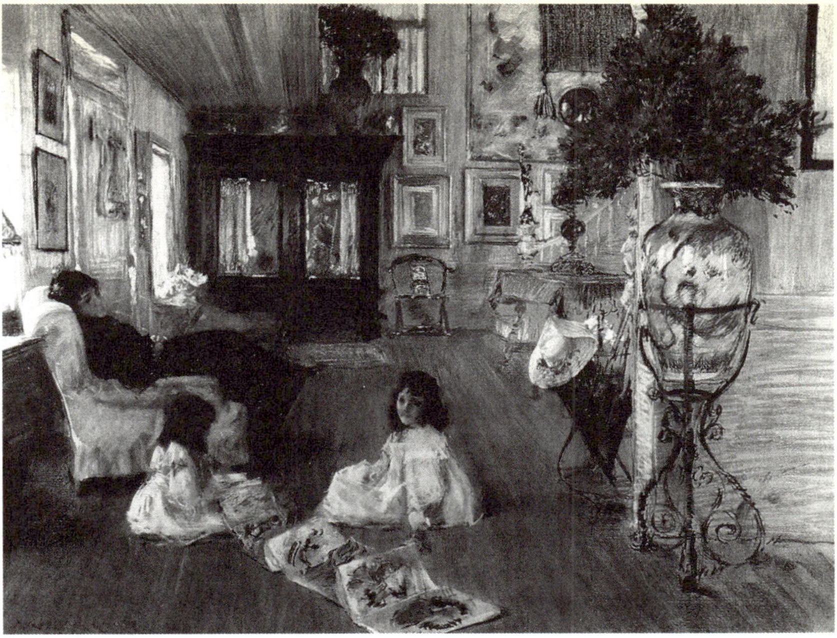

12 *William Merritt Chase,* The Hall at Shinnecock, *1892*

picture book. Cosy, too, watches art unfold as her father paints them from his position in the dining-room, and by following her cue we discover the artist himself reflected in the mirrored door of the antique Dutch kas (a reminder that Shinnecock was the first white settlement on Long Island). While Chase's family is his ostensible subject here, he conflates his artistic process pictorially and metaphorically with his domestic life and, in so doing, inverts traditional hierarchies. The living hall becomes a studio, the piece of furniture a painting, the female model the viewing subject, and the male artist the figure within the frame. Chase's clever composition invokes memory of Velázquez's *Las Meninas*, yet the pastel medium supports the indications that he has abdicated masculine control.[20]

While the family living space at Shinnecock functioned as the artist's workplace, Chase depicted his summer studio as a setting for domestic life. In *A Friendly Call* – also inspired by Velázquez – Alice entertains a female 13
visitor on the banquette that lined the west wall; in *Ring Toss*, Dorothy, 14
Hazel, and Helen play a childhood game amidst their father's canvases. Both of these paintings received favorable notice in Chase's lifetime, yet the link they posited between domestic content and studio context failed to impress his critics. Royal Cortissoz praised *The Friendly Call* (which won the Shaw Prize in 1895) for its technique and picturesqueness but referred to the setting, in feminine terms, as "a prettily decorated room rather than a studio."[21] Similarly, William Howe Downes described in detail the atti-

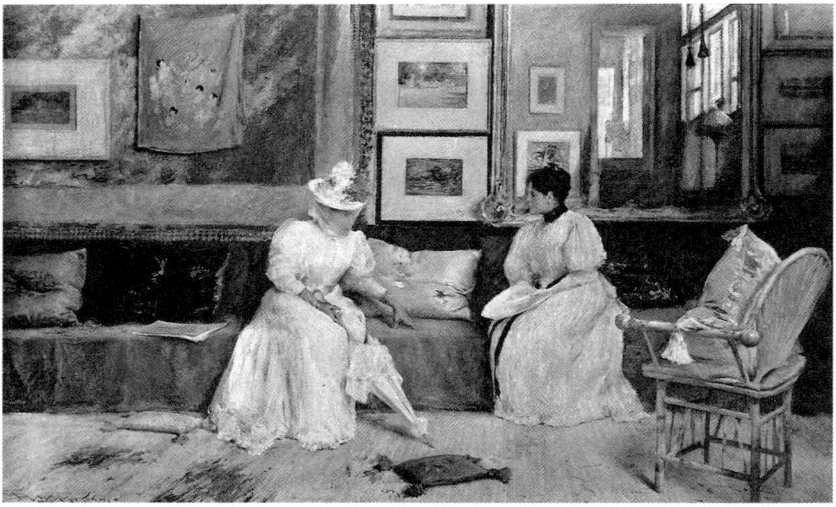

13 *William Merritt Chase,* A Friendly Call, *1895*

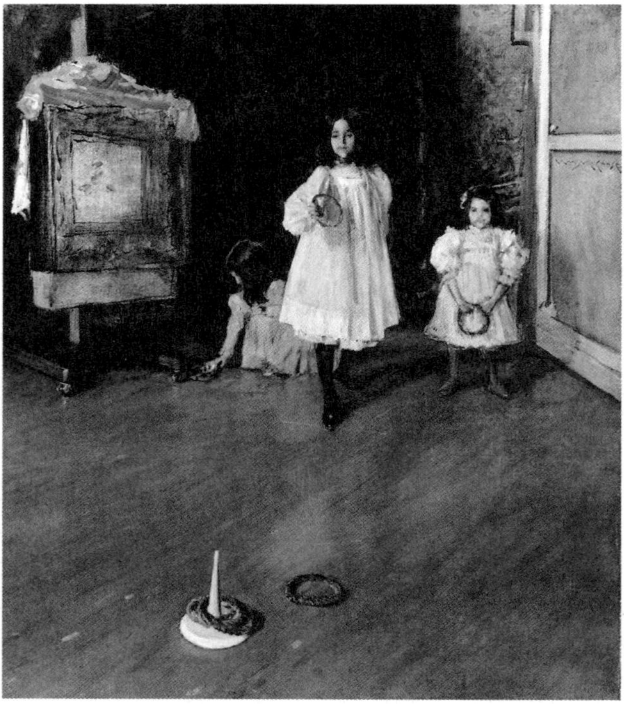

14 *William Merritt Chase,* Ring Toss, *c. 1896*

tudes of the "three dainty little maids at play" in *Ring Toss* and then noted, as an afterthought, "The accessories – an easel, an unfinished canvas, etc. – indicate the character of the room."[22] Rather than increasing respect for his technically facile observations of modern life, Chase's domesticated studio pictures seemed to deny his artistic power as impresario of the scene.

If signs of the artist's presence gradually receded to the background in Chase's images of domestic life at Shinnecock, his family appeared increasingly to dominate – one might even say to colonize – his studio space. In 1896, the painter experienced what Nicolai Cikovsky, Jr, describes as a "crisis of confidence" that led him to give up the Tenth Street studio, sell his vast collections, and threaten to abandon teaching altogether.[23] Although precipitated by financial difficulty, such actions coincided with a pictorial separation of professional and private life. Before 1896, Chase frequently depicted his wife and daughters pursuing their own activities in the Shinnecock studio. After that time, he either returned them to the domestic sphere (*For the Little One*, Metropolitan Museum of Art, New York) or represented them as visitors or models in his workplace (*Did You Speak to Me?*, Butler Institute of American Art, Ohio; *Alice in the Shinnecock Studio*, The Parrish Art Museum, New York). Signs of an impending crisis can be seen in *Ring Toss* in the dark background, the two canvases (one barely begun, one turned against the wall), and the empty space that separates the artist from his youthful subjects.

Despite his apparent retreat from the domesticated studio, Chase's wife and children remained his favorite models. For three decades, until his death in 1916, they inspired, critiqued, and validated his artistic life. The artist recorded their relationship vividly in pictures and also in letters, written in the summer of 1903 when he was teaching classes in Europe after the closing of the Shinnecock School. In nightly missives, Chase reported to Alice about the paintings he had seen, people he had met, progress of his students, and how he longed to have her in bed beside him so he could give her "a *tight* squeeze." On more than one occasion, the compulsive spender proudly told his wife that he had seen many beautiful objects, but hadn't bought anything. And, lest an unusually haphazard piece of penmanship from Munich make her suspect, the bon vivant assured her in a postscript, "*I have behaved myself to your liking*."[24] Although Chase may have sometimes felt his bohemian impulses held in check by Alice, he never ceased to value her collaboration. "In his last illness," she wrote, "his favorite amusement was to review with me the European galleries, asking me to recall what I thought the most interesting in each canvas, and living over in his memory the pictures he loved best."[25] The autonomy women possessed in Chase's studio and home life may help to explain why his celebrity as a painter was never equalled by his sales.

The fact that Chase's domesticated studio pictures failed substantially to alter his reputation as a painter of surfaces suggests that he did not strike an acceptable balance of power between the sexes. Although the painter's turn (via French Impressionism) toward American nature freed his art from association with an effete European culture, equation of the Shinnecock studio with rural leisure preserved its negative feminine connotations. John Higham has shown that Americans in the 1890s rejected passive gentility and actively embraced an ideal of "the strenuous life."[26] For a male painter to advance his art life by identification with home life, domesticated studio pictures had to display a masculine power of mind.

While Chase's domestic life spilled over into his studio life, Edmund Tarbell's home and family were controlled by his artistic vision. When the artist (whose great-grandson described him as "a patriarch of patriarchs"[27]) met his future wife, Emeline Arnold Souther, she was a student at Boston's newly-founded Museum School. Family history has it that Tarbell instantly fell in love and that he returned home early from studying in Paris because she was seeing another man.[28] When the couple finally married in 1888, Emeline abandoned any professional aspirations she may have had. According to one biographer, Tarbell "made the narrow Victorian rule that there would be only one painter in their family."[29]

Emeline did, however, serve as a model for her husband's early work. *In the Orchard* (Daniel J. Terra Collection) shows her sitting at the far right with her brother and sisters in a plein-air landscape.[30] Tarbell's representation of his young wife reveals his pride and his possessiveness; while her direct gaze commands the viewer's attention, her body is almost entirely concealed from view. Confined as she appears in *In the Orchard*, Emeline expressed no dissatisfaction with her consignment to the domestic sphere. When asked if she would marry an artist again if she had her life to live over, she reportedly replied, "Yes, if I could find another Tarbell."[31]

Having established a reputation in America as a master of plein-air painting, Tarbell turned his artistic vision inward. By the end of the century he could afford models and a studio and had begun to construct modestly sized images of what Trevor Fairbrother describes as "quiet-mannered contemporary people in tastefully decorated rooms."[32] In the controlled studio environment, the artist labored diligently to reproduce the appearance of figures and objects (in his words, to "make it like") and, according to his critics, created abstract beauty in the process. John E. D. Trask claimed in 1918, "Had Tarbell contributed nothing to the world but this group of interiors his high place as a painter would, nevertheless, be fixed securely for all time."[33]

When studied as a group, Tarbell's interiors allow us to reconstruct his studio interior and his domestic ideals. The room itself consisted of a long wall with three low windows flanked perpendicularly by a solid wall on the left and a door that opened inward on the right. Within this space, the artist arranged and rearranged a small number of props and models in compositions that increasingly simulated contemporary homes. Tarbell's spartan workplace possessed a frugal aspect characteristic of Boston interiors.[34] Equally important, it exemplified the turn-of-the-century preference for a "stripped [as opposed to decorated] studio," which Sarah Burns describes as an "index of sincerity and asceticism in art, . . . a rejection of urban luxury, of the suffocating accumulation of things associated with cosmopolitanism, consumerism, and the feminization of American culture."[35]

Although the studios of Chase and Tarbell bespoke different tastes and characters, their careers followed similar courses. In mid-life, both painters freed themselves from contemporary European models and found inspiration in seventeenth-century art. While Chase turned from Whistler to Velázquez, Tarbell moved from Degas (and also Whistler) to Vermeer. Their new models were venerated as modern old masters, artists who captured the truth of natural appearances as revealed through light. Extolling Tarbell's first Vermeeresque composition, *Girl Crocheting* (Canajoharie Library and Art Gallery, New York), Kenyon Cox wrote, "It seemed to eclipse his own previous works . . . making them look like mere paint while it alone looked like nature."[36] He stressed that the Bostonian did not imitate the Hollander's subjects or technique, but rather brought his point of view to the environment and people of the present day.

For contemporary critics, Tarbell's later interiors possessed beauty of both form and content that satisfied the spiritual cravings of a materialistic age. Charles Caffin claimed their power to stir the viewer's imagination were a sign of imagination (as opposed to simply observation) on the artist's part. In praise of *Girls Reading*, he wrote, 15

> To me "Girls Reading" seems a lesson in the holiness of beauty. In the hush that pervades the room, the pensive tenderness of the various silhouettes of dark against light; in the reverence . . . that impregnates the harmony of the whole, I discover, idealized with inexpressible charm, the possible beauty of the home life.[37]

Compared to *The Breakfast Room* with its combined connotations of artfulness and sexuality, *Girls Reading* linked formal beauty to domesticity. Francis Hamilton commented, "Here is an American interior, simple yet finely harmonious, that may well serve as a source of inspiration to the professional or amateur decorator," and went on to say, "A woman sewing or reading is domestic charm personified."[38]

The ideal womanhood portrayed in Tarbell's domesticated studio pictures seems to have had some reference to real life. While Emeline remained at home, the artist began, around 1905–6, to have their children model for some of his interiors. Josephine, the eldest of the four, appears at age fifteen as the central figure in *Girls Reading*. In later life, she reminisced,

> We all posed for father and enjoyed doing this for him because he was so good to us and we wanted to show our appreciation. I was asked by a friend if I was paid much and I was shocked at this question because I was so proud to do something for father and I really enjoyed it. When I was taken out of school to pose for father some people thought he was neglecting my education. I think the knoledge [sic] I received from father while I was posing was a greater help to me than any formal schooling I could have received.[39]

Although she is modestly situated at the rear of *Girls Reading*, Josephine's white dress and pink bow and sash make her the painting's focal point. Her rapt attention, signaled by alert glance and forward-leaning pose, adds psychological energy to this vision of female domesticity and reflects her youthful dedication to her artist-father.[40] Tarbell's youngest daughter, Mary (who lived her entire life with her parents except for a two-week marriage), shared her sister's adulation. She declared succinctly, "Everything he did was beautiful."[41]

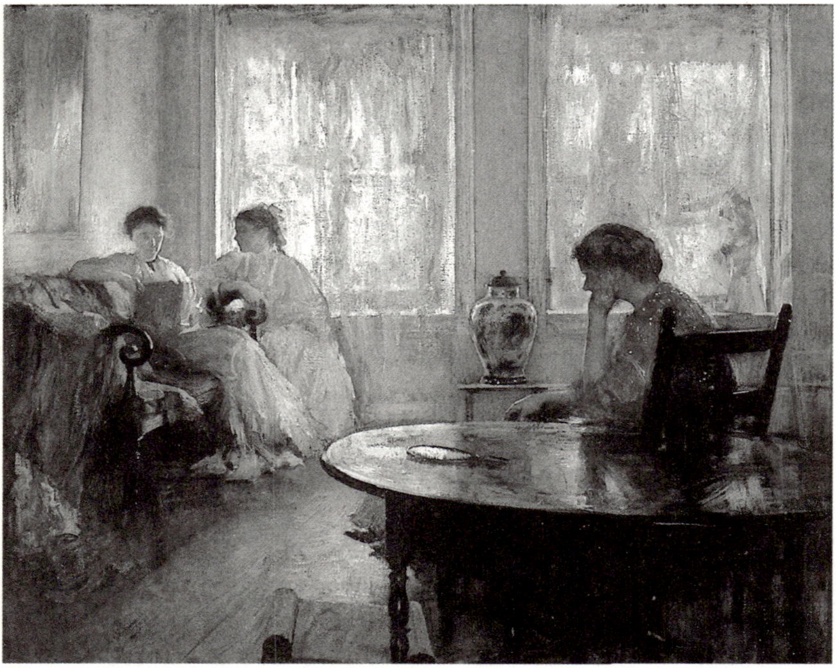

15 *Edmund C. Tarbell,* Girls Reading, *1907*

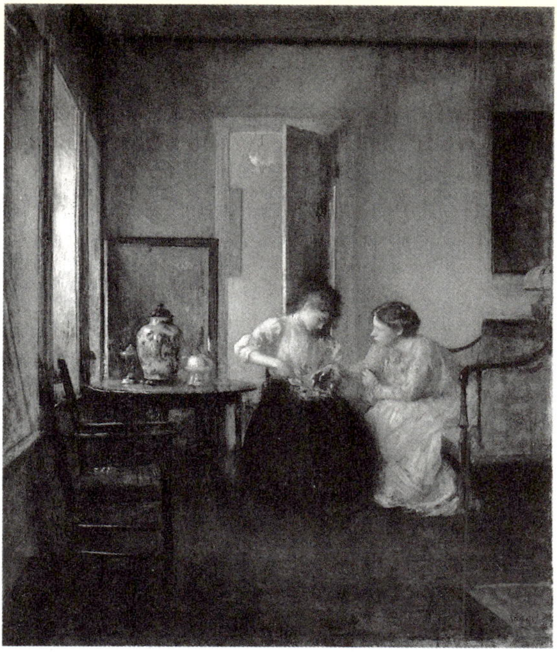

16 *Edmund C. Tarbell,* New England Interior, *1906*

The domesticated studio pictures of Tarbell exemplify both the devotion of his immediate family and a concept of family, broadly defined, peculiar to the region with which he proudly identified. *New England Interior* shows Josephine again, on the left, with a professional model, Charlotte Barton.[42] The painting's title derives not from the action, which appears to be sewing, but from the furnishings, which also figure prominently in *Girls Reading.*[43] Most notable among them are two of Tarbell's prized possessions: a New England gateleg table, symbolic of Puritan ancestry, and a Chinese porcelain jar, suggestive of the China Trade.[44]

In late nineteenth-century New England, such relics of colonial America functioned as "emblems of wealth and aristocracy." According to Celia Betsky, nostalgia for moral and material purity was subsumed in this period by reverence for genealogical purity and "conservationism snuggled up to conservatism."[45] Tarbell himself did not descend from a line of merchants (like other *nouveaux riches* he bought his antiques from a dealer), but he could trace his lineage to seventeenth-century Groton. Virtually every lengthy article written about the painter in his lifetime makes mention of this fact. To viewers outside New England, Tarbell's art clearly manifested his region's peculiar brand of snobbery. A hostile New York critic observed, "He probably belongs to the Back Bay section . . . and puts the family above the person."[46]

Tarbell's proudest expression of his New England origins was the summer home in New Castle, New Hampshire that he purchased for his family in 1902. The artist expanded and remodeled the residence; under his direction a modest white farmhouse on the Piscataqua River was transformed into a country estate with a gardener, a cook, three maids, a groom, and a coachman. In this rural retreat, Tarbell indulged a much publicized passion for golf that linked him to the country's new athleticism. He also added a studio to his property, a separate building close to the house with one large room and a northern light.

A photograph of Tarbell painting in New Castle represents his artistic enterprise in terms of the domesticated studio. Taken in 1907 by R. D. McDonough of Portsmouth but probably arranged by the painter, this ostensibly candid image derives compositionally from the highly praised *Girls Reading*. The gateleg table and Chinese jar appear together now in the foreground. To the left, in the far corner of the Sheraton sofa, a book absorbs the attention of Mary and her younger brother, Edmund, Jr. Seated opposite the children in a Chippendale chair, Tarbell bends over his easel, and behind him the recently begun *Portrait of Mr and Mrs Frederick Prince* (William Wood Prince Collection) and the more finished *Preparing for the Matinee* (Mr and Mrs George J. Arden Collection) signal the promise of future production (in contrast to Chase's studio consumption). In this artfully constructed photograph, domestic life, New England heritage, and studio practice are drawn together formally by the three legs of Tarbell's easel. Art constitutes a hub around which life revolves.

At New Castle, Tarbell began to compose domesticated studio pictures in the context of his own home. His climactic work in this genre is *My Family* of 1914. Ostensibly a group portrait, it shows (left to right) Josephine, Mary, Mercie, Edmund, Jr, and Emeline (again bodily confined) together in the living hall. This colonial revival interior with exposed beam ceiling, antique mantel, and diamond pane windows was the centerpiece of the painter's remodelling project. Conceived as a work of art in its own right, it contains, in this representation, his signature antiques and, through the open window, a view of the studio roof.

While Chase's domesticated studio pictures often give the impression of stopped action, Tarbell's family appears still, silent, and isolated from one another. What unites this frozen group is neither any activity represented (reading, sewing, thinking) nor a neurasthenic condition, but the artist's idea of life as art. We see them in the act of modeling, in which, by Josephine's account, all participated willingly. Corroborating her recollection, a family friend observed, "[Tarbell's children] fitted into the fabric of his life and the composition of his paintings as perfectly as if he had conceived them in a vision." Equating biological and pictorial creation as achievements of the artist, he continued, "One is hardly able to tell where

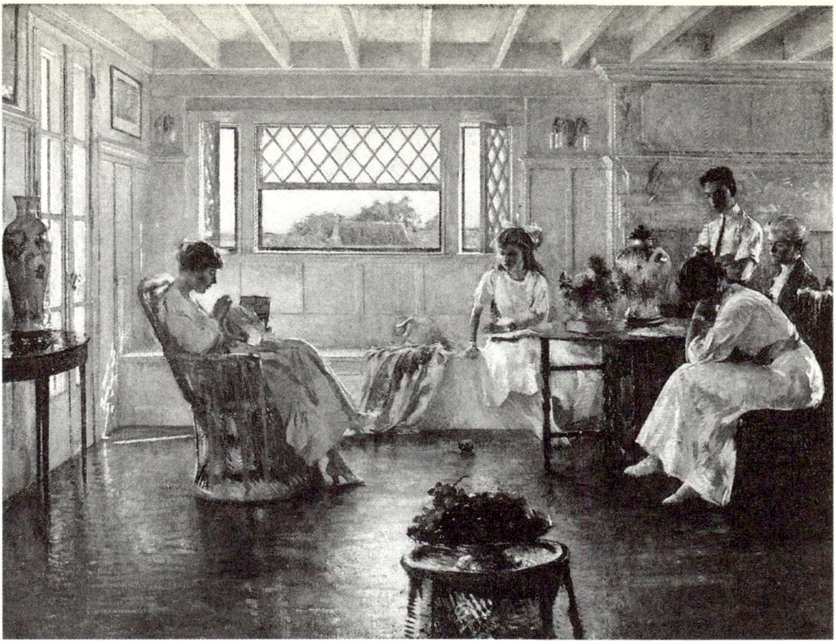

17 *Edmund C. Tarbell,* My Family, *1914*

the genius of the father lies – in the fortunate conception of his children, or in his exquisite taste and adaptation in working them into his pictures."[47]

The family's complicity in Tarbell's aesthetic arrangement of their home life is nowhere more evident than in a concerted (albeit unsuccessful) effort by Josephine, after the artist's death in 1938, to turn their New Castle estate into a historic property. In numerous letters of appeal to preservation societies, art museum directors, personal friends, the Smithsonian Institution, and even First Lady Eleanor Roosevelt, she stated her case plainly and practically:

> So often the result of a man's life in making a beautiful home is broken up after his death only to be restored to its original condition later on. This time there seems to be a chance to keep father's home as he left it, if we only knew how.[48]

Rather than seeking to sell the property or change it according to her own designs, Josephine sought to preserve the family home as a testament to her father's art.

On the surface, Tarbell's *My Family* and Chase's *Hall at Shinnecock* have much in common. As genre paintings, both show upper-middle-class Americans at leisure in an aesthetic environment. As interiors, both contain furnishings that allude to the nation's colonial history: Chase's Dutch kas, Tarbell's gateleg table and Chinese jar. As portraits, both depict the artist's wife and children in the living hall of their summer home.

Read as domesticated studio pictures, however, these works reveal a deeper level of meaning rooted in the individual character of the two families represented. In the *Hall at Shinnecock*, Alice and the girls are immersed in art. Paintings line the walls of the room, Koto studies a picture book, and Cosy watches her father in the act of painting. Both Koto's book and Cosy's gaze reach out to Chase, and his own reflected image in the mirror makes the artist part of this domestic scene. In Tarbell's picture, a different relationship prevails. Emeline and the children are depicted not with works of art, but with studio props, which also read as household furnishings and signs of New England ancestry. The members of this family do not look at art, rather they are art; their domestic life takes the form of a finished picture. Tarbell himself remains determinedly outside the composition, literally, in front of the foreground still life, and metonymically, under the windowless studio roof.

While Chase moved himself into the domestic sphere, Tarbell transported his family into the realm of art. Their different constructions of the domesticated studio – one participatory, one more patriarchal – reflect the character of both their home lives and the generations to which they belonged. Chase, who flourished in the gilded age, exemplified the genteel tradition in America. Cosmopolitan and bohemian, his love of beauty and passion for consumption linked him with women more than men. Tarbell, thirteen years younger, came to artistic maturity in the progressive era, a period anxious to restore the masculine character of the nation. Hard-working and conservative, he believed, as one admirer phrased it, "that painting was the work for virile manhood."[49] The admiration accorded Tarbell's domesticated studio pictures, in contrast to those of Chase, hinged on American attitudes toward gender as much as art per se.

As modernists, Chase and Tarbell strove to create abstract formal beauty in their pictures; as Impressionists, they looked at American life and found its most attractive aspects in the domestic sphere. By conflating studio life and home life, each, in his own way, sought to advance his aesthetic project through appeal to cultural desire. While Chase's wife and children looked at pictures, socialized, and played in his workplace, Tarbell's read, sewed, and dutifully posed. In such representations of model-families, American viewers read the feminine or masculine character of the artist. For a male bastion of critics and patrons, the successful painter of domesticated studio pictures was the man who kept women under his control.

4

Psyche and Sympathy: Staging Interiority in the Early Modern Home

SUSAN SIDLAUSKAS

ACCORDING to Walter Benjamin – epic chronicler of nineteenth-century Paris – the domestic interior was "the universe for the private citizen."[1] The visual evidence seems to bear him out, for the image of the interior flooded not only French, but British and American architectural journals, pattern books, photography albums, and manuals that advocated interior decoration as a form of self-expression. In popular illustrations of the new apartment house, or *maison à loyer*, façades were sheared off in order to demonstrate that the social class of the occupants was inversely proportionate to their height from the street. In the new domestic melodramas, the naturalistic setting virtually assumed the stature of a protagonist.[2] Across nineteenth-century urban culture, then, the domestic interior would seem to have become the transparent, even inevitable, metaphor for bourgeois identity – a metaphor ratified through the sheer multiplicity and diversity of its expression.

The role of advanced painting in this account of the rise of the interior – and of the visualization of interiority – was more equivocal, and more dynamic, however. Rather than simply illustrating the visible signs of cultural change, a number of key paintings of the mid- to late nineteenth century *enacted* the instabilities that were its consequence. Such an achievement depended upon pictorial structures that exploited the interior's accessibility as a sign, even as they subverted its commonplace associations with comfort and safety. Such paintings gave shape to the containment that defined interiority, yet at the same time breached its pictorial and psychological frame by actively soliciting the engaged response of the viewer. Every viewer who stands, and who stood, before these paintings enacts that duality yet again, for the spectator's presence violates the intimacy that the interior was assumed to contain and protect. Benjamin himself alluded to the janus-faced nature of the interior: on one hand, a sanctuary from which the world could be safely observed – "a box in the world-theatre," as the critic put it; on the other hand, a stage on which one's most intimate feelings could be acted out with the greatest authenticity.[3]

The canons of realism legislated against picturing those feelings through

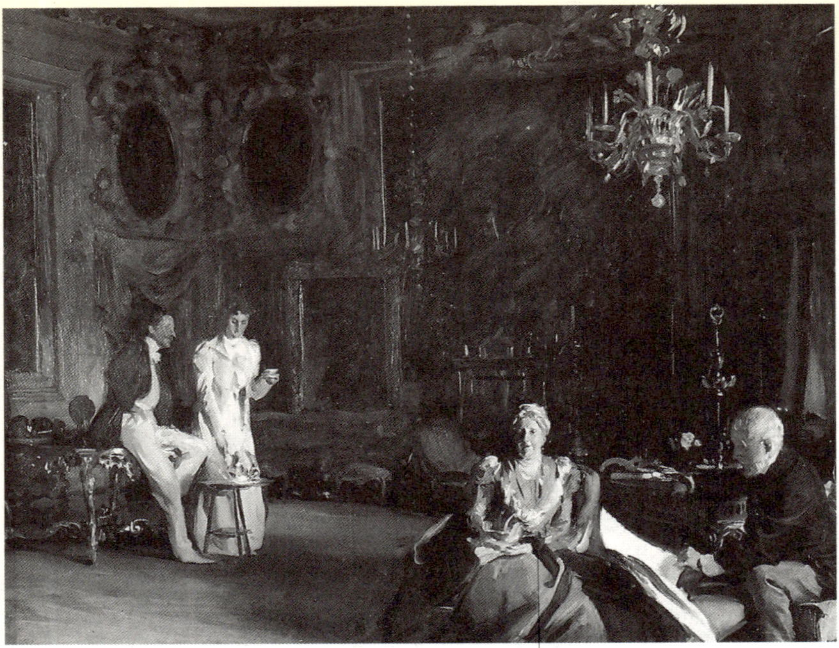

18 *John Singer Sargent,* Interior in Venice, *1889*

narrative or allegorical means, however. One group of painters offered an alternative: they represented the *externalization* of feeling, or identity, by seizing upon the most revelatory nuances of a person's relation to his or her intimate setting. Rather than illustrate this dynamic relation through an accumulation of detail or narrative signs, these painters intervened at the most basic level of pictorial structure: they fundamentally altered the relation between figure and ground.

Members of the new bourgeois class were anxious to represent both their psyches and their status through an expressive, and legible, relation to their intimate surroundings. The calculated juxtaposition of the body to the house through the mediums of architecture, decoration, furniture arrangement and the somatic expressions of gesture, posture and personal adornment constituted nothing less than the enactment of a private identity. This was a new notion in the culture, and it demanded a new pictorial expression. And if the relation of the body and the house seemed inflected by ambiguity and instability, so too was its analogue in paint: the relation of figure to ground.

Consider, for example, the overarching shadow and asymmetric figure placement of John Singer Sargent's *Interior in Venice* (1889); the open space and uneven figure distribution of James Tissot's *Too Early* (1873, Guildhall Art Gallery, London); and the yawning spaces at the centers of Edgar

Degas's *Interior* (1868, Philadelphia Museum of Art), Sargent's *Daughters of Edward Darley Boit* (1884) and of William Merritt Chase's *Hide and Seek* (1888). The indistinct architectural boundaries of Adolph Menzel's *The Artist's Sister with Candle* (1847, Bayerische Staatsgemäldesammlungen, Munich) offer another variant of disequilibrium, as does the jarring emphasis on *internal* boundaries within the tightly constricted space of James Abbott McNeill Whistler's *Harmony in Green and Rose: The Music Room* (1860–61), of Degas's *The Bellelli Family* (1859–60) and of Edouard Vuillard's *Mother and Sister of the Artist* (1893). And finally, there are the oppressive distortions of scale and perspective in the architecture and figures of *Ennui* by Walter Sickert (1914).

In discussions about pictorial composition, the formulations of body and house, and figure and ground, often are used interchangeably. They are allied, certainly, even interdependent. But they are not identical. And it is in part the spectator's response to the distance between the two formulations that gives these paintings their particular potency. More precisely, the pictorial fusion of figure and ground on the surface of the canvas is inevitably in tension with the spectator's psychological resistance towards wholly merging a body with its surroundings.

In her book, *On Longing*, Susan Stewart has argued that the imaginative relation between the body and its surroundings must always be in doubt.

> The body presents the paradox of contained and container at once. Thus our attention is continually focused upon the boundaries or limits of the body; known from an exterior the limits of the body as object; known from an interior, the limits of its physical extension into space.[4]

In representations of the body within a domestic space, then, we are contending not with one interior, but with *two*: the body itself and the container that surrounds it. The instability that Stewart describes seems to have found one of its first pictorial expressions in the domestic interiors of the nineteenth century. In several of the paintings just mentioned, body and space seem to be competing for primacy. In Sargent's *Daughters of Edward* 23
Darley Boit, empty space threatens to overwhelm the figures who stand at its periphery; while in many of Vuillard's paintings, figures seem enervated while their surroundings – wallpaper, upholstery, floor-coverings – teem with life. And in Degas's *Interior* and Sickert's *Ennui*, space and figure are 19
locked in a tense equipoise that seems perpetually on the brink of dissolution.

At first glance, the pictorial structures within all these paintings seem random and idiosyncratic – even aberrant. But in fact, they conform to a fairly predictable mix of asymmetry, imbalance, and distortion: precisely the features that, among others, have come to be identified as the early signs of "modernity" in painting.[5] The compositional strategies employed here

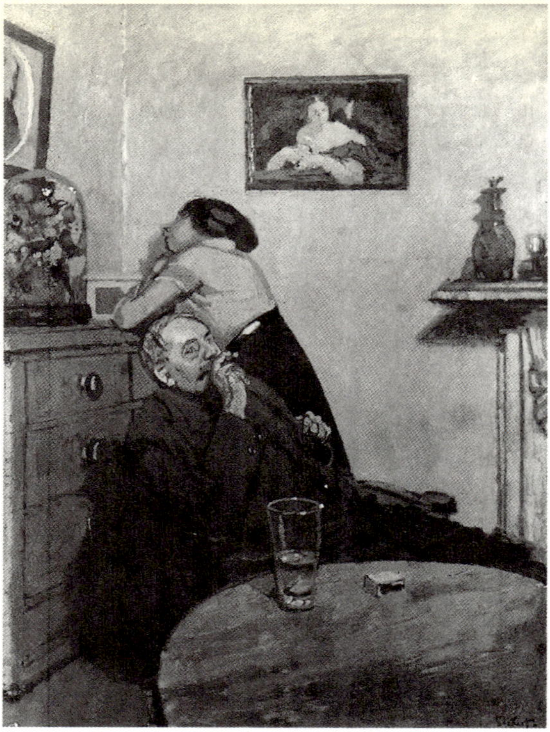

19 *Walter Sickert,* Ennui, *1914*

would later become, in a more reductive form, fundamentals of the vocabulary of abstraction: the identification of figure and ground, the emphasis on "negative" space, the expressive distortions of space, scale and perspective, and the schematic treatment of physiognomy. Even the absorptive, non-specific, engagement that would be demanded by abstraction finds a precedent here, for these images do not *narrate* stories of psychological discomfort, alienation between the sexes, or the isolation of children; they act out their effects through figural and spatial arrangements that were calculated to provoke a bodily empathy on the part of the sentient viewer.

Conventions for perceiving and describing space in these years suggest that when spectators viewed painted figures stranded on opposite reaches of a gaping space, pressed into a corner, subsumed into the furniture around them, or divided from their intimates by an assertive drapery, they were cued to experience a visceral response, a bodily empathy for the discomfort of their protagonists. The visual provocations to unease and disorientation were thus translated into an imagined experience of another's psychological state. In architectural treatises, manuals on decoration, descriptions of theatrical settings, and novels, readers/viewers were encouraged to project themselves imaginatively into whatever space was described or represented. The idea was that one didn't merely see space, one could *experience* it through a visceral response to the imagined effects of light and shade, proportions, perspective and scale.

César Daly, an architectural theorist, editor and critic, was contributing to a larger nineteenth-century attempt to combine aesthetics and science when he formulated his roster of "aesthetic geometry," a series of shapes that were thought to elicit predictable physiological responses in the responsive viewer. "Movement of Lines! Equilibrium of masses!" Daly proclaimed. "Is there not, in effect, in the universality of these figures, the proof that at the base of human instinct exists the conscience of a permanent symbolic relation between, on the one hand, certain considerations of lines, and on the other hand, the static and dynamic conditions of bodies?"[6]

The mental animation of architectural forms, as well as the voids they enclosed, was advocated by some of the earliest writings to emerge from the nascent field of art history. Cast as the psychological notion of "empathy," Heinrich Wölfflin used the idea to characterize the sentient viewer's response to art and architecture. In 1886 Wölfflin wrote that, "Our own bodily organization is the form through which we apprehend everything physical." These judgements take place, he argued, through a "process of unconscious endowment of animation," in which architecture, as an "art of corporeal masses, relates to man as a corporeal being." Wölfflin explicitly linked symmetrical compositions to positive responses. "Likewise," he continued, "it is also known that a severe injury to the equilibrium can have a depressing effect. We ourselves feel fear and anxiety when the restful effect of balance cannot be found."[7] What might Wölfflin have thought of the asymmetric figure arrangement of Sargent's *Daughters of Edward Darley Boit*, or the claustrophobic perspective of Vuillard's *Mother* 22
and Sister of the Artist, paintings that are nearly contemporary with his own formulations?

If we extend both Daly's and Wölfflin's formulations about the animism of physical space to the painted interior, we might imagine that any figure represented within that space becomes a surrogate for the spectator's own empathic response: a substitute through which the viewer can vicariously "experience" the imagined discomfort of a space too compressed or too attenuated, a furniture arrangement too confining, or another figure too near, or too far away. Of course, the nature of the response will differ with each historical viewer; nonetheless, a quality of heightened engagement or curiosity seems to characterize many viewers' responses to these paintings.

Sargent's *Daughters of Edward Darley Boit*, Vuillard's *Mother and Sister of the Artist*, Degas's *The Bellelli Family*, Whistler's *Harmony in Green and Rose*, and Chase's *Hide and Seek* each represent distinct positions within a shifting relation between body and house, figure and ground; a dynamic, often unstable, interdependency that was being played out not only in nineteenth-century visual art, but in Antoine Sardou's and the younger Alexandre Dumas's domestic melodramas, in Daly's treatises on modern urban and suburban housing, in the "realist" settings of Emile Zola's *Thérèse Raquin* (1867) and Gustave Flaubert's *Sentimental Education* (1869), in Edmond and Jules de Goncourt's two-volume analysis of their home and possessions, *The House of the Artist* (1880), and in photographer Eugène Atget's comprehensive *Intérieurs Parisiennes* of 1900. By the turn of the century, the imaginative fusion of the body with its surroundings would find its expression in the "Overture" to Marcel Proust's *Swann's Way* (1912), in writer Paul Bourget's essays on "the new psychology" (1886), in the theories of "neurasthenia" formulated by Dr Jean-Martin Charcot, and in the all-over decorative program of the Art Nouveau style, which depended upon the idea that the boundaries between inner psyche and outward aesthetic expression were growing ever more indistinct.[8] The paintings described below may be understood as the preconditions for the imaginative body/space fusion of Art Nouveau. While the expressivity of the works by Degas, Whistler and Vuillard depends upon the compression of figure, space, and object, the paintings by Sargent and Chase instead emphasize empty space at the expense of the figures. In different but related ways, each artist produced an image of disorientation and discomfort, in which a pictorial instability between figure and ground enacted a psychological discomfort – between body and house.

In Degas's *The Bellelli Family*, his aunt Laura, her husband Baron Gennaro Bellelli, and their daughters Giulia and Giovanna, are all positioned frieze-like in a shallow space that gives shape to their emotional confinement. In an extraordinary presentation for the ostensible head of the family, Degas encases the Baron in a taut frame created by the intersection of the fireplace frame with other axes of the room's decoration.[9] His entrapment is compounded by the massive, averted chair in the right foreground. The Baron is separated by the table from the pyramidal configuration of Laura, Giovanna and Giulia, an isolation tempered only by the oblique glance that Giulia directs towards, but not at, her father. Baron Bellelli's slightly forward-leaning posture, at odds with the evident impossibility of release, enhances the sense of impotence. Figures punctuate, rather than dominate, the space of the room, and chairs and tables become agents of confinement and restraint.

Degas simultaneously exploits and critiques the tendency of the middle class to define itself through their possessions; here, possessions divide the members of the family, rather than protecting and affirming their stature and identity. Degas subtly intensifies the analogy between persons and their possessions by juxtaposing Giulia's fragile limb to the stick leg of the chair she sits upon. This visual passage anticipates a short story by Degas's friend

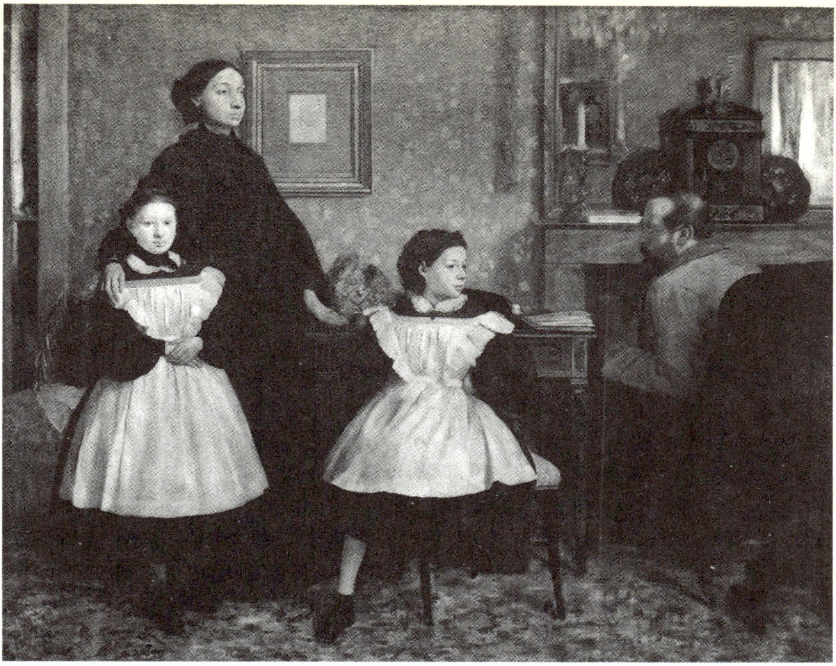

20 *Edgar Degas,* The Bellelli Family, *1859–60*

the critic Edmond Duranty, called *Bric-à-Brac* (1876), in which the author describes an overcrowded drawing-room in which the massive forms of its stiffly-costumed human inhabitants are indistinguishable from the large armoires and over-decorated wing chairs that surround them. The expressive and economic inseparability of a person from his or her surroundings would become a central tenet of Duranty's later manifesto, *The New Painting* (1876), an essay made influential in part by its descriptions of unidentified but unmistakable interiors by Degas.

A similar animacy of objects and furniture is also apparent in *Harmony in* 21
Green and Rose by Whistler. Here, Whistler puts Degas's means to even more ambiguous ends. The identity of the figures is unclear, as is the reason for the proximity of the three female figures – one a mirror reflection – looking in different directions. What is most relevant to us here is that while the configuration of the space – and the mirror that partially reflects it – is only vaguely defined, the draperies assume the stiffness of walls, becoming partitions that compress and further isolate three already stranded figures.

The sense of simultaneous compression and isolation is even more concentrated in Vuillard's *Mother and Sister of the Artist.* Madame and Mademoiselle Vuillard are portrayed in what appears to be a kitchen, or dining-room, which is modestly furnished and sparsely decorated. No shared domestic task explains their somewhat uncomfortable proximity.

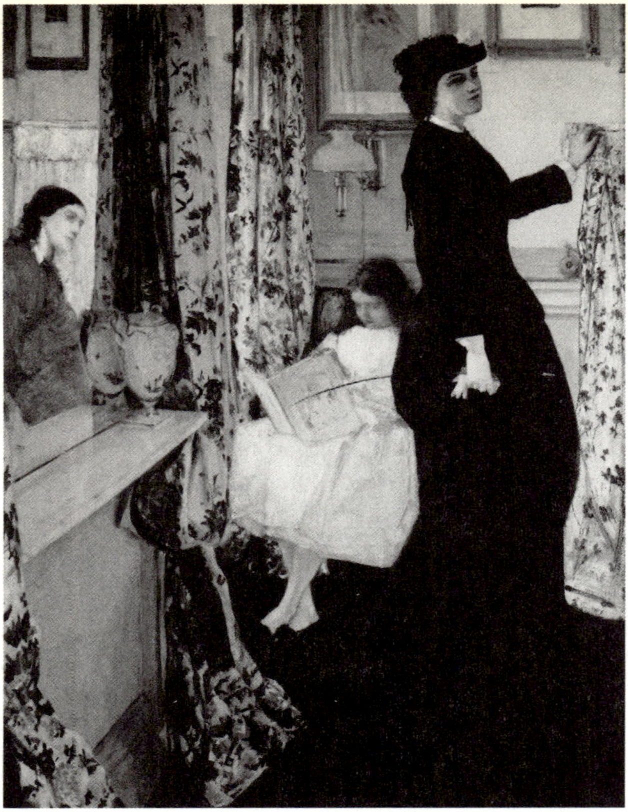

21 *James Abbott McNeill Whistler,* Harmony in Green and Rose: The Music Room, *1860–61.*

Vuillard's mother, always a dignified, stalwart presence in his paintings and drawings, here sits as if implanted: the only real anchor in a space of remarkable instability and shifting perspectives. The artist's sister Marie, on the other hand, seems only tenuously attached to the floor beneath her, and *too* closely attached to the flanking wall. Her figure is contracted, hunched over to conform to the space in which her brother has placed her. If she were to rise from her awkward position, her head would pierce through the top frame. As Vuillard has painted her, she is a fragile caryatid, bearing the weight of the painting on her back.

The spectator is swept into the room by an expanse of floor that abruptly rears up and flattens, so that it appears to be a surface floating behind the figures rather than a plane beneath them. There is no conventional vanishing point. Instead, the viewer's visual trajectory is halted by the massive chest of drawers whose solidity mimics the blocky form of Madame Vuillard. The bureau is oversized; its breadth fills the portion of the rear wall that we see, exaggerating its narrowness and adding to the all-

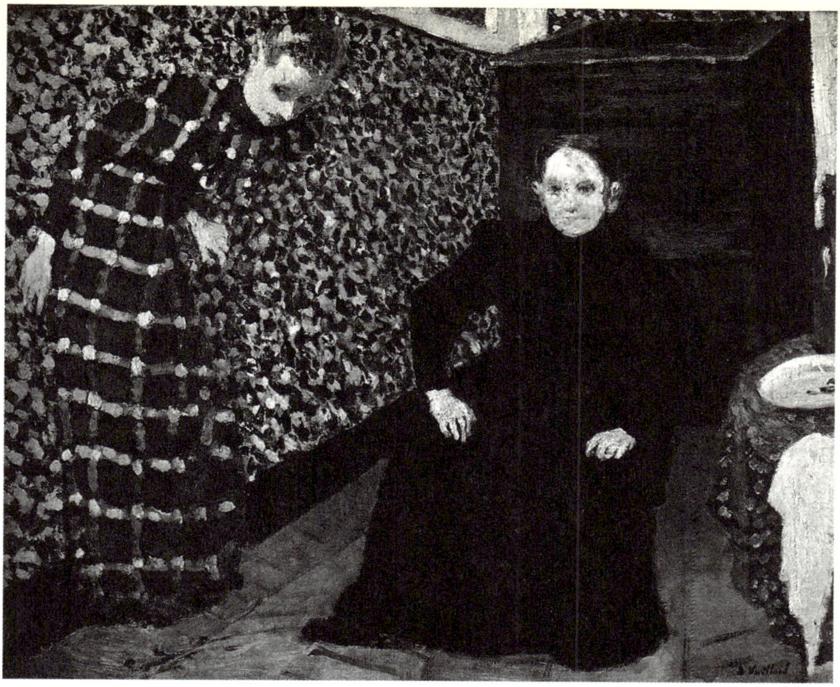

22 *Edouard Vuillard,* Mother and Sister of the Artist, *c. 1893*

over sense of constriction. While these planes appear to contract as they are observed, Madame Vuillard seems impervious to the forces of perspective and appears, in contrast, to expand. Like the wallpaper that surrounds Marie, the bureau behind her mother is a near-animate presence; it even appears to have adopted some of the physiognomy of its owner. One is reminded of Duranty's *Bric-à-Brac*, whose emphasis on the interchangeability of humans and furniture would be pursued even further by the Symbolist writer Paul Bourget. Writing in 1886, Bourget insisted that not only did furniture suggest an owner's temperament, it had a temperament of its own.

> The surface of a room, the shape of an object, its color, can inspire sympathy, or even antipathy . . . objects become signs of a great number of small actions.[10]

In Vuillard's double portrait, each woman arrogates a different perspectival space. While the stability of Madame Vuillard is reinforced by the bureau behind her and the perspective lines (or floorboards) that rise straight up beside her, the floor beneath Marie tilts precipitously upward, intensifying the sensation that she is unable to secure a place to stand. Marie's feet are nearly invisible; she barely skims the surface of the floor, hovering above the baseboard and pressing up against a wall which offers her no real support. A trail of black from the baseboard behind Marie's hem rises upward to skim her dress, further binding her to that unstable surface.

The arrangement of the brushstrokes, as well as their scale and color, moreover, act to disrupt this small space, psychologically and pictorially. The daubs around Marie are large and appear randomly shaped and placed, and repeat the vivid hues of her dress. As the strokes move to the area around her mother, however, Vuillard diminishes their scale, mutes their intensity, and replaces the golds and oranges with muddy browns, black and beiges. Through these pictorial adjustments, Vuillard reinforces the perception that his mother commands her environment. But even the assertive plaid of her dress does not allow Marie to stand out from the surfaces of the room. While the wallpaper seems disturbingly alive, Marie seems almost spectral. Her visual autonomy, as well as her femininity, are so severely undermined that her form challenges the very notion of corporeal presence. The confusion of the animate and inanimate is distilled in Vuillard's decision to paint Marie's left hand in exactly the same ochre tones as the writhing wallpaper pattern that surrounds it.

Vuillard's painting was produced during a moment of particularly acute anxiety about all things female: biology, sexuality, artistry, psychology and decorum. While caricatures of the "New Woman" deplored her aggressiveness and masculinity, as well as her stance as a threat to the stability of the bourgeois family, the womanly arts of embroidery, tapestry making, and jewelry design were promoted by the Women's Art Exposition of 1892, organized in part to revive France's flagging decorative arts industry. While the exposition seemed to support women's talents, the authors were careful to insist that they must exercise their talents only at home, so as not to disrupt the equilibrium of their families. Critics suggested that women should become "artificers of the interior," and design themselves with the same aesthetic acumen that they bestowed on their upholstery and decor: one object within a wholly-integrated design program.[11]

There is another, more immediate, context for Vuillard's pictorial fusion of his sister to her setting: his own work in the avant-garde *Théâtre de l'Oeuvre*, or Theater of the Work, widely considered the first Symbolist theater in Paris. Working with the founder, his childhood friend Aurélian Lugné-Poe, Vuillard designed playbills for productions that favored the rather gloomy psychological dramas of Scandinavian playwrights Ibsen and Strindberg. More importantly, Vuillard also designed several stage settings and the lighting that animated them. While almost no visual evidence remains of his designs, we can reconstruct some of their effects through contemporary accounts of the theater's productions. We know that for the performance of a poetic piece by the Belgian author Maurice Beauborg, Vuillard stretched a green scrim across the stage. His intervention not only created an eerie effect, but rendered the boundaries between actors and

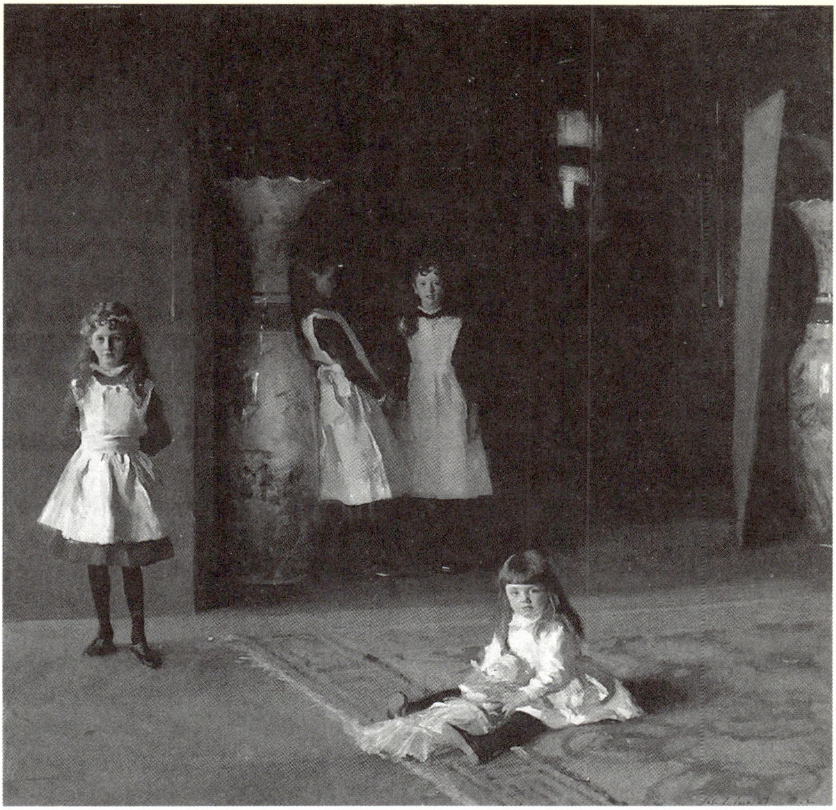

23 *John Singer Sargent,* The Daughters of Edward D. Boit, *1882*

their surroundings indistinct. Atmosphere was emphasized over detail, and the theater's productions became famous for their almost abstract fusions of light, color, and sound.[12]

Despite their obvious differences in scale, treatment and effect, Sargent's *Daughters of Edward Darley Boit* and Vuillard's *Mother and Sister of the Artist* share something significant. Each painting compromises the corporeal presence of its human subjects by placing at least some figures in a nearly antagonistic relationship with their surrroundings. While Vuillard depended upon a too-lively wallpaper pattern and a disorienting perspective, Sargent's method was to allow a palpable emptiness to dominate the composition with such force that it challenged the pictorial and psychological autonomy of those figures who perch at its edges.

We have evidence that the audiences for late 1870s' and early 1880s' painting did respond to the evocative powers of empty space. Writing on J. Bertrand's painting *Marguerite of Faust* (1878, present whereabouts unknown) a critic made an explicit connection between its unusual figural arrangement – a gaping space with figures on either edge and an infant stranded in the middle – and the despair of the protagonists:

> The reader will observe the peculiar composition which the artist has used, the focus of the scene being quite vacant, and the personages arrayed centrifugally around the edges; this blank emptiness of his stage gives our painter a very appropriate expression of austerity, of cheerlessness, of desolation.[13]

Sargent's *Daughters of Edward Darley Boit* visualizes the fragility of the ties that bind. Mary Louisa, Florence, Jane, and Julia, with her doll "P-Paul", are asymmetrically dispersed in the cavernous entrance hall of their family's Paris apartment. The eye is ineluctably drawn to the shadowy reaches of the room beyond the four girls, the archway of which is flanked by two enormous vases and a free-standing red screen. The vases, the screen and the blue and white rug upon the floor are the only decorative touches in a rather austere setting. The sisters seem adrift in this monumental space, detached from one another: "lost in space" as one scholar once put it.[14]

The vases are too oversized to humanize the setting; nearly architectural in scale, they cannot be consigned to the category of bibelot. Other than the vases, which stand sentry-like in the hall, signs of the parents' presence are entirely suppressed. And yet there are virtually no compensating childish props. Only Julia, who was three years old at the time of the portrait, is allowed a doll, and "P-Paul" is held carefully in her lap. The hem of its dress merges neatly with the rug's border, as if even the area for girlish play must be firmly demarcated. The area in which the sisters are fixed seems both prefatory and transitional; its *raison d'être* seems to depend on its relation to *other* spaces. As such, the foyer is at once confining and unprotected, suspended somewhere between private and public. Not only its function, but its boundaries are ill-defined. There is an absence of comforting corners or enclosing walls, and thus the eye travels vainly to locate the limits of perception.[15]

Sargent's painting anticipates with extraordinary prescience a passage in Henry James's *American Scene* (1907), in which the author complained about the lack of definition in American domestic architecture, believing it to be truly injurious to the psyche. Even though the Boit girls were painted in a Parisian apartment, James's prose evokes Sargent's interior.

> This diffused vagueness of separation between apartments, between hall and room, between one room and another, between the one you are in and the one you are not in, between place of passage and place of privacy, is a provocation to despair which the public institution shares impartially with the luxurious "home" . . . Thus we have every part of every house visible, visitable, penetrable, not only from every other part, but from as many parts of as many other houses as possible . . . Thus we see systematized the indefinite extension of all

> spaces and the definite merging of all functions; the enlargement of every opening, the exaggeration of every passage, the substitution of gaping arches and far perspectives and resounding voids for enclosing walls, for practicable doors, for controllable windows, for all the rest of the essence of the room-character, that room-suggestion, which is so indispensable to occupation and concentration.[16]

The very palpability of Sargent's "resounding voids" threatens to dissolve, or to permeate, the figures that interrupt it. In 1933, the psychoanalyst Eugène Minkowski grappled with how to describe the near-physical presence of darkness. He wrote,

> This obscurity is not at all the simple absence of light, as we know it; it has something very positive about it. It seems much more material to me, much more "filled" than light space, which, as we have seen, fades away, so to speak, before the materiality of the objects which are in it. Precisely because of this it does not spread out before me but touches me directly, envelops me, embraces me, even penetrates me, completely, passes through me, so that one could almost say that while the ego is permeable by darkness it is not permeable by light. The ego does not affirm itself in relation to darkness but becomes confused with it, becomes one with it.[17]

Sargent concentrates the darkness in the center of his canvas, and so destabilizes the very place the spectator expects to find stability, an expectation intensified by the square format of the painting. Here, Jane and Florence Boit seem poised on the edge of nothingness, transfixed. It is as if a too-rapid movement could tip them backwards into the pictorial counterpart of the "abyss" so often alluded to by Sargent's friends Henry James and Edith Wharton. While the figure of Jane constitutes the painting's approximate center, she seems ill at ease and remote, both pictorially and psychologically. Washed in shadow, she nearly merges with the encroaching darkness of the room beyond. Even the white of the pinafore – brilliant on Mary Louisa – is a muted chalky grey. The line of white reflected off Jane's shoe is the only suggestion of where her feet are located; thus, the spectator remains uncertain of where the young girl's body ends and the shadowy architecture begins.

Even Jane's posture seems calculated for discomfort. She stands stiffly, with her shoulders thrust slightly forward, as if at attention. Her hands hang limply at her sides, and her eyes are glazed and widened; she seems wary without being entirely alert. Her lips are parted, but slack, another suggestion of hesitation and movement or feeling arrested. Jane seems completely detached from Florence beside her. The vase Florence leans upon could only be a fragile support, despite its monumentality. Her shoulders nestle in to fit its curve, but the arc of her back seems strained and

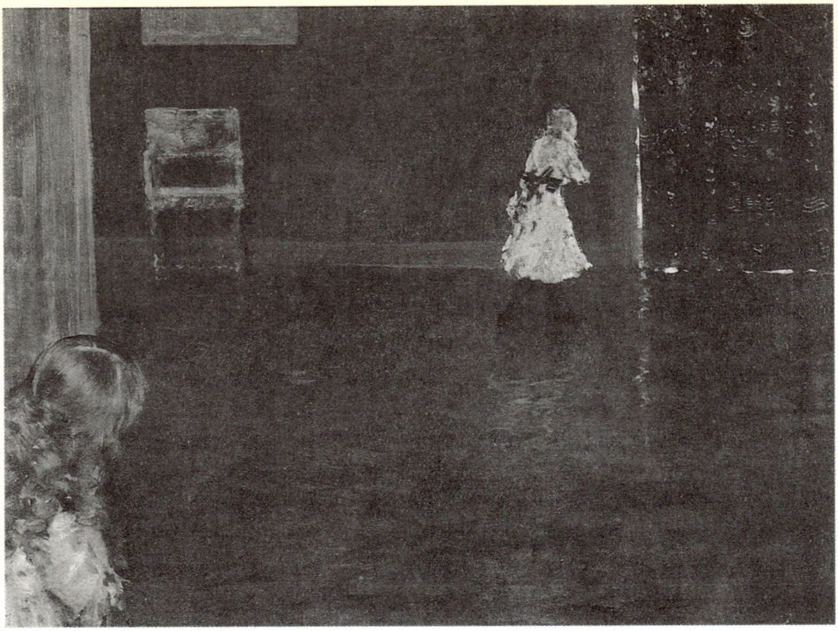

24 *William Merritt Chase,* Hide and Seek, *1888*

uncomfortable. Mary Louisa stands, isolated before the blank wall, with a gravity beyond her years. Far away from her in the foreground, Julia is the only sister who engages the viewer without reserve, and she seems remarkably still for one so young.

There is no evidence to suggest that the image of alienation that Sargent created had a basis in the actual family life of the Boits. Instead, the painting seems to be the artist's interpretation of the general isolation of childhood, perhaps encouraged by his own experience, which seems by all accounts to have been rather grim.[18] The theme of the equivocal nature of childhood was also taken up by William Merritt Chase, who produced *Hide and Seek* six years after Sargent painted the Boit sisters. In *Hide and Seek*, one small girl peers around a curtain at a companion who is retreating towards the right rear corner. The girls are fixed at either terminus of a diagonal that spans a daunting expanse of empty space. The sense of a great distance derives not only from the void between the two girls, but from the different handling each of them receives. The golden curls of the girl in the lower corner are rather naturalistically painted; a warm light reflects off rounded coils of hair. Though her head is turned to face into the room, making her face inaccessible to us, she nonetheless seems substantial, solid and rounded. Her white dress is rendered in some detail; vivid blue laces dangle from her elbow, for instance. Her companion, on the other hand, is a ghostly apparition, schematically drawn and thinly painted. She is the antithesis in paint of her more present companion. It is as if the thinness of the brushstrokes and lack of definition give material form to her immanent disappearance from sight.

Chase created another ironic comment on the act of perception by the way he framed the view which is the focus of the nearer girl's attention. Because of the way she peers around the sheer curtain that edges the left side of the painting, it is as if she stands in a different perceptual space from her playmate, looking at a *picture* of her disappearing friend. The chair parallel to the rear wall adds to this impression. The only piece of furniture in the room, it is as sketchily painted as the retreating girl. In spite of its lack of solidity, however, it provides an important compositional anchor: a square which is part of a pattern of rectangles that ties the composition together, in spite of its "emptiness". Chase uses a stream of light as a connective agent across the darkness. White light spills from beneath a distant doorway on the right, is funneled into a narrow band which skims the doorway and runs along the baseboard to intersect with the vertical of the curtain wall. The floor is subtly articulated. Watery wriggles of brownish-red color appear to undulate across the floor, and there is a constant play between surface attention and deep space. The sensation of distance is so overwhelming here as to constitute the *subject* of the painting.

Both Chase's and Sargent's works address the marginality and isolation of childhood, a theme Henry James would take up in *What Maisie Knew* (1897). In the preface, James wrote movingly of the "great gaps and voids" in the child's mind between what is seen of the adult world and what is understood. Thus he describes young Maisie's dilemma:

> Only, even though it is her interest that mainly makes matters interesting for us, we inevitably note this in figures that are not yet at her command and that are nevertheless required whenever those aspects about her and those parts of her experience that she understands darken off into others that she rather tormentedly misses.[19]

Both the symbolic and material utility of the bourgeois interior would be irrevocably compromised by the destruction of World War I. For many artists, the effects of the war were most poignantly distilled in the image of a home rent asunder, its interiors exposed to view. When James's fellow expatriate Edith Wharton traveled through the French countryside in 1915, she described the broken-down structures of domestic life: "Every window-pane is smashed, nearly every building unroofed, and some house-fronts are sliced clear off, with the different stories exposed, as if for the stage-setting of a farce . . .'[20]

Consider this: if the physical structures that gave shape to private life – the cherished possessions, favored corners, connecting passageways – could be obliterated, or at least fundamentally altered, what then of the identity that those structures had helped to define? This was a question that would surface in the work of many post-war writers, for whom the exercise of defining a self seemed to become more and more internalized – a vision held privately rather than acted out. Virginia Woolf, for instance, enunciated a distrust for all domestic trappings in a world where they seemed to have lost much of their meaning. In her diary, she wrote, "[I] thought how a house should be portable like a snail shell. In future perhaps, people will flirt out houses like little fans; and go on. There'll be no settled life within walls."[21]

Woolf's writings attest to the emergence of a new conception of the individual mind – a new shape, we might say. Rather than being imaginatively projected out onto an architectural space, interiority assumed a rational structure of its own, which was often described as a series of rooms or chambers. Here is Woolf's description of the magnetic, yet elusive, Mrs Ramsay in *To the Lighthouse*:

> [Lily Briscoe] imagined how in the chambers of the mind and heart of the woman who was, physically touching her, were stood, like the treasures in the tombs of the kings, tablets bearing sacred inscriptions, which if one could spell them out, would teach one everything, but they would never be offered openly, never made public. What art was there, known to love or cunning, by which one pressed through to those secret chambers.?[22]

In the early decades of the twentieth century, the painted image of the interior may no longer have served as the vehicle for self-expression; but the three-dimensional interior became the site for a new kind of artistic collaboration that mirrored some cultures' shift in emphasis – from the private to the public, from the individual to the collective, from the everyday to the utopian. The collaborative design of the "abstract interior" in the work of De Stijl, the Russian Constructivists and the artists of the Bauhaus was conceived as a vehicle for social change.[23] The irregularities and unpredictability of the human body, and psyche, were rigorously edited out of the abstract interior, as they would be excised from much early modern architecture. Walter Benjamin identified the impetus for one of its leading spirits in this way: "The work of Le Corbusier seems to arise when the "house" as a mythological configuration approaches its end." As Anthony Vidler argues in "Homes for Cyborgs," his contribution to this volume, the need for a psychically and physically responsive architecture would resurface with a vengeance in the so-called "intrauterine" designs of Surrealists Tristan Tzara and Matta Echaurren. Their critiques of modernism's reductiveness anticipate some of the debates of our own day, as the domestic interiors painted over a century ago by Degas, Vuillard, Sargent and Chase are evidence of how the en-visioning of irresolution and ambiguity satisfies, indeed anticipates, our postmodern sensibilities.[24]

5

The Ideal Swedish Home: Carl Larsson's Lilla Hyttnäs

MICHELLE FACOS

FEW homes are more familiar to international audiences than that of turn-of-the-century artists Carl and Karin Bergöö Larsson. Featured in popular magazines and on greeting cards, the rooms of the Larsson family home appeal to a nostalgic longing for an idealized, pre-industrial past while simultaneously providing inspiration, almost a century after their design, for post-modern architectural innovations.

Although Lilla Hyttnäs has been open to the public for several decades, most people know it through Carl Larsson's watercolor illustrations. These were first exhibited in the USA in 1895, in Sweden in 1897, and in Germany in 1898. In 1899, twenty-four of the watercolors were collected and published in *A Home*, with an introduction by the artist. *A Home* has gone through more than a dozen Swedish printings, making it one of the best-selling picture books in the history of Swedish publishing. Printed reproductions of these paintings appear on the walls of many Swedish homes, often in a child's room or hallway, and the book has been translated into more than half a dozen foreign languages, including Japanese; it has undergone multiple printings in German and English. The enduring attraction of the Larsson home is also evidenced by the large numbers of people making the pilgrimage to Sundborn, the village in central Sweden where Lilla Hyttnäs is located, by recent exhibitions of the *A Home* watercolors in the USA (1982) and Japan (1994), and by the release of a Carl Larsson line of home furnishings by the Swedish design firm IKEA.

Why is Lilla Hyttnäs so popular? The answer lies in its complex relationship to time and history, class and culture, memory and experience. Because Lilla Hyttnäs underwent constant modification in both structure and furnishings since its acquisition by the Larssons from relatives in 1888, what will concern us here is Lilla Hyttnäs as it appeared in the middle of the 1890s, as Larsson recorded it in his *A Home* illustrations.

Carl Larsson's illustrations of life at Lilla Hyttnäs were conceived as private mementoes in 1894, but by Christmas 1898 when he began his introduction to *A Home*, Larsson envisioned them as a model for a reform of domestic decor linked to a desire to improve the character of those who dwelled in modern houses. This shift in intention related to Larsson's engagement with Sweden's National Romantic movement, which was concerned with the preservation of indigenous culture and the realization of social democracy in Sweden.

The Larssons' ideas about the powerful effect of milieu on the personality came from England. The pernicious influence of industrialization on English society and the therapeutic potential of domestic decor absorbed John Ruskin and William Morris. Their theories arrived in Sweden through the polemics of Ellen Key (particularly *Beauty for All* and *Individualism and Socialism*) and the newspaper articles of Edmund Gosse published in *Ny Illustrerad Tidning* during the late 1870s.[1]

In his first public lecture, delivered in London to the Trades Guild of Learning in 1877, Morris articulated a concern for the beautification and improvement of living conditions in England's cities and towns consonant with that later espoused by Carl Larsson. He declared that a revival of the decorative arts on a popular level

> will make our streets as beautiful as the woods, as elevating as the mountain-sides; it will be a pleasure and a rest, and not a weight upon the spirit to come from the open country into a town; every man's house will be fair and decent, soothing to his mind and helpful to his work: all the works of man that we live amongst and handle will be in harmony with nature, will be reasonable and beautiful: yet all will be simple and inspiriting . . .[2]

From England then, came the idea that surroundings affect the individual's temperament and character; the Larssons embraced the Arts and Crafts movement principle that aesthetic reforms in the home and work environments could ameliorate social conditions. Their exposure to Morris's ideas through the articles of Gosse in the 1870s would have been reinforced during the 1880s when they lived in Paris, where Ruskin and Morris enjoyed tremendous popularity.

The Larsson family modelled the Arts and Crafts revival that Ruskin, Morris, and their followers considered the salvation of modern society: each family member designed, constructed, and embellished the home according to his/her individual inclinations and capabilities. Their activities mirrored the growing interest in indigenous material culture, which August Strindberg considered integral to the Swedes' rediscovery of their national character.[3] This gave rise to the formation of groups dedicated to encouraging native decorative arts in the final decades of the nineteenth century. Foremost among them were Friends of Handicrafts (*Handarbetets vänner*) and The Association for Swedish Crafts (*Föreningen för svensk hemslöjd*), which sought popular support by establishing chapters in many provincial towns. John Kruse, founder of the latter group, expressed ideas that could as easily have come from Morris:

> Industrialism's entire development has, in its way and in our time, shown to what extent the human spirit . . . with the help of scholarship, could dominate the forces of nature and make them into their willing servant . . . What happened to the old, beautiful dream of the free, strong and harmonious development of mankind, equipped with a wealth of accomplishments and talents . . . What can be done in order to have yards again inhabited by contemporary Swedes? A home of one's own and the renaissance of the old arts and crafts are sufficient answers.[4]

Although turn-of-the-century socialists emphasized collective action, they also valued certain aspects of individualism. This emerged at Lilla Hyttnäs in the subordination of its idiosyncratic and eclectic decor to a very personal sense of style and in the unique contributions made by family members. Lilla Hyttnäs became synonymous with the "Larsson style." As one contemporary observer noted, "'Carl Larsson' is written on every wall."[5] Walter Benjamin has observed that at the end of the nineteenth century, the house assumed a new role as an "expression of the personality," and Lilla Hyttnäs exemplified this trend.

Carl Larsson asserted that his motives in publishing *A Home* were altruistic. In his introduction, Larsson informed the reader, "You will soon notice that it is my interest in how things are for *you* that is the real reason these paintings have come out in book form."[6] Clearly, Larsson's message was not aimed at the dwindling number of peasants, who were exemplars of the kind of cultural continuity Larsson and his National Romantic colleagues esteemed. Rather it addressed the burgeoning ranks of the working classes and especially the bourgeoisie, whose striving after urbanity and novelty threatened the survival of traditional Swedish culture. Larsson felt that his home epitomized moral values that needed cultivation within this constituency.

To Larsson, Lilla Hyttnäs manifested honesty and simplicity in its design and execution because of its continuity with indigenous cultural traditions. While there are elements of Lilla Hyttnäs that correspond to furnishings found, for example, in the designs of British architect M. H. Baillie Scott, virtually everything illustrated in *A Home*, from the stuccoed exterior to the living room's big picture window, had local, Swedish precedents. This fact has often been overlooked even by Swedish scholars eager to elevate Lilla Hyttnäs from a provincial curiosity by association with the English Arts and Crafts movement. The English influence discernible to contemporary visitors occurred primarily in the renovations made after 1900, when the Larssons made it their main residence. By the time *The Studio*, to which the Larssons were charter subscribers, began publication in 1893, the rooms of Lilla Hyttnäs, as they were recorded in *A Home*, had largely been completed. The resemblance between Scott's interiors, as illustrated in *The Studio*, and those of Lilla Hyttnäs, can be attributed to the fact that they were informed by a similar Arts and Crafts movement aesthetic.

The professed simplicity of Lilla Hyttnäs's tradition-inspired interiors belied the sophisticated taste and aspirations informing their conception and the concomitantly complex relationship which they had to the socio-cultural context in which they functioned. Theodore Adorno declared the importance of the interior for understanding the social topography of an era,[7] and Lilla Hyttnäs embodied many of the contradictions of an industrializing society. It was at once peasant and bourgeois, individualistic and democratic, traditional and modern.

The acquisition, design, and furnishing of Lilla Hyttnäs was a direct response to what Walter Benjamin has described as the nineteenth century's invention of private, domestic space as a retreat from the industrial world to which bourgeois fortunes were inextricably linked.[8] The dialectic of daily life at the time seemed to require that homes become more quiet, intimate, and unique as the urban environment became more noisy, hectic, and impersonal. Lilla Hyttnäs conformed to this model, both in terms of its interior design and its geographical location.

Lilla Hyttnäs was situated in the province of Dalarna, the center of traditional Swedish culture, whose inhabitants were resistant to change. The untainted, pre-modern charm of this province was indebted to its successful opposition to land reforms which initiated a radical transformation in Swedish agriculture and virtually destroyed village life in the late eighteenth and early nineteenth centuries. Dalarna villagers clung tenaciously to age-old collective practices in everything from breadbaking to farming; native costumes were still worn there. By the end of the nineteenth century, Dalarna, with its village-specific dialects, had become a refuge from the outside world – one where time seemed suspended. While not a tourist attraction itself, Sundborn was an ideal escape from the cosmopolitan bustle of Stockholm (four hours away by train).

At the turn of the century, many among Sweden's bourgeoisie extended Benjamin's notion of the home as a retreat from modern, city life by purchasing summer homes. Their pastel colored, gingerbread cottages sprang up primarily along the coasts near Sweden's two largest cities, Stockholm and Gothenburg. In resorts like Marstrand and Varberg on the west coast and Sandhamn and Dalerö in Stockholm's archipelago, affluent urbanites experienced the rejuvenating effects of nature. This flight to nature was fostered by the prevailing primitivist discourse in which immersion in nature was understood as psychically and physically therapeutic. According to the contemporary poet Gustaf af Geijerstam, "Every person . . . conceals a deeper need for quiet . . . It is the primitive which we city dwellers seek in rural life during the summer, the primitive and its peace."[9]

Larsson, like all National Romantics, considered this reconnection with nature in cultural terms. For them it was less of an escape by affluent urbanites from the noise and filth of the city than a re-establishment of bonds with their heritage. Swedish intellectuals enthusiastically endorsed *friluftsliv*, which Norwegian philosopher Arne Naess has defined as "a positive kind of state of mind and body in nature, one that brings us closer to some of the many aspects of identification and self-realization with nature that we have lost." At the same time, it reified the National Romantic (and bourgeois) urge to appropriate nature, which "presupposes a culture, the privilege of those who have ancient roots."[10] Love of nature manifested itself in the four illustrations in *A Home* depicting the Larsson family enjoying various outdoor activities. "Yard and Brewery House" showed the Larsson children sledding and skating in a snow-blanketed landscape, "A Good Bathing Place" depicted them swimming (nude) on the village outskirts on a summer day, and "Crayfishing" and "Breakfast Under the Big Birch" recorded the Larsson family dining al fresco. Nature played a visible role even in the interior scenes, where bouquets of wildflowers, potted plants, glimpses of trees through windows, and painted floral motifs abound.

The Larssons resisted parvenu behavior by refusing to establish themselves in a trendy resort and by asserting their heritage by refurbishing ancestral property. Still, their enterprise constituted a bourgeois urge to distinguish themselves from the working and peasant classes by asserting cultural privilege. But instead of indulging in the raw declaration of affluence communicated by coastal cottage building, the Larssons pursued a more sophisticated strategy analogous to later manifestations of bourgeois culture, which the sociologist Pierre Bourdieu has described as

> symboliz[ing] a squandering of time and a competence which can only be acquired by long frequentation of old, cultivated people and things, that is, membership in an ancient group, the sole guarantee of possession of all the properties which are endowed with the highest distinctive value because they can only be accumulated over time.[11]

While Lilla Hyttnäs conveyed the impression of a home whose character resulted from several centuries of gradual growth and acquisition, it was, in fact, a modern confection produced within the span of a decade.

Until 1901 when they made it their permanent residence, the Larssons followed the same pattern as much of Stockholm's bourgeoisie: they lived in Stockholm and used Lilla Hyttnäs as their summer home. For Carl Larsson, this situation was undoubtedly a sign of upward social mobility and economic prosperity, one which supports a sociological reading of Lilla Hyttnäs. As a child of Stockholm's working poor, Larsson was always self-conscious about his improving material circumstances. His watercolor illustration (now in the collection of Prins Eugens Waldemarsudde, Stockholm) recording the visit of a member of the Swedish royal family, fellow artist Prince Eugen, to Lilla Hyttnäs announced the arrival of the Larssons in the highest echelon of Swedish society. Lilla Hyttnäs demonstrated the propensity of Sweden's increasingly affluent bourgeoisie to amass capital and lavish it on the embellishment of the domestic sphere. Both in the text and illustrations of *A Home*, Larsson evidenced his utopian mindset by privileging activities that presupposed access to leisure and required an investment of time and energy (something working-class Swedes had little of), for the acquisition and enjoyment of culture.

Ernst Bloch has labeled these familial cloisters "dream appearances" because of their attempt to compensate for the harsh, pressing realities without by creating fanciful retreats within.[12] This modernist alienation initially attracted Carl Larsson to Lilla Hyttnäs. In *A Home*, he admitted, "Here I experienced that unspeakably sweet feeling of seclusion from the noise of the world . . ."[13] In so far as Lilla Hyttnäs represented a domain whose qualities of lightness, openness, simplicity, and casualness emerged in dialectical opposition to the evolving urban environment, it conformed closely to Bloch's conception of a "dream appearance."

Carl and Karin Larsson created a refuge at Lilla Hyttnäs radically different in character from those of their contemporaries. Whereas most Swedish bourgeois interiors of the time evidenced alienation from the social sphere in their orientation toward physical comfort (in overstuffed furniture), isolation (with heavy draperies concealing the outside world), and fantasy (with cohesive period rooms encouraging an imaginative flight to exotic times and places), the Larsson home conformed to the Arts and Crafts ideal of providing a sense of psycho-emotional well-being and a holistic integration of the residents with their habitat, but did so in a way that reinforced, on one level, the very divisions they were trying to bridge. They addressed the separation of public and domestic spheres by reintegrating working and living spaces under one roof, an act that further obviated the need for contact with the outside world. Still, to many Lilla Hyttnäs offered a therapeutic mechanism for confronting the unpleasantries of modern life. According to one journalist:

> When we were tired of work and worries, [Larsson's] peek into these sunny, peaceful scenes from Sundborn's little world soon returned us to our right equilibrium, chased away our feeling of despondency, and gave us a brighter and healthier outlook on life.[14]

When he presented his private realm to the public for the first time in *A Home*, Larsson proffered it as a model of domestic and social reform, intentionally broadening its significance to one with suprapersonal implications.

Despite its participation in discourses derived from the international Arts and Crafts movement, Lilla Hyttnäs expressed the specificity of

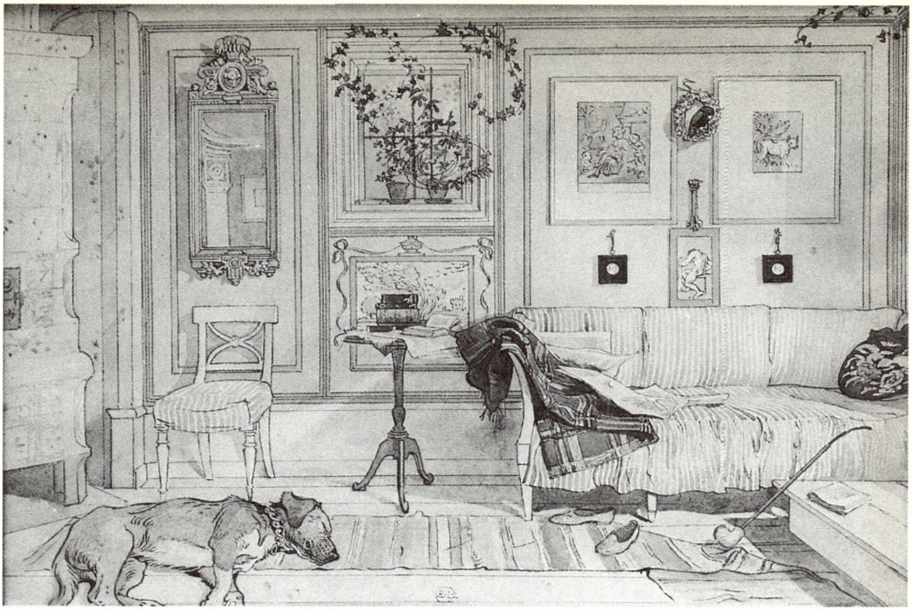

25 *Carl Larsson,* The Lazy Corner, *from* A Home, *c. 1894*

Swedish cultural history, since its decor derived from indigenous styles. This choice reflected the rise of nationalism in Sweden during the second half of the nineteenth century, a phenomenon resulting from compulsory and universal schooling that indoctrinated a generation with a patriotic education. Among the historical periods figuring prominently in primary schooling of the day was the reign of Gustav III (1746–92), a king whose biography and popularity combined the charismatic and tragic qualities of a John Kennedy with the grand cultural aspirations of a Louis XIV. Assassinated at the age of thirty-six, this beloved king strove to make Stockholm a leading European cultural center by inaugurating his spare interpretation of the Louis XVI style and by promoting continental culture.

Typical of the Gustavian style were partitioned walls, lightly draped windows, small scale furniture either painted or in light woods, and textiles with simple check or stripe patterns. The Swedish nobility immediately emulated this style in their manor houses and apartments. The Larssons' fascination with this period evidenced, on the one hand, their desire to elevate their own social status by association and, on the other, their commitment to promoting a Swedish national identity through the appreciation of indigenous history and culture. Carl Larsson's illustrations of the Gustavian interiors of Lilla Hyttnäs stimulated public interest in this style which was so closely linked to one of Sweden's most important historical periods.

The simplicity associated with the Gustavian style had important moral implications for Larsson and the National Romantics, since honesty and modesty were identified by them as hallmarks of the Swedish temperament. In his introduction to *A Home*, Larsson implored, "Therefore, o Swede, save yourself in time, return to simplicity and honesty . . . Then you will be happy in the feeling of being yourself . . ."[15] Swedish intellectuals found confirmation for this self-image in the observations of outsiders like the French Enlightenment philosopher Baron de Montesquieu, who more than a century earlier had written: "If we travel toward the north, we meet people who have few vices, many virtues, and a great share of frankness and sincerity.'[16]

Larsson and his National Romantic compatriots recognized that aesthetic choices were related to ethical ones, and like simplicity, authenticity was promoted not for its own sake, but because of its link to a Swedish national identity. In accordance with this ethos, none of the furnishings in the Larsson home were industrially produced copies of foreign or antique originals. Larsson bemoaned the tendency of his contemporaries to "follow foreign patterns, yesterday Parisian and Berlinian, today, English and American,"[17] and to purchase shoddy, soulless factory-made furnishings. He felt it exacerbated the alienation afflicting the fashion conscious bourgeoisie.

The spare, light-filled interiors of Lilla Hyttnäs contrasted starkly with typical bourgeois homes of the time, with their dark, heavy furniture and ornately patterned walls. In comparison, Lilla Hyttnäs's decor harked back to the Biedermeier era of the 1830s and 1840s, by which time the Gustavian style had filtered down from the aristocracy to the bourgeoisie. Because the Larssons' antiques were simple in design and Swedish in origin, they were perceived to be in harmony with their peasant furnishings, many of which were rescued from neighboring farmsteads. In *Mamma and the Small Girls' Room*, the tripod washstand, dressing table, and corner beds were examples of the local peasant furnishings the Larssons promoted as utilitarian and beautiful. Larsson's children – robust, Scandinavian cousins of Kate Greenaway's storybook children (with whom Larsson may have been familiar) – confront/ignore the viewer with disarming informality. In Sweden, nude children were commonplace within the boundaries of house and garden. Here, as in all of the *A Home* images, Larsson invites us to take his place as a member of the family. For a moment, our own alienation dissipates as we participate imaginatively in the intimate dramas of Lilla Hyttnäs.

The particular kind of eclecticism which Lilla Hyttnäs represented gave it paradigmatic importance on a number of fronts. It functioned as a "dream appearance," as a prototype of patriotic interior design, as an exemplar of tasteful individualism, and, in its egalitarian mixture of aristocratic and peasant styles and reduction of all objects to their use and aes-

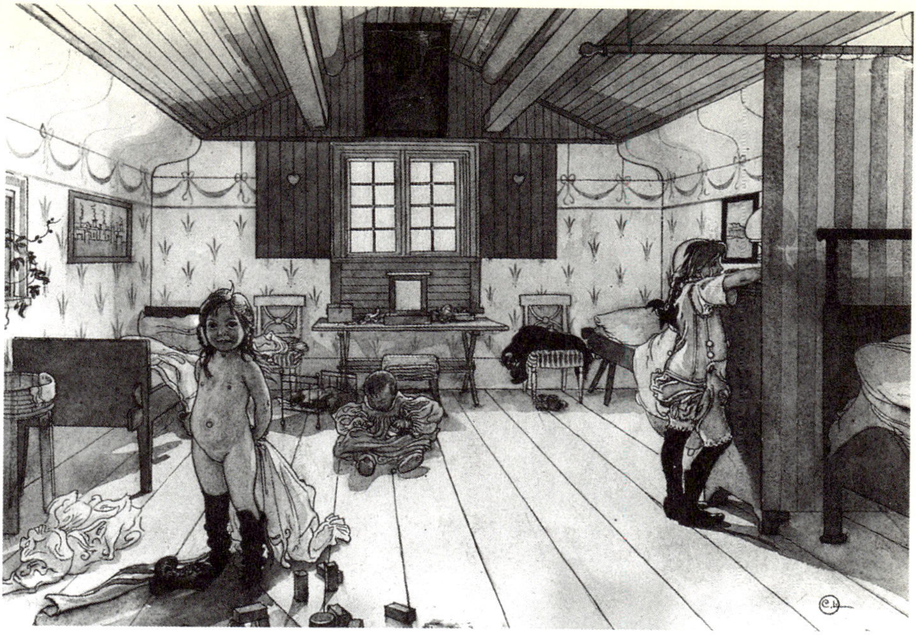

26 *Carl Larsson,* Mamma and the Small Girls' Room, *from* A Home, *c. 1894*

thetic value, Lilla Hyttnäs anticipated the social democratic political ideology that guided Sweden through much of the twentieth century.

The Larssons' resolve to revive peasant culture was as noteworthy at the time as were their efforts to promote the Gustavian style. In an era of rapid industrialization and concomitant pressures to be "modern," the urge to obscure one's peasant past was compelling. Native costumes, folk art, and rustic furnishings were considered embarrassing reminders of the primitive origins of the emergent bourgeoisie. This trend began to shift in the late 1880s, as increasing numbers of Swedish intellectuals subscribed to aspects of folkish ideology which elevated the peasantry to the status of guardians of national identity.[18] The Lilla Hyttnäs enterprise dovetailed with this current of thought, which has prevailed in the twentieth century. This idealization allowed the bourgeoisie to approach peasant culture while remaining distant from it, a situation Bourdieu identifies as characteristic of the relationship between these social groups.

The peasant furnishing of Lilla Hyttnäs enhanced its role as a "dream appearance" by appealing to the childhood memories of most Swedes who, even by the 1920s, were no more than a generation away from the land. Peasant cottages were part of the landscape, if not of one's experience. The Larssons recontextualized familiar domestic objects from the murky log cabins in which they originated to the light-filled rooms of Lilla

Hyttnäs. In this way they created an idealized and generic vision of the Swedish childhood home. Here there was no evidence of grime or privation; the cozy rooms and healthy children bespeak happiness and prosperity. All the viewers had to do was to substitute their own family members for the Larssons' in order to personalize these images and temporarily escape from the problems of modern, urban life.

While the revival of peasant culture was literally conservative in its zeal to sustain traditional ways of life, it was linked, in Sweden as in England, to progressive political ideas. Swedish National Romantics worked together with Social Democrats in order to realize a totalizing program of individual freedom, health and happiness; social equality and harmony; symbiosis with nature; and preservation of indigenous culture.

While Lilla Hyttnäs was intended as a refuge from cosmopolitanism, thereby functioning on one level as a manifestation of the social alienation precipitated by industrial capitalism, it also functioned as a microcosmic model of progressive social ideas. Unlike most bourgeois homes of the time, it contained no drawing-room outfitted with valuables to impress visitors; it was emphatically not a museum-like showplace. The fact that the value of an object for the Larssons was directly connected to its use and aesthetic value, was consistent with the egalitarian and democratic impulses championed by Larsson and his progressive colleagues. The equanimity with which the furnishings of Lilla Hyttnäs were treated was evidenced by the Larssons' practice of modifying objects to accommodate the needs and whims of the Larsson family – locks were removed from antique cupboards and installed on doors, Rococo chairs were painted in bright colors to match the decor, a Baroque chest was embellished with a portrait of young Brita Larsson wearing a nightgown. The value of all objects in the Larsson home were connected to their beauty and utility, not their age or status.

Not only did the Larssons' emphasis on indigenous design embody the idea that nations (as well as individuals) needed to be secure in their identity and accepting of their heritage, but the blending of elements from various social and historical settings provided a conceptual model for egalitarian and democratic political reform. The Larsson ethos was made explicit with aphorisms painted by Carl over doors and on cupboards. One of these, "liberté, égalité, fraternité," became the official motto of Sweden's Social Democratic party, and established its ideological link to French Republican ideals.

Larsson's success in making Lilla Hyttnäs the visual representation of progressive ideology elevated the house to a showplace of social idealism. Throughout the twentieth century images of Lilla Hyttnäs have constantly confronted Swedes – in schoolbooks, magazines, and advertisements. It was universally acclaimed as the ideal Swedish home; and it was the home itself that provided the model of a rapidly changing Swedish society. In a 1928 parliamentary session this vision was articulated by Representative Per Albin Hansson:

> The home's basic framework is cooperation and a feeling of belonging . . . Adopted for the larger "folk home" this would mean dissolving all social and economic differences that now divide citizens into privileged and disadvantaged, dominating and dependent, rich and poor, haves and have-nots, plunderers and plundered.[19]

This vision of the home as a societal ideal determined the course of Sweden's political evolution in the twentieth century and was prefigured in Carl Larsson's illustrations of the cooperative atmosphere of Lilla Hyttnäs. The importance of the Larsson home was immediately recognized by contemporaries. One admirer noted that it was "a symbol for a newly awakened Swedish sense . . . that exists in the general consciousness. One which is invisible, but whose development will be felt long into the future."[20]

Like many products of the Arts and Crafts movement, Lilla Hyttnäs was a manifestation of the peculiarly modernist paradox of egoism and altruism that Emile Durkheim identified in 1897 as complementary aspects of a single social state. It simultaneously attested to Larsson's material success and his desire for democratic and egalitarian social reform. Similarly, while Lilla Hyttnäs represented the decentering of bourgeois culture and a distancing from dominant class tastes, it was made possible by subscribing to bourgeois values of comfort, consumption, and cultural acquisition.

What is unique about Lilla Hyttnäs is that it manages to be all things to all people; its protean possibilities allow visitors and viewers to make of it what they wish. Firmly rooted in Swedish history and culture, it transcends these bounds, appealing particularly to those cultures (American, German, Japanese) most radically transformed by modernization and industrialization. These cultures possess a proportionately large segment of members who are well educated enough to be aware of their alienation and affluent enough to assuage it by the construction of "dream appearances." For them, as for Swedes, Lilla Hyttnäs functions as a locus of yearning for an idealized, pre-industrial past that provides both a conceptual and material template for attaining the comfort and happiness associated with an imagined earlier time.

6

Frank Lloyd Wright's Kindergarten: Professional Practice and Sexual Roles

DAVID VAN ZANTEN

WOMEN were important in Frank Lloyd Wright's career in Oak Park, Illinois (1889–1909). He emerged as an architect building homes in an increasingly woman-dominated suburb; his chief draftsman, Marion Mahony, was one of the first university-educated American women architects; Wright's aunts, Jane and Ellen Lloyd Jones, had been his first clients in 1887 and were important clients again in 1902; their work as experimental teachers paralleled that of his mother, Anna, and his wife, Catherine, and was basic to his own architectural education.

It would seem fruitful to examine Wright's early work in this context, that of the turn-of-the-century American suburb and its female ethos. Nancy Cott and Gwendolyn Wright have outlined this on a broad plane and Leonard Eaton, Norris Kelly Smith, and Anthony Alofsin have started more focused work.[1] In this short sketch, I would like to focus on Wright's Oak Park practice, working from the research of Eaton and Smith to suggest a chain of hypotheses: 1) that Wright's conscious commitment to the suburb is distinctive and fundamental to his whole enterprise in Oak Park; 2) that within this commitment is the assumption that his objective was to teach as well as provide a professional service, and to teach through design exercises that were lucid, elastic, and nurturing; and 3) that this conception of design as nurture is essentially feminine and led him into a conflict between the (organizing) urban and the (nurturing) suburban, eventually frustrated him so much that in 1909 he dramatically threw it all over.

For Wright to propose nurture as his basic manner of professional practice was to reverse the method established in Chicago, the city of corporate organization, especially by Daniel Burnham, who insisted upon a quasi-military specialization and delegation and the insertion of authorized details.[2] Nurture was the function of the suburb: after the men left each morning for the quantified, competitive, gridded, industrially fabricated Loop, the women set to homemaking and childrearing in the nature-filled suburb. And this distinction between organizing and nurturing was the difference between business and art, as Wright himself would state in his 1898 business card.

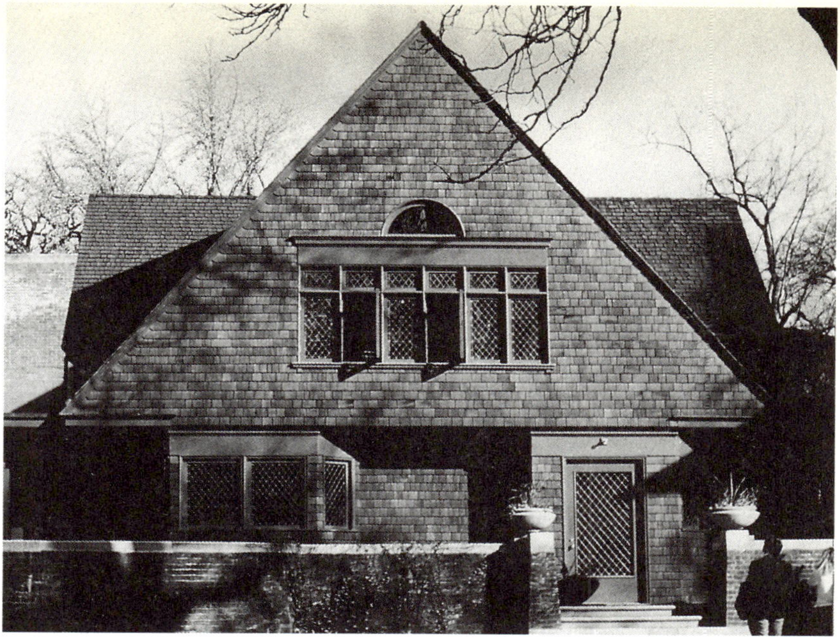

27 *Front Façade of Frank Lloyd Wright Home (facing Forest Avenue), Oak Park, Illinois*

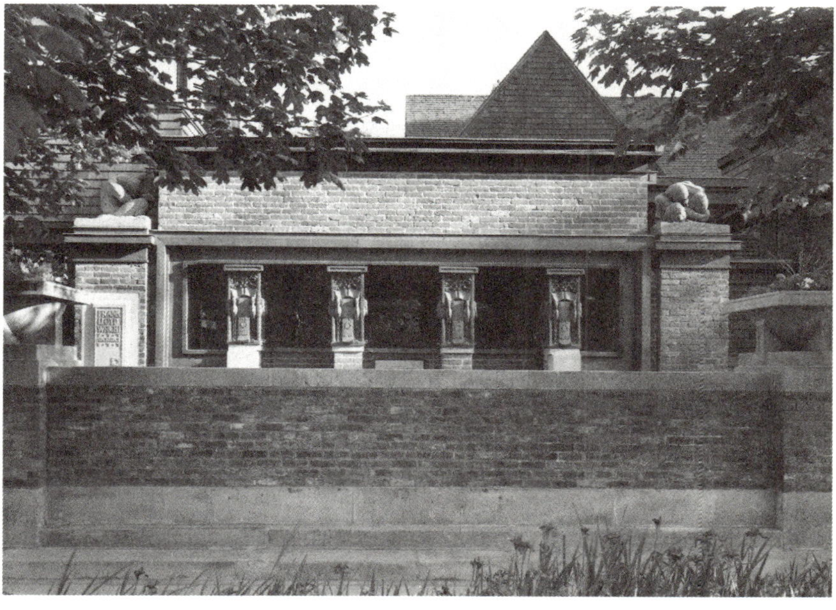

28 *Studio Façade, Frank Lloyd Wright Home and Studio,* restored to the year 1909

In 1898 Wright added a separate and very strikingly designed office, with a drafting room accommodating about twelve draftsmen, to his home in Oak Park. The new structure had a separate, monumental entrance on Chicago Avenue, as well as a library intended to be open to the public as "a free circulating art library." Wright's office had previously been in the Loop (first in the Schiller Building, then in Steinway Hall, and finally in the Rookery), and it was unheard of in Chicago for an ambitious architect to establish himself in the suburbs. His friends and competitors – Dwight Perkins, Myron Hunt, Robert C. Spencer – all worked out of Loop offices, although they were all principally domestic architects living in and designing for the elite suburbs. One leading Prairie School firm came out of the Loop – Thomas Tallmadge, a leading citizen of Evanston, and Vernon Watson, a respectable resident of Oak Park, working extensively after 1905 in both localities from offices at 188 Madison Street. A few lesser-known architects who did maintain suburban offices, such as Eben Ezra Roberts in Oak Park, worked only in the immediate vicinity and maintained offices in the local bank building near the railroad station.[3]

Wright explained his initiative in a business card and it was reproduced in the 9 February 1898 issue of *Construction News*:

> The practice of architecture as a profession has fine art as well as commercial elements; . . .
>
> To develop in a better sense this fine art side in combination with its commercial condition the architect should place himself in an environment that conspires to develop the best there is in him. The first requisite is a place fitted and adapted to be protected and set aside from the distractions of the busy city. The worker is enabled on this basis to secure the quiet concentration of effort essential to the full success of a building project – the intrinsic value of which is measured by that effort.
>
> To practice the profession of architecture along these lines, in the hope of reaching these better results, a complete architectural workshop has been constructed in Oak Park . . .

Wright's structure was domestic in scale and intimate, with its principal space – the drafting room – dominated by a large brick fireplace. It was less a "workshop" than a "living room" as Alfred Granger labelled it in *House Beautiful* in 1899 or a "studio" as Robert C. Spencer called it in *Architectural Review* in 1900.[4] The latter designation has stuck to this day. Living room and Studio expressed the collegial atmosphere that Wright tried to cultivate among his draftsmen and delineated in his 1908 article "In the Cause of Architecture."

> These young people have found their way to me through natural sympathy with the work, and have become loyal assistants . . . The few draftsmen so far associ-

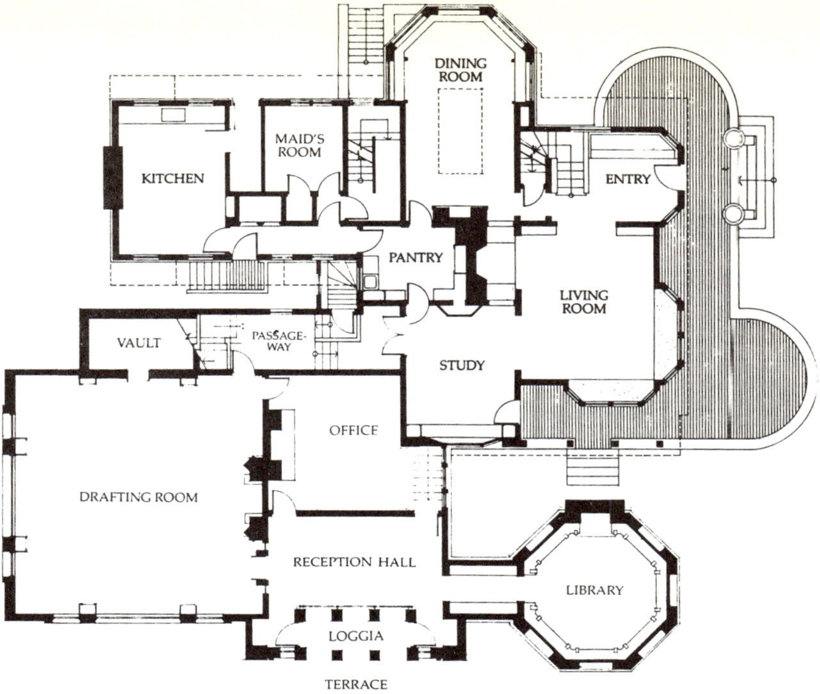

29 *Studio Addition Floorplan, Frank Lloyd Wright Home and Studio*, 1898–1909

> ated with this work have been taken into the draughting room in every case almost wholly unformed, many of them with no particular previous training, and patiently nursed for years in the atmosphere of the work itself, until, saturated by intimate association, at an impressionable age, with its motifs and phrases, they have become helpful.[5]

For about a year and a half Wright established profit-sharing.[6] Most importantly, the method of design he developed in the Studio around 1900 – his "Prairie Style" – functioned as a geometric system of composition that the draftsmen could use individually to elaborate Wright's general indications.[7] There was no production line or division of labor, Wright wrote in 1908; instead he tried having each draftsman carry a selected design through from beginning to end:

> This year I assign to each a project that has been carefully conceived in my own mind, which he accepts as a specific work. He follows its subsequent development through all its phases in drawing room and field, meeting with the client himself on occasions, gaining an all-round development impossible otherwise, and insuring an enthusiasm and a grasp of detail.

Significantly, Wright's system of Prairie design was already in 1900 linked by Robert C. Spencer to the abstract block compositions taught in the kindergarten method of elementary education established in the USA during the 1860s[8] and adopted by Wright's mother in raising him. Spencer's observations have usually been understood narrowly by historians, as explaining the specific aesthetic characteristics represented in Wright's style. It would seem logical, however, to propose in the context of the educational concept of his Studio that Wright saw it as pedagogical, as a way of achieving compositional lucidity and comprehensibility so as to structure the draftsman's individual elaboration of a scheme. That is to say that Wright saw the Studio on Chicago Avenue as the professional mirror of the kindergarten maintained by his wife Catherine in the great vaulted playroom on the opposite side of the Oak Park house or of the kindergarten education he himself had received from his teacher-mother Anna (living in Oak Park next door on Chicago Avenue), or of the experimental kindergarten-oriented Hillside Home School his aunts established in Spring Green, Wisconsin (housed in the large building that Wright erected for them in 1902–3). The principle of the kindergarten was to educate children not by discipline and memorization but by play – by recognizing play as the reflection of the natural curiosity and enthusiasm that might be harnessed by a sensitive teacher to become learning. A basic component was the "gift," the carefully designed toy of abstract form that might guide the child's creativity without restricting it: cubic blocks, for example, to be set in patterns on a grid. (It is play with these blocks that is often cited as influencing Wright's own sense of design.) At the Hillside Home School this method was expanded to constitute an entire pre-college program.[9]

Wright was not the only architect considering the establishment of the kindergarten paradigm in architecture at that moment: in 1902–3 Louis Sullivan was publishing his "Kindergarten Chats," in the *Interstate Architect and Builder* in Cleveland, addressed to young draftsmen, citing the kindergarten as the model for design education as well as demonstrating what he meant, more broadly, in his essays.

I have described Wright's attitude in the Studio as nurturing and noted how he shared design responsibility – even profits – with his draftsmen. He tried to be very giving, as his mother, wife, and aunts were with their numerous children, and as was the whole ethos of the suburb. But as is well known, Wright's commitment collapsed in 1909 and he abandoned his wife and children, his Studio and his men, his whole suburban world, to flee to Europe with an Oak Park client's wife. Afterwards he was sad, if unrepentant, in describing how he had left, as Anthony Alofsin has documented. But he was angry at his former draftsmen, who went out on their own after 1909 and who (he felt) merely copied his style. In 1914 he published an article entitled "In the Cause of Architecture," reflecting bitterly on the optimism of six years before:

> Half-baked, imitative designs – fictitious semblances – pretentiously put forward in the name of a movement or a cause, particularly while novelty is the chief popular standard, endanger the cause, weaken the efficiency of genuine work, for the time being at least; lower standards of artistic integrity permanently; demoralize all values artistically; until utter prostitution results.[10]

What went wrong? Were not the Studio draftsmen *supposed* to learn and apply Wright's system? Even in the optimistic delineation of his 1908 article there was a note of condescension when he called his draftsmen "assistants" and "helpful." Wright was a powerful, willful artist and – in the end – wanted willing executants more than grateful pupils. There was always too much of the Burnham in him. The basic problem seems to have been that the nurturing of six children, twelve draftsmen, and dozens of Oak Park clients was not, in the end, what he wished to do, regardless of his mother, wife, and aunts.

A look at the position Wright was now in leads us back to his great predecessor: Henry Hobson Richardson, with his office in his house in Brookline, Massachusetts. Here had been a man who did big work in a quiet, collegial setting, creating a new seemingly "American" architecture in friendly collaboration with powerful businessmen and grateful draftsmen. He had died young in 1886, and Root, Sullivan, and Wright were in awe of his accomplishment. But Wright discovered that this could not be reproduced in Chicago in 1900. Patrician Brookline was not middle class, domestic Oak Park. Richardson's apprentices were fundamentally different from Wright's callow kindergartners. Architecture had ceased to be crafted and nurtured; with Burnham it had come to be produced.[11]

Writers have never ceased to be struck by the distinction between the suburbs and the city in the industrial age but are usually quick to attribute this to a simple dichotomy between wealth and order versus poverty and chaos. It would be more interesting to explore such distinctions as marks of social (and sexual) structure. The emerging downtowns and suburbs of the industrial city around 1900 were social zones of unstated and only symbolically indicated meaning. Wright's problem is that in abandoning the Loop (the conventional professional zone) he stumbled into another zone (that of the suburb-home-nursery) just as structured as the first, and just as hostile to him, although for different reasons. By 1909 all he could do was to flee to the unappropriated territory of Europe, then Wisconsin.[12]

7

"Hi Honey, I'm Home": Weary (Neurasthenic) Businessmen and the Formulation of a Serenely Modern Aesthetic

JOYCE HENRI ROBINSON

Happy the man who, far from business and affairs,
  Like mortals of the early times,
May work his father's fields with oxen of his own,
  Exempt from profit, loss, and fee . . .
    Horace, Epodes 2.1–4[1]

If we can take Horace at his word, it appears that businessmen have been wearied by the demands of the forum for a very long time. Horace's usurer, who utters this rather plaintive refrain, dreams of returning to the countryside where men work the fields "like mortals of the early times" and are free from the concerns of "profit, loss, and fee." Implicit in every sad song bemoaning the fate of the exhausted merchant is, of course, the denunciation of the workaday world of city life. The inevitable corrective and cultural corollary to the quotidian routine of the forum is the restorative realm of the pastoral which, if not always available to the weary businessman in actuality, has since ancient times been presented to him through the distancing artifice of bucolic poetry and painting. As noted historian of the pastoral Renato Poggioli reminds us, it is when civilization "tires man's heart" that pastoral poetry most often appears and offers the exhausted city dweller "moral relaxation and emotional release."[2]

The quest for an uncomplicated moment of felicity in the midst of a highly complicated society is the concomitant to life lived in the city, and since ancient times (as Horace reveals) the onward and increasingly fast-paced march of civilization has been habitually accompanied by the laments of weary sojourners longing for a realm of pastoral calm. This atavistic yearning for the rehabilitative delights of the pastoral is nowhere more provocatively visualized than in Henri Matisse's *Bonheur de vivre*, which remains, undoubtedly, modernism's most familiar evocation of an idyllic golden age. The painting celebrates humankind's original harmony with nature, a harmony that is expressively communicated in the gently curving forms of the landscape and the female nude, that crucial denizen of Arcadia. The image appears to be aesthetically and psychologically fully consonant with Matisse's ideas about his art as expressed in his 1908 essay, "Notes of a Painter," in which the artist includes the weary *homme d'affaires* among the designated recipients of his serene art:

> What I dream of is an art of balance, of purity and serenity, devoid of troubling or depressing subject matter, an art which could be for every mental worker, for the businessman as well as the man of letters, for example, a soothing, calming influence on the mind, something like a good armchair which provides relaxation from physical fatigue . . .[3]

Matisse's language is both gender and class specific. The beneficiary of his restful art is the mental or intellectual worker (*travailleur cérébral*): more specifically, the definitive male bourgeois, the businessman. Why is the *homme d'affaires*, the businessman, one of the chosen recipients of the pastoral delights of Matisse's art? Was this merely an entrepreneurial strategy on the artist's part, a bold announcement of hoped-for patronage?

As Joseph Masheck has shown, Matisse's language and his "prosperously bourgeois outlook" echo a familiar topos, found in the writings of Reynolds, Hume, Goethe, and Baudelaire, of the fatigued gentleman whose prosperity enables him to procure refreshment through poetry and art.[4] What Matisse adds to these earlier aesthetic musings is the understanding of the refectory role assumed by the decorative pastoral landscape in the creation of a serenely restful art. Though Matisse, in many ways, inaugurated a modernist attitude toward the production of art in the twentieth century, he was himself a child of the nineteenth century, and the roots of his pastoral, and I would argue "domestic" outlook, as expressed in the famous "businessman" passage and in the *Bonheur de vivre*, are to be found there. This essay examines the cultural and artistic origins of this serenely *domestic* aesthetic which is indebted to late nineteenth-century writings on interior decoration, domesticity and the housewife, and the decorative landscape.[5] To begin, however, we must investigate that most prominent of Matisse's weary designees: the *homme d'affaires*. Could it be that there is something we don't know about the turn-of-the-century businessman and his need for soothing pastoral interludes to punctuate his frenetic life?

Medical literature written during the second half of the nineteenth century provides an important clue about weary businessmen and more generally about exhausted "brain-workers." In 1869, the American neurologist George Beard published *A Practical Treatise on Nervous Exhaustion* in which he discussed the symptomology and treatment of the recently identified nervous disorder, neurasthenia. Most simply defined as nervous exhaustion, neurasthenia was believed to result from the overcharging of the nervous system in confrontation with the incessant stimulation of urban existence. An inevitable psychological and physical counterpart to civilization and modernity, neurasthenia was labelled an "American disease" by Beard and proudly viewed as a kind of medical signifier of America's "advanced" status.[6] Convinced that the disease primarily affected the middle and upper classes, the "higher orders" within American society, Beard singled out male "brain-workers" as especially susceptible to the debilitating condition because of the increased mental exertion demanded by their occupations. Indeed, for Beard, neurasthenia was a "sign of mental superiority" and a natural, even socially acceptable, concomitant to the challenging arena of the marketplace.[7]

Though *A Practical Treatise on Nervous Exhaustion* was not translated into French until 1895, Beard's work was well known to the European medical community and the "maladie de Beard" was popularly diagnosed throughout the 1880s and 1890s.[8] French neurologists discounted Beard's contention that neurasthenia was a distinctively American phenomenon, citing the increasing number of European cases as ample proof of the condition's universality. Important texts on the mental disorder were published in France throughout the 1890s; each more or less echoed Beard's original findings, though in some cases, additional and more recent scientific evidence was supplied to shore up the author's findings.[9] The symptoms of neurasthenia were multiple and wildly variant and ranged from ticklishness, stomach upset and insomnia to physical enervation, anxiety, and impotence. Cerebral fatigue or "over-pressure" was among the most often-cited neurasthenic complaints and was attributed to the excessive intellectual work demanded of the brain-worker.[10]

> Intellectual work is one of the most fatiguing forms of nervous activity . . . Every man of average intelligence who exceeds ten hours a day in intellectual work, and, above all, who doesn't vary this work and combine it with some sort of physical activity, puts himself in the most favorable condition for nervous exhaustion.[11]

Our author, Fernand Levillain, informs us that it is not only the musical composer, the artist, the writer or the scientific researcher who suffers from nervous exhaustion. "The calculations and strategies of business, preoccupations of a financial nature, political discussions and matters . . . lead to the same result, intellectual fatigue and exhaustion due to an excess of mental excitation."

European writers were generally more willing than Beard to allow for a hereditary component in the development of the nervous disorder. Ultimately, they differentiated two essential types of neurasthenics: accidental or "shock" (typified by the fatigued businessman and the overworked scholar) and degenerate or hereditary.[12] For males, the leading cause of accidental neurasthenia was mental fatigue ("surmenage intellectuel"), and the man who dealt with troublesome pecuniary matters on a routine basis, the *homme d'affaires*, was highlighted as the most likely of all intellectual workers to succumb to the debilitating condition. Females, believed more likely to exhibit a natural propensity for the disease, were advised to avoid the excessive intellectual stimulation of the marketplace and counseled to remain within the protective confines of the domestic interior in order to safeguard their fragile nervous systems.[13] One of the primary accidental causes of neurasthenia in women purportedly was the willful violation of their roles as mothers and wives; that is, their willful departure from the calm sanctity of the home.[14]

Fortunately for the fatigued mental worker and the overly ambitious female, shock or accidental neurasthenics responded well to treatment. For the female neurasthenic, there were several recommended cures, the most famous of which was the "rest cure" developed by American neurologist Silas Weir Mitchell in the 1870s.[15] Entailing several weeks of complete isolation and bed rest (often in a country setting), Mitchell's infantilizing cure, which was widely promulgated in French treatises on the disease, apparently was reserved for only the severest cases. For the male brain-worker, the recommended cure was far less punitive, yet equally pastoral in nature.

> Those who work to excess, deskworkers, scientists and men of letters, occasionally succumb to bouts of mental depression . . . In general, these forms of neurasthenia are not very serious, even less so when hereditary influences are entirely lacking. Rest of the overtaxed brain, visits to the countryside or to the mountains, and several weeks of well-conducted hydrotherapy, are sufficient to restore the nervous system's equilibrium.[16]

The palliative effect of hydrotherapy, rest, and sojourns in the countryside was forthrightly proclaimed in French treatises on the nervous condition.[17] The rest cure, taking the waters, a day in the country: all were meant to bring serenity to the weary mind and spirit.

While neurasthenic businessmen might on occasion visit the healing waters in Vichy, they could hardly be expected to return to a domestic routine (as many neurasthenic women were advised to do) in order to mitigate the nervous tension produced by the tedious environment of commerce. Popularizing medical treatises from the period were eminently more practical. What was recommended for the weary and overworked businessman was that he retire, after a hard day's work, to a restful domestic environment within the city. In *La Neurasthénie et son traitement*, published in 1895, Émile Laurent tersely stated this prescriptive advice, noting that the "neurasthenic must lead a calm life sheltered from agitation."[18] For Laurent, a moderate lifestyle was recommended to corroborate the calming influence of the domestic retreat.

> I forbid them to drink, to smoke, even to love . . . in excess, of course. I allow them what one would allow a sensible man who is mildly ill: a half liter of wine daily, one cup of coffee without alcohol, and *Venus once a week* (emphasis added).[19]

The pleasures of Venus, while not prohibited, were to be experienced in moderate doses. Other doctors advocated the domestication of the love goddess and recommended that the male neurasthenic procure as part of his treatment a *femme au foyer*, a housewife, who would provide for him a serenely calm oasis, a private interior realm for physical and mental rehabilitation.

Advice books for the young mistress of the house written in the final decades of the nineteenth century encouraged her to create a psychologically and emotionally serene environment for her husband. Clearly, this kind of domestic advice participated in the ever-prevalent "ideology of separate spheres" which identified the female's domain as the interior, while the male was inevitably associated with the exterior realm of the forum.[20] Reiterating this commonly-held belief in 1892, Jules Simon pronounced that while man was made "to fight and work outside," it was the woman's task "to maintain order in the house and there organize happiness."[21] Like Ruskin's "angel of the house," she provided a shelter from the mental headaches and tribulations of quotidian existence; and, thus, the foyer, the interior, was identified as an important site for male recuperation.[22]

Handbooks and popular articles on interior decoration also aided the housewife in her creation of a quiet and restful enclave within the urban jungle. Implicit in such writings was the belief that the decoration of the home fell within the purview of wifely activities and the related assumption that such domestic activity was undertaken primarily for the benefit of the male occupant of the home. Typical of this pervasive opinion regarding the nineteenth-century female's aesthetic mission is the argument proferred by Jacob von Falke in *Art in the House* (1879):

> . . . the husband's occupations necessitate his absence from the house, and call him far away from it. During the day his mind is absorbed in many good and useful ways, in making and acquiring money for instance, and even after the hours of business have passed, they occupy his thoughts. When he returns home tired with work and in need of recreation, he longs for quiet enjoyment, and takes pleasure in the home which his wife has made comfortable and attractive . . . She is the mistress of the house in which she rules, and which she orders like a queen. Should it not then be specially her business to add *beauty* to the *order* which she has created? [original emphasis][23]

It is clear from this and other writings on the decorative in the second half of the nineteenth century that order, beauty, and serenity were the pre-eminently desirable qualities in domestic decoration. While public decoration might be expected to challenge the mind and provoke thought, the decor of the home was intended to calm, rather than excite, the mind and nerves of the city dweller.

The *femme au foyer*'s salubrious mission was often referenced in contemporary journals such as *Art et décoration* and *L'Art décoratif*, which featured any number of articles discussing the "psychology of rooms"[24] and recommending appropriate colors and lines for the creation of a restful and welcoming interior, a wonderfully domestic variant on the modernist expressive self-sufficiency of pictorial elements. The desired goal, simply stated, was the creation of a pastoral realm for physical and mental refection in which the decor contributed to, rather than detracted from, the refreshing of the weary brain-worker.

> The function of décor is not to arouse particular emotions, but to give the milieu a character in accord with the man who must live there, without compelling his thoughts to focus on the image of a concrete reality, without forcing them to be objective when the hour of subjective refuge awaits them.[25]

Not unexpectedly, this French author had the tired intellectual worker in mind when he advocated the creation of a decor that would not inspire analysis or force the weary brain to decipher its mysteries. Simply stated, the decor of the home should not encourage or inspire intellectual effort of any kind, since the fatigued businessman was forced to exhaust his mental energies on the diurnal routine of the forum. Concomitantly, paintings destined for the interior, it was believed, should not inspire mental headaches but participate in the restful ambiance of the domestic environment. Arts and Crafts architect M. H. Baillie Scott, an advocate of integrated and harmonious home design, ardently expressed this conviction in his *Houses and Gardens* (1906) in which he clearly privileged the place of the (weary) man of the house.

> If we imagine, for instance, the tired man of business returning to his suburban home in the evening, it can hardly be supposed that he will be prepared to make the special mental effort involved in an inspection of his pictures; but whatever decorative quality they express in conjunction with their surroundings will at once enfold him as in an atmosphere which soothes and charms like harmonious music.[26]

The ubiquity of this belief that interior decoration and paintings destined for the domestic interior should calm the fatigued viewer is further evinced in the writings of the quintessentially world-weary Vincent Van Gogh. Regarding his *Bedroom at Arles*, Van Gogh noted to Theo that color was to be "suggestive here of *rest* or of sleep in general." "In a word," he concluded, "looking at the picture ought to rest the brain, or rather the imagination."[27]

Another source for this homely pastoral aesthetic are critical writings from the 1890s on the decorative landscape, a modern genre of landscape whose intent, according to critics, was not to elevate or teach the spirit, but "to make it serene again."[28] This mission was made clear in critic Alphonse Germain's article of 1891, "Le paysage décoratif," in which he outlined the transformative power of the decorative landscape and identified the domestic interior as its intended site.[29]

> What better way to transform our depressing hovels into oases where the spirit can rest after the worries of mundane existence . . . Oh, to forget the ugliness of the street when we stand before an idealized landscape . . .[30]

The choice of "oasis" to characterize the foyer is clearly purposeful and suggests a transformation of the domestic realm into a place of refuge, a pastoral shelter, as it were, via the idealized landscape. Germain, along with Raymond Bouyer, was the principal critic responsible for formulating the stylistic parameters of this new decorative genre which was envisioned as a kind of modern apparition of the heroic landscape minus the thought-provoking intrusion of didactic subject matter. The primary stipulation for the decorative landscape was that it contain the "skillful lines of the Old Masters," and both Germain and Bouyer recommended that young artists consult Poussin and Claude in their creation of a modern synthetic landscape. Such esteemed ancestry suggests the conservative nature of the decorative landscape as envisioned by Germain and reveals the true intention of his article, which was to ground the nascent decorative landscape tradition in the French past. For Germain, the decorative landscape as practiced by the young Nabis artists, whom he derogatorily labeled "deformers," was merely an ornamental distortion of the natural world.[31] The critic scoffed at the "néo-traditionnisme" advocated by Maurice Denis, the most vocal proselytizer for the young followers of Gauguin, and excoriated the apologist's primitivizing, non-western definition of the "decorative." Galvanized by Denis's writings, which he believed had effectively co-opted the "decorative" for the modernist agenda and corrupted the term by associating it with Japanese, Byzantine, and Egyptian art, Germain essentially reclaimed the decorative for the French race. Promulgating a far more parochial understanding of the decorative landscape than would Denis or fellow Symbolist critic Albert Aurier, both Germain and Bouyer ultimately defined the genre as the serenely expressive rearrangement of natural forms via the heroic landscape tradition of Poussin.

Germain believed that the *paysage décoratif* could serve as an integral component of a decorative schema within the domestic setting and was convinced of the *affective* power of interior decoration on the mind and soul of the dweller.

> In general, our contemporaries do not give the decoration of the home the importance it merits and are not sufficiently convinced of its influence on character. Lines and hues exert as considerable an influence as that of pure air, spectacles of nature and flowers . . . It is, therefore, necessary to surround oneself with harmonious and serene effects, luminous colors with nuances evoking feelings of happiness and calm, and ornament inspired by nature.[32]

This belief in the expressive autonomy of formal elements (here within the context of interior decoration) and in the power of line and color to influence "character" derives from Charles Blanc's highly influential *Grammaire des arts du dessin* (1867) and from the more contemporary writings of Charles Henry. Germain's short-lived critical support of the Neo-Impressionists in the early 1890s had familiarized him with the psycho-physical system of Henry (which essentially codified and provided scientific verification for Blanc's traditional and vaguely defined ideas[33]), linking linear movement, the emotional value of color, and viewer physiological response. Ultimately, Germain believed that the soothing formal qualities and idyllic theme of the decorative landscape could appease and provide solace for the weary spirit; as such, its destination was the private interior where it participated in the creation of a domestic pastoral oasis.

Throughout the early years of the twentieth century, critics continued to praise the restorative power of the conservative decorative landscape, repeatedly linking the genre, as had Germain, with idyllic pastoral themes. Writing of the little-known painter Jean-Francis Auburtin in 1912, critic Louis Vauxcelles (best remembered for providing the "Fauve" group with its moniker) identified the decorative pastoral landscape as an important means of placing "a little calm joy and hellenic fantasy on the walls of homes." This task was undertaken, not unexpectedly, "to comfort the worried soul of men overtaxed by their miserably frenetic and brutal condition."[34]

To accomplish this comforting mission, the decorative landscape had to be serene, rather than frenetic, and produce sensations of calm and well-being, not anxiety, if it were to succeed in creating a restful interior for the weary (male) viewer. According to conservative commentators, many decorative landscapes featured in late nineteenth-century interiors were not successful in achieving the requisite state of serenity. A cartoon bearing the caption "Serpentine painting" from an 1894 issue of *Revue illustrée* under- 30
scores the popular perception of the goal of domestic decoration as restful and the failure of the tentacular forms of Art Nouveau interiors in this enterprise. In the cartoon we see the typical petit-bourgeois male who, on contemplating this "decorative panel for a dining room," has become incapacitated by the undulating movement of the female nudes, overstimulated, as it were, by this vision of serpentine shrews.

According to historian Debora Silverman, there were artists and writers in *fin-de-siècle* France who created interiors that were deliberately designed to arouse the senses and activate "nervous vibration."[35] The most notorious example is, of course, Des Esseintes in Huysmans's *À Rebours*, who crafted his decor around images of Odilon Redon and Gustave Moreau in order to "shake up his nervous system by means of erudite fancies, complicated nightmares, [and] suave and sinister visions."[36] Silverman argues that though the interior did function as a therapeutic refuge from the metropolis throughout the closing years of the nineteenth century, the "overstimulated citizen . . . transported with him the propensity for animating the interior." "No longer," she concludes, "could the interior be construed as a stable and static historical setting."[37]

Silverman's analysis of the *fin-de-siècle* redefinition of interior decoration via the "new psychology" of Charcot and Bernheim highlights, I believe, the effete (aristocratic) exception that proves the (bourgeois) rule. The "peinture serpentine" cartoon encapsulates the pervasive bourgeois belief that the interior should provide a stable, calm environment, and humorously demonstrates the conservative reaction to the mentally exhausting *fin-de-siècle* interior. Similar attitudes are amply evident in the critical response to Siegfried Bing's model rooms in his *Maison de l'Art Nouveau*, which offered the French public a glimpse of the latest in home design in 1895. Featured in Bing's Paris gallery was a dining-room designed by Henry Van de Velde that included decorative paintings by the Nabis artist Paul Ranson and dinnerware designed by Édouard Vuillard. In the Ranson panels the theme of young women working in the fields might certainly be construed as pastoral and, therefore, appropriate for an idyllic decorative landscape; however, the ornamental deformation and contorted meanderings of the trees and human figures (echoing the arabesques of Van de Velde's inlaid copper decoration) made them, it was suggested by more than one observer, inappropriate for the intended domestic setting. René Boylesve commented that in front of such an image he would barely be able to make it to the meat course before having to beat a hasty retreat from the table, while Camille Pissarro described the Ranson panels as "odious."[38] Perhaps most telling, however, was the response of *Le Figaro* critic Arsène Alexandre who, though he found Ranson's panels "simple and skilled," said of his visit to Bing's gallery: "I left exhausted, sick, exasperated, my nerves on edge and my head full of dancing nightmares."[39]

The major plaint levelled against Bing's decorative ensemble was its eclecticism, which was identified by the critical press as a sign of its pastiched internationalism. Critics generally agreed that the French innate understanding of decoration – the French taste, that is, for simplicity, moderation, and harmony – had been tainted by the pernicious example of the meandering and menacing forms of foreign art. What has previously

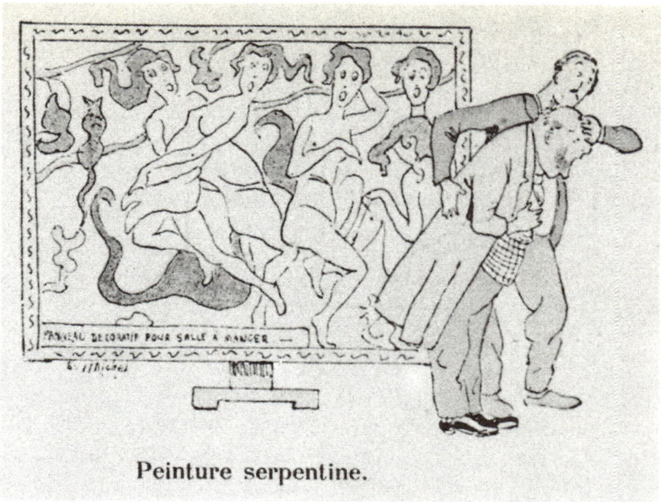

30 *Avelot,* Serpentine Painting, *from* Revue Illustrée, *1 May 1894*

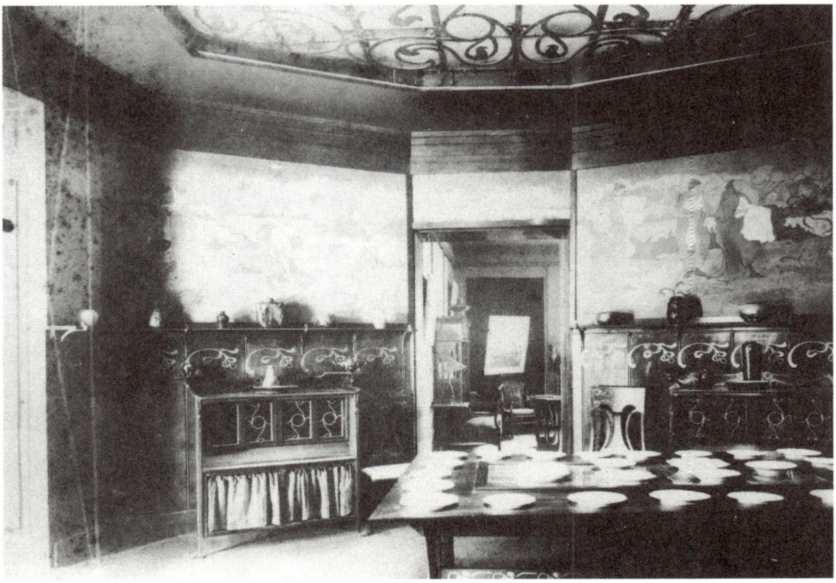

31 *Henry Van de Velde, Dining Room, Maison de l'Art Nouveau, 1895*

been perfunctorily dismissed in this negative critical response to Bing's *Maison* is its inflection by the language of medical discourse. Alexandre's account, which includes terms such as "undigestible" and "unhealthy," suggests a quite visceral and immediate physical response to the undulating environs of this modern interior. Alexandre was especially troubled by Van de Velde's smoking room with its "wall coverings composed of enormous arabesques that enter your head and swirl about," while Boylesve likened the room to the interior of a yacht, regretfully noting the absence of "the requisite paraphernalia for seasickness."[40] Another critic deemed the entire Bing Salon the product of a "neurasthenic millionaire," furthering the critical assessment of the "unhealthy" influence on the mythical (and unfortunate) dweller of this Art Nouveau domicile.[41]

Implicit in this response is the converse belief in the rectitude of the well-ordered and restful bourgeois domestic interior. In the *fin-de-siècle* period, there was one universally acclaimed artist who, it was believed, could provide the perfect thematic and formal recipe for the creation of a domestic pastoral decorative art, and that was Pierre Puvis de Chavannes. Serenely divorced from the anxious present, Puvis's idyllic imagery offered viewers suffering from a general "life fatigue" a brief respite from the chaos of the city.[42] This notion of Puvis's work as a kind of quiet haven in the midst of the urban maelstrom appears throughout the critical literature in the late 1880s and 1890s. It is noteworthy, and indeed telling, that the catalogue essay for Puvis's important one-man exhibition at Durand-Ruel in 1887 opened with the following:

> You live amidst agitation, noise and the hectic crowd, surrounded by a feverish atmosphere. Suddenly, a drapery parts, and you are in peace and calm; what a sensation of well-being![43]

For Roger-Ballu, Puvis's "serene work," unlike the militant art of most of his advanced contemporaries, was the perfect panacea for an exhausted and enervated viewing public. It is not unusual that Puvis's art appeared restful and quiet, from "another era," in the words of one critic, in the privacy of the Durand-Ruel gallery. Yet, even at the annual Salon, which Émile Zola likened to a department store and which most commentators characterized as a bustling fair or bazaar, Puvis's entries were said to have had a similar effect. In a survey of contemporary art written some ten years after Puvis's death, Julius Meier-Graefe recalled the throngs who each year fought their way through the noise and bustle of the Salon to find the work of Puvis. As long as Puvis was alive, he recalls, people went to the Salon to see his pictures, despite the "audacities" of the annual event. "When one got to him through the tumult of the rooms, all the trumpets of the big and brutal musicians and all the squealing of the little pipers seemed to cease. It was like coming into a church."[44]

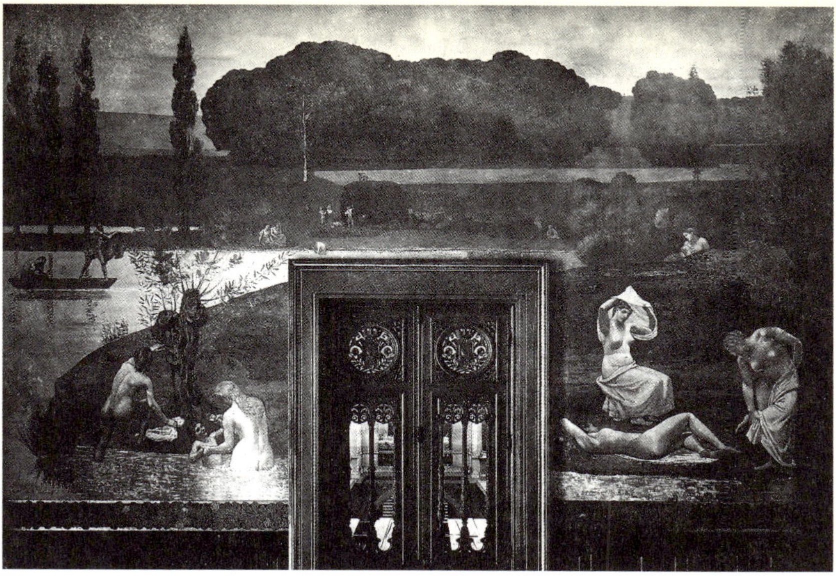

32 *Puvis de Chavannes,* L'Eté, *Salon d'arrivée, Hôtel de Ville, Paris, 1891*

Though Puvis was arguably the most visible and esteemed *public* artist of the Third Republic, his art provided both the thematic material and the stylistic formula for a quintessentially private art. Roger Marx was one of many critics who applauded the artist's abstemious classicism as well as the salubrious pastoralism celebrated throughout his decorative oeuvre. In particular, Marx praised *L'Été*, publicly enshrined in Paris's Hôtel de Ville, for its power to "take us away from ourselves" and to provide a brief respite from the fever and anguish of city life. When viewers gather around the Hôtel de Ville panel, Marx writes, they forget the malaise oppressing society, distanced as they are (visually and psychologically speaking) from the vortex of modern affairs, distanced as well, he notes, from "the contagion of modern neurasthenia."

> . . . one senses that [the panel] was executed in isolation, far from the whirlwind of human affairs and the turmoils of life; the contagion of modern neurasthenia has not broken its spell; healthy and suspended above the world, it counters our pervasive pessimism with the comforting vision of another, better world.[45]

The decorative pastoral landscape as essayed by Puvis and many of his followers images the bucolic existence enjoyed by an ancient society before the founding of cities and modern commerce. As such, it provided the perfect visual panacea for a neurasthenic age. The nervous disease, after all, was a highly visible signifier of urban modernism and cultural advancement; that is to say, it was intimately linked to modern civilization. Thus, for a world-weary late nineteenth-century audience, the pastoral mode, with its emphasis on the halcyon existence of a pre-civilized world, effectively served as the cultural antidote to *fin-de-siècle* decadence and malaise.

In *L'Été* we see a serenely pastoral environment and the calm existence of an ancient society before the founding of cities and modern commerce. As befits the nature of the envisioned activity, the surrounding landscape is bucolic and shelters the arcadians from the harsh realities of life beyond this delightful place. In this decorative panel both the necessary labor and earned leisure that accompanied the construction of humankind's earliest societies are incorporated. Befitting its decorative function, the accessible pastoral iconography demands little in the way of mental cerebration from the viewer, and the thematic interest is evenly dispersed across the picture plane. Rather than focusing on one dominant figural group, the spectator's gaze is thus invited to wander unimpeded throughout the comforting environment.

Throughout all of Puvis's pastoral landscapes, women serve two functions: they are presented either as active and robust caretakers of the hearth (*femme au foyer*) or as visual emblems of rest and calm (bathing nymph). Often, as in Puvis's panels at the Musée de Picardie in Amiens, these female realms are in turn contrasted to the male-dominated realm of work on (as opposed to in) the city. Even within this early bucolic society, the workaday world of the "city" is disassociated from "home," the locus of rest and calm stability. In *L'Été*, leisure and the feminine realm are literally foregrounded, while the mundane realm of the masculine is effectively removed and is merely a distant backdrop.

Puvis maintains this ideological bifurcation of the male and female spheres – males identified with work, females with home and/or leisure – throughout his decorative landscapes, though it is clear that his allegiance (as a decorative painter) lies with the serene domain of female leisure and rest. In *Doux pays*, a panel painted for the private home of Léon Bonnat in 1882, the identification of the pastoral with females resting in nature is further evidenced. Here young male children join the women in their idyllic (homey?) surrounds, while the masculine realm of arduous activity is remotely referenced and serves as a visual antithesis to the feminine realm of pastoral calm. In 1895, Bonnat spoke in glowing terms of the decorative panel recalling that on days when he was "tired and listless," the *Doux pays* brightened his soul and forced his "somber imaginings" to evaporate.[46] This was, in essence, the mission stipulated by Germain in his essay on the decorative landscape, and both he and other critics interested in the genre believed that Puvis's pastoral decorations could indeed restore serenity to the weary spirit. Roger Marx, who applauded Puvis's ability to image a world distanced from the "contagion of modern neurasthenia," similarly recognized the transformative power of the decorative landscape.

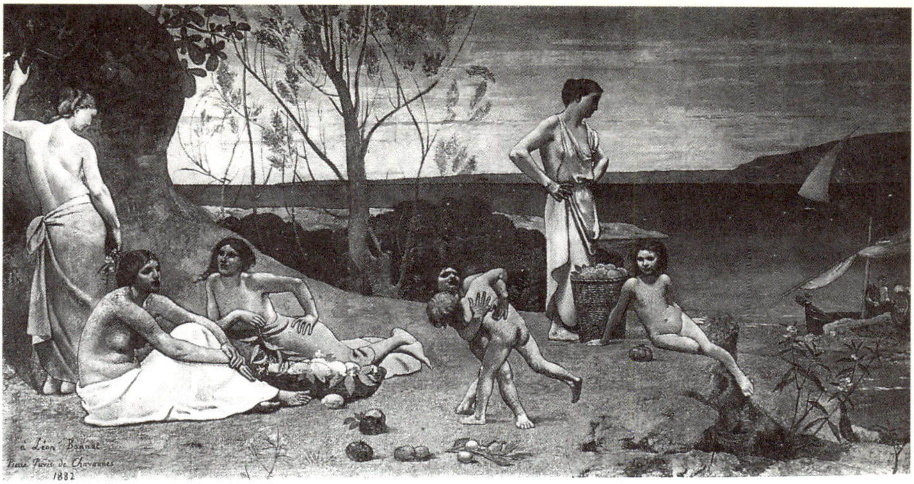

33 *Puvis de Chavannes,* Doux pays, *1882*

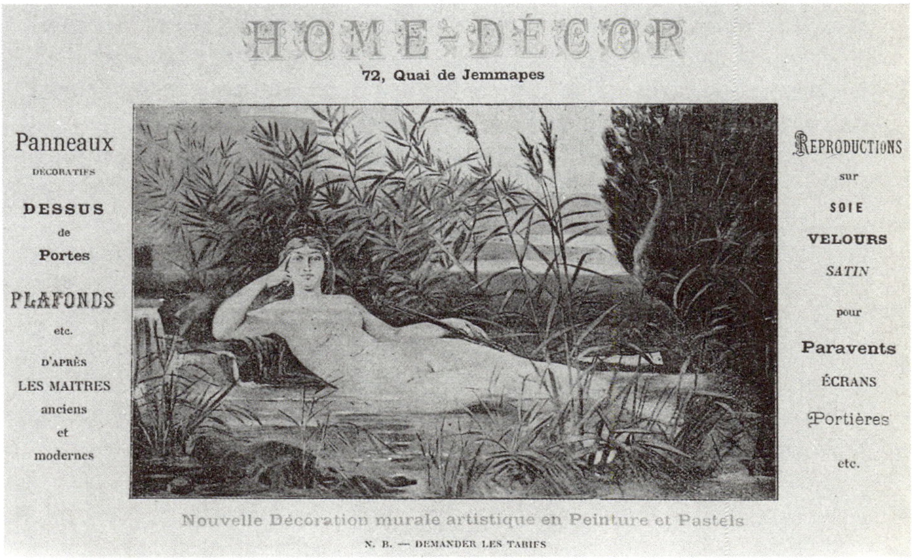

34 Home Decor, *from L'Estampe et L'Affiche, 15 February 1899*

> At the sight of so much calm and harmony, our soul [has] to rediscover the secret of lost tranquility, and [falls] back under the illusion of a possible joy of life.[47]

Puvis's decorative landscapes, like Matisse's *Bonheur de vivre*, image a peaceful enclave sheltered from the world of business and mental fatigue; accordingly, they highlight that quintessentially restful denizen of Arcadia, the female nude. At the turn of the century, the female's socially designated role was to provide comfort and rest for her weary (neurasthenic) husband, either as *femme au foyer*, as keeper of a calm, structured interior, or as decorative nymph, that gently-curving hieroglyph of serenity. The cultural linkage of these two seemingly disparate female roles is succinctly evidenced in an 1899 advertisement for decorative panels featuring a reclining curvaceous nude intended, presumably, to function as part of the consumer's "Home Decor". In an article entitled "Le Feminisme et le bon sens," written for an 1895 issue of *La Plume*, Victor Joze further demonstrated this linkage in suggesting that the female remain as nature intended her, as "mistress of the house or bacchante."[48] While the nymph reigns supreme in the *Bonheur de vivre*, both apparitions of the desirable female lurk throughout Matisse's oeuvre. In *Luxe, calme et volupté* (1904–5), they commingle peacefully as the beach at Saint-Tropez is transformed into a modern-day isle of Cythera. Many years later, they reappear in that paean to domesticity, *The Music Lesson*, their roles neatly juxtaposed within the sheltering protection of the arcadian world of nature. The domestic and pastoral realm of rest and beauty as envisioned by Matisse is, ultimately, a "masculine dreamworld," to borrow once again from Renato Poggioli.[49] Within this pastoral world of dreams, the female – in either guise – provides domestic comfort and serenity and contributes to the creation of a private interior haven distanced from the neurasthenic chaos of the city.

This dream of a simpler, happier existence away from the "contentious forum" is the real key to understanding the pastoral.[50] If the nineteenth-century businessman was unable to live the bucolic life as envisioned by Horace's usurer, he could at the very least recreate (or have recreated for him) the pastoral place of delight *chez lui* via the decorative landscape. For the world-weary *homme d'affaires*, the proper domestic interior embodied an ambiance of restful leisure (*otium*), visually and emotionally providing a retreat from the world of business (*negotium*). Arcadian pleasures were, thus, literally close to home, and it is this domestic serenity that we find celebrated in Matisse's modernist aesthetic.

8

Domesticity, Decoration and Consumer Culture: Selling Art and Design in Pre-World War I France

NANCY J. TROY

AMONG the social expectations that affected the presentation and reception of art in nineteenth-century France, the delimitation of the boundaries between the public and the private was especially crucial, although deeply problematic." So writes Martha Ward in a recent study of exhibition practices of the Impressionist period that explores how the private domain came to be seen as a bulwark protecting the contemplative experience of works of art from the onslaught of crass commercial practices and debased tastes associated with the public sphere. "While the 'dealer and critic system' expanded rapidly," Ward continues, "artists also increasingly took the initiative for their own promotion, and Salon organizers began to adapt practices from the private domain. The distinction between public and private proved to be chronically unstable and required constant renegotiation with the actual conditions of artistic production and consumption."[1] Where the Impressionist painters emphasized decorative features of their installations in order to secure a discursive context within the private sphere, Ward notes that the Neo-Impressionists insisted instead on the presentation of their paintings as autonomous objects and therefore favored neutral settings rather than decorative ensembles; correspondingly, they embraced rather than rejected the public sphere, choosing as their principal venue the Société des Artistes Indépendants.[2] In the early twentieth century, the presentation and marketing of art and design continued to be structured by the competing discourses of the private and public spheres. Yet, I want to suggest, the domestic settings that had previously functioned as aestheticized spaces deemed appropriate for the presentation of fine and decorative art themselves became associated with commerce. As a result, the private setting modelled on the home no longer functioned unproblematically as a protected site where art could escape the taint of commerce.

This essay focuses on three examples of exhibition interiors from the years around 1910 in which aspects of the discourse of domesticity were engaged – in various and even contradictory ways – in order to sell art and design, and, simultaneously, to mask the commercial nature of that very practice: the Maison Cubiste, Daniel-Henry Kahnweiler's gallery, and Paul Poiret's couture house. It is my contention that the issue of decoration was crucial to the discourse of domesticity and that, in order to understand why domesticity was alternately embraced or held at bay for the purposes of selling works of art or maintaining their elevated status during this period, it is necessary first to appreciate how, between 1890 and 1914, decoration was displaced from its central position as a highly valued aspect of the fine arts to the marginal position that it still occupies today. The positive values attached to domesticity in the late nineteenth century changed considerably with the denigration of decoration in the pre-war period, especially within the influential Cubist movement: these changes can be illuminated by examining a series of interrelated circumstances that seem to have converged on issues of gender construction. I therefore propose to begin by exploring the relationship between, as well as the distinctive features of, Cubist and Art Nouveau attitudes to decoration and the decorative arts in order to point out how gendered notions of commerce and consumer culture functioned to construct the modernist concept of the "merely" decorative.

In their 1912 book, *Du "cubisme"*, an explication of the fundamental tenets of Cubism that functioned in some circles like a manifesto of the movement, Albert Gleizes and Jean Metzinger condemned decorative painting as "the antithesis of the picture." The authors explained:

> The decorative work of art exists only by virtue of its *destination*; it is animated only by the relations established between it and the given objects. Essentially dependent, necessarily incomplete, it must in the first place satisfy the mind so as not to distract it from the display which justifies and completes it. It is an organ.

The Cubist picture, on the other hand, is an easel painting or *tableau de chevalet* that

> carries within itself its own *raison d'être*. You may take it with impunity from a church to a drawing-room, from a museum to a study. Essentially independent, necessarily complete, it need not immediately satisfy the mind: on the contrary, it should lead it, little by little, toward the imaginative depths where burns the light of organization. It does not harmonize with this or that ensemble, it harmonizes with the totality of things, with the universe: it is an organism.[3]

It was in order to distance Cubist art from the dependent nature of decoration that Gleizes and Metzinger emphasized Cubism's essence as easel painting. By insisting on the internal coherence and structural independence of the easel painting, they in effect rejected the Art Nouveau approach to decoration that had emerged in the 1890s, according to which a painting was no different than any other decorated object insofar as it was conceived as an integral part of a larger ensemble of designs, its integrity subordinated to that of the setting in which it was to be seen.

"The term *décorative*," Rioux de Maillou had written in 1895, "implies a subordination, the necessity of staying within a given boundary, of orienting oneself in a direction, determined by the manner of being and the character of the object to be decorated."[4] At the same time, and in parallel terms, the writer Octave Uzanne equated decoration with femininity, celebrating "woman's ability to adorn both her own body and the interior spaces in which she naturally belonged."[5] As Debora Silverman has shown, Uzanne and others associated with the officially sanctioned craft revival of the 1890s "hoped to facilitate what [Uzanne] called the renewal of female interior arts, 'intimate and decorative.'"[6] The dichotomy that Gleizes and Metzinger constructed between decoration and Cubism was thus built on the foundation of a pre-existing idea about gender that they extended to the point that, for them, impotence and decoration marked the feminized, domestic interior as the site of passive, sensual satisfaction while independence, potency and art qualified the masculine sphere of the active intellect.[7] With this schema in mind, one might consider the Cubist painters' participation in an ambitious display of decorative art featured at the 1912 Salon d'Automne not as an inexplicable departure from their expressed disdain for decoration but instead as an effort to redefine decorative art itself, and the domestic interior in particular, as appropriate sites for men's artistic activity.

Holding this proposition in abeyance for the moment, it is important to point out that during the 1890s the nature of the relationship between art and decoration was quite complex. In that decade, not only had proponents of decoration succeeded in convincing several artists' societies to establish sections for decorative painting in their annual salons, indicating a substantial degree of acceptance of decoration amongst the membership of those societies, but at the same time decorative painting was being practiced by numerous vanguard artists, including Paul Gauguin, Maurice Denis, and Édouard Vuillard. The decorative aspect of their work, its relative flatness resulting from the deployment of large areas of unmodulated colors or repetitive patterns, far from being denigrated as appealing only to the senses, was in fact celebrated at the time as the source of "synthetic, symbolic and ideistic" values, precisely the values customarily attached to easel painting.[8] Clearly, then, not everyone believed that decorative painting was inherently incapable of conveying meaning or intellectual content. Indeed, the contribution of decorative, Symbolist works of the 1890s to the development of highly intellectualized abstract styles of easel painting in the early twentieth century has long been appreciated. It thus appears that during the 1890s, decoration was a contested field that was being both claimed as a site of high art and ideistic values, and used to structure and

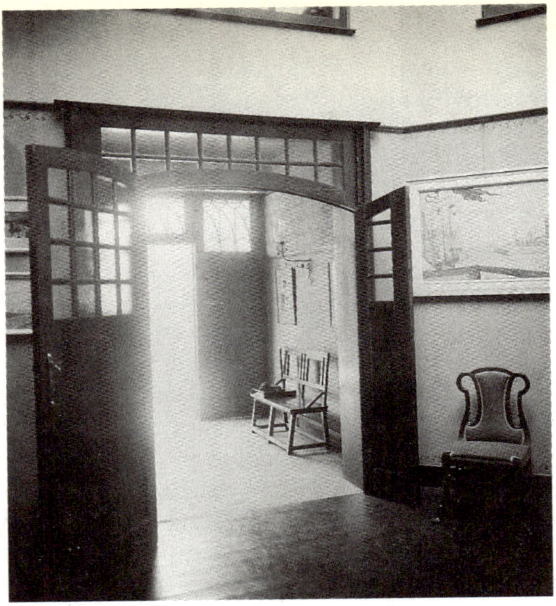

35 *Henry Van de Velde, Hall of the Artist's Home "Bloemenwerf", Uccle, 1896*

channel sensual experience within the domestic interior conceived as an Art Nouveau ensemble.

The gendered discourse that characterizes the Cubist appraisal of decoration was shaped by these earlier artworld debates, but it also has to be understood in the context of the emergence in the late nineteenth century of a culture of consumption whose emblem was the department store.[9] The department store has often been described as a cathedral of modern commerce, and it has also been likened to the museum in its aestheticized display of consumer goods and commodities designed for the middle-class home. By displacing both the religious connotations of the cathedral as well as the aesthetic claims of the museum to the realm of the marketplace, the department store threatened both the moral integrity and the high art status of decoration and the decorative arts that together formed the theoretical foundation for the work of Henry Van de Velde, for example, as well as other early proponents of what came to be known as Art Nouveau.[10] It was apparently through this new nexus of associations with the department store that decoration and the decorative arts became inextricably linked to the feminine arena of consumption. The commercial dimension of the feminization of the decorative arts worked to construct decoration as separate and distinct from the fine arts; decoration was gendered feminine not simply because it was sometimes produced by women and often associated with the female sphere of the domestic environment but also, and perhaps more importantly, because it was tied up with the equally feminized realm of consumer culture.

Despite the espousal of a morality of design by such decorators as William Morris and Henry Van de Velde, or the ideistic notions attached to decoration by the Symbolists in the 1890s (and later by Matisse, whom Joyce Robinson discusses in this volume), in the early twentieth century the aim of decoration, as Gleizes and Metzinger implied in *Du "cubisme"*, was still widely understood to be the satisfaction of the senses rather than the engagement of the mind. And while decorative art continued to be identified with commerce and the crafts, easel painting enjoyed the stature of an intellectual enterprise that ever since the Renaissance had guaranteed its appropriateness for the fine artist concerned with the expression of profound truths. Accompanying and amplifying these associations is the issue of gender, which I believe might account for certain aspects of the Cubist enterprise, including in particular the Maison Cubiste.

Displayed at the Salon d'Automne in 1912, the Maison Cubiste included a façade as well as three rooms of a domestic environment that was distinctive for its informality and eclecticism. In the principal interior, the *salon* 36
bourgeois, the exhibition audience encountered a diverse collection of decorative elements contributed by a rather large number of male and female artists, including André Mare (furniture), Roger de la Fresnaye (woodwork, fireplace, chandelier), Jean-Louis Gampert (wallpaper), André Versan (lighting fixtures), Marie-Thérèse Lanoa (rugs), Sabine Desvallières (firescreen), and Maurice Marinot (enamelled glassware). Among the smaller objects were bookbindings by Mare and a tea service for six by Jacques Villon. Inserted above mirrors in the four corners of the room were oval paintings by Marie Laurencin, each depicting the head of a young woman. While the decorative features of the interior were contributed by women and men, the fine art objects were the work of men only. Easel paintings by Marcel Duchamp, Fernand Léger, Gleizes, Metzinger, and La Fresnaye hung on the walls, and sculptures by Raymond Duchamp-Villon and Ernest-Frédéric Weild were also displayed.

The disparate character of the decorative objects shown in the *salon bourgeois* immediately distinguishes this interior from a characteristic Art Nouveau ensemble. Indeed, all the stylistic features of the Maison Cubiste were conceived as a reaction against what André Mare described as "the errors of 1900."[11] Instead of the thoroughly feminized Art Nouveau style, marked by softly curving lines and muted colors, the Cubists based their work on the more ample forms and classicizing demeanor of the early nineteenth-century Louis-Philippe style. That there is a difference in the gendered associations attached to these styles seems evident in light of the terms Mare used to exhort his Cubist collaborators:

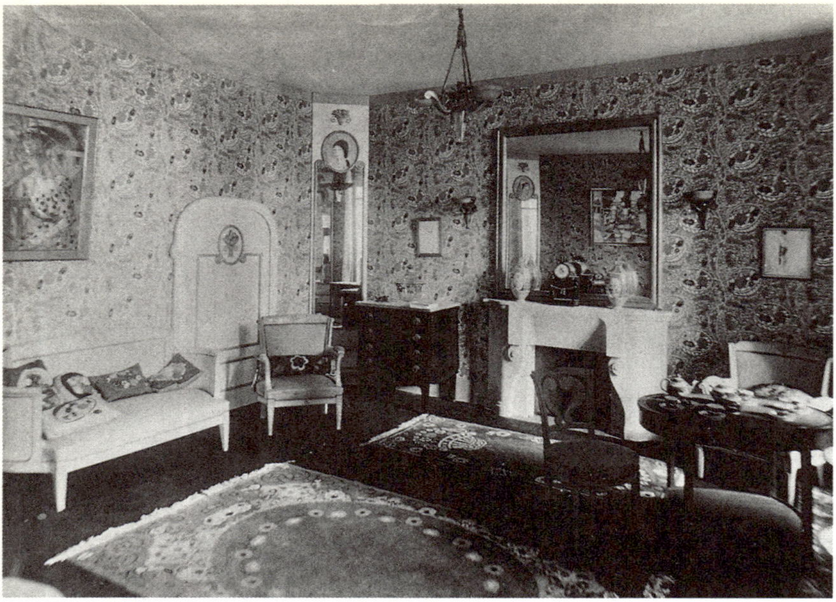

36 *André Mare et al., Salon Bourgeois, Maison Cubiste, 1912*

> 1) Return to very simple, pure, logical and even slightly cold lines, whereas the period that preceded us was horribly tormented. 2) Return to very fresh, very pure, very daring colors, whereas that same preceding period always contented itself with washed out, discolored, anemic tones. Have a vigorous and naïve drawing technique ... To summarize, make things with a slightly severe line, the coldness of which will be mitigated by a pleasant, brightly colored decor, and the whole in a very French tradition.[12]

Not only was the Louis-Philippe style associated with the middle-class orientation of the bourgeois monarchy, as distinguished from the eighteenth-century aristocratic affiliations of French Art Nouveau, but critics also aligned it with the contemporaneous German Biedermeyer style. Indeed, nationalist issues complicate the gendered readings of styles at this point, such that Art Nouveau, a notoriously international movement, came to be vaunted as peculiarly French, whereas the Cubists' version of Louis-Philippe, because of its relation to German styles, was rejected as alien to the true French tradition. To the extent that the delicacy of Art Nouveau was associated with French taste, feminine characteristics were equated with Frenchness; the heavy lugubriousness associated with German design was read not only as alien to feminized French taste but also as appropriate to the non-aristocratic character and entrepreneurial spirit of the German people.[13]

Entrepreneurship was in fact a feature of the Maison Cubiste, which was designed to promote the sale of paintings as well as furniture. The stylistic eclecticism of its decorative components may have been considered an acceptable by-product of the artists' collaboration insofar as it might have encouraged middle-class consumers, perhaps daunted by the cost of a totally harmonious (Art Nouveau) ensemble, to consider purchasing individual objects instead. That same eclecticism also established an appropriate setting for the display of Cubist easel paintings as objects that were stylistically similar to one another yet comparable in their individual integrity to the adjacent furniture and therefore equally suited to the middle-class domestic interior. Applauding these features of the *salon bourgeois* as beneficial for the marketing of Cubist paintings, Fernand Léger remarked in a letter of 7 August 1912 to André Mare, "Your idea is absolutely *splendid* for us, really *splendid.* People will see Cubism in a domestic setting, which is very important . . . If you can exert influence about the placement in the gallery at the [Salon d']Automne, do, it is important." Presumably thinking of its potential for drawing the attention of a particular class of buyers, he even praised Mare's choice in naming the *salon bourgeois*: "*Your title is perfect.*"

When the Maison Cubiste is viewed through the lens of the discourse of domesticity, it becomes clear that the Cubist artists involved in its creation effectively confused every gendered code that they invoked. As the independent, Cubist organism was imbedded in a simulated bourgeois environment designed, like the department store display, to arouse desire on the part of the consuming audience, so the masculine force of the *tableau de chevalet* was overwhelmed by the feminizing associations of decoration and the decorative arts. The gender implications of the Cubists' rejection of Art Nouveau and embrace of Louis-Philippe were not openly addressed in the critical reception of the Maison Cubiste, the components of which were seen less as appeals to familiar bourgeois characteristics of French culture than as signs of capitulation to an alien commercial culture. As a result, the artists' aspirations to reform French decorative arts traditions were regarded as dangerous signs of foreign encroachment on the national terrain of the arts. The artists who created the Maison Cubiste never managed to reconcile the contradictions they thereby engaged, and I believe these issues have clouded our appreciation of the role these artists played in early twentieth-century French modernism ever since.

At this point it is important to clarify the commercial status of the Cubist artists who are under consideration here. Both Gleizes and Metzinger had been associated with the Abbaye de Créteil, an abortive attempt in the early years of the twentieth century to establish a utopian artists' community free from "the commercialism, the corruption and intrigues in the arts controlled by a bourgeois society."[14] Although the

Abbaye's attempt to operate outside the boundaries of the commercial art world can be understood in straightforward terms as an effort at social reform, it can also be explained as an attempt to establish an alternative to the dominant art institutions of the period.[15]

The failure of officially sponsored salon exhibitions to engender sufficient sales of works by younger artists goes a long way toward explaining the rationale not only for the Abbaye de Créteil but also for several subsequent efforts by artists who would eventually become identified with Cubism either to circumvent or to gain a measure of control over existing venues for the display and sale of their work. These efforts include the successful rigging of the 1911 Salon des Indépendants hanging committee by Gleizes, Metzinger, Le Fauconnier and Léger, which enabled them to place their work together in Salle 41 and hang works by their associates in adjoining rooms. By insuring the cohesion of their work, they managed to establish their group identity as a movement in the public eye.

The year following their strategic intervention at the Indépendants, these artists also participated in a major private exhibition mounted by the Société Normande de Peinture Moderne, an organization founded in Rouen in 1907 with the Duchamp-Villon brothers among its most prominent members. Committed to the interrelationship of the arts, including poetry, music, painting, sculpture and the decorative arts, the Société Normande worked to create exhibition opportunities that would promote the group identity of its membership. In 1911, for example, the Société sponsored two exhibitions that included the work of Mare, Duchamp-Villon, La Fresnaye, Villon, and others who eventually contributed to the Maison Cubiste. In October 1912, the Société mounted the Salon de la Section d'Or, one of the most important Cubist exhibitions in pre-war France. These latter exhibitions, as well as the group manifestations at the Salon des Indépendants and the display of Cubist works in the Maison Cubiste at the Salon d'Automne, amounted to a major strategic effort on the part of Cubist artists who could not depend upon private dealers to control the marketing of their art.

Lacking contractual arrangements for the sale of their work, Gleizes, Léger, Metzinger, Duchamp-Villon, Mare and their collaborators were compelled by market conditions to create an audience for their work in the public domain of the officially sanctioned salons and smaller exhibition venues of their own devising. Their situation needs to be distinguished from that of Picasso and Braque, whose work has invariably been presented as the paradigm against which to measure the production of every other artist associated with the Cubist movement.

As Malcolm Gee may have been the first to point out, during the pre-war period, "painters associated with the *avant-garde* were effectively split into two groups according to whether they had acquired the backing of an influential dealer – those who had failed to do this were evidently in a far weaker position from a financial and career point of view."[16] Following Gee, art historians have recently begun to appreciate the degree to which commercial considerations might account for stylistic differences between the Cubist painters who regularly exhibited in the salons and those, like Picasso and Braque, whose work was occasionally shown publicly abroad but in Paris was available only in the gallery of a private dealer. The presence or absence of a need to create an audience and appeal directly to potential consumers must be taken into account in discussions of the hermeticism of Picasso and Braque's style as opposed to the legibility of Gleizes and Metzinger's, or Picasso and Braque's silence as distinguished from the public voice represented by Gleizes and Metzinger's *Du "cubisme"*, for example. Both sets of oppositions engage the problem of situating the artist's work, making it known and accessible to a certain public, conceived as narrow and elite in the case of Picasso and Braque, or broad and bourgeois, in the case of the salon Cubists.

At this point I want to entertain the notion that the oppositions I have been delineating might be clarified if they are read in the context of the gendered discourse of consumer culture. It has long been accepted that Daniel-Henry Kahnweiler was the most innovative and successful dealer in advanced art in pre-war Paris, and that his practice as a dealer was predicated on his disdain for paid publicity and refusal to appeal to the crowd. Describing the opening of his gallery in 1907, Kahnweiler later recalled, "There was nothing – no publicity campaigns, no cocktail parties, nothing at all. And I'll tell you something even stranger: I didn't spend a cent on publicity before 1914, not one cent. I didn't even put announcements in the papers; I didn't do anything."[17] As noted above, the practice of shunning the public salons in favor of private exhibition venues was pioneered by the Impressionists and other private exhibiting societies as well as certain dealers active in the second half of the nineteenth century. Kahnweiler adopted their strategic use of the private sphere, but whereas the Impressionists' exhibition spaces had been decorated as ensembles and designed to evoke the intimacy of the feminized, domestic interior, Kahnweiler's gallery was installed in a manner that marked it as a masculine space. Purposely distinguishing his gallery from the venues of the officially sanctioned salons as well as the ornately furnished, palm-bedecked interiors of other dealers, Kahnweiler used plain sackcloth on the walls to render his as an ostentatiously undecorated space.

Kahnweiler secured the vanguard status of his artists, most notably Braque and Picasso (who painted a quintessentially hermetic portrait of the dealer in 1910) but later also Léger and Gris, by protecting them from the increasingly obvious commercialism of crowded exhibitions in large public spaces. After 1909, his artists never participated in public exhibitions in

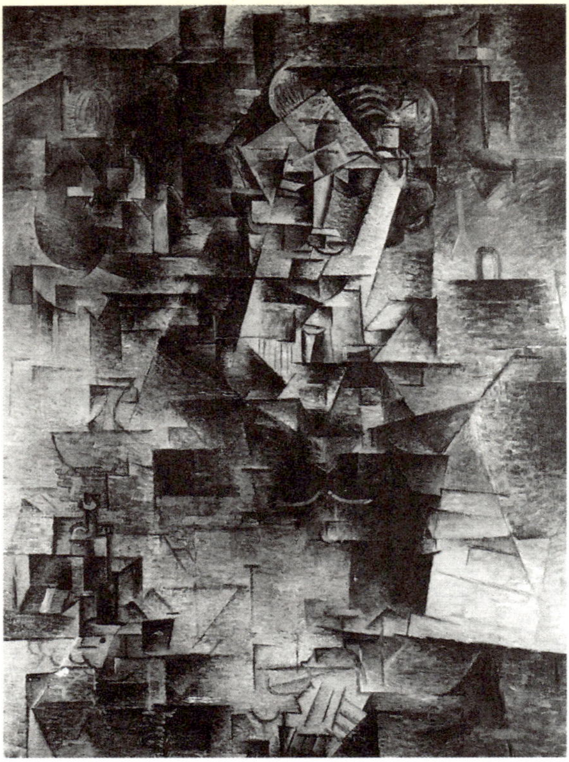

37 *Pablo Picasso,* Daniel-Henry Kahnweiler, *1910*

Paris, and instead of mounting shows, Kahnweiler simply hung their pictures in the gallery. According to Kahnweiler, this "shows you the absolute contempt in which we held not only the critics but also the general public."[18] Abstention from the salons was part of a strategy designed to promote what Kahnweiler described as "a distinctly discrete and aristocratic attitude."[19]

Kahnweiler's strategy clearly demonstrates a desire to insure that works by his stable of artists would be available only to a small, well-informed and self-selected circle of critics and collectors in a private atmosphere visibly different from the domestic environment of the middle-class home. Just as clearly, it steers a course diametrically opposed to that chosen by the artists who constructed the Maison Cubiste at the Salon d'Automne of 1912.

Kahnweiler's success as a entrepreneur, and therefore also some degree of the success of his artists, appears to have been based at least in part on the dealer's ability to divorce his business practices from anything that might be associated with the overlapping discourses of domesticity, decoration and consumer culture. In order to sell works of art by vanguard artists to the clients to whom they might reasonably be expected to appeal, he had to eschew the range of commercial practices associated with establishments appealing to much larger markets. If salons, like department stores, attracted enormous audiences to their vast and often highly orchestrated displays of disparate objects, if they issued extensive catalogues and generated highly visible accounts in newspapers and popular journals, the private dealer maintained the distinctiveness of his products by not advertising and by suggesting the elite character and intellectual self-sufficiency of the works of art he displayed. Whereas the salons required intensive campaigns on the part of artists seeking even a modicum of control over the presentation of their work in order to assure its coherence before a largely uninformed public, the private dealer's stock, like his audience, was pre-selected; there was no need for further organization to assure the integrity of the objects Kahnweiler displayed, and he therefore simply put them up at random on the sackcloth-covered walls of his gallery.

Yet Kahnweiler did not develop these strategies in a vacuum. Indeed, certain of his commerical practices were paralleled by those of Paul Poiret, a couturier, collector and patron of the arts who was especially innovative in exploiting modern art for the benefit of his multifarious commercial enterprises. Among the many artists with whom Poiret associated and whose work he collected and promoted were Constantin Brancusi, André Derain, Raoul Dufy, André Dunoyer de Segonzac, Paul Iribe, Marie Laurencin, Fernand Léger, Georges Lepape, Francis Picabia, and Pablo Picasso.[20] In addition to his principal business as a dress designer, during the pre-war period Poiret was involved to some (still ill-defined) degree in a commercial art gallery situated on the premises of his couture house, called Galerie Barbazanges; he also manufactured a luxuriously packaged line of perfumes named after his eldest daughter Rosine, and ran a loosely organized decorative arts school that furnished designs for his decorative arts atelier and marketing outlets, named after his second daughter, Martine. The interlocking and mutually reinforcing character of his various enterprises struck even contemporary observers as a brilliant marketing strategy. In a 1912 article describing the interior of the newly inaugurated Martine boutique, a correspondent for *Vogue* remarked that while it was common practice to combine the sale of millinery, bags, belts, caps and other apparel accessories, "certainly couturiers have never before insisted that chairs, curtains, rugs and wall-coverings should be considered in the choosing of a dress, or rather that the style of a dress should influence the interior decorations of a home."[21]

Poiret's entrepreneurial success in promoting this *Gesamtkunstwerk* approach to domestic design and female adornment was secured by his ability to obfuscate the commercial nature of his art-related activities. In order to sell clothes, perfume and furnishings to the aristocratic and wealthy bourgeois clients for whom his products were designed, like Kahnweiler he had to avoid cheap publicity and any other practices associated with mass marketing techniques. Instead, the haute couturier maintained the distinctive allure of his products by not advertising, at least not to large audiences, and by appropriating the fine arts to promote the originality, uniqueness and aesthetic quality of his designs. To that end, Poiret made a practice of hiring fashionable painters and graphic artists to create his business stationery, change of address announcements, and two *de luxe* albums of dress designs which he managed to exhibit not only in the Galerie Barbazanges but also at the Salon d'Automne. In 1909, he commissioned a fashionable architect as well as decorators and painters to renovate an eighteenth-century mansion to serve not only as his home, but more importantly as the headquarters of his businesses, in which several hundred assistants were employed. A contemporary observer described the façade of the house, noting the contrast between its calm and noble *ordonnance* and its actual function as a "commercial establishment, and a very prosperous one at that. Yet there is no name in gold letters, large or small, no marble plaque engraved with a name that is famous among *mondaines*; and this is already the first original act of this couturier artist: not to have followed the example of so many others by defiling a superb architecture."[22]

Although Poiret's marketing strategy, designed to attract a wealthy, aristocratic clientele, was distinctive for its luxury and expense, in its disdain for conventional paid publicity and refusal to appeal to the crowd, it was based on some of the same elitist assumptions as Kahnweiler's. Both the art dealer and the couturier were caught in the web of contradictions that united elite and popular culture, the private and the public spheres. To become recognizable as a movement, and therefore marketable as a style, Cubism, like fashion, required not only adherents, but also audiences and dissemination. The dealer's ability to establish an elite position for Picasso and Braque was predicated in part on the broader appeal of those who might be called the "public" Cubists: Gleizes, Léger, Metzinger, and their circle, who depended on the interest generated by exhibitions in the public sphere in order to sell their work.

The photographs of Poiret's mannikins posed in his couture house that Edward Steichen made for publication in *Art et Décoration* in 1911 are symptomatic not only of Poiret's approach to advertising but of his enterprise as a whole in the way they confound art and commerce: Steichen's soft-focus camera style created a mysterious, feminized aura of aestheticism that undermined the fashion photograph's usefulness in conveying detailed information, and directed attention away from any strictly commercial purpose.[23] To that same end, Poiret invited a fashionable young architect, Louis Süe, to design the interior of his *hôtel* and arrange the artworks it contained in a manner that would provide a stylistically appropriate environ-

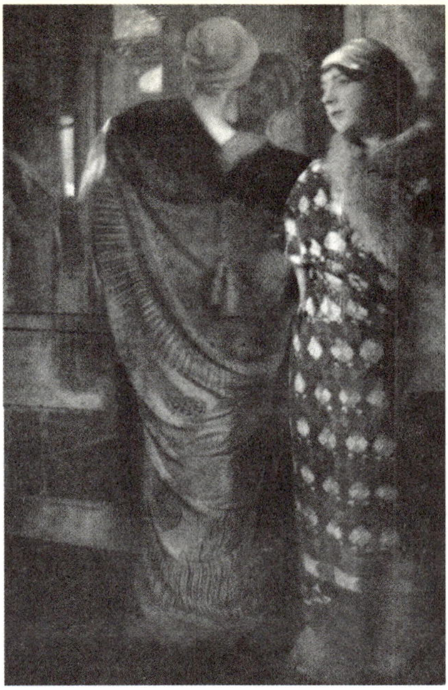

38 *Paul Poiret, Battick and Negus models, 1911. Photographed by Steichen*

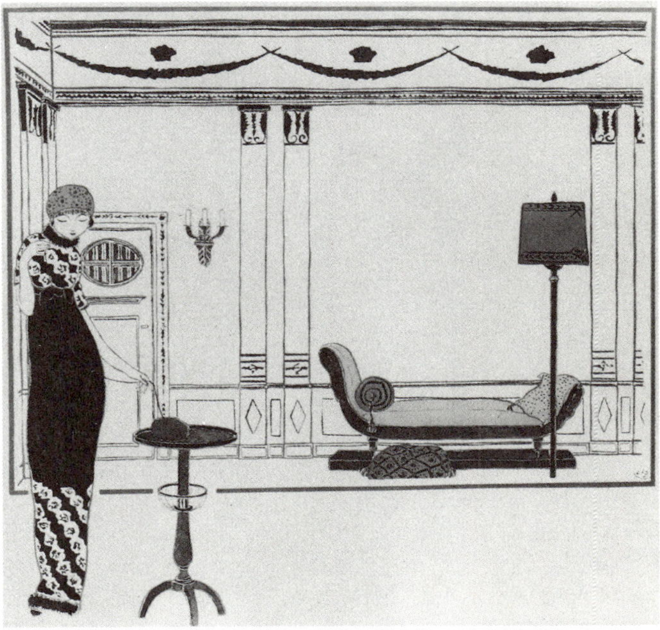

39 *Georges Lepape, plate 2 of* Les Choses de Paul Poiret vues par Georges Lepape *(Paris, 1911)*

ment for the clothes being sold there. In Süe's harmonious salons, traditional in style but with modernist overtones as conveyed by one of the images in Georges Lepape's album, Poiret's controversial clothing apparently looked reasonable, not disjunctive, outrageous or threatening, as it reportedly did when seen on the street or in interiors not specifically crafted for its enhancement. According to an account written in 1911, "One sees these gowns in a modern setting where the design of the furniture and the colors of the wall coverings reflect the same aesthetic tendencies. The paintings offer the same vivacious colors, the drawings the same naïve elements, a bit delicate in outline."[24]

The carefully controlled environment Süe created for Poiret included a small proscenium stage as well as a formal garden in which fashion shows were presented. At the same time, Poiret's home also functioned as a highly theatrical setting for the extravagant costume parties he staged and in which he performed the starring role. The most famous of these fêtes, the *Thousand and Second Night*, was held on 24 June 1911. For that occasion, Poiret and his wife required their 300 or so guests, mostly artists and patrons of the arts, to dress up in oriental costumes comparable to those Poiret was designing for actual theater productions. Anyone who failed to appear in proper attire was outfitted on the spot in clothes supplied from Poiret's ample stocks.

The *Thousand and Second Night* enabled Poiret and his guests to act out a fantastic evocation of the Orient staged like an extravagant fashion show, a theatrical performance on the grounds of his maison de couture. As Poiret later recalled, "My house was closed [off] by tapestries, in such sort that glances from the street could not penetrate. The guests were received as in a theatre by a squad of old gentlemen in evening dress, who were no jokers, and most carefully scanned the arrivals," to insure that no one would "disfigure the ensemble of the fête." From the entrance, guests proceeded through the house until they came upon "the great tragedian De Max . . . [who] told stories taken from the *Thousand and One Nights* . . ."[25] In the garden, seated on Persian carpets under a canopy painted by Raoul Dufy, who also created the hand colored invitations, Poiret played the role of a despotic Sultan, holding a whip in one hand and a scimitar in the other. Guests were brought to him in order to "make their obeisance according to the tradition of Islam."[26] After his favorite, played by his wife Denise, and his other concubines were released from their golden cage and while drinks of all sorts were being served, a series of spectacles was performed by acrobats, a pythoness, a monkey merchant, and several exotic dancers. As Peter Wollen has noted, the event "firmly established Poiret's reputation as *Le Magnifique*, after Suleiman the Magnificent. From then on, alongside the all-pervasive influence of the Russian Ballet, the Oriental look dominated the fashion world and the decorative arts."[27]

In contrast to the Maison Cubiste, which put the private sphere on public display yet failed in its effort to market Cubist paintings by placing them in a decorative arts context whose particular features undermined the discourse of domesticity, in his couture house Poiret successfully transformed the domestic sphere into a stage on which to deploy art, design and theater in order to present orientalism as a marketable commodity. Eliding the distinctions between the anti-commercial elitism of Kahnweiler's gallery and the commercially motivated, public appeal of the Maison Cubiste, Poiret's couture house was maintained as a circumscribed, private realm in which interior design and the proximity of an art gallery functioned simultaneously to mask and to promote the commercial purpose of his enterprise: selling clothes. Unlike the anti-decorative, anonymous and masculine environment of Kahnweiler's gallery, but equally distinct from the ambiguously gendered Maison Cubiste (with which they nevertheless shared many stylistic features), Poiret's carefully composed interiors embraced the feminine sphere of bourgeois domesticity in order to market his dresses as part of what we might call a totally designed "life style," rather than a range of mere commodities.

Epilogue

The discourse of domesticity that structured Poiret's marketing strategy failed to protect him when his exclusive designs became established fashions and were copied for mass production and sale in the USA at cut-rate prices. To his horror, in 1913 Poiret discovered that false labels, available by the thousands, were being sewn into cheap dresses that easily passed for original creations.[28] At the very moment that his entrepreneurial dream was being realized, Poiret awoke to a nightmare of uncontrollable proliferation and consumption. Indeed, the marketing strategy that he had employed to position his clothes as unique creations in the realm of elite culture – the exploitation of art, architecture, interior design and theater – made his designs fashionable and in the process provoked the production of that very profusion of examples against which elite culture defined itself. Here the logic of fashion worked to collapse the private into the public sphere, eventually forcing Poiret to modify his elitism in order to manage his engagement in the mass market.

Poiret's strategic response to the particular conditions governing the merchandising of French fashions in America took place in the public arena dominated by the large-scale department store rather than the carefully controlled context of the couturier's private mansion. Indeed, the department stores through which Poiret reached a broad American audience were themselves important players in the game of exploiting French haute couture fashions at the low as well as the high end of the market.

Macy's followed its Fall 1913 shows of original French fashions with "American-made copies of the Imported Gowns," claiming, "We are in a position to duplicate any of these models accurately at far less than the cost of the originals."[29] Similarly, Gimbel's advertised Paris designs at one-tenth the usual price, proclaiming, "Without exception, these Suits are unapproached in New York or in Europe, for they are our latest specialty. Yes, we had the Suits made in New York, but they are true to the original Paris models."[30] Another outlet vaunted "Chic Style, Perfect Fit and Superior Workmanship at Very Moderate Prices . . . Individual Adaptations and Reproductions Are Assured."[31]

Faced with these challenges to his attempts to maintain an elitist position even in the mass market, Poiret immediately realized that the discourses of high art would not be sufficiently powerful to control the forces unleashed by American commerce. Compelled to do battle on a field defined in terms of industry rather than art, he appealed to American law and publicly threatened to sue "anyone who places a false label in imitation of my trademark on any article of merchandise."[32] Poiret also organized a Syndicate for the Protection of the Great French Couture, which under his direction instituted a set of controversial rules designed to regulate access to the members' seasonal shows, to control the publication of photographs of new models, and to prevent shipments for legitimate clients and commercial outlets from falling into the hands of wholesale copiers. After the outbreak of war in August 1914, as access to the American market gained new urgency for French couturiers facing drastic reductions in both domestic and foreign trade, Poiret's entrepreneurial problems were exacerbated when the Syndicate blacklisted two American customers with German names, one of whom turned out to be the agent responsible for purchasing the wedding gown of President Wilson's fiancée. The incident raised an uproar in the USA, threatened to destroy the Syndicate and caused Poiret and his colleagues to redouble their efforts to appeal to American buyers. In November 1915, for example, the Syndicate overcame a myriad of war-induced obstacles to stage a week-long "Fête Parisienne" in the ballroom of a fancy New York hotel, for which Poiret commissioned his friend Roger Boutet de Monvel to write a two-act play that served as a culturally acceptable vehicle for the presentation of 80–100 examples of the latest, genuine French fashions.[33]

At the same time, however, Poiret was transforming his commercial practices in response to the unique conditions of fashion marketing in America. In October 1916, in the pages of *Vogue* magazine, he advertised a collection "produced exclusively for the women of America," and described the models as "genuine reproduction[s]," which, he claimed, gave American women "the opportunity to own a PAUL POIRET creation without paying the usual excessive price." As a hybrid devised to reconcile the contradiction between art and industry, the genuine reproduction represented a pragmatic capitulation to the forces of American commerce. At the same time it exposed the fundamental instability of the logic of fashion, poised on the point where distinctions between private and public, elite and mass culture, the original and the reproduction, collide and dissolve. Unlike the creators of the Maison Cubiste, who also grappled with these ambiguities, Daniel-Henry Kahnweiler never faced this dilemma, because his own elitist definition of the private sphere avoided any association with the feminized discourse of domesticity and he was therefore able to maintain the commercial viability of his gallery by means of a fiction, a space in which high art could be protected from the volatile realms of fashion and consumer culture.

9

Forgotten Ties: The Suppression of the Decorative in German Art and Theory, 1900–1915

JENNY ANGER

> During these times of ferment around the turn of the century the words ornament and decorative were not yet dirty words in the criticism of painting . . .
> Admittedly this is a sensitive, not to say neurotic point in twentieth-century criticism. There is nothing the abstract painter used to dislike more than the term "decorative," an epithet which reminded him of the familiar sneer that what he had produced was at best pleasant curtain material. The abstract art of the twentieth century looks for an ancestry far removed from the humble craft of decorative design.
>
> *E. H. Gombrich, The Sense of Order, 1979*[1]

In modernism, the decorative and the abstract have long been held to be opposites. Adolf Loos articulates an extreme version of modernism's objection to the decorative, for example, in his essay "Ornament and Crime" (1908). In this infamous, widely-published article, Loos argues that the more refined man is, the less inclined he is to decorate – whereas children, Papuan natives, and criminals write graffiti, tattoo, and draw everywhere with reckless abandon.[2] In an earlier article, "Ladies' Fashion" (1902), Loos includes women with his underdeveloped, excessively adorned primitives: "The clothing of woman is distinguished externally from that of man by the preference for ornamental and colorful effects and by the long skirt that covers her legs completely. Both of these factors show us that in recent centuries woman has been severely retarded in her development."[3] Naomi Schor has shown that the excesses of the purist aesthetic that Loos and his fellow modernists prescribe are forever mapped onto the feminine, specifically "the *ornamental*, with its traditional connotations of effeminacy and decadence . . . [or] the *everyday*, whose 'prosiness' is rooted in the domestic sphere of social life presided over by women."[4]

Despite modernism's abhorrence of the decorative understood in these terms, the supposedly separate spheres of decoration and pure form have nevertheless had intersections, which the dogma of separation has taken great pains to account for. Wassily Kandinsky's central modernist text, *Concerning the Spiritual in Art* (1912), exemplifies the hermeneutic effort undertaken to erase decorative traces from "pure" painting. Much of Kandinsky's text confidently constructs a foundation for an art of pure composition driven by "inner necessity" and based on musical and synesthetic models. However, he expresses trepidation at completely forsaking representation:

> If today we already began completely to destroy the bond which ties us to nature, to rush head long into liberation and to content ourselves exclusively with the combination of pure color and independent form, we would produce works which would look like geometric ornamentation, which, to put it crudely, would resemble a necktie or a carpet.[5]

As the epigraph from Ernst Gombrich's "study in the psychology of decorative art" suggests, Kandinsky's position is typical within modernism, not merely for its desire to divorce itself from the decorative, but also for its "neurotic" compulsion to do so. Rather than accepting this division, art historians have begun to track the seemingly inevitable and repetitive elision of the decorative in the discourse of art. Norma Broude recognized some years ago, for example, that it is often said that great modern artists, that is, male artists, "raise" the "merely decorative" to the level of "significant form."[6] Mark Cheetham recently characterized this *Aufhebung* (sublation) as the "rhetoric of purity," which raises the "feminine" into a more "pure" and "masculine" art, and he situated this process as central to modernism, not as an occasional aberration of it.[7]

The inevitability of this move becomes the focus of the present essay. I address the disappearance of the decorative from the modern aesthetic from two perspectives. First, I concentrate on the conflicted writings of early twentieth-century German critic Karl Scheffler in order to examine discourse on the decorative from its most visible period – when, as Gombrich says, "the words ornament and decorative were not yet dirty words." I contrast Scheffler's initial embrace of the decorative with his later erasure of it as a positive aesthetic, and I analyze the transformation in terms of gender and consumer culture, both of which organize the shift in fundamental ways. Second, I explore ways in which Scheffler's – and others' – abandonment of the decorative may be implicit in the modernist aesthetic as initiated by Immanuel Kant. It is the coincidence of this aesthetic with the commercialized and strictly-gendered cultural field at the turn of the century that necessitates the expulsion of the "feminine," the decorative, and the commercial from modernism. Surveying this field, I argue that the suppression of the decorative obscures the extent to which the discourse of abstraction is partially grounded in the very discourse it vehemently suppresses. But even more, I suggest that the aesthetic of pure abstraction which finds its source in Kant depends structurally upon this repudiation – not once and for all, but ever and ever again – and that this process becomes deeply imbricated in contests of power, especially those of gender and capital. In other words, Kandinsky's ideal of "pure color and independent form" and the decades of abstract painting that followed in its wake depend wholly on "feminine," commercial decoration *and* on the invisibility of this dependence.

Before proceeding, I must briefly address the problem of definition, which is a leitmotif of this essay and of the discourse on the decorative in general. By the word "decorative," I invoke the decorative arts, decorative design, and ornament, including ornament as adornment in addition to ornament as linear structure in design. Instead of trying to tease out these distinctions, I draw attention, on the one hand, to the traditional modernist objection to this entire field, and, on the other, to the common trope used to define that field, namely, function. The decorative and ornamental are generally considered to be inessential and functionless. Nonetheless, the decorative arts are supposed to embody a meeting of function and formal qualities in art. It is their utility that separates them from "high art," which in the tradition of Kant serves no function, or, more specifically, appears "purposeful without end." This apparent confusion of terms, hinging on function, is crucial, I suggest, to the persistence of the modernist aesthetic. The imprecision and mobility of the term "decorative" – signifying at once an exterior embellishment and an interior, linear structure, a useless arabesque and a useful curtain – allow, as we shall see, for its repetitive usurpation and the denial thereof by "pure" modernism.

I

> Abstraction is therefore the essential domain of the ornamentalist.
>
> Karl Scheffler, "Meditations on Ornament," 1901[8]

Karl Scheffler's work is an instructive example of the process of suppression because he so clearly articulates the general shift from avidly supporting to denouncing the decorative, elucidating the gendered and economic stakes of that suppression as he proceeds, and because however influential Loos's essay "Ornament and Crime" may have been, Scheffler's very different early theories of decoration were perhaps equally constitutive of modernist thinking about pure form. Peg Weiss has documented the importance of Scheffler's early writing on the decorative for the development of Kandinsky's theory of pure abstraction. Based on Scheffler's and Kandinsky's shared interests in the emotional valence of musical and coloristic correspondences and on Kandinsky's explicit reference in *Concerning the Spiritual* to Scheffler's essay "Notes on Color," Weiss perceives that "[t]he call to abstraction through ornament was perfectly clear to Kandinsky." Interestingly, Weiss repeats the dismissal of the decorative that concerns me here. Apparently empathizing with Kandinsky, she

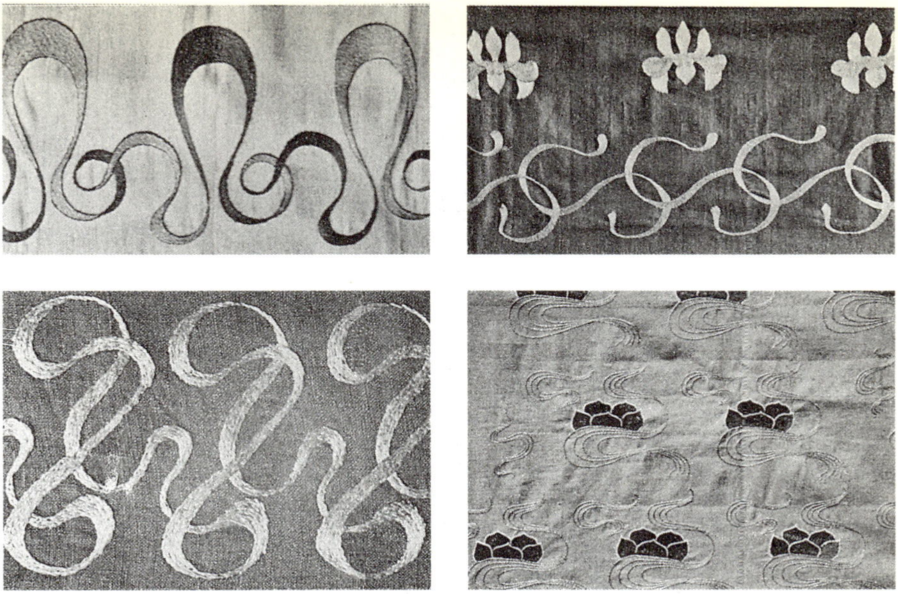

40 *Marie Closset, four embroidery patterns, from* Die Kunst, *1909*

writes: "He often felt himself almost plagued by decorative ideas, yet he clearly recognized in them their great potential . . .," and he perceived at last that his " 'decorative' work could indeed serve as a bridge to the end goal of 'fine art' with a higher significance."[9] Despite – or perhaps because of – this dismissal, Weiss demonstrates the relevance of Scheffler's theory of ornament for thinking abstraction in painting.

At the onset of his career Scheffler was critic and Berlin correspondent for *Dekorative Kunst*, the Munich Jugendstil journal co-founded and edited by Julius Meier-Graefe from 1897 to 1900, and a regular contributor of increasingly lengthy essays for *Die Kunst*, the journal *Dekorative Kunst* merged into in 1900, where he championed the decorative as an aesthetic significant to modernism. Scheffler spoke from an important center of the decorative arts movement, which its supporters considered to be *the* modern movement. Scheffler's and his colleagues' writings were always juxtaposed with illustrations of or designs for functional decorative objects, including posters, embroidery, book covers, rugs, wallpaper samples, stained glass, curtains, and fixtures of all kinds. The abundance of these images, with text often running continuously between unrelated illustrations, effected a kind of ornamental *Gesamtkunstwerk* (total work of art), which embodied the authors' praise of the decorative. This format facilitated a radical analysis of abstraction conceived out of decoration, as for example in Scheffler's description of Henry Van de Velde's designs in 1898: "a rhythmic interlacing of line, a circumscription of form, a purely musi-

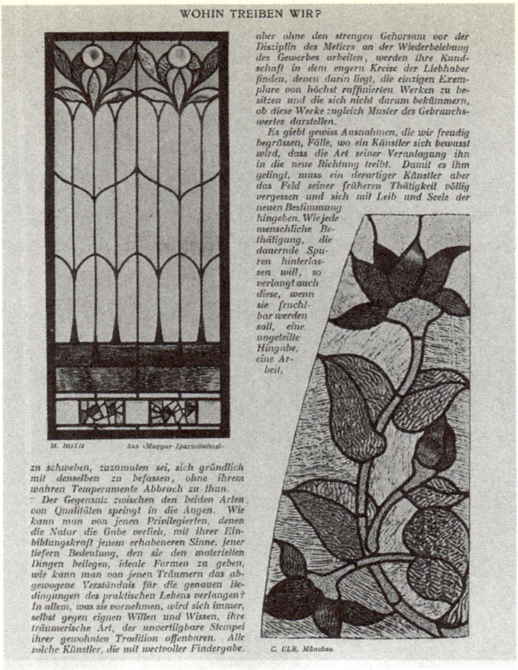

WOHIN TREIBEN WIR?

aber ohne den strengen Gehorsam vor der Disziplin des Metiers an der Wiederbelebung des Gewerbes arbeiten, werden ihre Kundschaft in dem engern Kreise der Liebhaber finden, denen darin liegt, die einzigen Exemplare von höchst raffinierten Werken zu besitzen und die sich nicht darum bekümmern, ob diese Werke zugleich Muster des Gebrauchswertes darstellen.

Es giebt gewiss Ausnahmen, die wir freudig begrüssen, Fälle, wo ein Künstler sich bewusst wird, dass die Art seiner Veranlagung ihn in die neue Richtung treibt. Damit es ihm gelingt, muss ein derartiger Künstler aber das Feld seiner früheren Thätigkeit völlig vergessen und sich mit Leib und Seele der neuen Bestimmung hingeben. Wie jede menschliche Bethätigung, die dauernde Spuren hinterlassen will, so verlangt auch diese, wenn sie fruchtbar werden soll, eine ungeteilte Hingabe, eine Arbeit,

M. ROTH Aus »Magyar Iparművészet«

zu schweben, zuzumuten sei, sich gründlich mit denselben zu befassen, ohne ihrem wahren Temperamente Abbruch zu thun.

Der Gegensatz zwischen den beiden Arten von Qualitäten springt in die Augen. Wie kann man von jenen Privilegierten, denen die Natur die Gabe verlieh, mit ihrer Einbildungskraft jenem erhabeneren Sinne, jener tiefern Bedeutung, den sie den materiellen Dingen beilegen, ideale Formen zu geben, wie kann man von jenen Träumern das abgewogene Verständnis für die genauen Bedingungen des praktischen Lebens verlangen? In allem, was sie vornehmen, wird sich immer, selbst gegen eignen Willen und Wissen, ihre träumerische Art, der unvertilgbare Stempel ihrer gewohnten Tradition offenbaren. Alle solche Künstler, die mit wertvoller Findergabe.

C. ULE, München

41 *M. Roth and C. Ule, Stained Glass, interspersed with text by S. Bing, "Wohen treiben wir?", from* Dekorative Kunst, *1898*

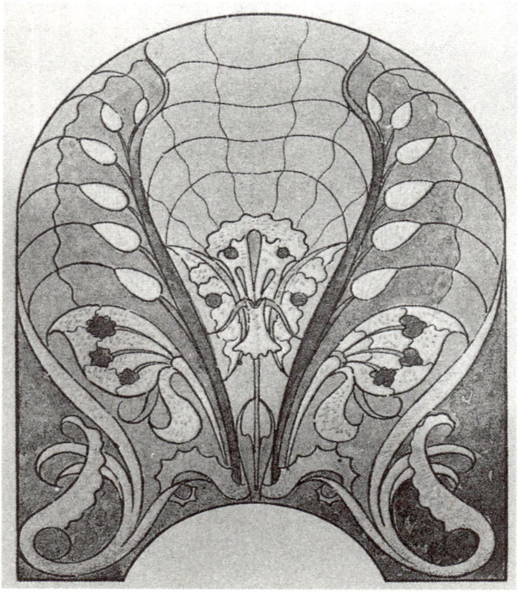

42 *R. Evaldre, Stained Glass, from* Dekorative Kunst, *1898*

cally experienced variation of figures, a flow of movement. It is the most strongly architectonically experienced ornament of the whole modern movement."[10]

For art historians schooled on the polarization not only of the decorative and the abstract, the feminine and the masculine, but also of consumer culture and high art, it comes as a surprise that the early Scheffler finds pure abstraction sometimes most compelling in commercial settings such as shop window displays. In his first review of the Berlin scene in 1898 he writes that in the autumn, decorative art is rarely exhibited, so one must instead check out department store windows. The only area of "general summer bloom," he reports, is that of Woman's toilette, and he raves in particular about a window display at the Petrus department store:

> At PETRUS's there are some arrangements of silk and lace . . . These . . . net laces and net embroideries are beautiful in their clear drawing and full of painterly variations in their intertwining of thread. It is a stirring pleasure to find these delicacies on the hems of these radiant clothes surfaces, or to trace an enticing, blooming web over its colorful background.

In addition, he claims that the lace, despite its coming from a 400-year-old industry, "feels more modern" than other art industry products that are brand new.[11] In 1898 it was unproblematic to invoke terms like modern, clear drawing, and painterly – terms one now associates with high art – to describe fabric and lace displayed for women in one of the novel department store windows. Since these particular referents were not illustrated, the reader/viewer continues the process of abstraction by imagining a rendering of the display synchronized with the imagery which does accompany the text. Scheffler feminizes the modern again when he reviews the newly completed façade of Alfred Messel's Wertheim department store, which also was not originally illustrated but is shown here. Scheffler deter- 43
mines that the "pleasing, modern sight" of the wide open structure was demanded by the need to display everything for the "covetous gaze of Woman." In other words, spare, modern architecture, as pleasing as it is, is an answer to demanding women, specifically to female window shoppers. The pleasure is not limited to women, however, as Scheffler reveals, exclaiming: "Was sind das für Auslagen! [What displays those are!]"[12]

As modernism became more firmly established ideologically, however, Scheffler's position shifted to that of his more widely remembered and conservative book, *Woman and Art* of 1908, in which he vehemently disassociates the abstract and the decorative, the masculine and the feminine. The discrepancies between this and the earlier Scheffler provide some insight into the eventual erasure of the decorative as a positive aesthetic in modernism. In a formulation analogous to Otto Weininger's popular theories from *Sex and Character* of 1903,[13] Scheffler asserts in *Woman and Art*

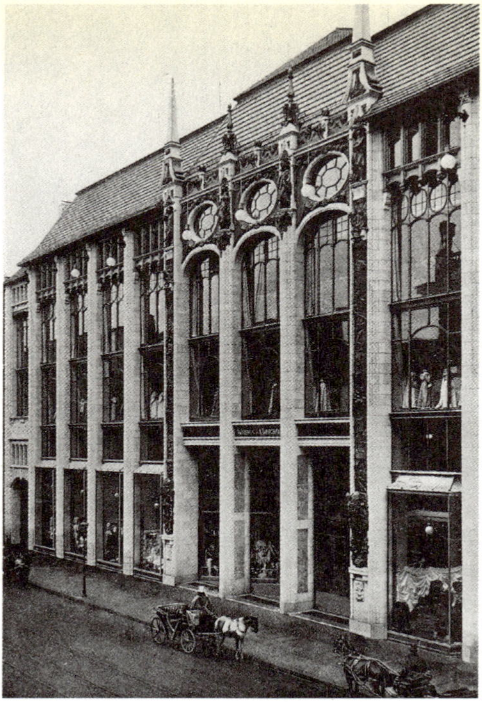

43 *Alfred Messel, Warenhaus Wertheim, Leipziger Strasse façade, 1896*

that "Woman" cannot understand "pure form," because she thinks too amorphously. Man, on the other hand, can condense and therefore can create and appreciate abstract form. Scheffler says that Woman's talents are decorative and ornamental; she excels, for example, at table-setting, make-up, and house decoration, although she apparently cannot complete her toilette without the help of men because, as Scheffler wryly notes, the famous clothing designers are men. Further, Scheffler advises fathers to keep daughters away from the arts and crafts schools, which were founded to provide German industry with skilled artisans, because the young women will face bitterness due to their lack of ability, the "lure" of prostitution, and the threat of becoming masculine – albeit without ever having enough masculinity in them to create proper form. He implores fathers to "Just look at these joyless, manly, embittered girls in the art workshop, listen to their talk, observe them . . .!"[14] Scheffler writes forcefully, as he also did in the Munich journals, but the urgency with which he pushes his new agenda is markedly different from the tone of his earlier columns, and the discrepancy calls for attention.

Scheffler's attack on Woman here is striking in contrast to his earlier writing for the journals, in which he praises things feminine (which were occasionally designed and made by women as well as generally produced for women). It is precisely the turn against commodity culture, displaced onto Woman, that leads to Scheffler's complete turn against decoration and ornament by 1908. Confident in 1901, he wrote that "the future belongs to industry" and that art should take advantage of mass production so as to create fine things for all, to create a true art of the people or *Volkskunst*.[15] In an article on Otto Eckmann's latest carpets, Scheffler encourages customers to pride themselves on selecting goods based on quality, whether artists' names are attached or not.[16] However, by 1902 Scheffler has already become more pessimistic about the possibility of industry's making quality arts and the public's having the ability to select them. He admits that previously he had radically underestimated the complex problem of the art schools' curriculum, where "aesthetics crosses profane utility, social and cultural philosophy cuts across economic politics, democratic altruism meets aristocratic egotism head on, and the zigzag movement of progress must overcome the curve of tradition." He insists that the artistic capacity of a people is part of the national welfare, but he laments that statesmen only consider art when they can measure its marketability. Unfortunately, he continues, despite some good teachers the majority of art school students learn only to imitate and choose to imitate only that which will sell well. Industry exploits the rare, talented students, and degrades even fine, enduring work into "seasonal ware." He contrasts the ideal of simplicity with the taste for excess that was instilled in the masses by manufacturers. Finally, he asserts that "the seed of the whole problem is that all of the big powers pursue *Industriepolitik*," and he cites with some disdain the English, who market fine art at home and in continental capitals and "sorry factory work" to their colonial customers.[17]

The evolving disillusionment articulated here elucidates *Woman and Art*. Scheffler's recommendation in the book that daughters not be sent to arts and crafts schools seems to have as much to do with his frustration with the poor work and exploited class of artisans produced by those schools as with doubts about women's artistic ability. In the book, "Woman" is unable to focus on essential form in the same way the masses are carried away by "excess." Scheffler, by the time of *Woman and Art*, has lost faith in any possibility of mass social redemption through the general availability of fine aesthetic and utilitarian products, but he blames "Woman" for that failure. Convinced of consumerism's inevitability, he attempts to shore up high art against it, an art he now conceives of as pure abstract form stripped of its history in ornament. Scheffler collapses mass culture, Woman, the decorative, and ornament as the collective enemy of high art, a new category in his writing created by a disarticulation of elements that had been mutually constituting. But his "purist" assault was far from independent of consumer culture. This displacement of anxiety and blame onto Woman was rather an easily consumable and popular product for a population struggling with the heavily contested entry of women into arts schools in ever increasing numbers, and experiencing two critical changes in 1908, the year the book was published: women's first legal membership in German political parties, and significant gender-equalizing education reforms, also achieved after many years of struggle.[18] For decades the book was a standard reference for the opposition to women in art and to so-called feminine practices in art. To ensure the perpetuation of this popular position, Scheffler abandoned his writing on decorative arts for the Munich journal and in 1906 took over the helm as editor of the Berlin journal, *Kunst und Künstler*, a high art monthly committed to contemporary German painting and prints, especially to the increasingly conservative German Impressionism.

Scheffler was by no means alone in his new embrace of an abstract ideal purified of ornament. Meier-Graefe, his editor during the early years of *Dekorative Kunst*, canonized the aesthetic of universal, essential form in his three-volume study, *Modern Art* (1904). Notably, Meier-Graefe's shift also appears to be linked to commercial disillusionment, in this case his own financial failure. As Nancy Troy details in her account of the decorative arts movement in France, Meier-Graefe had left his editorial position with *Dekorative Kunst* in September 1899 to open his own decorative arts boutique, La Maison Moderne, in Paris (a poster for which is illustrated here). Despite his efforts to make fine goods generally available, he was forced to liquidate the merchandise at half price and then sell the floundering store in April 1904, during which time *Modern Art* was in production.[19] In this foundational art history text, Meier-Graefe's aesthetic concerns about the "vulgarization" of the "pure work of art" are woven together with disgust in the commerce of art, which he calls "a frantic, absurd, and unhappily, thoroughly dishonest traffic . . ." He is nostalgic for some universal aesthetic value in art that he believes the market has replaced with exchange-value: "In the form to which it is confined today – that of picture or statue, a marketable commodity – it could only exercise an influence by fulfilling the purpose of other marketable things: that of being purchased."[20] As with Scheffler, the assertion of a pure form independent of the market can only be made in explicit opposition to commercialism.

Theorists from Theodor Adorno and Clement Greenberg to Peter Bürger and Andreas Huyssen have long posited that modernism was defined against "mass culture" or the "culture industry," other names for the increasing commodification of western culture in the early twentieth century. Modernism thus defined itself against an Other, an Other which has often been equated discursively with femininity, as Huyssen, in particular, shows.[21] But Scheffler's writing demonstrates that this Other first emerges when it is exiled from the terrain it helps to create. Examples of this expulsion abound, implying that personal misfortune and changes of

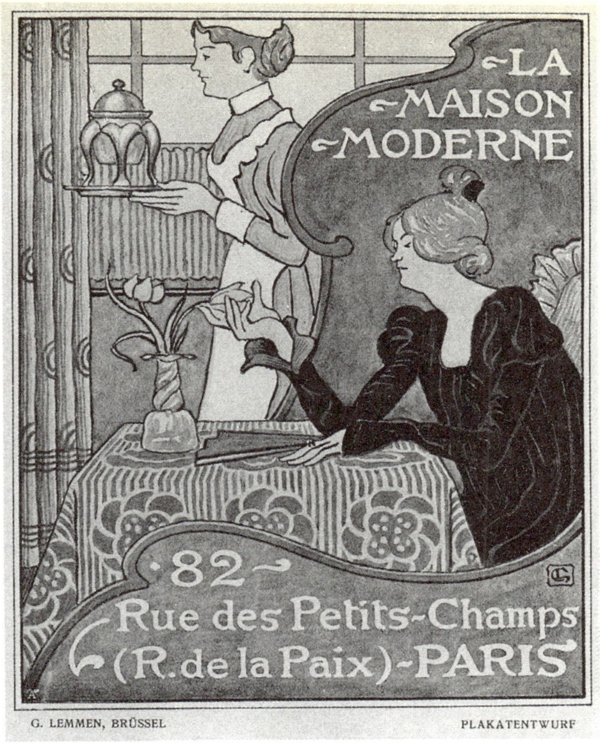

44 *Georges Lemmen, poster design for La Maison Moderne, from* Die Kunst, *1900*

heart are not all that condition it. Leaving Scheffler's particular case I will address this repetition more specifically.

II

> . . . if light-filled shop windows with the most outstanding products from all the industries of civilized peoples not only encourage one to purchase but also speak purely to our aesthetic sense . . . then that is solely to the credit of the modern department store organism.
>
> Leo Colze, *Berlin Department Stores*, 1908[22]

Modernism's intensive focus on an ideal essential form is, to begin with, neither natural nor inevitable but rather historical. As Michel Foucault argues in *The Order of Things*, the modern episteme generally speaking is focused on essential, internal structure. Foucault theorizes that the end of the eighteenth century brought about the same type of change in grammar, in natural history, and in the analysis of wealth – namely that an essential, inner truth became the focus for the analysis of each, an inner truth which is necessarily constructed. Foucault describes at the same time a crisis of representation, because the interior depth of things is an "always inaccessible point . . . beyond our gaze . . ." Citing Kant as one of the thinkers at "the threshold of our modernity," Foucault writes that "Kant avoids representation itself and what is given within it, in order to address himself to that on the basis of which all representation, whatever its form, may be posited."[23] Kant's idealist aesthetics, which sought to establish the conditions that define a universally valid form – while avoiding a description of what this looks like – inaugurates the legacy of modernist aesthetics. I cite in passing Charles Baudelaire, who has so often been read as valorizing the "eternal and immutable" within the ephemeral, Clive Bell and Roger Fry's principle of "significant form," and Clement Greenberg's adulation of pure paint in painting.[24] All of these point to an ideal, an essential in the tradition of Kant.

Modernist artists were equally invested in representing essences and had to contend with the disruption between surface and interior concomitant with the crisis of representation Foucault describes. He writes that "it is from the depths of the force that brought them into being and that remains in them . . . that things – in fragments, outlines, pieces, shards – offer themselves, though very partially, to representation."[25] One could say generally that Cubism, experimental photography, and modernist novels took up "fragments, outlines, pieces, shards" as a means to represent the inner truth of things. Full disclosure is promised and always deferred; oscillation between the surface and the projected essence is all one can achieve. The department store façade is a site where this crisis of representation is oddly illuminated.

Scheffler originally conceived of abstract decorative form – while it was still acceptable to do so overtly – from shop window displays. His characterization of the "covetous gaze of Woman," in fact, may not have been his own invention but could rather have been lifted from Émile Zola's popular novel, *The Ladies' Paradise* (1883), which was translated into German and proliferated into dozens of editions by 1900.[26] Both Scheffler and Zola thematize the deferral of disclosure inherent in the crisis of representation and curiously located in commercial display. Neither describes the shop window in any direct, mirroring sort of way, but each prescribes means of representation that were taken up in the aesthetic realm, and, indeed, in the marketing realm. As late as 1976 one Alton F. Doody writes, "The principles and techniques described in *The Ladies' Paradise* are as pertinent to retailing today as they were one hundred years ago . . . *The Ladies' Paradise*, therefore, is a pragmatic guide which can be used in our time to increse the merchandising effectiveness of almost any retail store."[27]

Zola's text clearly demonstrates the ambivalence produced by the representation crisis. After his protagonist Denise Baudu arrives in Paris and is introduced to her uncle's dingy, old-fashioned shop across the street from the glamorous new department store, she has a moment to herself:

> . . . what most interested Denise was The Ladies' Paradise opposite, the windows of which she could see through the open door . . . [T]he great shop seemed alive and in full activity.
>
> Denise began to feel as if she were watching a machine working at full pressure, communicating its movement even as far as the windows. They were no longer the cold windows she had seen in the early morning; they seemed to be warm and vibrating from the activity within. There was a crowd before them, groups of women pushing and squeezing, devouring the finery with longing, covetous eyes. And the stuffs became animated in this passionate atmosphere: the laces fluttered, drooped, and concealed the depths of the shop with a troubling air of mystery . . . But the furnace-like glow which the house exhaled came above all from the sale, the crush at the counters, that could be felt behind the walls.[28]

Initially it appears that all this, the goods and the interior mechanism of the store at work, could be "seen" from across the street through the windows. Nevertheless the mixture of metaphors turns the representation upon itself: on the one hand, the "great shop seemed alive" and "the stuffs became animated in this passionate atmosphere"; but, on the other hand, the store is "a machine working at full pressure," exuding a "furnace-like glow." This "glow" appears to be "exhaled," but the mechanical metaphor reveals that the store is not really alive but is rather generated, both by the commodity exchange mechanism operative within ("the furnace-like glow . . . came above all from the sale") and by the "longing, covetous eyes" of the customers outside the store. In the resulting "passionate atmosphere," "the laces fluttered [and] drooped, [but they nevertheless] concealed the depths of the shop with a troubling air of mystery," troubling in its ever promised and never deliverable essence.

Another passage in *Ladies' Paradise* underlines the problematic which already underpins the previous quotation:

> . . . the last window especially attracted [Denise's and her brothers'] attention. It was an exhibition of silks, satins, and velvets, arranged so as to produce, by a skillful artistic arrangement of colours, the most delicious shades imaginable. At the top were the velvets, from a deep black to a milky-white: lower down, the satins – pink, blue, fading away into shades of a wondrous delicacy; still lower down were the silks, of all the colours of the rainbow, pieces set up in the form of shells, others folded as if round a pretty figure, arranged in a life-like natural manner by the clever fingers of the window dressers. Between each motive, between each coloured phrase of the display ran a discreet accompaniment, a slight puffy ring of cream-coloured silk.[29]

The "skillful artistic arrangement of colours" and the "pretty figure, arranged in a life-like natural manner by the clever fingers of the window dressers" point to the constructedness of the supposedly animate form. Notably, this constructedness results in an extremely abstract rendition of shades of color in a visual plane; the musical allusions of "motive," "phrase," and "accompaniment" demonstrate further that this is a description of "pure" abstract form.

The modernist aesthetic of pure abstract form is not supposed to be related to, much less predicated upon purchasability; nevertheless the reliance persists. In his study of Berlin department stores from 1908, for example, Leo Colze confirms the contemporary aesthetic significance of display windows. In the epigraph above Colze credits the modern department store "organism" with creating a site – the "light-filled shop windows" – for display of the most outstanding products from all over the world. At one and the same time, he continues, this site both "encourage[s] one to purchase" and "speak[s] purely to our aesthetic sense." Explaining how display windows become the "main motif" of the department store genre, architectural historian Julius Posener writes: ". . . the main principle of the exterior architecture [is] to place the wares before the eyes of the public in the most advantageous manner, to show them what is to be found inside already there from the street."[30] It is this promise of the interior, of the essence, from the outside that seems to entice both aesthetic observer and potential shopper.

How could shop windows exercise such aesthetic power? The ambiguity of the shop window as revealed in the passages from Zola in fact finds parallels in Kant's strained negotiation of an aesthetics insistent upon representing inaccessible inner form. In the *Critique of Judgment* (1790), Kant establishes that essential form is that which "constitute[s] the proper object of the pure judgment of taste." He writes:

> Even what is called ornamentation (*Parerga*), i.e., what is only an adjunct and not an intrinsic constituent in the complete representation of the object, in augmenting the delight of taste does so only by means of its form. Thus it is with the frames of pictures or the drapery on statues, or the colonnades of palaces.[31]

Jacques Derrida devotes extensive attention to this passage in *The Truth in Painting*, because it is impossible to discern where the proper object of taste ends and these *parerga*, or things extrinsic to the work (*ergon*) begin.[32] Crucial to the problem at hand is that Kant's examples of appealing form, which should be intrinsic, are to be found in the outside, adjunct *parerga*. The distinction between inside and outside therefore disintegrates even as that distinction remains constitutive. The incessant oscillation from surface to interior in the department store display mirrors the instability of this construction.

The trope that brings the shop display and the modernist aesthetic into explicit juxtaposition is function, which is articulated in terms of interest. The selling of commodities is a most interested rather than disinterested project, but it is the appearance of disinterest that appeals both to the buyer and to the modernist aesthetic sense. The surface effects of displays appeal sensually while promising and never delivering use-value. Kant's essential is defined from the outset as wholly independent of interest: "The pleasure, which the judgment of taste determines, is without any interest."[33] "Interest" in Kant is always bound with the existence of the object, that is to say one's capacity to covet or possess it, which in turn is always related to the projected purposefulness of the object. Following this formulation, pure aesthetic contemplation cannot coincide with the possessability of useful goods: "The assessment of the beautiful has only a formal purposefulness, i.e., a purposefulness without end [*Zweckmässigkeit ohne Zweck*]." "Objective purposefulness," on the other hand, is usefulness, positioned by Kant outside of the object.[34] In this sense the ornamental exterior is functional, in the mode of the decorative arts, and therefore cannot be apprehended purely aesthetically. However, here, too, Kant's ambivalence asserts itself: he distinguishes between "free beauty (*pulchritudo vaga*) and merely dependent beauty (*pulchritudo adhaerens*)," the latter apparently including embellishment or adornment insufficient in itself.[35] Remarkably, though, Kant's examples of free beauty, which exhibits "finality without end," are themselves *parerga*. That is to say, his examples for the ideal object – which appears to have a purpose but stops short of ever fulfilling it – are in those decorative supplements that should, according to his logic, be outside the object: "So designs *à la grecque*, foliage for framework or on wallpapers, etc., mean nothing in themselves; they represent nothing, no Object under a definite concept, and are free beauties."[36] The construction of decoration as useless in this latter instance facilitates conceptualizing useless, disinterested inner form. The seamless shifts in the decorative's position – inside/outside, useless/useful – enable Kant's foundational aesthetic.

The ambivalence of the shop window display, legible in all these registers, becomes, finally, a material condition of the conceptualization of abstract high art. While most early twentieth-century abstract painting aims to repress it, the shopping series by Blaue Reiter painter August Macke makes visible this condition of Kandinsky's ideal of "pure color and independent form." In *Fashion Shop* (1913), Macke reduces the figures – not 45
surprisingly, stylish, female window shoppers – to simple, flat shapes of saturated color. These shapes are echoed by those of the displays, which suggest feathered hats and outfits with long, narrow skirts, fitted bodices, and wide, sweeping lapel collars, similar to and therefore referring back to the shoppers' attire. Indeed the central figure becomes difficult to distinguish from the ground of the painting: for example, the yellow form

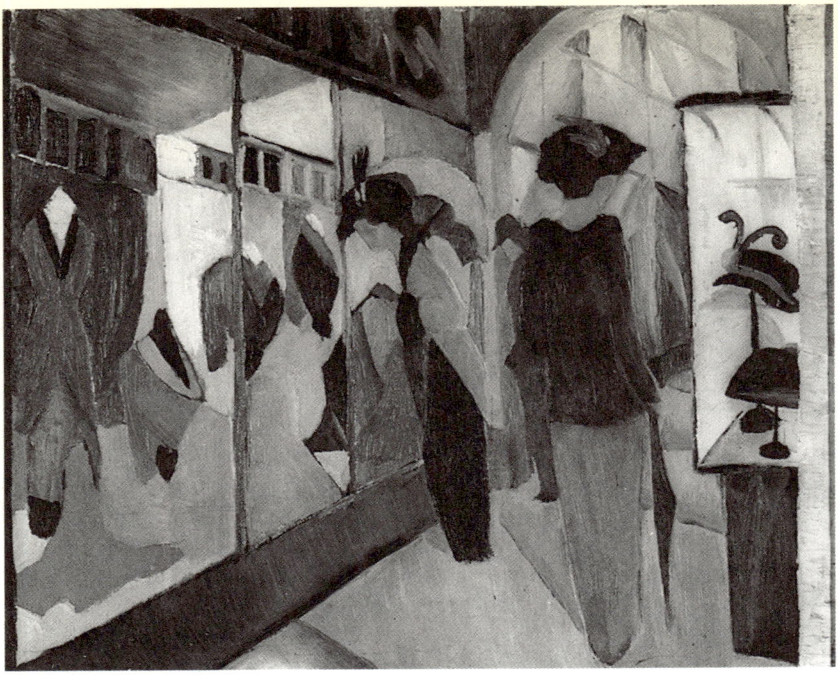

45 *August Macke,* Modegeschäft (Fashion Shop), *1913*

below her face shoots forward, uncontained by the display behind her as it logically should be, and the red, brown, black sequence (forming a triangle whose apex is her left cuff) reads as a series of flat shapes that works against the perspective the orthogonals would establish. A more "purely" abstract example might be Paul Klee's *Mirroring Window* (1915). Here one can see a precursor of Klee's famous "magic square" paintings, constructed of modules of free-floating color. Drawing on the modernist metaphor of depth, Will Grohmann canonized these works as the "innermost circle" of Klee's art.[37] At the same time one is encouraged by Klee's title to read orthogonals, which meet in the upper left corner to constitute a display case, and abstracted fabrics or goods reflected around the space and against the window which is the plane of the picture itself.

The confluence of modernist aesthetics and commodity aesthetics in these readings is troubling, I suggest, only because modernism maintained the supposed "purity" and "disinterest" of the aesthetic ideal so successfully – though all the while it was grounded in the "impure," the functional, the decorative. This becomes, perhaps, less of a leap if one considers Jean-Joseph Goux's modern epistemic model, that of the general equivalent. He proposes that ". . . certain categories of semiotics, linguistics, and structural psychoanalysis overlapped those already in place in the economic domain," most specifically the "phenomenon of exchange." An "excluded, idealized

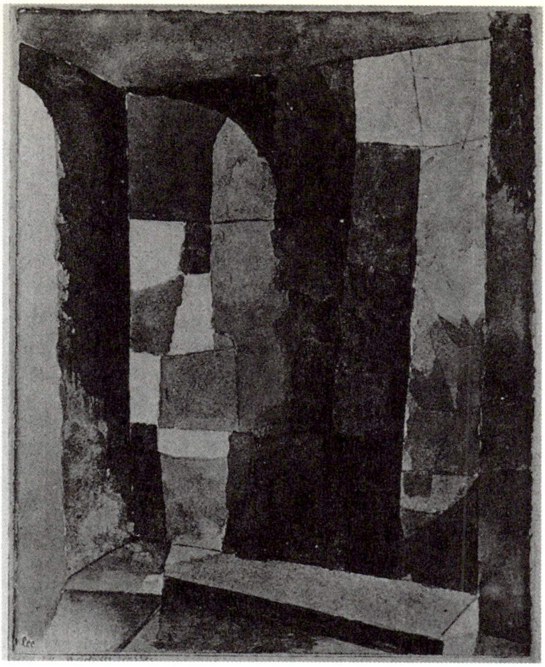

46 *Paul Klee,* Spiegelndes Fenster (Mirroring Window), *1915*

element" is set apart (e.g., the Father becomes the general equivalent of subjects, language that of signs, the Phallus that of objects, all on the model of gold in the economic domain). This setting apart enables comparison, allows for "equivalence posited despite difference, the maintenance of an ideality throughout changes in materiality, etc."[38] Exchange-value, apparently detached from use-value in the aesthetics of commercial display, is abstract and ideal. It is useless and ornamental to the object, and it is simultaneously the idealized element. One recalls that Meier-Graefe lamented that modern art was reduced to its exchange-value, but then his voluminous study praised pure form in art as miraculously free of exchange-value. Following Goux, it appears that ideal form and exchange-value may refer to the same idealized element – that which is set apart as the idealized "general equivalent" – even though "pure" art is traditionally defined against commercial exchange.

Abstract painting may be a site where Foucault's and Goux's models coincide. In Foucault's spatial model one wants to approach the interior though it is visually inaccessible. Therefore one substitutes visible, surface abstractions for the idealized essence within. Ornamental, non-functional exchange-value facilitates the substitution, as Goux's theory suggests. Suddenly ornament becomes the essence and its genesis is correspondingly erased. Some turn-of-the-century theorists, like Scheffler and Meier-

Graefe, hailed the decorative arts as *the* modern movement, at least initially. Since the movement was bound up in capital, both theorists deserted it and tried to construct abstract art against it. Willfully forgetting the arts' common history, these writers contributed to the persistent myth of pure disinterest which demands that abstraction and ornament be read as separate. Regardless of this myth, however, the decorative is always supplemental in the Derridean sense – that is, it may appear extraneous, but it is in fact essential to the object's completion. For this reason the theorists of modernist "purity" could never complete their obsessive expulsion of the decorative. That Kant conceived of the disinterested ideal by way of ornament and decoration and that department stores marketed decorative arts and fabrics in abstract displays are tied together in the history of what art made of them both.

10

"A Room of One's Own": The Bloomsbury Group's Creation of a Modernist Domesticity

CHRISTOPHER REED

> Good God! to have a room of one's own with a real fire and books and tea and company, and no dinner bells and distractions, and a little time for doing something! It's a wonderful vision, and surely worth some risks.[1]

This passage might be taken as the manifesto of the loosely knit circle of artists and authors who banded together in Edwardian London and came to be known as the Bloomsbury group. The lines could be seamlessly inserted in *A Room of One's Own*, Virginia Woolf's now-famous 1929 feminist tract, which described women's oppression under patriarchy in terms of denied space. But these words are not Woolf's, and the reference is not to rooms for women. The text appears in a 1909 letter from Lytton Strachey to Duncan Grant, which expresses the longing of these two gay men to escape conventions of bourgeois domesticity they found as stifling as did their female counterparts. For Bloomsbury's members, men and women alike, "a room of one's own" came to symbolize the struggle to create the new and more enabling forms of domesticity they associated with modern life.

Alienation from the conventional home and the determination to imagine new forms of domesticity are recurrent themes in Bloomsbury's letters, memoirs, and fiction. "I feel desperately homesick, – but for what home?" was how Lytton Strachey phrased the problem. E. M. Forster traced his anti-military and anti-patriarchal beliefs to his childhood eviction from the family home. "It has so happened that I have been deprived of a home," Forster wrote; "If I had been allowed to stop on there I should have become a different person, married and fought in the war."[2] Forster's *Howards End* takes its title from the remarkable house that confers on the characters in the novel the will to resist the violence and oppression associated with patriarchal domesticity. In Virginia Woolf's *Flush*, as well as in her autobiographical essays, daughters escape from their fathers' houses to find personal and professional fulfillment in radically different kinds of homes. This shared emphasis on domesticity may be what bound the women and men of Bloomsbury into a community that, for better or for worse, remained far more cohesive than most avant-garde groupings.[3] Although yearnings for a new kind of home affected all of Bloomsbury's members, however, it was the artists of the group who embodied these desires through the construction and decoration of a series of domestic spaces conceived as the settings for a new way of life.

As early as 1904, Vanessa Bell, the painter who was Woolf's older sister, reacted to their father's death by packing up her siblings and abandoning the home she had overseen since her teenage years when the premature deaths of her mother and older half-sister left her, in her father's words, "mistress of the house." Describing Vanessa's break with this past many years later, Woolf's language turns violent. "She had sold; she had burnt; she had sorted; she had torn up. Sometimes I believe she had actually to get men with hammers to batter down – so wedged into each other had the walls and the cabinets become." Leaving the old house in upper-crust Kensington empty, they moved to a far less fashionable neighborhood, chosen, Woolf recalled, when "Vanessa – looking at a map of London and seeing how far apart they were – had decided that we should leave Kensington and start life afresh in Bloomsbury." Bell herself asserted, "All that seemed to matter was that at last we were free, had rooms of our own and space in which to be alone or to work or to see our friends."[4]

As important as the physical accommodation of rooms of one's own was the new look that the house at 46 Gordon Square gave to the domestic life it contained. "It seemed as if in every way we were making a new beginning in the tall clean rather frigid rooms," Bell later recorded. No known visual documents remain from this period, but letters and memoirs emphasize the new house's contrast with the dark woodwork and heavy red velvet interiors of the Kensington home. A letter from Bell to Woolf offers the most intriguing evidence of a conscious determination to make the look of 46 Gordon Square reflect the aspirations of its new inhabitants:

> I have been hanging pictures in the hall. I hope you'll approve . . . On the right hand side as you come in I have put a row of celebrities: 1. Herschel – Aunt Julia's photograph. 2. Lowell. 3. Darwin. 4. father. 5. Tennyson. 6. Browning. 7. Meredith – Watts' portrait. Then on the opposite side I have put five of the best Aunt Julia photographs of Mother. They look very beautiful all together.[5]

Visitors to 46 Gordon Square, then, entered between the literally patriarchal legacy of this "procession of educated men" (to take a phrase from Woolf's *Three Guineas*) and an alternative matriarchal heritage of artistry and beauty represented by the pioneering photographer Julia Margaret Cameron's misty pictures of her beautiful niece, Vanessa and Virginia's mother.

This visualization of the sisters' liminal position between traditions would become the hallmark of Bloomsbury's domestic spaces. Attempting to imagine ways of living appropriate to its determinedly unladylike women and unmanly men, Bloomsbury relied on imaginative recombinations of available conventions. The domestic focus of Bloomsbury's art along with its fondness for pastiche – both of which have been judged by critics as signs of artistic failure – might better be seen as strategies that acknowledge the reality that subordinate groups cannot recreate their situation outside or free from the constraints of the dominant culture. Rather, Bloomsbury represents an instance of subcultural negotiation of existing conventions in order to create an alternative space within the culture it inherited.

The importance of this ideal of alternative space is evident in the many accounts of the Gordon Square house left by the men and women who came to refer to themselves – and it is significant that their sobriquet took the name of the new neighborhood – as Bloomsbury. Numerous memoirs attest to the importance of the house as a refuge from the tea-table society of Kensington, with its emphasis on marriage and its insistence on domestic propriety. From Virginia Woolf's 1906 short story, "Phyllis and Rosamond," which contrasts the lives of two sets of sisters, one living in the parents' "great ugly house" in Kensington and the other in "the great tranquil squares" of Bloomsbury, to her 1935 play, *Freshwater*, which ends with the young Victorian actress Ellen Terry, dressed as a man and clutching Julia Margaret Cameron's camera, escaping "to Bloomsbury – number forty six Gordon Square," the house symbolized the determination of ambitious women to forge a new way of life. So important did the house become to Bloomsbury's group identity that in 1916, when wartime financial strictures forced the Bells to give it up, Vanessa's husband, Clive, borrowed the vocabulary of French tourist guides to suggest to his wife, "Perhaps our friends would like to save 46 Gordon Square as a 'monument historique'."[6] In fact, Bloomsbury economist John Maynard Keynes took over the lease, and the house remained a center of the group's London activities.

By 1916, Bloomsbury's social identity as a group had solidified around its pacifist resistance to England's involvement in World War I and its rejection of patriarchal prescriptions of heterosexual monogamy. Concurrently, Bloomsbury's aesthetic identity had coalesced around the ideals and imagery of French modernism. These two identities, the social and the aesthetic, were not unrelated. In the catalog to the second of the influential exhibitions Bloomsbury organized to promote modern art in London, Roger Fry described the artists he christened the "Post-Impressionists" as "modern men trying to find a pictorial language appropriate to the sensibilities of the modern outlook." After Fry's death, Woolf in her biography challenged those who interpreted his aesthetics as a realm distinct from life:

> [W]ere they distinct? It seems as if the aesthetic theory were brought to bear upon the problems of private life. Detachment, as he insisted over and over

> again, is the supreme necessity for the artist. Was it not equally necessary if the private life were to continue? That rhythm could only grow and expand if it were detached from the deformation which is possession . . . It was difficult to put that teaching into practice. Yet in his private life he had forced himself to learn that lesson.[7]

This belief that the look of modern art reflected new ways of thinking and being allowed Bloomsbury to make modernism the expression of its ambition to visualize new ways of life. Beginning in 1910, when Fry first exposed London to recent Parisian art, Bloomsbury's artists turned their attention to the creation of the modernist home.

Bloomsbury's widely travelled artists and critics were well positioned to exploit their knowledge of the French avant-garde in the service of the new domesticity. They looked, in particular, to Matisse, as is evident in Duncan Grant's first domestic decoration: a 1910 mural for Keynes's apartment at King's College, Cambridge. Although subsequently covered over, the mural is revealed in photographs to have depicted a fanciful harvest scene where workers gathering grapes frame a Matissian ring of whirling, naked figures. Where Matisse's paintings (as analyzed by Joyce Robinson in this volume) were conceived to sustain the conventional businessman, however, Grant's mural embodies a more specific aspiration to create a refuge from hegemonic heterosexuality for the economist who was also his lover. This aim connects the three stylistically rather disparate elements of the mural: the spinning dancers derived from Matisse, the semi-nude women whose static solidity and distinctive headgear evoke the murals of Piero della Francesca, and the nude men whose active muscularity alludes to Michelangelo. While the relationship of these three sources may escape modern viewers, their combination exemplifies Bloomsbury's way of setting up housekeeping in the gaps between existing traditions. In this case Parisian modernism is juxtaposed with Victorian Aestheticism to create an affirmation of homoeroticism that is both historically grounded and up to date.

From the Victorians – including such Cambridge scholars as John Addington Symonds, Oscar Browning, and Goldsworthy Lowes Dickinson – came an image of the Mediterranean as the last locus of the ancient traditions of "Greek love," in which homoerotic attraction became the basis for uplifting bonds between men. Symonds' *A Problem in Greek Ethics* (which appeared anonymously in Havelock Ellis's 1897 *Sexual Inversion*) and Dickinson's 1896 *The Greek View of Life* were, according to Noel Annan, "part of the working library of liberation" for educated gay men in Britain through the 1930s, while Symonds' 1883 *Life of Michelangelo* broke new ground in challenging the heterosexualization of the artist's love poetry. Like "the philosophers of Athens," Symonds insisted,

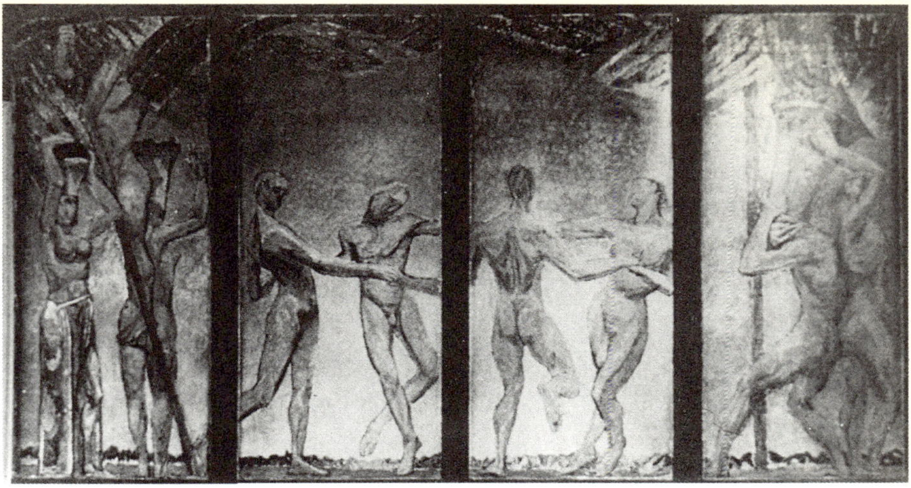

47 *Duncan Grant, mural for John Maynard Keynes, King's College, Cambridge University, 1910*

Michelangelo "showed no partiality for women, and a notable enthusiasm for the beauty of young men." Grant's absorption of these ideas is evidenced by a letter he wrote from Italy to Strachey in 1907, in which he describes his perceptions of the Italians' casual appreciation of male beauty, then concludes, "I suppose they've been educated by Michel Angelo."[8]

For Bloomsbury's men, the legacy of the Aesthetes was not just textual but personal. Keynes was friends with Dickinson, and he studied under the gregarious and charismatic historian of Italy, Oscar Browning, who popularized notions of Greek love at King's College – indeed Keynes tried to get Browning's old rooms, and Grant's first plans for the mural were devised for that space.[9] Inspired by such ideals, Grant and Keynes travelled together to Greece and Turkey in 1910, and to Sicily and Tunis in 1911, where Keynes photographed Grant nude, posed in such classical settings as the temple at Bessae in imitation of the pictures of youths, naked or loosely draped, that photographers like Wilhelm von Gloeden circulated as postcards and in art magazines.[10] While such pictures were furtively collected by older Aesthetes, Grant's sprawling vision of arcadian sensuality – like Bell's entryway – proclaimed Keynes's home the site of a new kind of domestic life.

Frank acceptance of homosexuality was one of the beliefs that united Bloomsbury's members and distinguished their sensibility – in contrast to the tortured Aesthetes – as "modern". For Grant, assiduously copying Pieros and Michelangelos, however, the links between modern life and modernist styles of painting remained elusive until the fall of 1910. What brought them together was the first Post-Impressionist exhibition. Always laconic, Grant simply recorded, "We were wildly enthusiastic about the exhibition." Vanessa Bell was more specific:

> It is impossible I think that any other single exhibition can ever have had so much effect as did that on the rising generation . . . here was a . . . sudden liberation and encouragement to feel for oneself which were absolutely overwhelming . . . [I]t was as if one might say things one had always felt instead of trying to say things that other people told one to feel.

The rhetoric of escape is clear here, but again it is not Matisse's temporary relief from the workaday world. Bell here proclaims a permanent rejection of conventional norms, articulating for herself the catalog's insistence that Post-Impressionism was defined by "the resolve of each artist to express his own temperament, and never to permit contemporary ideals to dictate to him what was beautiful, significant, and worthy to be painted."[11]

Although logistical problems meant that Matisse's paintings were (in Fry's words) "quite inadequately represented" in the exhibition, he starred in the catalog as the ultimate realization of the Post-Impressionists' willingness to forsake public approval in favor of complete self-expression through abstract form. Somewhat paradoxically, Matisse's status as the most advanced modernist made him, in Fry's terms, the most "primitive" as well, an appellation that signified affinity not so much with African art as with Italian painting from before the Renaissance. Fry's advocacy of modernist painting, in fact, drew much of its authority from his status as an expert on the painters known as the "Italian primitives," and his defenses of the avant-garde Parisians asserted their "attempt to go behind the too elaborate pictorial apparatus which the Renaissance established in painting" to rediscover "the principles of primitive design." Fry warned, "When you can draw like Tintoretto, you can no longer draw like . . . Piero della Francesca." Cézanne, on the other hand, Fry compared to "primitive Italian artists, such as Piero dell Francesca."[12]

Fry's fusion of French modernism with Italian primitivism – especially as both were yoked to a call for art "to regain its power to express emotional ideas" and "to give to the rendering of nature its response in human passion and human need"[13] – offered Grant a style of art to match his aspirations for a new life in defiance of the strictures on passion in force in barely post-Victorian England. Significantly, it was only after Fry framed Matisse and modernism as a reassertion of primitive power that Grant evinced much interest in either, though he had seen examples of Matisse's work while studying in Paris early in 1909. Now, however, echoes of early Matisse – *Le Bonheur de vivre* (now at the Barnes Collection), which Grant could have seen when he visited the Steins' apartment, or the sculpted *Le Dos* and preliminary versions of the monumental *Dance* mural (now at the

Hermitage Museum), which he could have seen when he was taken to Matisse's studio – reverberated in the poses and handling of Grant's spinning dancers.

In assigning these canonic images as sources for Grant's work, however, art historians have overlooked an entry in the 1910 Post-Impressionist show that connects directly to Grant's domestic focus. Ignored amid the riot of avant-garde painting and sculpture was a selection of painted ceramic vases commissioned from modernist artists, including Matisse, by gallery owner André Druet in 1907. Matisse's vase may have been like – or even identical with – one from this series owned by the Steins, which features a ring of spinning dancers rendered in the same lively black outline that characterizes the center panel of Grant's mural (Grant's Matisse-inspired technique is especially apparent in the still-extant preliminary oil sketches). On his trip the following summer, Grant is known to have decorated Tunisian earthenware vases with black line-drawings of nude figures. It is tempting to speculate that the sight of Matisse's eminently domestic ceramics may have sparked in Grant both memories of the works he had seen in Paris and the determination to bring this aesthetic into the domestic realm.[14]

Whatever its precise sources, Grant's invocation of Matisse brought up to date older ideas of Italy as arcadia, free from the restrictions of bourgeois norms. Like Vanessa Bell's display of pictures in the front hall at Gordon Square, Grant's mural turns its domestic setting into a site for creative anachronism, as the collision of authoritative conventions – Parisian modernism and arcadian Aestheticism – opens up a space for new ways of life. This combination of the modern and the arcadian proved a compelling answer to Bloomsbury's demand for a new domestic aesthetic, and the Keynes mural can be seen as inaugurating a half-century of Bloomsbury's domestic decorations featuring abundant gardens and sensual nudes, redolent of Classical and Renaissance prototype, but rendered with the loose brushwork and bright colors of an exuberant modernism.

The space of this essay precludes more than a cursory analysis of these later projects. In 1912, Grant – assisted by Vanessa and Virginia's brother, Adrian, who was another lover – created a massive installation of wall-painting and decorated shutters in a house they shared with other
"Bloomsberries" (to use their own term) in Brunswick Square, London. 48
Overtly indebted to Matisse's *Dance I* (now at the Museum of Modern Art), which Fry had brought to London for the second Post-Impressionist exhibition, the flat figures engaged in the pre-eminently modern activity of tennis are startling in their anticipation of Matisse's much later cut-outs. Two years later, Grant, Bell, and Fry collaborated on a mural of colorful nudes – a dark red man, a yellow man, and a woman with blue hair – for the entrance hall of Fry's house outside London. Also dating from this period is

an unfinished mosaic in Fry's garden that, in an echo of Grant's 1912 mural, depicts a game of badminton.[15] These individual projects in Bloomsbury's own dwellings embody the group's determination to create for itself new forms of modernist domesticity. The history of Bloomsbury's efforts to take this vision public, however, reveals both the strength of the regulations enforcing patriarchal norms and the prejudice against the domestic as an arena for artistic accomplishment in the modern era.

The Omega Workshops, founded by Fry, Bell, and Grant in 1913, may be seen as another effort at the productive fusion of disparate traditions, in this case Parisian modernism and the guilds of the Arts and Crafts Movement, where, supervised by entrepreneurs like William Morris, art and decoration were combined in ambitious projects of aesthetic and social reform centered on the look of daily life. Fry had participated directly in such guilds, and it was his conviction that an organization for the production of modernist furnishings could provide financial support for ambitious but impecunious artists such as Duncan Grant. When the Omega set up studios and a shop in a Bloomsbury house that was reputed to have been a center for William Morris's Pre-Raphaelite guild, enrolled artists were paid a small but living weekly wage – about that of a clerk – for anonymous work on furniture, fabrics, and toys. To insure that the workshops enabled rather than supplanted the artists' careers, participants were limited to working three half-days per week. Fry often invoked Morris's example in his publicity for the Omega, asserting in his fund-raising materials, "The Post-Impressionist movement is quite as definitely decorative in its methods as was the Pre-Raphaelite, and its influence on general design is destined to be as marked." Fry's description of one of Grant's cushions embroidered with a cubist cat might be said to encapsulate the whole enterprise: "It was a mid-Victorian idea, but it was not treated in a mid-Victorian manner."[16]

The extent of the Omega's challenge to mid-Victorian manners can be gauged from records of the rooms it created, all, unhappily, now destroyed. Photographs and other records reveal startling transformations wrought on the look of the conventional British home. Entering a room furnished by the Omega was like stepping into a modernist painting. Picasso faces looked out from paper fans, while jagged cubist figures danced across inlaid furniture. The workshops' signature red chairs, bright abstract rugs, exuberant paper flowers, and knick-knacks painted with nudes and goldfish seemed to realize the interiors Matisse's paintings depicted. This effect was most striking when whole rooms were commissioned from the Omega. In one, massive flower baskets tower from skirting board to ceiling. In the vestibule of a mansion near Regent's Park, Vanessa Bell created in mosaic a cubist still-life derived from Picasso's *Pots et citron*. Matissian dancers by Fry, Grant, and Bell cavorted across the walls of a display of Omega furniture

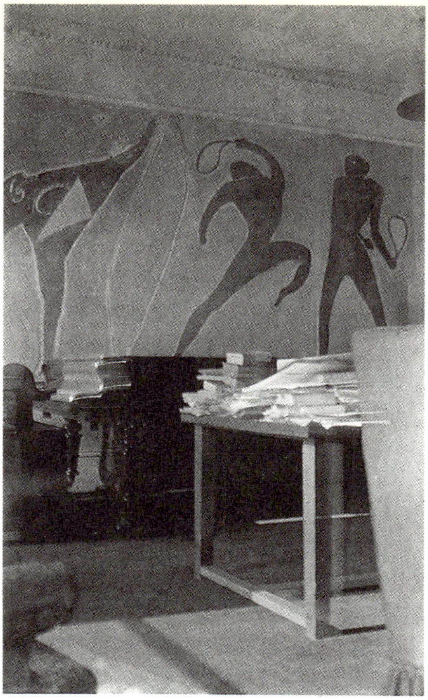

48 *Duncan Grant, mural at Brunswick Square, 1912*

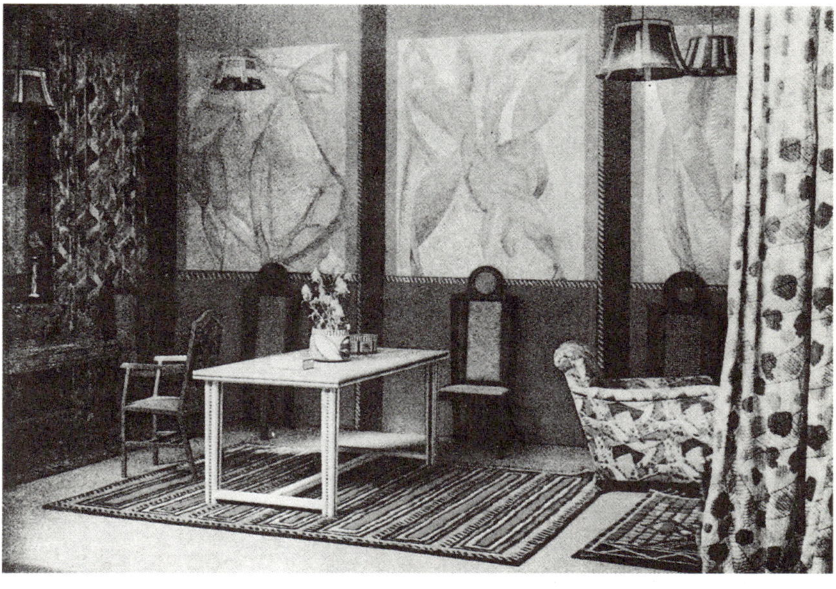

49 *Omega Workshop, Post-Impressionist Room at the Ideal Home Exhibition, 1913*

and fabrics at the otherwise staid "Ideal Home" show, where the visiting royal family is reported to have "deemed it the perfect example of how not to decorate a sitting room".[17]

Meanwhile, in the house at Gordon Square, Bell turned the walls and ceiling of her children's room into a colorful jungle of clouds and animals in abstract silhouette (again presaging Matisse's later work), a design so successful that in the winter of 1913 she recreated it upstairs in the Omega showrooms. The inspiration for this project dates back to the previous year, when one of Bell's letters records a visit by Grant, where he "lay on the floor and talked in a desultory way of . . . how we are to turn my studio into a tropical forest with great red figures on the walls, a blue ceiling with birds of paradise floating from it (my idea), and curtains, each one different." Bell's conception of this vision – extravagantly arcadian and modernist – as an antidote to the frigid formalities of England is suggested in her summary: "This is all to cheer us through London winters." For Fry, Bell's daring in realizing her vision was linked to the sexual revolution of which Bloomsbury was a part. Proclaiming the link between modernism and feminism, he publicized Bell's Omega installation in the newspapers, saying, "Some years ago, even the cleverest women consciously or unconsciously copied men. Now they seem never to do so . . ."[18]

Critical commentary on the Omega reinforced the idea that the new look of domesticity connotated new ways of life at odds with the conventions of English propriety. From the mild-mannered *News and Leader*, which observed that "the walls of the Post-Impressionist home will not be as the walls of ordinary homes," to the sensationalizing *Mirror* headline, "A POST-IMPRESSIONIST FLAT: WHAT WOULD THE LANDLORD THINK?", journalists emphasized the shock (or, perhaps, the horror) of the new. A photo caption in the *Mirror* ran, "Mr Fry thinking out some new futurist nightmare, something that will eclipse even the room above." Art critics were more specific in reproving the Omega's importation of Continental aesthetics. P. G. Konody of the conservative *Observer* complained that the "flirting decorations" that Bell and Grant painted for the exterior of the Omega showrooms "– gay, giddy and slight – might hold their places on some sun-baked wall within the equatorial belt, but . . . they affront the grave decorum of Fitzroy Square." Inside, he criticized the furnishings, "laden with formless wriggles that serve no useful purpose," and he mocked Bell's nursery (which he attributed to Fry), in which "the prattling infant is to be led, all unconsciously, into the gay groves of Post-Impressionism."[19]

Konody's imputations of a sensuality subversive of proper British restraint continues to animate critical reactions to the Omega more than a half century later. In 1985, the art critic of *The Listener* complained that the Omega artists "failed to discipline their instinctive exuberance and act on

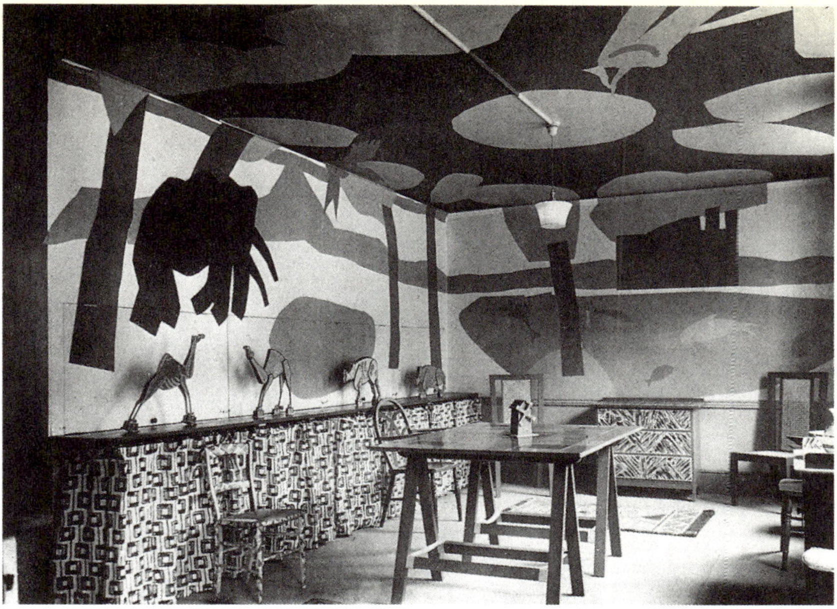

50 *Vanessa Bell, Children's Nursery, Omega Workshops Showroom, 1913*

the realization that their ideal of visual delight should be subtly expressed rather than brandished at the onlooker in such a relentless manner." Responding to recent exhibitions of Omega work, *The Guardian* in 1984 reported that Fry "of course went to Tuscany, or the South of France. It was there that he acquired his own cheap taste for flashy brush strokes and gaudy colors," which renders Omega products "as out of place in the English winter as a lemon yellow frock."[20] For Bloomsbury, such incongruity was exactly the point. Challenges to aesthetic propriety were part and parcel of broader challenges to convention, and modern art became the visual expression of aspirations to new ways of life, most literally in the application of modernist aesthetics to the stuff of everyday life.

For critics then and now, Bloomsbury's transgressions – of the boundaries of patriarchal propriety as well as of the border between fine art and design – provoked bitter attacks in which the authority of sexual and aesthetic conventions are mutually reinforcing. In 1914, the London version of the Futurist Manifesto inveighed against "the commercial acquiescence of English artists, the effeminacy of their art and their complete absorption toward a purely decorative sense." *Blast I*, the manifesto of the Futurist-derived Vorticist movement, condemned "Decorative Art" as "rightly despised." The year before, the Vorticists' leader, Wyndham Lewis, whose anti-domestic rhetoric is quoted in the introduction to this book, attacked the Omega's directors in explicitly gendered terms, claiming that their cooperative workshop was an attempt "to call in as much modern talent as they could find, to do the rough and masculine work without which they knew their efforts would not rise above the level of a pleasant tea party." Summing up this debate fifty years later, an English art historian explains, "Lewis refused to castrate his programme with even a hint of Omega-like desire to enhance the beauty of everyday surroundings."[21] Recent attacks on Bloomsbury in the American art press, meanwhile, ridiculed the group for "reject[ing] the respectable and conventional in favor of the perverse and esoteric." The same critic, attempting to explain why the English, in his view, failed to understand Cubism, blamed Bloomsbury's pernicious focus on "the more decorative aspects of Cubism" as manifest in the output of the Omega:

> [F]ar from advancing any real understanding of the Cubist aesthetic, this cozy, decorative use of its more superficial devices only served to blur its artistic importance. The Omega style – so typically Bloomsbury in the way it diluted and distorted modernism in the interest of aesthetic sociability – made Cubism look homey and insipid.[22]

What is clear in these attacks is the way domesticity becomes equated with femininity (or even castration and perversion) in a culture were the real and the important are conceived as prerogatives of masculinity, and the homey is, by definition, insipid.

For the members of the Bloomsbury group, excluded from conventional definitions of masculinity, identification with the feminized domestic realm allowed an inversion of conventional systems of value. As Virginia Woolf explained, in reference to her own work, "When a woman comes to write a novel, she will find that she is perpetually wishing to alter the established values – to make serious what appears insignificant to man, and trivial what is to him important."[23] In this light, both Bloomsbury's focus on the domestic and the nature of its domestic designs as subversive recombinations of incongruous traditions reflect an impulse to refashion the world in order to enable new ways of life – the ideal Woolf (and Strachey) conveyed with the image of "rooms of one's own."

Until feminist scholars, inspired by Woolf's writings, rekindled interest in Bloomsbury, dismissive assessment of the group's visual production were the critical norm. Renewed appreciation for Bloomsbury art and design had just begun when the youngest of the group's artists, Duncan Grant, died in 1978 at the age of ninety-three. For most of their working lives, the Bloomsbury artists retreated behind the high walls of secluded country houses in France and England, ceding the group's public identity to its writers. The proximate cause for this retreat was the onset of World War I, which destroyed the Omega's structure, though Fry was able to maintain the workshops as a haven for women artists, refugees, and the

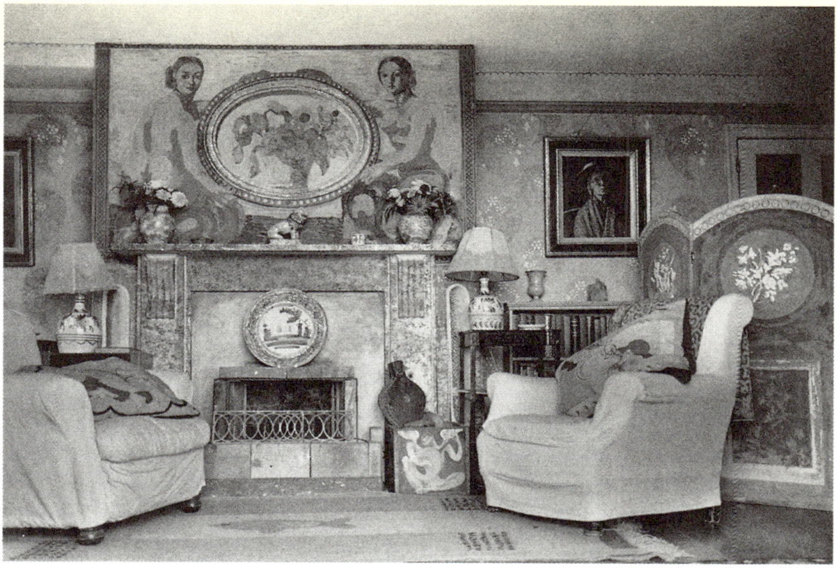

51 *Duncan Grant, Overmantel in the Garden Room, Charleston Farmhouse, c. 1928*

occasional draft-dodger, even as Grant and Bell were displaced to the country, where Grant, as a conscientious objector, was consigned to farm labor. Writing of this period, Bell later explained:

> The excitement and the joy had gone. The hostility of the general public was real now, no longer a ridiculous and even stimulating joke . . . All the world was hostile close round one [sic] and Bloomsbury had no changing atmosphere in which to move and expand and grow.

According to Woolf, during the war Fry became "oppressed by the conviction that art after the war must be esoteric and hidden like science in the middle ages – 'we can have no public art, only private ones, like writing and painting, and even painting is almost too public.'"[24] The most public phase of the Bloomsbury artists' careers was over, and though after the war they continued occasionally to exhibit their paintings and to design textiles and pottery, their aesthetic became increasingly nostalgic. Fry turned more and more to art history, while Grant and Bell gradually constricted their focus around their home in rural Sussex.

Half do-it-yourself palace, half self-imposed prison, Charleston, the farmhouse retreat where Grant and Bell spent the last fifty years of their lives, may be the hardest of Bloomsbury's domestic environments to assess. Virtually every surface – walls, doors, window frames, furniture – is covered, and sometimes recovered, with painted decoration, creating a Post-Impressionist *Gesamtkunstwerk*. The abundance and exuberance of the decorations at Charleston, however, are offset by a kind of studied insularity and willful provinciality that refuse to register any influence indicative of the world after 1914. Ambivalence over Charleston is evident even in Bloomsbury's assessment of its painters' creation. At Charleston, Fry said, he found "the only breathable atmosphere in England," but he also confessed to feeling excluded from a working partnership between Bell and Grant that became increasingly self-contained. Woolf admired the way at Charleston, "Nessa seems to have slipped civilization off her back, and splashes about entirely nude, without shame, and enormous spirit," but she also wondered – less admiringly – at her artist colleagues "looking at the pinks and yellows, and when Europe blazes all they do is screw up their eyes and complain of a temporary glare in the foreground."[25]

The terms of such criticism reiterate what this essay has argued were the basic tenets of Bloomsbury's domestic vision: Fry's anxiety over Bell and Grant's insularity bespeaks the anti-patriarchal ambition that the home should support community rather than coupledom, while Woolf's complaint articulates the aspiration that new forms of domestic life should sustain activist challenges to militarism and nationalism in the culture at large. If Charleston failed completely to realize Bloomsbury's ambitions, it, nevertheless, claims our interest today, if simply as evidence of a long-ignored domestic subcurrent within mainstream modernism. In the post-modern era, with its attention to gay and feminist identity, however, the nature of Bloomsbury's alternative domesticity seems a provocative early model of coalition across the lines of gender and sexual orientation. Likewise, the basic elements of Bloomsbury's art – the blurring of the boundaries around fine art, and strategies of pastiche – anticipate some of the most definitive characteristics of postmodern artistic practice. The ambivalent legacy of this final embodiment of Bloomsbury's aspirations to rooms of one's own stands as an inspiration to those concerned with issues of domesticity today.

11
Homes for Cyborgs

ANTHONY VIDLER

> The cyborg is resolutely committed to partiality, irony, intimacy, and perversity. It is oppositional, utopian, and completely without innocence. No longer structured by the polarity of public and private, the cyborg defines a technological polis based partly on a revolution of social relations in the *oikos*, the household. Nature and culture are reworked; the one can no longer be the resource for appropriation or incorporation by the other.
>
> *Donna Haraway, "A Manifesto for Cyborgs"*

If, for the first machine age, the preferred metaphor for the house was industrial, a "machine for living in," the second machine age would perhaps privilege the medical: the house as at once prosthesis and prophylactic. In the Corbusian "home of man" technology took the form of more or less benign "object-types" and perfectly controlled environments that allowed for the full play of the natural body in nature. The line between nature and the machine, between the organic and the inorganic, seemed crystal clear; organicism was a metaphor, not a reality. Now, the boundaries between organic and inorganic, blurred by cybernetic and biotechnologies, seem less sharp; the body, itself invaded and reshaped by technology, invades and permeates the space outside, even as this space takes on dimensions that themselves confuse the inner and the outer, visually, mentally, and physically. "L'homme-type," the modulor muscleman, has through a combination of prosthetic devices, drugs, and body sculpture emerged as Cyborg, a potentially gender-free mutant, and its home is no longer a house. As Walter Benjamin presciently observed, "The work of Le Corbusier seems to arise when the 'house' as mythological configuration approaches its end."[1]

In the terms introduced by Donna Haraway, cyborg culture, a product of late capitalist technology, is at once an all-embracing and controlling reality and a utopia full of promise. The totalizing and hegemonic power of "modern production seems," in Haraway's words, "like a dream of cyborg colonization of work, a dream that makes the nightmare of Taylorism seem idyllic." But it also, she argues, opens up the possibility of a political struggle over the different boundaries it cuts through: the boundaries between the human and the animal, the animal-human organism and the machine, the physical and the nonphysical. "Late twentieth-century machines have made thoroughly ambiguous the difference between natural and artificial, mind and body, self-developing and externally designed. . . . Our machines are disturbingly lively, and we ourselves frighteningly inert."[2] For Haraway, it is precisely in the interstices of these differences, in "the simultaneity of breakdowns," that the "matrices of domination" might be cracked open and, in the "pollution" that results, a new political and social practice opened up. Such a practice, she hopes, will create the conditions of a gender independence through the construction of what Alice Jardine has dubbed "Technobodies" by means of medicotechnologies of reproduction, transplants, and the like.[3]

The implications of this metamorphosis for architecture are more radical than even Reyner Banham – author of *Theory and Design in the First Machine Age* (1960), an optimist in technological "Futurism" and supporter of the London-based Archigram group, from the 1960s – would have envisaged. No longer are we fooled by the promise of the house as a bubble-container that frees its human contents from the vicissitudes of external environment: neither Buckmaster Fuller's Dymaxion dome nor the spacesuit reflects the infinite permeability assumed by the contemporary skin, the interchangeability of body part and technical replacement, or the spatiomental reconstruction implied by the cyberspace. This complex and impure system of existence, indeed, offers neither the luminous promise of technological utopia nor the dark hell of its opposite. The sleeper in *When the Sleeper Wakes*, H. G. Wells's turn-of-the-century dystopia, was faced with a clear confrontation between the scientific and the social; the hacker in William Gibson's *Neuromancer* no longer knows the difference between waking and sleeping.

Cyborgs and their homes, of course, have a respectable prehistory in the modern period, in the monstrous merging of animal and human so characteristic of surrealist imagery. As Haraway writes, "The cyborg appears in myth precisely where the boundary between human and animal is transgressed. Far from signalling a walling off of people from other living beings, cyborgs signal a disturbingly tight coupling."[4] Thus the gentle horse-headed women and boys that populate Leonora Carrington's *House of Fear* and its illustrations by Max Ernst seem deliberately to transpose the attributes of the centaur and the unicorn in gender and implication. As Carrington herself remarked, "A horse gets mixed up with one's body . . . it gives energy and power. I used to think I could turn myself into a horse."[5] From the figure of Fear, in the Castle of Fear, who "looked slightly like a horse," in Carrington's text and Ernst's collage, through the Oval Lady, who holds the secret of turning herself into a living version of her rocking horse, to little Francis, a mask for Carrington herself, who grows a horse's head, these equine presences play on the register of sexual and mental ambiguities with evident autobiographical reference. It was, after all, Father who burned the rocking horse to punish the Oval Lady for even desiring to be a horse, and Francis whose horse's shape at once displayed his shame at failing to be woman and his androgynous desire. Carrington's horse-people seem to prefigure Haraway's separatist cyborgs.

Carrington's homes for androgynes are equally filled with a mixture of organic and inorganic objects: thus Uncle Ubriaco's workroom in "Little Francis" was "a spacious apartment on the ground floor filled with half-constructed constructions and wholly demolished bicycles. The walls were lined with bookshelves that held books, spare tires, bottles of oil, chipped figureheads, spanners, hammers, and reels of thread."[6] A series of books – *Man and Bicycle*, *Intricacies of Pedals*, *Tobson's Essays on Spokes and Bells*, *Free Wheels and Ball Bearings* – was piled beside a heterogeneous collection that included starved cockroaches in a small cage, a string of artificial onions, a spinning wheel, ladies' corsets of a complicated pattern, and a great many cogwheels.

For Carrington and the Surrealists in general, these semiorganic and dream objects were arrayed to counter the implacable rationalism of purely technological modernism, epitomized in the shape of the Father, who, in the "Oval Lady," seemed "more like a geometric figure than anything else," and who achieved grotesque proportions in the character of Egres Lepereff, "The Great Architect," in "Little Francis." Based on Serge Chermayeff, appointed a surrogate parent during Carrington's stay in London, this designer of guillotines for the execution of boys like Francis espoused "good machinery and efficient planning," which "are always artistically moving." "My platform . . . was pleasing," purred the Architect, "though utterly devoid of anything save the merest mechanical necessities. It was a symphony of pure form." Francis himself was less certain that "architecture . . . in modern art is the nearest form to pure abstraction," observing innocently, "But if you build abstract houses, the more abstract you make them the less there'll be there, and if you get abstraction itself there won't be anything at all."[7]

Surrealism's antipathy to modernism, reflected in the well-known quarrels between André Breton and Le Corbusier, was, on the surface, based on this suspicion of abstraction. For Breton, modernist functionalism was "the most unhappy dream of the collective unconscious," a "solidification of desire in a most violent and cruel automatism." The argument was elaborated by other Surrealists: Dalí in his exaltation of the Art Nouveau, with its "terrifying and edible beauty"; Hans Arp's championing of the "elephant style" against the "bidet style"; Tristan Tzara's indictment of modern architecture as "the complete negation of the image of the dwelling." All posed a volatile and elusive sensibility of mental-physical life against what was seen as a sterile and overrationalized technological realism: the life of the interior psyche against the externalizing ratio.

Le Corbusier himself summarized the opposing positions succinctly in his only contribution to a quasi-Surrealist journal – a note on the work of the psychologically troubled artist Louis Soutter, in an article published in *Minotaure* in 1936. To Soutter's remark, "The minimum house or future cell should be in translucent glass. No more windows, these useless eyes. Why look outside?," Corbusier replied, "This affirmation of Louis Soutter . . . is the very antithesis of my own ideas, but it manifests the intense interior life of the thinker."[8] For Le Corbusier, looking always, as Beatriz Colomina has observed, toward a universally transparent exteriority, the attempt to reenvision the objects of daily life metaphorically was misguided, leading to a dangerous imbalance in the human "technico-cerebral-emotional equation," the creation of a "sentiment-object" rather than an object of use. As Benjamin noted, it was in this debate that the essence of modernity might be summarized: "To embrace Breton and Le Corbusier – that would be to draw the spirit of contemporary France like a bow which strikes with knowledge to the heart of the present."[9]

Against the cold rationalism of the modernists, the Surrealists called for an architecture more responsive to psychological needs: what Tristan Tzara termed an "intrauterine architecture" was conceived as a radical criticism of the house of Corbusian and Miesian rationalism. "Modern architecture," Tzara argued, "as hygienic and stripped of ornaments as it wants to appear, has no chance of living." Against the horizontal extensions and the dissolution of the barriers between public and private implied by the Domino model, Tzara posed the maternal and sheltering images of "uterine" constructions which, from the cave to the grotto and the tent, comprised the fundamental forms of human habitation:

> From the cave (for man inhabits the earth, "the mother"), through the Eskimo yurt, the intermediary form between the grotto and the tent (remarkable example of uterine construction which one enters through cavities with vaginal forms), through to the conical or half-spherical hut furnished at its entrance with a post of sacred character, the dwelling symbolizes prenatal comfort.

Entered through "cavities of vaginal form,' these conical or half-spherical houses were dark, tactile, and soft. They imitated the play-constructed shelters of childhood.

> When one returns what was torn away during adolescence and childhood, man could possess those realms of "luxe, calme et volupté" that he constructed for himself beneath the bed covers, under tables, crouching in cavities of earth, above all at the narrow entry; when it is seen that well-being

> resides in the *clair-obscur* of the tactile and soft depths of the only hygiene possible, that of prenatal desires, it will be possible to reconstruct the circular, spherical, and irregular houses that mankind has conserved from the time of the caves to the cradle and the grave, in his vision of intrauterine life which knows nothing of that aesthetic of castration called modern. This will not, in valorizing these arrangements with the acquisitions of actual life, be a return to the past, but a real progress, based on the potentiality of our most strong desires, strong because latent and eternal, the possibility of being liberated normally. The intensity of these desires has not changed much since the stage of man's savagery; only the forms and satisfactions have been broken up and dispersed over a larger mass, and, enfeebled to the point of being lost, with their acuity, the sense of true reality and quietude, they have, by their very degeneration, prepared the way for that autopunitive aggressivity that characterizes modern times.[10]

In Tzara's mingling of popular psychology and primitivism – his observations on architecture were published in *Minotaure* following Michel Leiris's illustrations of Dogon huts in 1933 – we can identify a double nostalgia. On the one hand, the return to archetypal forms marks an identification with the origins of civilization and an explicit critique of its technological results, human and material; on the other, the notion of womb *as* origin displays a familiarity with Freudian explanations of desire and the repressed or displaced routes of homesickness: "There is a joking saying that 'Love is homesickness,'" Freud had written in 1919, "and whenever a man dreams of a place or a country and says to himself while he is still dreaming: 'This place is familiar to me, I've been there before,' we may interpret the place as being his mother's genitals or her body" (U 368). It is no doubt in this light that we may interpret Tzara's desire that "the architecture of the future will be intrauterine if it has resolved the problems of comfort and material and sentimental well-being, if it renounces its role of interpreter-servant of the bourgeoisie whose coercive will can only separate mankind from the ways of its destiny."[11]

Such nostalgia, however, hardly evoked the comforting images of hearth and home that were, during the same period, being raised by philosophers of the *Heimat* from Tessenow to Heidegger. For the apparently warm and all-enclosing interiors of intrauterine existence were, as Freud pointed out, at the same time the very centers of the uncanny. At once the refuge of inevitably unfulfilled desire and the potential crypt of living burial, the womb-house offered little solace to daily life.[12]

Thus, Matta Echaurren's "intrauterine" design for an apartment dedicated to the senses, published in *Minotaure* 11, in 1938, was a deliberate 52
attack on the commonplaces of the bourgeois home. The perspective view shows materials and forms that merge nature and the inorganic, the

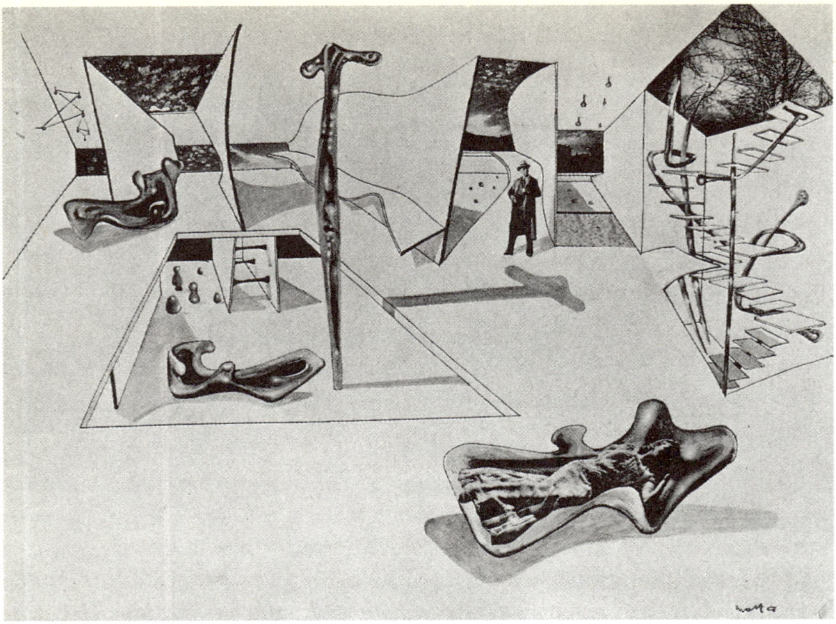

52 *Matta Echaurren, Mathématique Sensible, Architecture du Temps, from* Minotaure *11, 1938*

mathematical and the tactile. It was, Matta noted, "a space that will bring into consciousness human verticality." A true vertigo machine, composed of "different levels, a stair without a handrail to overcome the void," it was also a space of psychological interaction. Its columns were "psychological Ionic"; its furnishings "supple, pneumatic." Matta specified inflatable rubber, cork, paper, and plaster for the soft areas, all for better contrast, framed in an "armature of rational architecture." The whole space simulated a kind of artificial womb.

> Man looks back at the dark pulsions of his origin which enveloped him with humid walls where the blood pulsed close to the eye with the noise of the mother . . . we must have walls like damp sheets which deform themselves and join with our psychological fears . . . the body insinuated as into a mold, as into a matrix based on our movements.[13]

It was the task of the architect, Matta concluded, "to find for each individual those umbilical cords that put us in communication with other suns, objects in total freedom that would be like plastic psychoanalytical mirrors." Frederick Kiesler's "Endless House," designed in multiple versions between 1924 and 1965, was similarly conceived. Hans Arp spoke of this "egg"-like form as if it were the egg of Columbus: "In his egg, in these spheroid egg-shaped structures, a human being can now take shelter and live as in his mother's womb."[14]

This blurring of lines between the mental and physical, the organic and inorganic, was, for the Surrealists, one of the characteristic pleasures of Art Nouveau. Dalí's celebrated eulogy to Gaudí's "edible" architecture had stressed its images of metamorphosis, of all historical styles merging into each other, of the intersection of the biological and the constructional, building and psychoanalysis, architecture and hysteria, in order to produce the ultimate object of desire, or at least its reification. Characterized by its mimesis of the digestible – gates with panels like pieces of calves' liver, columns with bases that seemed to say "eat me!," buildings that as a whole might be assimilated to cakes – it was an architecture that, in Dalí's words "verified that urgent 'function,' so necessary for the amorous imagination: to be able in the most literal way possible to eat the object of desire."[15] Opposed to modern functionalism in every way, the Style 1900 discovered its real functions in the appetites and desires.

A "traumatism" for art, this style equally modeled itself on the postures of human trauma and psychosis. Using Charcot's photographs of female hysterics at the Salpêtrière, Dalí drew a "psycho-pathological parallel" between these images of "ecstasy" and the carving of the Art Nouveau.

> Invention of "hysterical sculpture." – Continuous erotic ecstasy. – Contractions and attitudes without antecedents in the history of statuary (I refer to the women discovered and understood after Charcot and the School of the Salpêtrière). – Confusion and ornamental exacerbation in relation to pathological communications: precocious dementia. – Close relations to the dream; reveries, day dreams. – Presence of characteristic oneiric elements; condensation, displacement, etc. – Blossoming of the sado-anal complex. – Flagrant ornamental coprophagy. Very slow, exhausting onanism, accompanied by a huge feeling of guilt.[16]

The well-known theory of Surrealist-inspired ecstasy that followed, summarized in Dalí's collage *Le phénomène de l'exstase*, with its focalization of ears ("always in ecstasy") and juxtaposition of Charcot's photographs with Art Nouveau sculpture, also included a telling image of a tipped chair, empty as if having thrown its contents out of the picture.

This uncanny property of objects to adopt the characteristic behavior of their owners, thence to take revenge, the habit of the inanimate to take on the characteristics of the animate, and vice versa, had already been recognized by Freud. In a passage that seems to anticipate Ernst's collages, he speaks of the naïve story of the haunted table from the *Strand Magazine*:

> I read a story about a young married couple who move into a furnished house in which there is a curiously shaped table with carvings of crocodiles on it. Towards evening an intolerable and very specific smell begins to pervade the house; they stumble over something in the dark; they seem to see a vague form gliding over the stairs – in short, we are given to understand that the presence of the table causes ghostly crocodiles to haunt the place, or that the wooden monsters come to life in the dark, or something of the sort. It was a naive enough story, but the uncanny feeling it produced was quite remarkable. (U 367)

This sensation, evoked, Freud explains, by an "over-accentuation of physical reality in comparison with material reality," was the precise equivalent of Dalí's architecture of "hyper-materialism." Le Corbusier characterized the sensibility, accurately enough, as a disturbance in the balance of "our technico-cerebro-emotional equation," an overinvestment of "sentiment" in objects, to the extent that "the feeling for cause and effect falters. We are seized by disquiet because we no longer feel well-adapted; we revolt against our enforced servitude to the *abnormal*."[17]

And yet, of course, modernism's own object imaginary was hardly less disquieting. Walter Benjamin, indeed, went beyond Dalí's simple opposition to make the conceptual link between the technical visions of modernism and the apparent antitechnical stance of Art Noveau. Benjamin, who cited Dalí on the "delirious and cold buildings" of Art Nouveau, formulated a vision of the Jugendstil that was, in reality, an "attempt of art to take the measure of technique."[18] Precisely because, Benjamin argued, the Jugendstil considered itself no longer "menaced" by technique, it could identify itself with technique. Thus he noted the correspondence between the curving lines of Art Nouveau and their modern counterparts, electric wires, which in turn paralleled the nerves of the modern city dweller: "In the characteristic line of the art nouveau are brought together – united in a montage of imagination – the nerve and the electric wire (and which in particular brings into contact the world of organism and of technique by means of the intermediary form of the neurovegetal system)."[19] For Benjamin, this intersection of technology and nature was represented by the displacement of symbols from romanticism to modernism.

Here we may begin to trace the affiliations of Surrealism and modernism on the level of technique, affinities that were announced by Benjamin himself in the aphorism: "The reactionary attempt that seeks to detach the forms imposed by technique from their functional context and to make natural constants out of them – that is to say, to stylize them – is found sometime after art nouveau, in a similar form, in futurism." The structure that united the two, in Benjamin's terms, was fetishism. For it was fetishism that, in its multiple displacements, "suppresses the barriers that separate the organic from the inorganic world," that is "at home in the world of the inert as in the world of the flesh."[20] Such confusions of identity were, as Sigfried Giedion noted, the inevitable product of the modern mechanization of the dwelling in its mission of repression against the bric-à-brac of the nineteenth century.[21] Giedion observes of the interiors of Ernst's *Une semaine de bonté*,

> Of the billowing drapes, of the murky atmosphere, Ernst's scissors make a submarine cave. Are these living creatures, plaster statues or models of the academic brush found reclining here or rotting? To this question no answer can or should be given. The room, as nearly always, is oppressive with assassination and non-escape.[22]

Surrealism and purism, indeed, fetishized precisely the same *types* of objects: what for Surrealists were "objets trouvés" or vehicles of oneiric desire and for Le Corbusier were "objets-membres-humains," or the physical extensions of the body. As Le Corbusier himself recognized,

> The new "Surrealists" (formerly Dadaists) claim to lift themselves above the brute nature of the object and are ready to recognize only relationships which belong to the invisible and subconscious world of the dream. Nevertheless they compare themselves to radio antennae; thus they raise radio onto their own pedestal . . . the supremely elegant relationships of their metaphors . . . are all the time very clearly dependent on the products of straightforward conscious effort . . . the finality necessary to polished steel.

To prove the point Le Corbusier cited de Chirico, writing in the first number of *La Révolution Surréaliste*, December 1924: "They are like levers, as irresistible as those all-powerful machines, those gigantic cranes which raise high over the teeming building sites sections of floating fortresses with heavy towers like the breasts of ante-diluvian mammals."[23]

In this dependency of surrealist fantasy on the real objects of the machine world, "type objects" and "sentiment objects" met in their common aim to overcome technique in its banal manifestations in favor of a technological imaginary that would transform technology into the human and vice versa, into the prosthetic and potentially critical devices of the cyborg. It was not by chance that Walter Benjamin identified Olympia, the automat doll of E. T. A. Hoffmann's "Sandman" and subject of Freud's analysis of the uncanny, as the ideal woman of the Art Nouveau. "The extreme point of the technical organization of the world," concluded Benjamin, "consists in the liquidation of fertility."

The modern cyborg was, in this way, anticipated by the automat, with its long tradition in romantic thought, from Hoffmann's Olympia to Mary Shelley's monster, from Villiers de L'Isle-Adam's *Eve future* to Duchamp's "Bride." These "celibate machines" were, as Lyotard has observed, all ruses, fabricated to obscure the essential impossibility of mechanically dominating nature, to blur the distinctions between the biological and the technical; the first such contraption was constructed by Hephaistos for Zeus and named Pandora,[24] that first "automate," as Alice Jardine has redubbed her, in order to expose the ruse of modernism.[25]

Conceived of in these terms, the objects of arthitecture become so many prostheses, extensions of the body tied to it in almost organic ways; instruments that, as Michel de Certeau has characterized them, might be defined according to their functions:

> Two main operations characterize their activities. The first seeks primarily to *remove* something excessive, diseased, or unaesthetic from the body, or else to *add* to the body what it lacks. Instruments are thus distinguished by the action they perform: cutting, tearing out, extracting, removing, etc., or else inserting, installing, attaching, covering up, assembling, sewing together, articulating etc. – without mentioning those substituted for missing or deteriorated organs, such as heart valves and regulators, prosthetic joints, pins implanted in the femur, artificial irises, substitute ear bones, etc.[26]

Of course, most of the object types conceived by modernism were prosthetic to one degree or another: Le Corbusier never tired of vaunting the claims of "objets-membres-humains," those type objects responding to type needs and type functions and operating as liberating extensions of our limbs – "chairs to sit on, tables to work at, devices to give light, machines to write with (ah! yes), racks to file things in." A "human limb object," properly designed to harmonize with the body, would act for all the world like "a docile servant. A good servant is discreet and self-effacing in order to leave his master free."[27]

The modernist prosthetic object was equally a master: the etiquette machines fabricated by Schreber for his children – to construct correct posture while lying, sitting, and standing – as well as the taylorized furniture of the Gilbreths were all so many devices to control the body for its own good, chastity belts for the machine age, bringing the organic into line with the social and economic systems of industrial production.

In such a context, architectural exploration, as the projects of Elizabeth Diller and Ricardo Scofidio have understood it, might best be limited to the precise dimensions of a controlled experiment. In a world of infinitely disseminated power – of surveillance, of the image, of the technological – the stylistic metaphor is as suspect as the functional solution. In their place, the minute and exactly calibrated interrelations of body and machine are subjected to a dispassionate scrutiny, transcribed as the automatic writing of a generation of readymades. These calculations take as their starting point the clearly distinguished systems identified by modernist technique: the system of the object, of the body, of the optical, and finally of the home.

Each of these is carefully unwrapped, disassembled, and confronted, as it were, defenseless, to the next. The sites of these strategic deployments emerge as so many battlefields, strewn with the disemboweled residues of yesterday's biotechnical encounters: "no-man's-lands" or homes for cyborgs.

Accordingly the "object types" of Diller and Scofidio neither serve nor dictate; they simply reveal. Peeling back the layers of consumer coverings, Bauhaus black or suburban veneer, they show the form of the guts inside. Televisions are transformed into biological analog through disemboweling, their tubes, wires, and connections left bare, as if to demonstrate their temporary, makeshift nature. On the one hand enfeebled and weak, cut open and wounded, these machines are at the same time threatening, as they parade the enormous power of the technologically constructed microorganism invading the house.

But these operations are not entirely neutral: beginning as a readymade, the unmade object is itself subjected to a subtle transformation and mutation that points not only to its internal nature but also to its expanded field of operation, its relation to the body. Thus a television screen, shifted from vertical to horizontal, is no longer the focus of a conventional view but now reflected in a mirror that takes its place. The screen, simulacrum of the real, is literally displaced through a simulacrum of itself, at the same time as its controlling (picture-frame) position has been unfixed and refracted through the action of the mirror. Similarly, chairs, which normally would image as well as serve comfort, are cut through in order to threaten the (sitting) body at its most vulnerable point.

Such objects are no longer subject to subjects; they counterattack. As in the collages of Max Ernst, they unionize in revolt, but now in the form of critical machines that pose new identities for their subjects. As apparatuses that both work on the fuse with once-separate bodies, they, like the cyborgs that "use" them, scramble all the recognized codes. Such objects fight back, they machine us as much as we machine them. Indeed, the only
resistance, as many of the visitors to Diller and Scofidio's 1990 installation 53–56
at the Museum of Modern Art realized, was to fall back on the commonplace reading of the objects, using a mirror carefully positioned to demolish narcissism for making up and envisioning a chair in the air as a misplaced seat. The network of relations established among objects becomes itself a phenomenal prosthetic for the body, to be refused by normalcy.

If, at one level, the body can be interpreted as a construction determined by the discursive practices of its surveillance and punishment, in the literal constructions of Diller and Scofidio the body both transcribes itself and is written on. The chair that leaves a message impressed on the buttocks – the right way round for another to read – is a machine for transcription. But, unlike Kafka's writing machine that inscribed the name of the punishment in the flesh of the victim, these architectural "magic writing pads" leave only temporary marks. In this way, the states of the modern body are mirrored in reactive structures. Cybernetic and biotechnical operations – hacking, probing – are given material life through the physical exploration of inside and out and the optical scanning of a myriad blind eyes that observe without knowing.

Here the optical networks set up by screen and camera, observer and observed, stage a voyeuristic space in which objects and subjects alike are trapped *en abîme*. But while the apparent trajectories of the eye, marked by the intersecting visual cones of so many lenses, seem to replicate the laws of true vision, in fact the space is traversed by the lines of a "pseudo-optics" established not so much by the geometries of real optical systems as by the psychology of the viewers. And viewers are equally absent in this simulated science where objects take their place, describing an optical scene that both includes and excludes subjects, or rather includes them in the form of a system of virtual signs. In this way an empty chair will "stand in" for its user, closing the system from the outside, as if obligingly supplying itself in the position of the hypothetical spectator of Goya's *Las Meninas*, no longer a technical instrument but a psychological contrivance.

No-body, then, can place itself at the central projection point in this optical system, which operates as a kind of literalization of post-Lacanian space. We who have become used to the diagram of our historically relative, rapidly changing perceptual structures, from Alberti's perspectival window to Nietzsche's labyrinth, are now presented with their archaeological reconstructions, each in conflict with the next, literalized by means of objects that project each system's sinister implications.

The gaze intimated by these layered and fractured cones of vision is, of course, no longer panoptical. In Alice Jardine's words, "We are no longer in the system of the panopticon described so accurately by Foucault . . . we are rather in a mode of self-surveillance: we watch ourselves as someone else."[28] From panoptical gaze to cyborgian gaze, Diller and Scofidio's intricately intersecting watchers shift attention from the written inscription of surveillance to the disseminated, three-dimensional network of glances and reflections. The carefully calibrated glances of the Dutch group portrait as described by Alois Riegl, the culturally precise meanings of perspective as symbolic form explicated by Panofsky, give way to three-dimensional hyperspatial constructions, in which fault lines figure as importantly as any completed sight lines. Where, in a pure cybernetic system as modeled by de Certeau, the privilege is given to writing, now boundaries are broken down and confused by their very inspection in three dimensions.

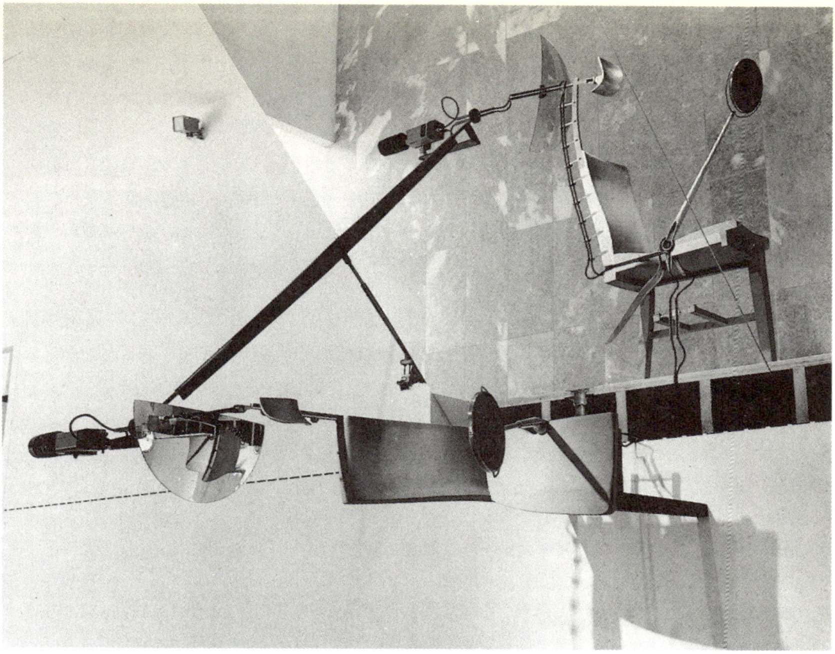

53 *Installation view from the exhibition,* Projects: Elizabeth Diller/Ricardo Scofidio. *1 July 1989 through August 1989. The Museum of Modern Art, New York*

By the simple but critical act of "realizing" the model in practice, Diller and Scofidio establish a host of half-completed, half-broken refracted lines between mechanical objects and organic subjects; this network *is* in a real sense the cyborgian construction. Emulating at the same time as provoking both inner "hacker" or "cyber" space and outer or body space, the apparatus acts for all intents and purposes as a complicated and imaginary prophylactic among its subjects. The machine-age bachelor mechanism was forced to construct a real barrier, as in the hymenal wall of Alfred Jarry's "island of lubricious glass," which took on the form of any sexual organ when touched.[29] The contemporary cyborg, in contrast, is already insulated by a deflected gaze of a constructed gender and needs no traditional home.

But the home of a cyborg is by no means a site of technological utopia. Describing "home" as a social location, Donna Haraway confronts the breakdown of the bourgeois domestic myth in the face of cybernetic industry:

> *Home*: Women-headed households, serial monogamy, flight of men, old women alone, technology of domestic work, paid homework, reemergence of home sweat shops, home-based businesses and telecommuting, electronic cottage, urban homelessness, migration, module architecture, reinforced (simulated) nuclear family, intense domestic violence.[30]

What for the post-war generation of architectural technotopias, from Archigram to high tech, simply signified burgeoning social opportunity – the unlikely communitarianism of the "global village" – emerges in reality as a suburban battlefield strewn with the dismembered nuclei of imaginary families and the wreckage of their "homes." In such settings, for better or for worse, there is, Haraway claims, "no 'place' for women." In their place, there are "only geometrics of difference and contradiction crucial to women's cyborg identities." Where, in the taylorized settings of the 1920s and 1930s, the home was to be retooled to produce a generation of engineers and technocrats, the woman smoothly integrating time and motion into the carefully calculated spaces of a "kitchen-house-factory," now the space of technological competency is reduced to the flat surface of the monitor, the breadth of two hands on the keyboard. In this context the spatial order of the home carries less and less meaning, and its traditional "rooms" and their furnishings even less. A "machine for living in" has been transformed into a potentially dangerous psychopathological space populated by half-natural, half-prosthetic individuals, where walls reflect the sight of their viewers, where the house surveys its occupants with silent menace.

In the Capp Street project constructed by Diller and Scofidio, where a domestic installation was inserted into an already existing San Francisco house, all these dimensions were explored: the space of each object was remapped as dining-table and chairs were lifted in the air, beds and chairs were split in two, all following the vectors established by their (traditional) uses exaggerated to cutting effect. Objects now acted out beyond their proper domains: chairs were attached to tables by locks and swings that emulated the presence of human arms; chairs were bisected by the locks of doors – all connected in ways they should not have been, in order to reveal their sinister interdependence in the domestic system. Domestic objects were now set free to map their own space of instrumentality; human agency was supplied by surrogate objects, themselves prostheses of objects in their dangerous extensions.[31] Like the dust traces falling on Duchamp's Large Glass, the phantom operations of absent inhabitants and living objects were also mapped in their deposits. The moving bed was tracked by films of dust beneath it; the presence of former drinkers marked by the rings of glasses on the table. The house was left as if an obsolete and already abandoned technological space – like the inside of an old radio – a readymade, found again to be reused at will, dust and all; the traces of non-occupation as well as of occupation seemed to provide a schematic archaeology by which to begin again.

Such an assemblage no longer prefigured a robotic future of unified and gleaming technology; rather it was composed in a present of uneven development, filled with the detritus of past systems of technical order. As

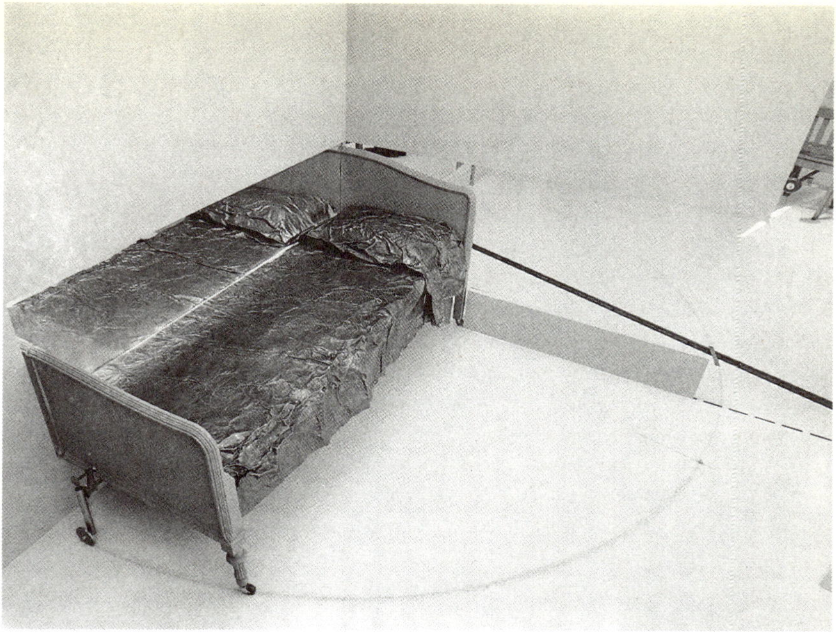

54, 55 *Elizabeth Diller and Ricardo Scofidio, installation views from* the withDrawing Room, *1987. The Capp Street Project, San Francisco*

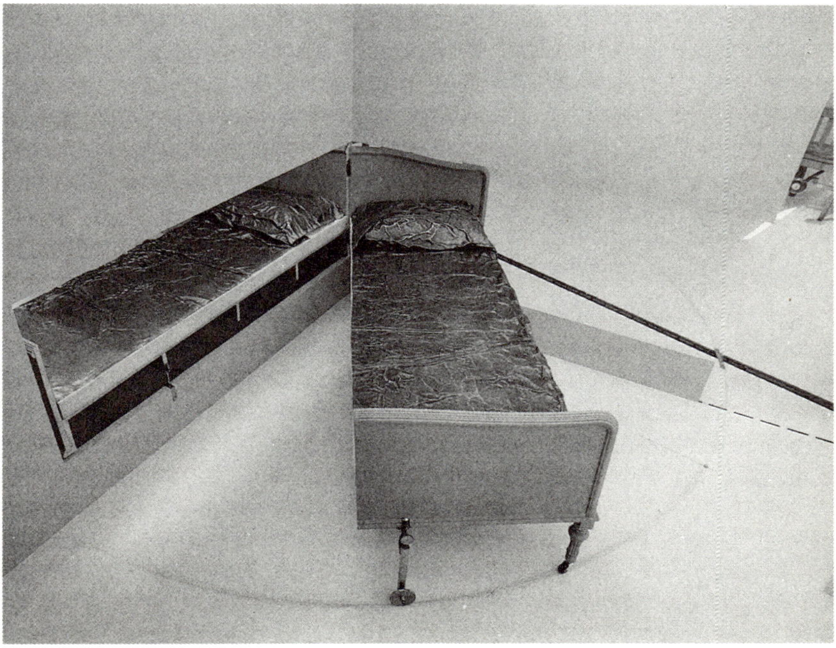

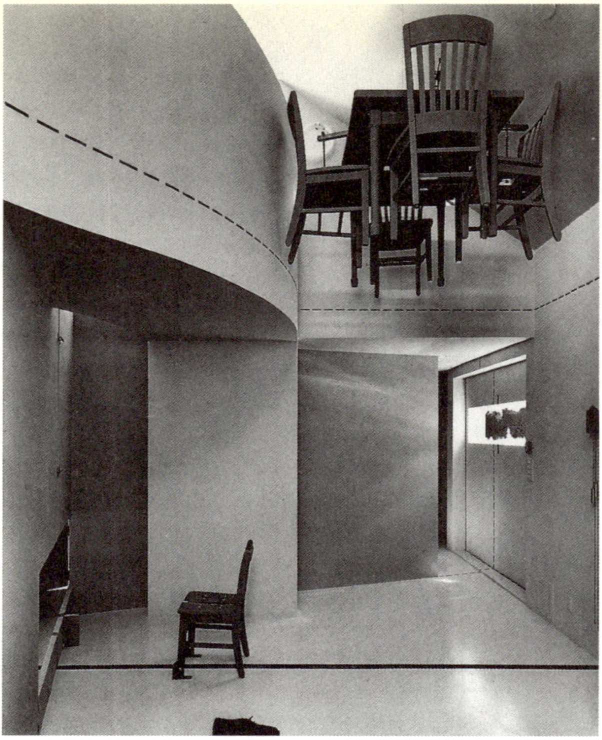

56 *Elizabeth Diller and Ricardo Scofidio, installation view from* the withDrawing Room, *1987. The Capp Street Project, San Francisco*

described by Michel de Certeau, this present takes on the characteristics of an open-cast mine, still operative in a terrain layered by the fragments of already obsolescent systems:

> Epistemological configurations are never replaced by the appearance of new orders; they compose strata that form the bedrock of a present. Relics and pockets of the instrumental systems continue to exist everywhere . . . Tools take on a folkloric appearance. They nevertheless make up a discharged corps left behind by the defunct empire of mechanics. These populations of instruments oscillate between the status of memorable ruins and an intense everyday activity.[32]

Despite the apparent homogeneity of the cybernetic system, it operates in the interstices, and with the help of every previous system of bodily and textual inscription. Thus the readymades "found" by Diller and Scofidio are neither pure types, as imagined by Le Corbusier, nor ironic counter-types, as re-represented by Marcel Duchamp. They are nothing more than junk, throw-away objects found in the street or at the local dump. Already useless to the system of technological utopia, they nevertheless have been recuperated by precise operations for another system, the cyborgian.

In this way, Diller and Scofidio construct environments that have all the air of those transitional wastelands described in contemporary science fiction: the "Night city" of William Gibson's *Neuromancer*, at once "a kind of historical park: reminding the most advanced Japanese technology of its humbler origins," and an "outlaw zone," "a deliberately unsupervised playground for technology itself."[33] Contemplating Diller and Scofidio's projects we are reminded of that other "Nighttown" depicted by Gibson in the short story "Johnny Mnemonic":

> The mall runs forty kilometers from end to end, a ragged overlap of Fuller domes roofing what was once a suburban artery. If they turn off the arcs on a clear day, a gray approximation of sunlight filters through layers of acrylic, a view like the prison sketches of Giovanni Piranesi. The three southernmost kilometers roof Nighttown . . . the neon arcs are dead, and the geodesics have been smoked black by decades of cooking fires.[34]

In the trusses of these abandoned domes lives a community of LO TEKS, dedicated to a reversal of progress into primitivism, transformed biologically into cyborgs of Darwinian regression, half-dog, half-human. Their city is a bricolage of junk held together by rough epoxy joints, taped to the rafters of this technotropia, "jury-rigged and jerry-built from scraps that even Nighttown didn't want." But where Gibson seems to celebrate, however savagely, a "neuromanticism" that points to a cybernetic sublime in these technological ruinscapes, Diller and Scofidio remain analytical and dedicated to the didactic dissection of the processes that construct this new world.

In this process, the selection of the everyday and well-used object – the old chair, the worn-out television – is deliberately calculated to lull suspicion. Old friends, thrown away after years of service, these objects are nothing but familiar – so familiar indeed as to become banal. But in their recuperation and necessary deconstruction they take on more sinister overtones. Returned from their proper burial, discovered in the wrong place, invested with an uncanny life of their own, they break the long process of deterioration and degradation that leads from the familiar, the ordinary, to the banal, returning once more to the status of the unhomely.[35] In the event, their effect is neither uncanny nor familiar, but rather a demonstration of the potential uncanny, an unveiling of the secret but ever-present reciprocities that bind people to objects in post-technological domesticity.

What Gibson calls "the consensual hallucination" of cyberspace, occupied by the disembodied consciousness of a hacker jacked into a matrix of spatially represented information – the public realm of the cybernetic – is now brought home. What Adorno epitomized as the dilemma of homesickness – the result of "distancing" – is now solved. The illustionistic virtuosity needed in order, as Adorno dreamed, to experience homesickness at the same time as staying at home is now technologically supplied.[36]

Private space is revealed as infinitely public, private rituals publicized to their subjects and these in turn connected to the public matrix. No longer sheltered from public surveillance by a well-defended private realm, the space of the domestic will now become, as Alice Jardine has hazarded, an agent of self-surveillance: "A lot of these ethical and political regimes will come together in self-surveillance; not all of it will be imposed from the outside . . . self tests . . . in the privacy of your own home . . . soon no-one will be able to touch anyone else, and I think it's going to be everyone."[37]

Thus it is that Haraway's cyborgian myth operates as much on the level of dystopia as of utopia; it is, as she explains, built out of irony, "the attempt to build an ironic political myth faithful to feminism, socialism, materialism."

> Irony is about contradictions that do not resolve into larger wholes, even dialectically, about the tension of holding incompatible things together because both or all are necessary and true. Irony is about humor and serious play. It is also a rhetorical strategy and a political method.[38]

Her attempt to pose the cyborg as "a creature of social reality as well as of fiction" that emblematizes the contemporary state of "lived social relations, our most important political construction," is a valiant effort to hold the unthinkable and the possible in the same frame, a counter to the gender divisions and relations that construct the (traditional) present.[39] Such irony, of course, can only be sustained in the active play of political and social experience; its difficult dialectic can rarely be incorporated in the positive spaces and aesthetic constructions of a material shelter. In the same way the "house" implied by Diller and Scofidio demands continuous consciousness of physical and psychological discomfort from its para-inhabitants; it converts the pabulum of Heideggerian nostalgia into a *Hausangst* that reveals the banal and everyday nature of the *unheimlich*; the dream of *Heimat* founders on the reality of the coffin-hotel in William Gibson's "zone".

12

Domestic Differences: Edith Farnsworth, Mies van der Rohe, and the Gendered Body

ALICE T. FRIEDMAN

According to her unpublished *Memoirs*, written while she was living in Italy in the 1970s, Edith Farnsworth met the architect Mies van der Rohe in Chicago in November 1945, at a dinner party at the home of mutual friends.[1] She was forty-two years old and single, a successful nephrologist at a large Chicago hospital. Mies, aged fifty-nine, was separated from his wife and three grown daughters in Germany; a former director of the famous Bauhaus and much admired within the field of architecture, he was virtually unknown beyond the art world and the academy. Mies was head of the Department of Architecture at the Armour Institute of Technology (later Illinois Institute of Technology), a position he had held since his arrival in the USA in 1938, but aside from some buildings on the campus of IIT, he had built nothing in this country. Mies was a man of great charm and a charismatic presence, and Edith, according to her *Memoirs*, was painfully lonely and bored. Over dinner, she mentioned that she was thinking of building a weekend house outside Chicago, and she wondered whether someone in his office might design it; Mies replied that he "would love to build any kind of house" for her himself. Thus each of them found the thing they believed they needed most: the architect now had an American client; the doctor, a friend who could help her create a retreat in which to escape the loneliness of weekends in the city.[2] The two immediately planned a trip to Plano to look at the site. Thinking back on that night, Farnsworth remembered her excitement: "The effect", she wrote, "was tremendous, like a storm, a flood or other act of God."

The experience of being a single, professional woman in the Midwest in the late 1940s played a critical role in Farnsworth's decision to build a custom-designed weekend house and it colors the entire history of the project, especially its reputation among her contemporaries. Evidence from a range of sources – from women's magazines, published books and private diaries – confirms the dominance of "traditional" marriage in 1950s' America, not only as a pervasive and powerful institution but as a virtually unchallenged vehicle for social and cultural activity in and around the home. For anyone outside the network of family life as it was narrowly defined by the period and enacted in both the burgeoning suburbs and in the city, the opportunities for either casual or formal social relations were severely curtailed. According to one survey, conducted in 1957 and published with the title *Americans View their Mental Health*, childless people, and particularly women, were viewed with compassion "as people who have missed the full richness of adult experiences." Moreover, in the popular imagination, single men and women were regarded with suspicion and could be subject to accusations of mental instability or homosexuality. The unmarried woman was seen as a "frustrated old maid" who had "failed so seriously in her understanding of a woman's role that she hadn't even established the marriage prerequisite of having a home". As such, she forfeited her place, both physical and symbolic, within American society, despite her not infrequent role as doting aunt or beloved eccentric, the latter being the role played by Edith Farnsworth in her own family.[3]

In this context, it is not surprising to read Farnsworth's recollections of the unhappy period in which she decided to build her house, a period of "tired, dull Sundays" when she would have nothing else to do but stretch out on the sofa and listen to the New York Philharmonic on the radio. A similar impression is conveyed by an unpublished autobiography, written in about 1959 by Anne Parsons, the unmarried daughter of Harvard sociologist Talcott Parsons, in which she complained of the loneliness of living as a single person in America:

> Life for the unmarried person after twenty five or so is simply not very easy because by this fact one is thrown out of all the better-worn social grooves so that even relatively simple things as what to do on Sunday become impossibly difficult.

In a letter to Betty Friedan, the author of *The Feminine Mystique*, Parsons wrote that for mainstream America the single woman was like "some sort of poison in the social system [that] has to be cast out," pointing to the gulf that separated her from her contemporaries, the "long spaces between my apartment and the suburban houses where I occasionally got invited for dinner to hear about the local school system . . ."[4]

Recognizing the fusion of the terms "family" and "home", Farnsworth approached the design of her own house as a typological problem, as a scientist would attack the morphology of an organism or disease. Having found a site on the banks of the Fox River some sixty miles west of the city, she began leafing through books and bulletins on modern architecture that she found on the "shelves of bookstores and the coffee tables of my friends." She marveled

> that I had been so slow to take an interest in architectural forms and purposes. The interest once found, the erection of even a small house in an out-of-the-

> way spot began to seem an action calling for a certain sense of responsibility. As in every other situation, there must be a really fine solution for an inexpensive weekend retreat for a single person of my tastes and pre-occupations and, conversely, it would be unbearably stupid to "put up" some contractor's cottage which could only ruin the site and remain as a token of empirical mediocrity.

Two key issues circulate through Farnsworth's narrative: questions about the domestic program, especially the contradiction between family life and singleness, and concern with cultural values, particularly the choice between taste and "mediocrity". These would resurface throughout the history of the project, structuring both Farnsworth's approach and experience as she was to represent them in interviews and in her writings, and shaping critical reaction to the house in both the professional and popular press. Because these concerns also loomed large on the broader American scene, fueled by the growth of suburban consumer culture and increased contact with Europe, the Farnsworth House, its client and architect were to become an emotional *cause célèbre* invested with meaning that went far beyond matters of architectural design. Although the principal players in this drama – Mies van der Rohe, Edith Farnsworth and the weekend house in Plano, Illinois – were in every respect atypical of the categories they were supposed to represent, they became the focus of intense debates hashed out in the press over American domesticity, sexuality and the politics of modern architecture.

Long before she met Mies, Edith Farnsworth had revealed an unusual interest in the arts and an affinity for European culture. Born in 1903, she attended classes in English literature and composition at the University of Chicago in the early 1920s, but focused her attention on the violin and travelled to Rome for further study.[5] In 1927 she returned to America, but made numerous trips to Europe until the outbreak of the war. She took her medical degree at Northwestern University in 1939 and maintained a successful practice as an internist in Chicago, but continued to pursue her interests in music and literature. Her interest in architecture came relatively late, given her broad travel experience, but once awakened, it developed quickly.

Returning from that first evening with Mies at the home of her friends, Farnsworth turned once more to her books and found illustrations of Mies's Barcelona Pavilion and Tugendhat House. Her perception of Mies's work was astute:

> I searched the sundry texts which lay about the apartment, and saw in them an architect whose austerity had kept him from popularity and whose manner was determined by his insight.[6]

Although the texts she consulted said very little about the work aside from commenting on his unusually luxurious materials, Farnsworth recognized in Mies's most important European projects both his minimalism and his single-mindedness in exploring the discipline of architectural design. Farnsworth, like everyone else, seems to have been unclear about what his "insight" may have been – the characteristically laconic Mies said little about this – but she was intrigued by what she read and heard. She was also pleased with Mies's enthusiasm for her project.

The visit to the site, which Mies agreed was beautiful, was the first of many "Sunday excursions" over the course of the next two years; sometimes the two were accompanied by "the boys" from Mies's office or by others. Mies and Farnsworth also began to socialize together in the city, and she frequently stopped by the office and even cooked dinners for the young associates in the practice.[7]

Although it was widely assumed that the two were romantically involved, there is nothing in Farnsworth's *Memoirs* to support that contention. Nevertheless, it is clear that for Farnsworth, a headstrong, proud and rather snobbish woman, the friendship with Mies represented a profound emotional and intellectual attachment. She immersed herself in Mies's world, struggling through the writings of philosophers who were important to him. She read the work of the Catholic theologian Romano Guardini in order, as she put it, to "lend myself to the concept of liturgy," a subject of concern to Mies as it affected architecture. In her enthusiasm, she recalled, she would read "anything which might enrich my own awareness, presumably by showing me how Mies had been enriched."[8]

Thus Farnworth became a "disciple", and when the model of her house was exhibited at the exhibition of Mies's work at the Museum of Modern Art organized by Philip Johnson in 1947, she felt proud of the project and of her role in it:

> it was the pivotal point of the exhibit, and I was happy as I boarded the train back to Chicago, reflecting that our project might well come the prototype of new and important elements of American architecture.[9]

Although she was no doubt unaware of it, Farnsworth had by this point made a critical transition from client to patron in the minds of her architect and his supporters at the Museum of Modern Art, blurring the boundaries between her own self-interest in the house and her enthusiasm for the larger intellectual and artistic implications of the project. By allowing an unusually long time to elapse in the design development phase and by taking part in the emotional life of the office, Farnsworth permitted financial, programmatic and scheduling questions to slide, a dangerous condition in any architectural project but one which was particularly grievous for a client of Mies, for whom theoretical and formal considerations always came before practical ones. This would come back to haunt her before long.

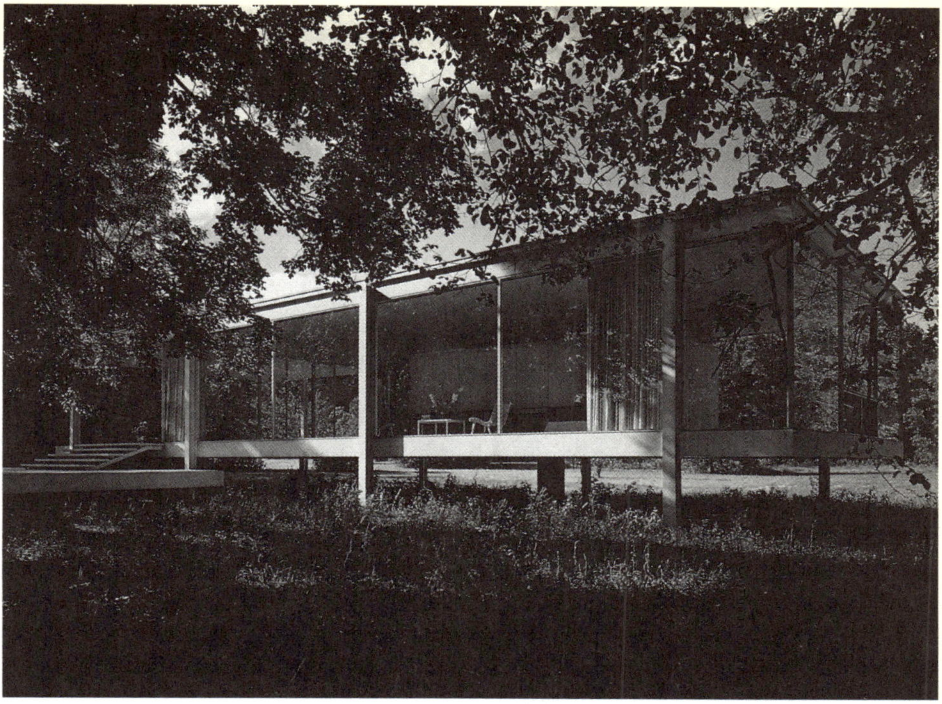

57 *Mies van der Rohe, Farnsworth House, Plano, Illinois, 1945–51*

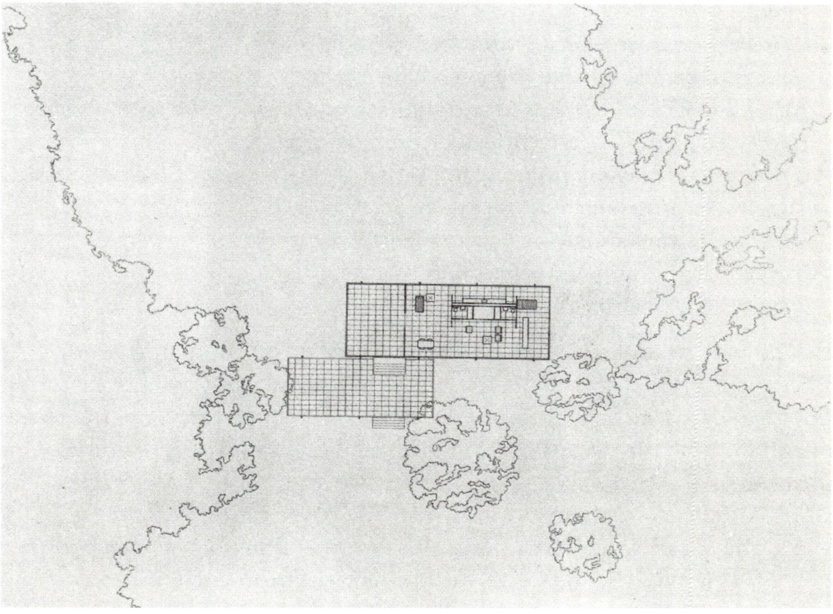

58 *Mies van der Rohe, Farnsworth House plan*

The house, with its open plan, glass walls and free-standing partitions, was as pure an exercise in architectural minimalism as Mies could have hoped for; he would later cite the fact that it was intended for a single person as a significant opportunity because programmatic concerns intruded so little in his thinking.[10] As the architectural historian Fritz Neumeyer has shown, Mies's work was shaped by philosophical concerns, in particular a search for architectural order and "truth" based on rational principles of design. His goal was to develop a language of form which reflected universal, rather than particular, aspects of human activity and concern.[11] Thus, while Farnsworth may have been, for Mies, an entertaining companion and a committed partisan, as a client she represented a means to an architectural end. Just as the Barcelona Pavilion, designed with no other function than to provide the King and Queen of Spain with a place in which to sign a guestbook, receive guests and drink champagne, was the perfect vehicle for Mies's thinking in 1929, so the Farnsworth House was to be a pure expression of ideas developed in his later career.

In his inaugural speech as Director of the Department of Architecture at Armour Institute on 20 November 1938, Mies made his views on architecture clear in his characteristically terse, aphoristic manner:

> The long path from material through purpose to creative
> work had only a single goal:
> to create order out of the godforsaken confusion of our
> time.
> But we want an order that gives to each thing its
> proper place, and we want to give each thing what is
> suitable to its nature.
> We would do this so perfectly that the world of our
> creations will blossom from within.
> More we do not want; more we cannot do.
> Nothing can unlock the aim and meaning of our work
> better than the profound words of St Augustine:
> "Beauty is the radiance of truth."[12]

Beauty was produced by plumbing the depths of the natural order. At Plano, the immediacy of nature at the riverbank site would permit an unprecedented closeness with the work of architecture and the interpenetration of the two. Mies was quite clear about how this might work in the case of the Farnsworth House. Farnsworth recalled that on one occasion, as the two of them stood by the Fox River on one of their Sunday visits, she asked what sort of materials he was thinking of using for her house. He replied that he wouldn't approach the problem in that way:

> I would think that here where everything is beautiful, and privacy is no issue, it would be a pity to erect an opaque wall between the outside and the inside. So I think we should build the house of steel and glass; in that way we'll let the outside in. If we were building in the city or in the suburbs, on the other hand, I would make it opaque from outside and bring in the light through a garden-courtyard in the middle.[13]

This statement, with its emphasis on the view of natural beauty from inside of the house, reveals an approach which was new to Mies and peculiar to his work in America. As in the project for the Resor House (1938) in Jackson Hole, Wyoming, which Mies represented with a photo montage showing a view of the Rocky Mountains through the living room windows, Mies's thinking for the Farnsworth House rested on a concept of uninhabited open landscape; the issue of privacy, of being seen from outside, was not considered. In European projects of the late 1920s and 1930s, by contrast, Mies explored the relationship between the glass curtain wall and the courtyard plan, most significantly in the Nolde House (1929), the House at the Berlin Building Exposition (1931), the Gericke (1932) and Hubbe (1935) Houses.[14] Mies's approach to the Hubbe House is particularly revealing since it was to be occupied by a single woman. His concern for the client's privacy offers a striking contrast to the Farnsworth House:

> Though she was going to be living in the house alone, she wanted to be able to maintain casual life and hospitality. The inner arrangement of the house is designed for this purpose as well, once again offering the necessary privacy in conjunction with the fullest freedom of open spaces.[15]

The Farnsworth House represented a radical departure from this view of the domestic environment. Issues of privacy, of sexuality and social life were repressed; for Mies, the house was a place for contemplation, an ordered place free of distractions. Speaking to an interviewer in 1959, he said that he felt the house had been misunderstood:

> I was in the house from morning to evening. I did not know how colourful nature really was. But you have to be careful inside to use neutral colours, because you have the colours outside. These absolutely change and I would say it is beautiful.[16]

In conversation with Christian Norberg-Schulz in 1958 Mies elaborated:

> Nature, too, shall have its own life. We must beware not to disrupt it with the color of our houses and interior fittings. Yet we should attempt to bring nature, houses and human beings together into a higher unity. If you view nature through the glass walls of the Farnsworth House, it gains a more profound significance than if viewed from outside. This way more is said about nature – it becomes a part of the larger whole.[17]

By the late 1940s, Mies believed in his architecture's ability not only to transcend nature but also to provide a framework for interpretation, a screen through which to look and understand. If Edith Farnsworth agreed in principle – or hoped she did, in the early days – it is clear that, for her, a great deal was lost in the translation from the model to the house in which she was supposed to live.

Relations between Mies and Farnsworth had begun to cool by the time construction was started in the summer of 1949: the two socialized together less, and Edith spent less time at the office. The reasons for this remain unclear, but the situation deteriorated as problems with the building became evident. When Farnsworth moved in in December 1950, the roof leaked badly and the heating system produced a film which collected on the inside of the windows. A local plumber, seeing that the systems were all gathered together in one inaccessible stack, suggested the house be named "My Mies-conception." The electrician advised that the entire system be redone. Nevertheless, according to Mies's office notes, he and Farnsworth were "still on good terms in February 1951."[18]

The final rupture was precipitated by disagreements over money.[19] With costs mounting to almost twice the original estimate of $40,000 (already a high figure considering that a house in a suburban development such as Levittown could be bought in 1950 for less than one quarter the price) and under pressure from family and friends, Farnsworth began to voice some of her concerns about the unconventional design and construction methods. Mies reportedly told her "to stick to her nephritis."[20] To add insult to injury, Mies seems to have decided at this point to charge a fee for his services, something that Farnsworth claimed had never been discussed and which members of the office later asserted he never planned to do; this was especially galling as Farnsworth had acted as his physician without fee.[21]

Having spent nearly $74,000, Farnsworth refused to pay any more bills or to take delivery of the furniture. She and Mies stopped speaking altogether. Fearing that Mies never really wanted "a friend and a collaborator . . . but a dupe and a victim," Farnsworth wrote a letter dated 1 March 1951 in which she informed him that she was turning the matter over to her lawyer. In July, Mies sued for the outstanding balance of $3,673.09. He also claimed he was owed fees of $15,000 and $12,000 for architect's and supervisory services. Farnsworth filed a counter claim in October 1951 which accused him of fraud, alleging that he had falsely represented himself as "a skilled, proficient and experienced architect," and demanding the return of $33,872.10, the amount she had paid to date above the original estimate.[22]

After a trial that dragged on until June 1953, Mies was awarded $14,000; Farnsworth's lawyers appealed, and the matter was finally settled out of court on 11 May 1956. But the most important battle was not fought in the courtroom, but in the press. Once the case was brought to the attention of the public, the architect and his costly building were treated with incredulity and derision. Farnsworth too was ridiculed. To her horror, crowds of people came on weekends to look at the house "reputed to be the only one of its kind" but in reality "a one-room, one story structure with flat roof and glass and steel outer walls."[23] She writes that she found it

> hard to bear the insolence and boorishness of those who invaded the solitude of my shore and my home . . . flowers brought in to heal the scars of the building were crushed by those boots beneath the noses pressed against the glass.[24]

Disdainful of the public yet furious at Mies, Farnsworth made statements in the press which fueled the public's curiosity and provided anti-modernist design journalists with the ammunition they needed. In an article by Elizabeth Gordon entitled "The Threat to the Next America," published in *House Beautiful* in April 1953, the author used her case as a starting point for a far-reaching denunciation of modernism:

> I have talked to a highly intelligent, now disillusioned woman who spent more than $70,000 building a 1-room house that is nothing but a glass cage on stilts . . . There is a well-established movement in modern architecture, decorating and furnishings which is promoting the mystical idea that "less is more" . . . they are promoting unlivability, stripped-down emptiness, lack of storage space and therefore lack of possessions . . .

Gordon pointed to "a self-chosen elite who are trying to tell us what we should like and how we should live." For her, such architectural totalitarianism and the denial of American consumerism paved the way for fascism:

> For if we can be sold on accepting dictators in matters of taste and how our homes are to be ordered, our minds are certainly well prepared to accept dictators in other departments of life. The undermining of people's confidence is the beginning of the end . . . So, you see, this well-developed movement has social implications because it affects the heart of our society – the home. Beyond the nonsense of trying to make us want to give up our technical aids and conveniences for what is *supposed* to be a better and more serene life, there is a social threat of regimentation and total control.
>
> Does it work? The much touted all-glass cube of International Style architecture is perhaps the most unlivable type of home for man since he descended from the tree and entered a cave. You burn up in the summer and freeze in the winter, because nothing must interefere with the "pure" form of their rectangles – no overhanging roofs to shade you from the sun; the bare minimum of gadgets and possessions so as not to spoil the "clean" look; three or four pieces of furniture placed along arbitrary pre-ordained lines; room for only a few books and one painting at precise and permanent points; no children, no dogs, extremely meager kitchen facilities – nothing human that might disturb the architect's composition.[25]

The following month, another author weighed in in the same magazine with a "Report on the American Battle between Good and Bad Modern Houses." Here too Farnsworth played a role. Citing the many rave reviews of the house in such journals as *Architectural Forum*, and *House and Garden*, the author asks "How about Dr Farnsworth herself on the subject of her house?":

> "Do I feel implacable calm?" she repeated. "The truth is that in this house with its four walls of glass I feel like a prowling animal, always on the alert. I am always restless. Even in the evening. I feel like a sentinel on guard day and night. I can rarely stretch out and relax . . .
>
> What else? I don't keep a garbage can under my sink. Do you know why? Because you can see the whole "kitchen' from the road on the way in here and the can would spoil the appearance of the whole house. So I hide it in the closet farther down from the sink. Mies talks about "free space": but his space is very fixed. I can't even put a clothes hanger in my house without considering how it affects everything from the outside. Any arrangement of furniture becomes a major problem, because the house is transparent, like an X-ray.[26]

While it is unlikely that these concerns were as grievous as Farnsworth made them sound in the thick of combat with Mies – she did, after all, remain in the house for over twenty years – they nonetheless contain critical indices for the meaning of the building in its time and place. Concerns over family, gender and the control of appearances, particularly in the domestic environment, loom large. Much of what was said against the house and modern architecture generally focuses on its disruption of the typology of the family home (children, dogs, ample kitchens, numerous possessions), and the vulnerability of its occupant to the prying eyes of others. Farnsworth complained more than once, in her *Memoirs* and to the press, about the problem of being looked at by people both inside and outside her home. In an interview published by *Newsweek*, 8 June 1953, she complained that Mies had wanted to build the interior partitions five feet high "for reasons of art and proportion" but that she had objected:

> "I'm six feet tall," she said, "and I wanted to be able to change my clothes without my head looking like it was wandering over the top of the partition without a body."[27]

The way the house acted as a stage for Farnsworth's single life and her middle-aged woman's body struck at the heart of American anxiety. As Lynn Spigel has shown, the popularity of television in the USA in the 1950s stemmed in part from American preoccupations with privacy, consumerism and family life. Through its ability to provide a close-up look at other people's lives and homes, television filled a need to know and compare, which was fueled by the ever-present lure of the marketplace through

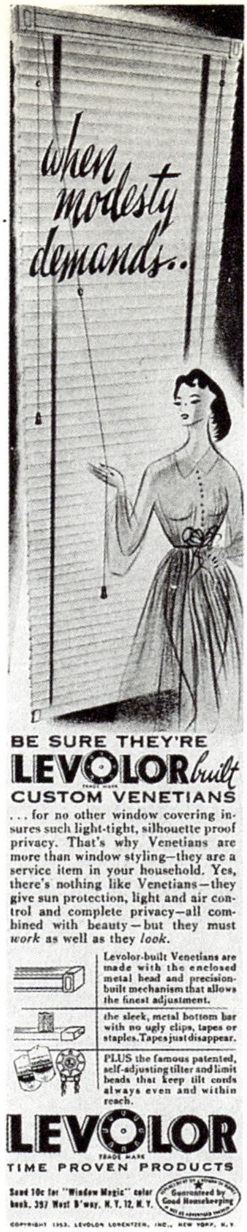

59 *"When Modesty Demands", an advertisement for Levelor Blinds, from* House Beautiful, *May 1953*

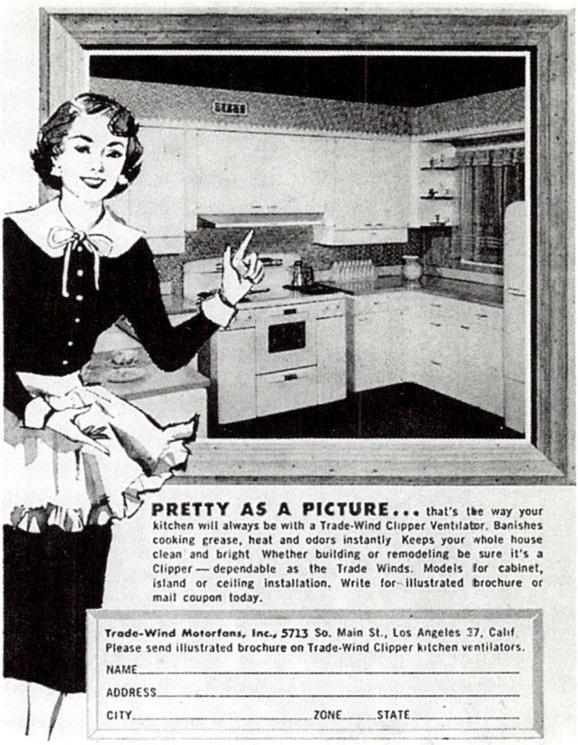

60 *"Pretty as a Picture", an advertisement for Trade-wind Motorfans, from* House Beautiful, *May 1953*

advertising. Moreover, television, like the picture window itself, blurred the distinction between public and private realms and problematized the very act of looking, particularly at women.[28] In this cultural climate, Farnsworth's insecurities found wide and attentive audience. Even the ads that appeared next to the article in the May issue of *House Beautiful* harped on this theme, showing women as the guardians of home and interior privacy, displaying their clean, modern kitchens which were "as pretty as a picture" thanks to modern ventilation systems, but having to draw the Levolor venetian blinds "when modesty demands."

Gendered language pervades Farnsworth's own expression of her doubts about the workability of the house. She complained that it had two bathrooms – including one for guests – but no bedroom. Guests would be expected to sleep on the sofa or on a mattress on the floor. While Mies may have seen this arrangement as liberating, for Farnsworth, the real-life occupant of the house, it was embarrassing. She complained that she and her guests would "inhabit a sort of three-dimensional sketch, I in my 'sleeping space' and he in *his* – unless sheer discomfort and depression should drive us together" [my italics].[29] In a house for a single woman, such an arrangement in fact represents a repressed rather than a freed sexuality, just as the doubling of the bathrooms suggests both social "propriety" (of a kind Farnsworth was ambivalent about, to say the least) and a desire to hide the female body and its functions. Despite pronouncements about freedom, Mies let it be known that the provision of a "guest bathroom" at the Farnsworth House was meant to keep visitors from "seeing Edith's nightgown on the back of the bathroom door."[30] Ultimately, this piece of women's clothing, this emblem of femaleness, sexuality and of the body, had to be hidden away precisely because it served as a reminder of the very things that Mies (and mainstream culture generally) wanted to efface in the identity of the middle-aged single woman. To display the nightgown was immodest and unfeminine, a disruption of the image of disembodied rationality that the interior arrangement so emphatically suggests.

The choice of furnishings also caused friction between architect and client, and here again the conflict raised broader issues concerning domesticity and gender. Mies's ideas about interior design are summarized by the poster for the Werkbund Exhibition on the Home, held in Stuttgart in 1927; here, in response to the question "how to live" (wie wohnen?), a large red "x" cuts across the image of a Victorian interior. As a number of writers have suggested, this aspect of Modernism cut to the heart not only of consumer culture generally but also of the means by which bourgeois women constructed identity and memory in the late nineteenth and twentieth centuries.[31] Given the close association of femininity and furnishings in the home, whether in the 1880s or the 1950s, Mies's repression of the domestic object appears, again, as a repression of women. As a single woman, and as a member of the American upper class, Farnsworth took the threat to the heirlooms and personal mementos in her home very seriously, and she had strong feelings about how what her house would say about her as a woman. She "could never consent to Mies's furnishing ideas," she wrote in her *Memoirs*. Apparently Mies had planned to put pink suede Barcelona chairs in her house and these, she claimed, would not only be too heavy but would "make the house look like a Helena Rubenstein studio."[32] Besides, she commented, "There is already the local rumor that its a tuberculosis sanitarium." As snapshots taken in the 1960s show, her own ideas about furnishing the house favored heirloom "antique" chairs in

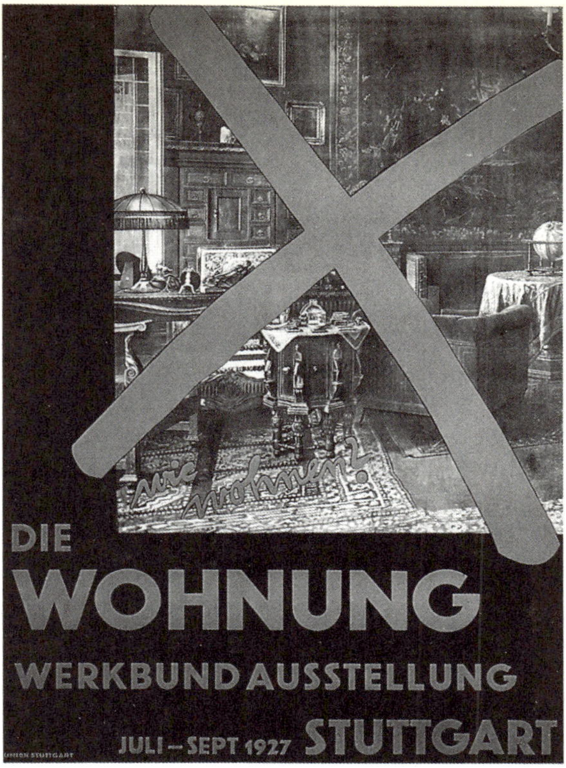

61 *Willi Baumeister,* Wie Wohnen? Die Wohnung Werkbund Ausstellung *(How to Live? The Dwelling Werkbund Exhibition), 1927.*

the dining-room and fu dogs on the terrace, suggesting continuity, American tradition and upper-class sophistication.

The severity of Mies's vision at the Farnsworth House is brought into sharp focus by comments made in 1931 by another Mies client, Grete Tugendhat, in response to a critique of her home by a critic of Mies. Replying to the question "Is it possible to live in the Tugendhat House?", she calls the spaces of the house "austere and grand":

> This austerity forbids merely passing time by "relaxing" and letting oneself go – and it is precisely this being forced to do something else that today's people, exhausted and drained by their professional work, require and sense as a liberation. For just as one sees each flower in this room in quite an uncommon way, and every piece of art seems more expressive (for example, a piece of sculpture standing in front of the onyx wall), so too a person appears, both to himself and to others, to be more clearly set off from his surroundings.[33]

Two points stand out in this statement. First, in the Tugendhat House, as in every other house by Mies, rich materials, colors, and works of sculpture play a defining role in the interior scheme in a way which is denied in the Farnsworth House; in Mies's idea of the Farnsworth House, the occupant, a surrogate for Mies himself, would focus on nature, not on objects in the home, just as Mies himself had done. Second, the experience of being "set off" from one's surroundings by an architectural stage was, at the Farnsworth House, inescapable; this was precisely what Farnsworth so resented. Neither at the Tugendhat House, nor at Philip Johnson's Glass House of 1949 in New Canaan, Connecticut (a work to which the Farnsworth House is frequently compared), was the rule of order so rigidly enforced or the gaze of the outsider so unrelenting. Socially, both the married Frau Tugendhat and the bachelor Philip Johnson were far more acceptable than Edith Farnsworth. And both were provided with enclosed places to enact their private lives: even Johnson's "Glass House," located on a remote estate surrounded by private property, was paired with an enclosed and almost windowless "Guest House" furnished in seductive pillows and soft fabrics. In Mies's view, it seems, the only part of Farnsworth's "private life" as a single woman that could possibly be worth hiding was her nightgown.

In the end, Farnsworth gave up the struggle, but she fought a good fight. She spent nearly twenty years in the glass house, working to make it a home; she battled Mies in court and in the press. Having sold the house and moved to Italy in the early 1970s, she looked back on the experience with bitterness. She had been for too long the object of other people's curiosity, too long a non-conformist. Now she wanted nothing more than to become invisible:

> Now I would prefer to move as the women do in the Old Quarter of Tripoli, muffled in unbleached homespun so that only a hole is left for them to look out of.

Best of all, she said, the world outside would not even know where the hole was.[34]

13

Robert Rauschenberg's Fabrics: Reconstructing Domestic Space

LISA WAINWRIGHT

When the American artist Robert Rauschenberg began to incorporate found materials into his canvases of the early 1950s, he challenged the stylistic hegemony of the Abstract Expressionists. Although scholars quickly marked Rauschenberg's move as a decisive moment in the history of post-war art, the artist had not abandoned the New York School's enterprise of exploring self in the moment of artistic process, he had simply shifted media. Equipped with the limitless bric-à-brac of consumer culture as his palette and informed by the spontaneity of Abstract Expressionism, Rauschenberg continued to create subjective content through acts of free-association.

If, then, it seems worthwhile to revisit Rauschenberg's work with Abstract Expressionism in mind, it is equally useful to explore just how the artist customized the New York School agenda. Pollock's flinging about of paint as a heroic means of asserting identity is clearly different from Rauschenberg's operation of collecting stuff as a means of constructing a personal narrative.[1] While Pollock indexed canvases with relentless sweeps of big painted marks, Rauschenberg carefully pieced together such items as old photographs, doilies, postcards, taxidermied barnyard pets, letters, newspaper clippings, and an array of cloth material. Rauschenberg's need to recreate self in the act of making art was informed by Abstract Expressionism, but his passion for using diaristic memorabilia as part of this process was of an entirely different sensibility. Indeed, collaging things from the everyday world afforded a much stranger result than painting on canvas, for Rauschenberg rendered his found objects uncanny by moving them into the artistic frame where they became both familiar (as recognizable objects) and unfamiliar (as ascribed with new meanings due to different contexts and in relation to other disparate objects). Caught between the *heimlich* and the *unheimlich*, Rauschenberg's combines became testament to a kind of intellectual and psychological restlessness, a condition facilitated by the collage technique he so often described as functioning in that uncertain "gap between art and life."[2] Although, like the Abstract Expressionists, Rauschenberg sought a subjective encounter through art-making, he relied on the materials of objective reality as a means of configuring this subjectivity.

While recent scholarship on Rauschenberg has attempted to reveal his thinking and pin down underlying themes in the work, for years scholars reveled in what they perceived as the absence of authorial presence in Rauschenberg's wide-open imaging. Art history canonized him at the threshold of Pop, describing his densely packed works as a testament to the dizzying effects of the mass media. Along with the look of his objects, which included such Pop tokens as Coke bottles and comic strips, it was Rauschenberg's social swing away from the Abstract Expressionist camp towards the group of painters, sculptors, musicians, dancers, and writers surrounding the composer John Cage that seemed to secure the context for future discussion of his work.

The artists in the Cage circle explored phenomena from the vernacular world – found sound for their music, discarded materials for their art and prosaic movement for their dance. Unlike the Abstract Expressionists who sought to generate content from a psychic excavation of the interior self, these young artists abandoned what they perceived as egocentric control in favor of random reorientations of data. Subsequently, early Rauschenberg scholars relied on this history. "There are no secret messages in Rauschenberg," Alan Solomon declared on the occasion of the artist's first retrospective at the Jewish Museum in New York in 1963, "no program of social or political discontent transmitted in code, no hidden rhetorical commentary on the larger meaning of Life or Art, no private symbolism available only to the initiate." Dean Swanson in the 1965 catalogue for the Walker Art Center's Rauschenberg exhibition wrote, "By incorporating actual fragments of reality in his paintings, Rauschenberg suggests that he is not solely responsible for the character of his work: he is, rather, a contributor in partnership with objects selected from life." And in the catalogue accompanying the major Rauschenberg retrospective at the National Collection of Fine Arts in 1977, both Joshua Taylor and Lawrence Alloway dismissed the notion that the artist's pictures admitted specific readings. On locating meaning, Alloway cautioned that one should not "expect that any given object in a combine-painting can be accounted for in terms of all the other parts. It is improbable that any single program will be supported by all the local bits."[3]

In this thematic brush-off by scholars and critics, one series of work was excepted. The use of fabric in Rauschenberg's art between 1953 and 1956 suggested to many a domestic trace. Alan Solomon readjusted his position in writing about *Charlene* of 1954: "The color reproductions in Charlene might be found on a parlor wall in Port Arthur [The Texas town that was Rauschenberg's childhood home]: the patches of cloth used for collage recall the country kitchen and attic, fabrics which might be used for house

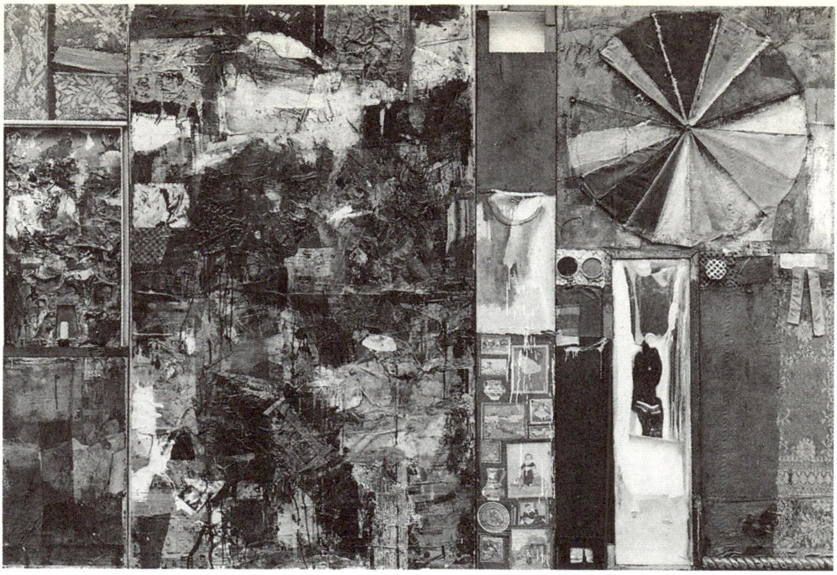

62 *Robert Rauschenberg,* Charlene, *1954*

dresses or curtains, doilies, lace, or India prints." Andrew Forge also saw in the material "a domestic and retrospective ring," as did Brian O'Doherty who felt it evoked the "sense of a diary." Even the artist admitted to the "souvenir quality" of the work, commenting on its "nostalgia," which he would later try to eliminate. While Rauschenberg scholars located a domestic theme in the telltale fabric signs, they failed to interrogate his domestic paradigm, and they ignored the significance of why Rauschenberg might have referred to domesticity at the height of Abstract Expressionism's bravura posturing.[4]

Rauschenberg began making art in the 1940s, early on introducing many of his mature themes and experimenting with a wide range of media, but his sustained use of fabrics began with the so-called red paintings of 1953–54. Although he had for some time been intermittently experimenting with collage, in these pictures he concentrated on it, and the interest finally culminated in the combines of the late 1950s. In the red paintings, rich red pigment threads around, serves as counterpoint, or at other moments obfuscates the fabrics, newspapers, photos, and other motley scraps building up the surface. It is, however, the worn fabrics that dominate. They seem stripped from the decor of an old home and reek with the nostalgia of attic trunks or family scrapbooks. The fragmentary and tattered look of the material, albeit organized in a gridlike composition, suggests time passed, yet such nostalgia is distanced by the evident insistence of the work as an artistic construction. The red paintings are ultimately not the stuff from the attic trunk, but an arranged sign for such paraphernalia.

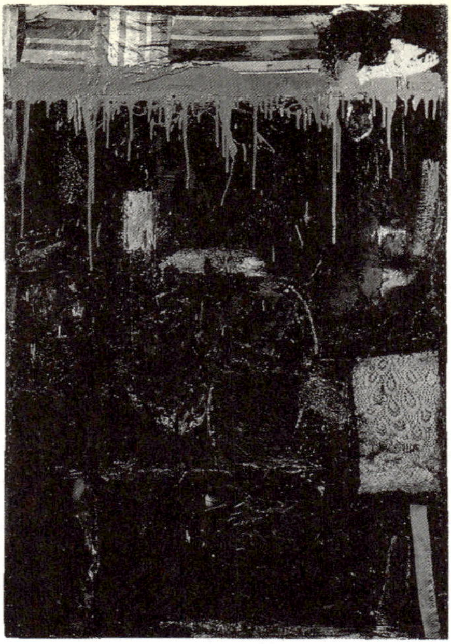

63 *Robert Rauschenberg,* Untitled (Red Painting), *1953*

In *Yoicks* (1953), Rauschenberg applied strips of polka-dotted mattress ticking in horizontal bands across the enormous canvas, punctuating the severe structure with bits of paper and dripping paint. When Walter Hopps described the fabric facade of *Yoicks* as conjuring up associations with "bedspreads," he touched on the work's domestic theme.[5] Included in the grid of fabric swatches in an *Untitled* piece, also from 1953, are two overtly homey scraps: at the lower right a bit of lace curtains seemingly borrowed from grandmother's parlor, and at the top edge of the composition a striped, tablecloth remnant perhaps removed from her kitchenette. The titles *Red Interior* (1954) and *Interior* (1956) again evoke domestic spaces, a suggestion confirmed by the sheer profusion of old fabrics and rich velvet squares in *Red Interior*, and the ornamental wall molding and man's hat, hung as if in a front hall entryway, in *Interior. Untitled [with shelf and colored glass light box]* (1953), which includes a shelf at its base and a stained-glass window (lit from behind) affixed to the top, hints of old Victorian homesteads. The floral motif of the illuminated decorative window complements the opulent but worn pattern of fabric and miscellaneous scraps of the central panel below. The piece evokes the same wistful domesticity as in *Red Interior* or *Interior*, although again the domestic sentiment, as it is conveyed through the piecemeal method of collage, reads as arbitrary construct.

Rauschenberg seems to have employed fabrics and nostalgic tokens to signal a comforting, domestic theme at a period in his life fraught with personal and professional insecurity. In the early 1950s, he had recently become a father and recently been divorced, he was out of cash and trying to maneuver a radically new aesthetic through the New York art world, and he was in his late twenties and discovering his homosexuality.[6] Rauschenberg seemed to reach back into childhood while piecing together his fabric façades to help him reconstruct another domestic space in which safely to discover who he had become and who he was becoming.

On a formal level, however, Rauschenberg's use of fabric contributed to a keen interest in dismantling the hierarchical ordering of high and low imagery. Comic strips, political posters, paint, magazine clippings, newspapers, reproductions of the work of the old masters, and fabrics function as equal and complementary signs in his pictorial fields. By introducing this wide range of material, Rauschenberg can be seen as reassessing a principal aspect of the modernist paradigm. Utopic painting driven by a singular vision of truth – that battleground of the avant-garde – no longer interested an artist energized by the pervasive melodrama of mass culture.

As a means of "moving out from Abstract Expressionism,"[7] a statement he claimed to have uttered each day before he started working, Rauschenberg turned to certain found materials as a way around a highly entrenched tradition. By turning his back on pure painting and soiling his canvases with junk, Rauschenberg began to disobey his "fathers." Using fabric only exacerbated the disrespect. Against the heavy weight of high culture, high modernism, and its attendant high masculinity (so perfectly incarnate in the well-known macho antics of the Abstract Expressionist men), Rauschenberg posed an alternative aesthetic some commentators identified as proto-feminist, and others underscored as gay.

To work with fabric in the 1950s carried important implications, for cloth was read as a gendered medium. Fabrics relate to the home: to curtains, clothing, and bedspreads and so cloth evokes the gender-assigned characteristics of domesticity and comfort. For artist Miriam Schapiro (discussed in the final essay in this collection), cloth signifies a feminine aesthetic as it belongs to the long-standing tradition of women's quilt-making. And while Schapiro has praised Rauschenberg's collages as "proto-feminist" for their featured use of cloth,[8] it might be more accurate to say that in fabric, Rauschenberg found a readymade sign for the familiar or *heimlich*. It was not a raw canvas Rauschenberg approached on which to enact an existential moment of heroic self-realization like Pollock or De Kooning, but rather a vaguely familiar collection of things he reoriented in intimate gestures of self-expression. He was taking care of home instead of going out exploring – he was drawn to associations of mother, not father.

Walter Hopps traced Rauschenberg's process of collecting memorabilia

– "taking care of home" – back to Rauschenberg's childhood, where the subject matter also originates. Hopps reported that Rauschenberg as a child built a small sanctuary with compartments where "he collected and arranged a great miscellany of things that were meaningful to him, obsessively adding jars and boxes and all sorts of found specimens such as rocks, plants, insects, and small animals. Using magazines or any printed matter, he drew, traced, copied, cut out, pinned up, and glued together images . . . which anticipated the physical and aesthetic form and complex juxtapositions of his future oeuvre."[9]

Charlene of 1953 and *Collection* of 1954 (whose title recalls Rauschenberg's childhood preoccupation), were the largest works of the mid-1950s and the culminating examples from the red series. *Collection* is just that: an assemblage of comic strips, art reproductions, newspaper advertisements, paint, and rich fabrics, whose general content seems like the accumulated junk of an overturned dresser drawer. The fabric and other found objects suggest a domestic theme, an implication reinforced by the inclusion at the center of the composition of an old photograph of a prim woman with a high collar and hair gathered neatly in a bun. Surrounded by memorabilia and positioned as a central icon, here emerges that protecting mother in her domestic realm who was merely implied in the fabric surfaces of related work.[10]

Charlene is even more chaotically structured than *Collection*, but it too highlights a photograph at its center: a face peering out from a patched surface of such items as torn clothing, newspapers, an image of the Statue of Liberty, embroidery samples, fine art reproductions, fabrics, paper, and thick impasto. The presence of a flattened umbrella at the upper right of the composition suggested to Andrew Forge "nothing if not an image of shelter," thus linking the work with the other combines referring to domestic space.[11] In both *Charlene* and *Collection*, however, the domestic pieces are still made vaguely strange, as they hover in relation to adjacent objects with other meanings.

Rauschenberg's use of rich material in the red paintings evokes an intimacy similar to that of the often psychologically charged domestic spaces depicted, at the turn of the century, by Bonnard and Vuillard. Indeed, Rauschenberg may have been directly influenced by the renewed interest in the Nabis around 1950. Irving Sandler has noted the influence on 1950s' art of Bonnard, Vuillard, Renoir, Soutine, Matisse, and the Fauves, most of whom were shown in depth in New York in 1950 and 1951. Sandler also makes the point that this second generation of gesture painters increasingly looked to art history as "a substitute for nature."[12] Rauschenberg's strangely familiar patterning, determined by appropriating from culture rather than nature, found company in the burgeoning second generation aesthetic.

After the red period, Rauschenberg expanded his palette of junk. The fabrics became easier to read as he shifted towards maintaining the integrity of his collaged materials. *Hymnal* and *Levee*, both works from this new period, follow the axial organization of the red paintings and include large squares of fabric as backdrops or components of a surface collage made up of more legible props. Although the collaged items are drawn from various realms – a Manhattan telephone directory and a graffitied valentine in *Hymnal*; a man's necktie, a Lucas Cranach portrait, and a diagram in *Levee* – paisley fabric backgrounds conjure up old-fashioned sitting-rooms where things are dark and worn, but somehow also familiar and reassuring.[13]

In this period, Rauschenberg's most aggressive use of fabric as a sign for comfort, security and domesticity occurred in a piece he constructed out of wildly painting on a pillow, sheet, and patchwork quilt. About *Bed* of 1955 70
he wrote,

> It wasn't programmed to be a bed painting. I was simply using the patterns that were already in the quilt as some sort of a challenge or threat – seeing what would happen working against or with them, and I wasn't doing very well. The quilt had so many nostalgic connotations that it remained much more direct than any of my actions so I thought the only thing to do is go along with that. So I added a pillow.[14]

Years later, he told Barbara Rose that,

> No matter how much paint I put on it, it just wouldn't seem like anything but a quilt to me. I had lots of exposure to quilts. I learned to crawl under my mothers' quilting table at "bees." . . . I loved crawling under the quilts. They were like big, beautiful tents.[15]

Rauschenberg connected the quilt in *Bed*, and by extension, his use of fabrics, with a memory of familiar shelter – a space formed beneath the canopy of his mother's quilt. *Bed*, like the other fabric works of the period, became redolent of domesticity and home. Indeed, the critic James Leggio went so far as to see *Bed*, with its "expelled" paint marks concentrated around the opening of the sheets at the top of the quilt, as a "tightly wrapped, womb-like enclosure, . . . alluding to childbirth."[16] Elaborating on the idea of domestic shelter both implied in the work's materials and made explicit by the artist's own commentary, Leggio's reading of an "abstracted womb" offers the ultimate contextualization of Rauschenberg's work in the realm of women's experience; and this would be a far cry from the dominant Abstract Expressionist mode.

Curiously, out of the gendered comfort seemingly evoked by the fabric material of *Bed* emerges a conflicted sense of the domestic. Again, those objects which appear to signal the familiar (mother's quilt) also issue the unfamiliar (the quilt now mutilated by an array of painted marks).

Prompted by the frenzied painting on top of the quilt, Alan Solomon remarked:

> How are our responses to the familiar and comfortable altered by the introduction of ominous and enigmatic associations? The thousand comforts of a patchwork counterpane (grandma, home, childhood, order) give way to the horror (joy?) of corruption (enrichment?) by paint (blood?), producing Exhibit A, an arena of violence (what crimes, what unconscious feelings, what essential disorder?)[17]

Solomon identifies a strange ambiguity built into Rauschenberg's principal domestic icon. On the one hand, the artist wished to conjure up comforting feelings about home. On the other hand, the sweet subject of domesticity was loaded with contradiction. "I have some bad feelings about Texas," Rauschenberg explained. "There's a lot of sadness about Port Arthur. And I had a terrible time in school. I didn't particularly have a celebrated childhood there."[18] Rauschenberg is left, then, with a profound anxiety about domesticity, an uneasiness which plays itself out through the conceptual indeterminacy of the props he continuously recontextualizes within his work.

It was Rauschenberg's relationship with his father that proved most difficult. He told Walter Hopps that his father was "physically violent, abusive and alcoholic," and in conversation with Jill Johnston in 1990, he repeated his father's dying words: "I never did like you, you son of a bitch." Altercations between father and son were evidently numerous. Ernest Rauschenberg was an avid hunter, for example, and gained a state-wide reputation as an accomplished bird-dog breeder; but Robert was a bad sportsman due to his nearsightedness, and found killing animals revolting (he was expelled from college for refusing to dissect a live frog). The characters of the two men were so fundamentally at odds, that Rauschenberg, named after his father, Ernest Milton, dropped his childhood name in 1947, in an effort in reinvent himself free of paternal identity.[19]

Rauschenberg may have collaged fabric and other autobiographic notes onto his pictures to rekindle childhood memories, but it was to reclaim a safe domestic space absent the father. In the very act of calling forth memories of childhood through fabric signs and other personal memorabilia, Rauschenberg attempted to design a narrative more suited to his needs. This desire to reconstitute his own sense of "home" became even more pronounced as Rauschenberg began to explore his homosexuality. Attempting to wed his gayness to concepts of domesticity only furthered the *unheimlich* effect of his work, a struggle already present as a result of his personal psychodrama about childhood and father. Even in *Bed*, the strangeness of the quilt's simultaneous exegesis of comfort and discomfort might derive from its commingling of domestic props with allusions to gay

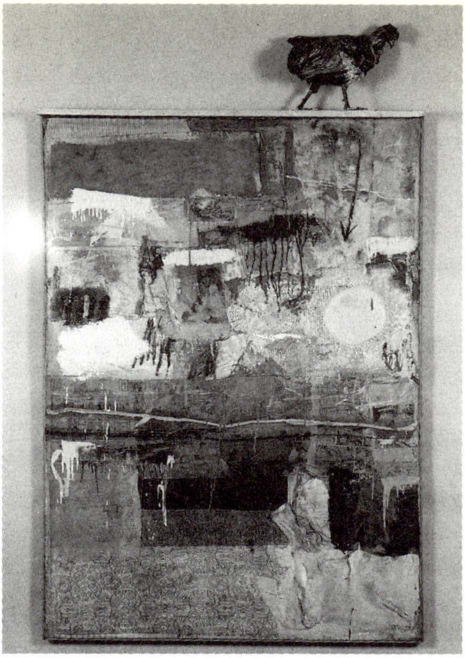

64 *Robert Rauschenberg,* Satellite, *1955*

sex. Rauschenberg constructed *Bed* after he moved in with Johns in 1955 and the work is sometimes read as a testament to their blossoming sexual relationship. If this is so, then memories of childhood signaled by *Bed*'s quilt conjoin with the experience of homosexuality, and like having sex on your mother's sofa, the gesture is loaded with apprehension.

There are several works from the 1950s where Rauschenberg brings together homosexual signs and "nostalgic" references to the domestic. The cluttered surface of *Satellite* (1956), for example, recalls the dense façades of *Charlene* and *Collection* completed the year before. Wallpaper patterns, crocheted doilies, old photographs, and an odd assortment of flowered fabrics signal the domestic, but a pin-up girl and messily arranged articles of clothing – including white tube socks – suggest an erotic edge.[20]

Rauschenberg frequently employed athletic socks in such works as the free-standing combine *Untitled* (1955) from the Panza Collection at MoCA, Los Angeles, *Forge* (1959), and *Slug* (1961). Art historian Neal Printz inter- 65
preted the sock motif's symbolism for Walter Hopps, explaining that these particular kinds of socks were sexual tokens within gay culture, functioning as fetish objects analogous to women's stockings in heterosexual ritual.[21] In his painting *Domestic Scene, Los Angeles* of 1963 (illustrated in Kenneth Silver's essay), for example, David Hockney depicted a gay couple's bathing scene, in which a nude man showering is assisted by his companion dressed

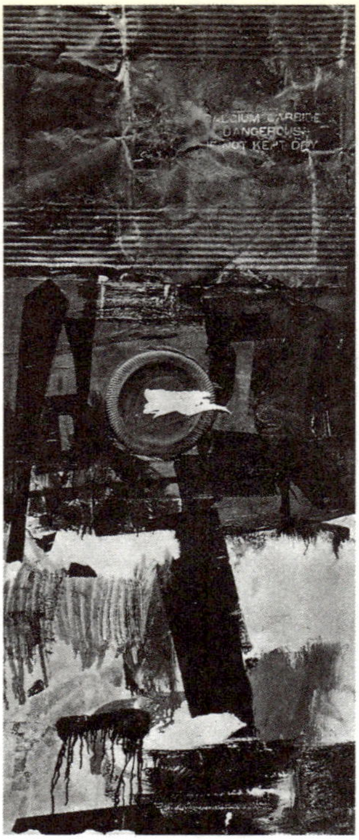

65 *Robert Rauschenberg,* Forge, *1959*

only in a frilly apron and athletic socks. Or in a more recent example, on the cover of a soft-core, gay video on foot fetishes, a caption reads, "Plenty of white sox [sic], clean, dirty and best of all, coming off to reveal stud feet underneath."[22]

In *Satellite,* Rauschenberg arranged the pair of athletic socks such that they seem animistically to embrace, echoing the pose of the couple juxtaposed in a photograph to their upper right. *Satellite*'s erotic signs are set against a backdrop of domestic familiarity so that Rauschenberg seems to reveal himself to mother, broaching the subject of sexuality within the domestic frame. He could here reminisce about childhood in the context of revealing his sexualized self.

In her book, *On Longing: Narratives of the Miniature, the Gigantic, the Souvenir, the Collection*, Susan Stewart explains that souvenirs of childhood, and really all souvenirs, function to retrieve a lost past, and yet this past is always ultimately contrived and thus negotiable. She writes,

> The souvenir must be removed from its context in order to serve as a trace of it, but it must also be restored through narrative and/or reverie. What it is restored to is not an "authentic," that is, a native, context of origin but an imaginary context of origin whose chief subject is a projection of the possessor's child-

> hood. Restoration can be seen as a response to an unsatisfactory set of present conditions . . . We thus might say that all souvenirs are souvenirs of a nature which has been invented by ideology.[23]

The accumulation of stuff in the Panza Collection's *Untitled* functions in the way Stewart describes: "Once the object is completely severed from its origin, it is possible to generate a new series, to start again within a context that is framed by the selectivity of the collector . . ."[24] In Stewart's terms, then, the familiar props in *Untitled* accommodate an unfamiliar narrative of Rauschenberg's own making.

Untitled is an elevated, collaged box construction propped up by back and side panels (also heavily collaged), and a single post. A taxidermied chicken appears under the box in the porch-like space created by the panels and post. An additional space is created to the left of the porch where a vertical board collaged with a single photograph of a man forms a right angle with a horizontal mirror below. Along with the presence of printed fabrics, and a scribbled child's drawing in the lower right-hand corner of the box, Mary Lynn Kotz pointed out a myriad of "autobiographical elements" in the work:

> There are photographs of Rauschenberg's former wife, Susan, his sister Janet, as a twelve-year-old girl and also in a newspaper clipping as the Louisiana Yam Queen; his parents as a young couple in Port Arthur, and in a newspaper story on their twenty-fifth wedding anniversary; and his son, Christopher, as a three-year-old . . . A magazine illustration of a small house surrounded by floodwaters is echoed by a snapshot of the Rauschenberg home in Port Arthur, and a published photo of the 1953 Miss America contestants is paired with a 1923 snapshot of Dora Rauschenberg [his mother] . . .[25]

While *Untitled* displays both male and female imagery, its principal female icon, the stuffed hen, rests underneath a bricolage of predominantly masculine motifs. Overall, the work appears as an altar to manhood, for Rauschenberg placed a pair of men's white Oxford shoes in the elevated box – regally positioned in a niche on high – and he featured, as the largest image in the combine, a photograph of a well-dressed man in a white suit adorning the adjacent vertical panel below. Walter Hopps viewed the work as an homage to maleness, regarding it as a pendant to the female version in Rauschenberg's well-known combine, *Odalisque*.[26]

Rauschenberg's conceptions of maleness in *Untitled*, however, are far from straightforward (or just straight), for while many of his depictions relate to family motifs and are the paraphernalia of the traditional home – family photos, newspaper clippings, etc. – the bold image of the natty man in Oxfords as a "handsome Dan" might appear as a gay intrusion into evocations of conventional domestic life. This theme is reinforced by the collaged panel above the chicken, where a well-built fellow in a photograph located between two references to childhood – Michelangelo's putti and the child's drawing – weeps openly. The inclusion of an image of Jasper Johns "near the white shoes,"[27] which have tucked inside them a pair of athletic tube socks, makes the reference to homosexuality specific to Rauschenberg's biography. Rauschenberg called upon a variety of "souvenirs" to reconstruct an alternative domestic paradigm, and through this process of choreographing props, he attempted to renegotiate the conflicted memories of his childhood around a more accommodating ideology. Nonetheless, as the combine enacts the process Stewart describes, seeing the past/home always from a perspective that distances us from it – "the souvenir speaks to a context of origin through a language of longing"[28] – the work is once again rendered somewhat unfamiliar and odd.

It was not until the late 1950s that Rauschenberg specifically paid homage to his domestic situation with Jasper Johns (his partner from approximately 1954 to 1961). The secret homelife he built with Johns in their loft on Pearl Street in New York only fueled his reexamination of the nature of domesticity. There are a number of homosexual motifs in *Double Feature*, many of which reoccur in related paintings from the same period. The inclusion of a torn back pocket and projecting umbrella fragment at the lower right of the composition, for example, hint at a homoerotic theme. Back pockets stuffed with colored scarves were a code in homosexual circles at the time, indicating gay identity as well as preferred styles of intercourse, and Rauschenberg used the sign in several works from the period.[29] The repeated use of umbrella sections as part of this coded sign might have evolved, in fact, from earlier work. In his 1955 review of Rauschenberg's show at Egan Gallery, Frank O'Hara referred explicitly to "sex organs (male and female) made from old red silk umbrellas."[30] In addition, the umbrella – flaccid when not in use and stiff when open – serves as a phallic reference.

The idea of homosexual coupling conveyed through the sub-culture language of the pocket/umbrella motif in *Double Feature* is also subtly treated in the work's title, which conjures up notions of doubling or pairing. That the picture reflects Rauschenberg's particular romantic situation may be implied in the stenciled words "JON" and "LOFT" which appear on the left side of the composition. Using anonymous text to refer to his lover and to their place of intimacy, he then, in stark contrast, places a characteristic black swatch of paint above the word Jon and allows its tendrils to drip down over the name. As the painterly mark derives from Abstract Expressionism's autobiographic style, it would appear that in *Double Feature*, Rauschenberg metaphorically caresses Johns' "sign" – JON – with his own – the painterly mark. The work becomes a memento about love and domesticity, albeit partially muted by the nature of its anonymous materials and the transparency of it as mere construction.

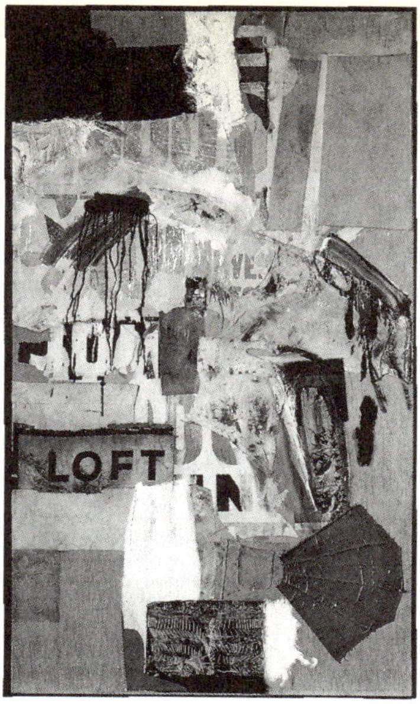

66 *Robert Rauschenberg,* Double Feature, *1959*

Jonathan Katz recently posited that Rauschenberg and Johns' partnership was vital to a sense of promoting community within an otherwise homophobic society. Katz's analysis relied on a sense of oppositional dynamics, where the artists' gay tropes – conceived through the mediated look of mass signage – evolved as a means of defying the privileged, "authentic," heterosexual male vocabulary of Abstract Expressionism. Katz claimed, "It was in response to Abstract Expressionism's dominance that Rauschenberg and Johns cultivated their most lasting contributions to American art."[31]

Rauschenberg's need to work against the established avant-garde, however, was more complex. It was not simply about jockeying for place in the art world, nor was it about asserting a feminist or gay agenda. His rejection of the conventional masculinity inscribed in Abstract Expressionism in favor of the nostalgia conjured up through materials relating to women and the home, derived from a personal need to locate a new domestic model. The indeterminacy of his collage medium, however, while allowing for renewed definitions of "home," could never accommodate any resolution – such is the fragmentary nature of collage. Rauschenberg's revelations about the domestic would remain uneasy. He would continue to be the son who wouldn't fit in because he fought with his father(s), and yet he could not shake the power of home. It is this unsettled sense of self that differs so dramatically from the ambitious and total assertion of identity at the core of the work of the Abstract Expressionists, and at the center of utopic modernism.

14

Master Bedrooms, Master Narratives: Home, Homosexuality and Post-War Art

KENNETH E. SILVER

Everyday life invents itself by poaching in countless ways on the property of others. *Michel de Certeau*

The Scene of the Crime

Eadweard Muybridge's photographs of nude male wrestlers have long occupied a special place in the gay imaginary. Their Greco-Roman precedents notwithstanding (or perhaps because of them), these chaste representations of forthright physical contact have served as a kind of soft-core pornography for generations of homosexual male spectators. Without the padded prostheses that characterize organized sports nowadays, or even so much as a jockstrap, two nineteenth-century guys roll on the ground in search of a stable relationship – the subduer and the subdued. Needless to say, Muybridge's serial images are, to a modern viewer, at the same time rather funny: as in many of the series in *Animal Locomotion* (1887), a gridded background is provided for the plotting of physical displacement, and it is the juxtapostion of this quasi-scientific *mise-en-scène* and the earnestness of the naked athletes' exertions that looks somewhat incongruous. Yet this has never managed to drain these pictures of their inherent interest for a homosexual audience, inasmuch as the depiction of nude men together – in such sharp contrast to pictures of nude women *en groupe* – are extremely rare. It may even be that the very matter-of-factness of Muybridge's photographs, in leaving a more personal elaboration up to the viewer, is helpful in their accommodation to a gay dream-space.[1]

Like homosexual men before and since, the English painter Francis Bacon found inspiration in these gridded, Whiteman-esque grapplers.[2] The protagonists of *Two Figures* (1953) are taken directly from Muybridge (although the lower man's body has been turned around, his face now coming into contact with the other man's, and their bodies, though blurred, now touching front-to-front), just as Bacon's schematic, perspectival box is a reworking of the photographer's grid. Yet, everything else has changed. Open to surveillance, Muybridge's photograph combines the laboratory

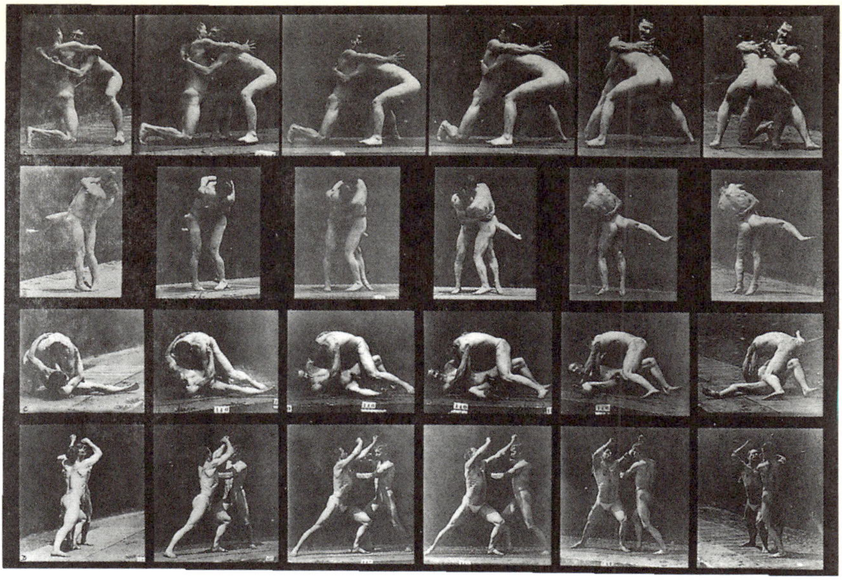

67 *Eadweard Muybridge,* Wrestlers, *c. 1887*

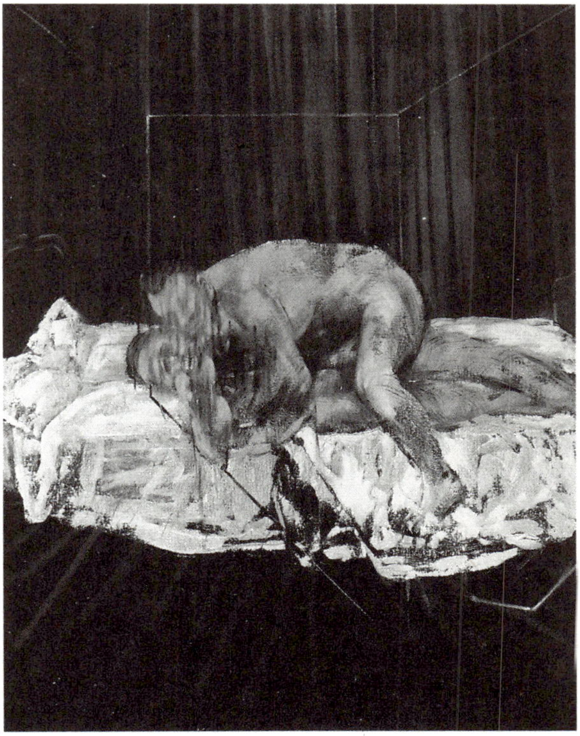

68 *Francis Bacon,* Two Figures, *1953*

and the great outdoors: the bright, warm, California sun that illuminates his motion studies – so helpful in a clear delineation of human form, against the light-on-dark grid – appears salubrious, recalling the ideas of turn-of-the-century public housing reformers, who believed that daylight would help alleviate disease in the slums. Bacon's painting, on the other hand, is nocturnal: what illumination there is results from a Baroque practice of placing white highlights against the darkness, a shorthand for the revelation that may come to the dark night of a soul, but which here speaks of things that cannot be shown in the "normal" light of day. Most importantly, Bacon has relocated his figures: what had been a thin mattress beneath the wrestlers in the photographic source has, in the painting, become a full-blown bed, complete with brilliant white sheets. With a few, thickly laid on strokes of paint, the protagonists have been given a home.

Bacon "domesticates" the Muybridge picture in other ways as well. Not only has the well-lighted, public place of science become the dark, private space of sexuality, but Muybridge's "document",[3] a transparent signifier of public scrutiny, available for a vast range of uses, has been turned into "art": the discourse of objectivity has been remade to serve the subjective. Muybridge's wrestlers are made to perform other work – dream work, subversive work – than that for which they were intended. Mark Roskill has written of *Two Figures*: "Whereas the imagery of the source connoted athleticism and muscularity in their various senses – man at the peak of his physical powers, exercising himself in a sport for the sake of his physique – the connotations of Bacon's image involves nudity in its shameful sense, and homosexuality."[4] Moreover, in taking Muybridge's men indoors, Bacon builds other kinds of walls around the couple than the physical. By way of "poaching" an icon from a narrative, isolating one particular moment in a temporal sequence, he constructs one particular reading – a gay one – from a multitude of possibilities. Once in the bedroom, physical exertion becomes sex; camaraderie, or rivalry, is made passionate; and spectatorship, which is at least offered the excuse of scientific observation in Muybridge, comes much closer to voyeurism.

As is obvious, this act of domestication at the same time unleashes its opposite: the wild and untamed (and, at the time in England, the illegal).[5] The intensity of male aggression, which is channeled into sport, and ritualized, in Muybridge's photographs, turns animalistic in Bacon. The rough application of paint, which blurs the faces of the two figures; Bacon's characteristic vertical striations on the dark ground, that fan out towards the bottom; and of course the showing of teeth, particularly those of the lower man, all contribute to a sense that this couple is enacting their sexuality as if they were caged animals. There is, in other words, a striking contradiction built into this domestic space. For if domesticity is meant to be a safe harbor, if home is where the heart is, it is also in Bacon's painting a

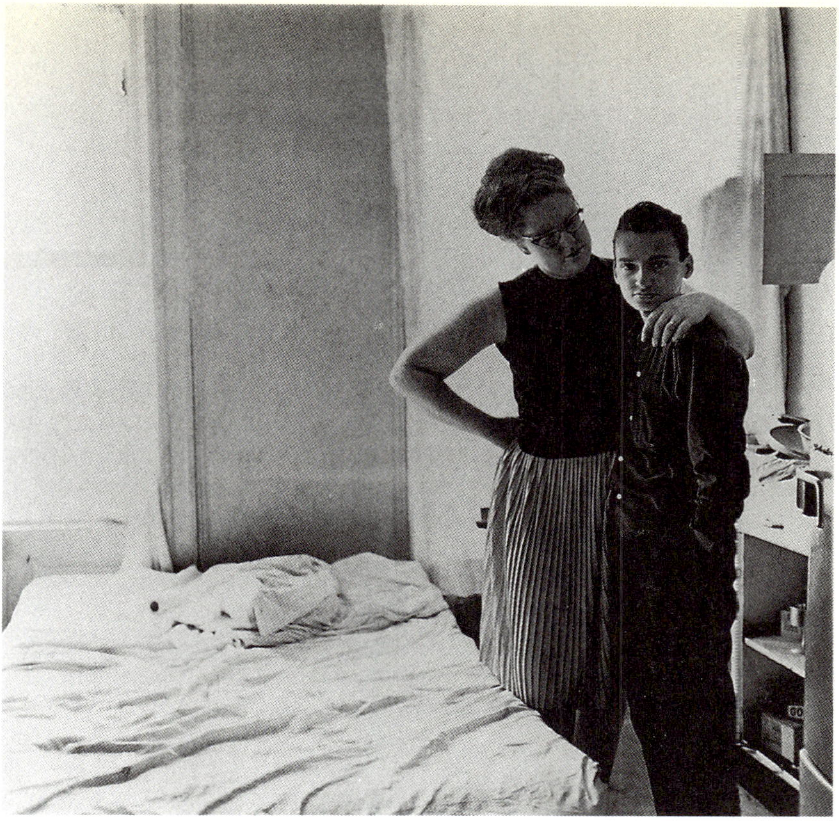

69 *Diane Arbus,* Two Friends at Home, N.Y.C., *1965*

private jungle, or perhaps more accurately a zoo, a place where the animal drives of certain men, deprived of expression in the public realm, are simultaneously contained and unleashed.

The gay conjugal bed cannot then, in Bacon's work, entirely overcome its discursive resemblance to the scene of a crime (to steal the image with which Walter Benjamin described Eugène Atget's photographs of Paris). Nor can it in the work of Diane Arbus.[6] If in Bacon's painting we are witnesses to the transgression as it is being perpetrated, in the American photographer's *Two Friends at Home, N.Y.C.* (1965) we are detectives, perhaps of the film noir type, arriving after-the-fact and as likely as not to misread the evidence. Once again the bedclothes are disheveled, except now the bed itself occupies the central place, as the protagonists have been pushed slightly to the right of center. This is obviously "the morning after," one of many such mornings, to which both the title of the picture and the details of domestic life – dirty pots and pans in the sink, open cupboard – attest. Although we recognize that the occupants – the perpetrators, as it were – are standing before us, that this is their space, not ours, we are not precisely certain how to interrogate them. For those of us who recognize at first glance that this is a lesbian couple, the bed is instantly charged with queer acts; for those who are not – and the title is discreet on this point – the much larger size of the "woman," who adoringly observes and embraces the much smaller "man," already causes a frisson that partakes of the Oedipal: is this in fact not merely a physically unconventional heterosexual couple – big woman, small man – but an incestuous one, mother and son having set up housekeeping? The unmade bed and messy kitchen suggest a disorder that we sense may be moral, but like one of Raymond Chandler's narrators, we still don't quite have it right, at least not until we realize that these are indeed two females. Yet, without the bed, outside the domestic space, as Arbus could have shown them – on the street, for instance – an interrogation (our quest for understanding what we see) would have been unlikely to proceed at all. We expect the public space, the space of Baudelaire's *flâneur*, and of Manet and Degas' roving eyes, to suture its own incoherencies; glimpses, fragments and pictorial puzzles are the stuff of the street, and, as such, are protection against a too-promiscuous, or overly-motivated surveillance. It is only the invasion of privacy into the domestic interior (even, as here, with the consent of those being portrayed) – and in the bright light of day, so different from Bacon's nocturne – that compels us to construct a plausible reading of the couple's relationship. Surely the unflinching directness of the "butch" partner, as she stares us down, is a challenge of this kind: "Do you get it yet?" she asks. "Now is it clear?"

Trespassing

The tortuous representation of homosexuality, and homosexual domesticity in particular, was compounded in its various twists and turns by a suppression that, although secondary to the homophobic impulse, was even more influential and wide-ranging. The domestic itself, as I have noted elsewhere, was written out of the critical construction of post-war American art.[7] The same domestic space that was mythologized and sold to a burgeoning post-war population, was under attack in the critical literature of American art. Andreas Huyssen has offered an incisive analysis of modernism's creation of an "other," composed of the female and the popular, which are equated;[8] in post-war American art criticism this equation was complemented by the construction of a hyper-masculinized modern artist.

In "The American Action Painters" (1952), a key text in the master narrative of Abstract Expressionism, Harold Rosenberg constructs an existential portrait of the new, American artist, a sort of aesthetic cave-man, who operates on instinct and nerve:

> At a certain moment the canvas began to appear to one American painter after another as an arena in which to act . . . The painter no longer approached his

> easel with an image in his mind; he went up to it with material in his hand to do something to that other piece of material in front of him. The image would be the result of this encounter.[9]

Yet, despite the "painting-degree-zero" quality of this context-less portrayal, Rosenberg has a quite specific context in mind as to the Scylla and Charybdis that await the imperiled artist on his journey: i.e. popular taste and the culture of domesticity.

The critic consistently returns to these hazards as the antithesis of the "authentic," high, modernist endeavor, as for instance when he decries the recent popularization of up-to-date good taste: "Unhappily for an art whose value depends on the authenticity of its mysteries," he laments,

> the new movement [i.e. Action Painting] appeared at the same moment that Modern Art *en masse* "arrived" in America: Modern architecture, not only for sophisticated homes, but for corporations, municipalities, synagogues; Modern furniture and crockery in mail-order catalogues; Modern vacuum cleaners, can openers; beer-ad "mobiles" – along with reproductions in articles on advanced painting in big-circulation magazines.

The current state of affairs, according to the critic, is – unlike the high-minded aspirations of those who believe in truly revolutionary art, whatever that might be – emphatically populist, vaguely feminine, and laughable, a "comedy of a revolution that restricts itself to weapons of taste – and which at the same time addresses itself to the masses: Modern design fabric in bargain basements, Modern interiors for office girls living alone, Modern milk bottles." As it so happens, modern design for the post-war family and home made its way into the Museum of Modern Art at the same time as, and even a bit before, Abstract Expressionist painting, in a series of exhibitions and books which included "Modern Rooms of the Last Fifty Years" (1947), "What is Modern Design?" (1950), "What is Modern Interior Design?" (1953), and "Art for the Family" (1954). This, at least in part, ought to be understood as the context for Rosenberg's description, in the same essay, of the kind of abstract art-making he finds empty and ultimately frivolous: "Satisfied with wonders that remain safely inside the canvas, the artist accepts the permanence of the commonplace and decorates it with his own daily annihilation. The result is apocalyptic wallpaper."

If one gets the feeling that Rosenberg's reiteration (in an essay purportedly about painting) of the popular and domestic hazards that lie in wait for serious American art is over-determined, that there is something else, unstated, lurking behind this anti-domestic diatribe, we are not the first to feel so. Fifteen years ago the critic Barbara Rose said of "The American Action Painters":

> I recall being puzzled by the article . . . Although it was obvious that Rosenberg was talking about something, I could not identify his subject as painting . . . In

> retrospect, I realize Rosenberg was not talking about painting at all; he was describing [Hans] Namuth's photographs of [Jackson] Pollock. All the metaphors were decipherable from the photographs: Pollock attacking his canvas spread out on the floor in front of him like a boxing ring or a bullfighting arena . . . Pollock pictured alone, isolated from any frame of reference save his own creation . . . what images could more poignantly conjure up a literary vision of the existential hero?[10]

Namuth's pictures of Pollock at work are, of course, among the best-known images of a modern artist that exist; published in *Art News* in May 1950 to accompany Robert Goodnough's article "Pollock Paints a Picture," they established him as the athlete-hero-aesthete, a distinctly new and very American type. And they did something else as well: they removed the artist entirely from a living space, from a studio that bore any traces whatsoever of home life. In a remarkable footnote to the above, Rose wrote:

> It is precisely this lack of domestic context, of course, that differentiates (at least until recently) the American from the European artist. The separation of the atelier from domestic quarters is typical of the New York School. Pollock's barn was the country equivalent of the industrial loft – a large, anonymous space with a pre-history that was not artistic . . . On the other hand, if Namuth had photographed Pollock's house, the photographs would have resembled the interior of Monet's or Matisse's studio: perfect order, a collection of books, records, art, and objects dear to the artist such as rocks and stones. This dichotomy between Pollock's domestic life, a model of order imposed by [Lee] Krasner's housekeeping ability, and the "mess" of the studio is striking.[11]

Rose does not really tell us whether she thinks that the representation of Pollock as a lone warrior of art – as a rugged, American individualist whose home life is, for all intents and purposes, non-existent – was a self-conscious construction or a reflection of a particular post-war American style; we can safely assume, I think, that it was something of both. In the case of Namuth's photographs of Pollock at work in the barn – the same series in which he hovers and lunges, hunkers down and jumps up around his canvas – there is now little question about the constructed aspect of the Pollock image. For a photograph has come to light which, for obvious reasons, was not going to help in the construction of Pollock-as-Prometheus: as Mr Pollock works at left, we find the artist Lee Krasner, Mrs Jackson Pollock, sitting in the corner of the barn at the rear right, hand on her hip and legs crossed, surveying the scene, perhaps giving advice, and – who can doubt it? – supplying moral support.[12] That is to say, home here intrudes upon the studio (Krasner even wears house slippers); the domestic interrupts and subverts the desired narrative of man-in-the-workplace, and thus was excised from the body of Pollock myth.

By its absence, then, the role of the domestic in American art was clear: it marked the limits of masculinity, the place of the spectator (the consumer rather than the producer) at the edges of the existential arena, the terra incognita of women. Yet, for Andy Warhol, an artist of the next generation, there seems to have been nothing *less* "incognita" than the world of women, nothing more familiar and beloved than the shared domestic – and psychic – space of mother and son. Warhol was not particularly secretive about the fact that his mother, Julia, lived with him for much of both their lives (Duane Michals, for instance, photographed mother and son at home, in 1958); their collaboration on a number of projects, including a number of commercial endeavors, was well publicized.[13]

Warhol was a "sissy" and proud of it, although we should not be fooled into thinking that his "effeminacy" was any more or less a construction than Pollock's "masculinity." Warhol was fully aware that his behavior was a form of throwing down the gauntlet, that his self-presentation as a "momma's boy" was scandalous: "You had to have seen the way all the Abstract Expressionist painters carried themselves . . . to understand how shocked people were to see a painter coming on swish," Warhol reminisced. "I certainly wasn't a butch kind of guy by nature, but I must admit, I went out of my way to play up the other extreme."[14]

Of course, Andy Warhol was but one of a large group of Pop artists who challenged the shibboleths and dogmas of Abstract Expressionism in the years after 1960, particularly the prohibitions against the popular and the domestic. Jim Dine, Claes Oldenburg, James Rosenquist, Tom Wesselmann, and Roy Lichtenstein, among others, including Warhol, iconographically trafficked in everything forbidden, from canned foods and Frigidaires, to dust mops and bedroom ensembles.[15] But Warhol went just a little bit further, and we might say, a bit "gayer," in contriving wallpaper – apocalyptic wallpaper, as it were – printed with the repeated image of a cow that he had found in a book. In 1966 he wallpapered Leo Castelli's New York gallery with it, and in 1970–71, for his retrospective at the Whitney Museum of American Art, he wallpapered the museum's huge 4th floor with his bright pink bovine heads on a yellow ground, on top of which he hung his paintings, transforming the space into something resembling a cozy home (if on a magnified scale).[16] It was as if Warhol knew, years after Action Painting's decline, the kind of shock-effect this could still have: in one of New York's bastions of modernism, Warhol's kitsch-looking retrospective seems to rejoice in restaging Harold Rosenberg's "comedy of a revolution . . . Modern design fabric in bargain basements, Modern interiors for office girls living alone, Modern milk bottles."

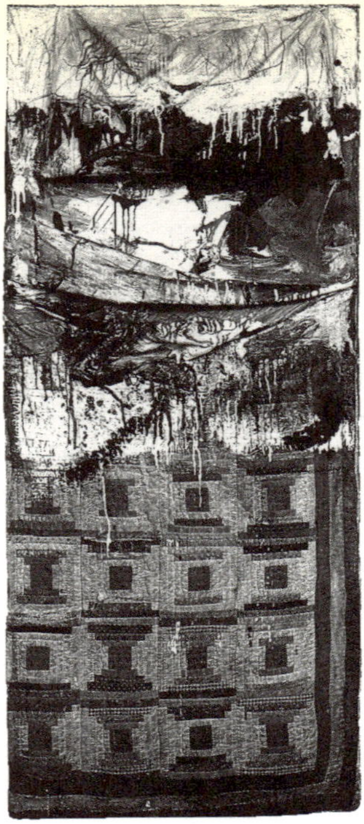

70 *Robert Rauschenberg,* Bed, *1955*

Undercover

But even earlier, in 1955, a year before Pollock's death, when Abstract Expressionism was at its zenith, thirty-year-old Robert Rauschenberg created a work that reaffirmed the claims of the domestic on modernism (this was a full seven years before the appearance of Pop art). *Bed* was clearly designed to be provocative, from its juxtapositions of raw and cooked – wild paint splatters vs. methodical, self-contained, Albers-like concentric squares; folkloric quilt vs. avant-garde abstraction – to the ontological uncertainty it makes palpable: is this a painting-as-bed or bed-as-painting? In which direction, it seems to ask, have we moved: from the studio to the home or vice versa?

Rauschenberg has literalized a certain suggestion in the art of Pollock – a kind of madness-for-paint, an exceeding of rational limits, a physicality that can no longer distinguish one physical space or spatial orientation from another, more or less the same conclusion that Allen Kaprow drew from Pollock's "legend" in 1958: "Pollock, as I see him, left us at that point where we must become preoccupied with and even dazzled by the space and objects of our everyday life, either our bodies, clothes, rooms, or if need be, the vastness of Forty-Second Street."[17] Rather than rendering Pollock as a painter's painter, locked in his workplace (alone, or otherwise), Kaprow gives us an artist with the doors of his studio flung wide open to the spaces of the world at large. While Pollock's advocates went to great lengths to distance his art from the banal – to distinguish his drips from the drip of the faucet, say – the younger generation of artists found it was precisely in this confusion of the ordinary and the extraordinary that aesthetic meaning might be produced. Rauschenberg himself made the canonical statement of this attitude: "Painting relates to both art and life. Neither can be made. (I try to act in that gap between the two.)"[18] Indeed, as it is here for Rauschenberg, the collapsing of the art/life binarism was more often than not understood as a breaking down of the spatial separation of artistic production from everything else – the separation which Barbara Rose found so striking in American art. Rauschenberg's *Bed* situates itself smack in the middle of these spatial (and rhetorical) fields, denying, or at least muddying the phenomenological waters of their difference, much as Lee Krasner's house slippers do in Namuth's photograph of her husband at work.

But this is not the only way in which *Bed* depends for its meanings on the "Pollock legend." There is also the question of sexuality. In Rauschenberg's work it is unclear, and quite deliberately so I think, whether this particular bed points to the renunciation of sex or its exhibition. In the first interpretation, the cot-size mattress, splattered with paint, makes us think of the monk's asceticism – all is sacrificed for the "vocation" of art (which in itself was somewhat scandalous in the highly practical, materialistic post-war American environment); the distinction between studio and home is collapsed in favor of the former. On the other hand, *Bed* can be seen as exhibitionistic, sexual writhings appearing indexically in the wild paint splattered on sheet, pillow, and upper part of the quilt; in this case, the rigors of the studio are subverted by the imperatives of desire, located in a sign of the domestic. But both "passionate" readings are nonetheless dependent on Pollock, in that the unspoken "truth" of Namuth's photographs is their sexual charge. Pollock's animal magnetism (as it used to be called), the virility he conveys in these black-and-white pictures (regardless of the "reality' behind them) have always been inextricable from the Pollock artistic legend. Does one dare say that, had he been less attractive – and less ruggedly stylish – the legend might have been, correspondingly, far less potent? That myth was intended from the start, anyway, as a hyper-masculinized corrective to the "sissified" representation of the visual artist in America, and Rauschenberg's *Bed*, which at once asserts the domestic and defiles it, again puts in play the terms of that discourse. Simply by making vertical what had been horizontal, by re-enacting the Pollock spatial re-orientation (i.e. from floor to wall), Rauschenberg's *Bed* acquires for itself the allure of Jack-the-Dripper.

The art historian Daniel Wheeler, opting for this second reading, has said of *Bed* that "the red-dominated paint dribbled over the patchwork quilt's own found colors and patterns seems to transform the bed into a lurid, Bacon-like scene of sadomasochistic mayhem," referring to works like Francis Bacon's *Two Figures*, discussed earlier in this essay.[19] But, while the two works may rightly be seen as linked, in a general way, through homosexual thematics – and this is implied, if not stated, in Wheeler's phrasing – it is obvious that, unlike Bacon's in 1953, Rauschenberg's of two years later offers no iconographic support for such a reading, as there are no figures represented, or even traces of figures, let alone *male* figures. Yet, the absence of men here cannot be explained by the fact that objectified males are more generally absent from Rauschenberg's scopic regime, or that Rauschenberg refrains, on principle, from the kind of visual poaching that we saw demonstrated in Bacon's use of Muybridge. To the contrary, the male body – especially the athlete's body, or the working man's – in the form of glances stolen from newspaper and magazine photos, and perhaps made by his own camera as well, is ubiquitous in Rauschenberg's art, in the combines, silkscreen paintings, and transfer drawings. There are handsome men, of great physical prowess, represented at least as far back as 1954, in *Bantam*, where a group portrait of the New York Yankees is inserted beneath a portrait of the young Judy Garland (and a nineteenth-century image of a woman gazing at herself in the mirror); in *Rebus* (1955), two sets of male sprinters in mid-stride; in *Interview* (1955), toreadors entering the ring; in *Small Rebus* (1956), a sprinter in one photo, and three gymnasts in another; in *Talisman* (1958), a Pittsburgh Pirate (presumably a runner on third base, preparing to run for home); the gold, silver, and bronze-medal weight lifters, on the Olympic winners' stand in Canto XXXI of *Dante's Inferno* (1960); another weight lifter, seen from the waist down only, with bulging, muscular thighs, in Canto XII; several batters during practice, and a crouching catcher, in *Shortstop*, *Overcast I*, and *Brace* (all 1962); a swimmer doing the crawl in *Sundog* (1962); the same swimmer, with the previous baseball players as well, in *Quarry* (1962); other baseball players in *Urban* (1962); football players in *Echo* (1962); firemen in *Tideline* (1963) and *Die Hard* (1963); hard-hats at a construction site in *Bait*, *Bicycle*, and *Windward* (all 1963); football players, and two swimmers (again doing the crawl stroke), in *Barge* (1963); a basketball player in *Yellow Body* (1968); and a photograph that the artist may have taken himself (and an image that may have some special significance for him, as it appears in no fewer than five works), of two men on a New York City Street, observed from the back: a construction worker (or perhaps a telephone or electric company, or street-repairman), who wears a construction helmet and a tight-fitting T-shirt; and a second man, stepping into an intersection, about six feet away. It appears in its entirety in an oil, pencil, and silkscreen work of 1963, *Untitled*, and then whole or in part in *Tracer*, 1963; *Persimmon*, *Skyway*, *Tree Frog* (along with the hard-hats from *Bait*), and *Press*, all of 1964; as well as in numerous other works. All this by way of saying that Rauschenberg's interest in looking at men, and in showing us that look, however surreptitiously, is one of the constants of his art.

Unlike Bacon, though, the images of men which Rauschenberg poaches from the media and the street are never domesticated – they are never brought indoors, never made intimate, or personal, or demonstrably sexualized. Only representations of women are. In the 1950s we find female pin-ups – the naked girls who were so popular on calendars, et al. – in a number of Rauschenberg's works, including *Untitled* and *Interview* (both 1955), and *Odalisque* (1955–58), as well as artistic nudes, such as Botticelli's *Birth of Venus* (in *Rebus*, 1955) and Titian's *Rape of Europa* (in *Small Rebus*, 1956). More significantly, in many of the same works of the early 1960s in which Rauschenberg's roving eye for male pulchritude is most clearly manifest, we find two Venus images drawn from art history: Velázquez's *Rokeby Venus* in *Crocus* and *Exile* (1962); *Bicycle*, *Barge*, and *Transom* (1963); and Rubens's *Toilet of Venus*, in *Tracer* (1963), and *Persimmon*, *Trapeze*, *Flush*, *Press*, *Retroactive II*, *Axle*, *Skyway* (all 1964). These two "toilette" images are, obviously, both domestic scenes (they take place in the bedroom/boudoir), and both Venuses admire themselves in mirrors (which at the same time allows us to see their faces, even though we view them from behind). Yet during, and just after, the period that Robert Rauschenberg was living in a building on Pearl Street in lower Manhattan with his real-life lover, Jasper Johns (they were together from 1955 to *c.* 1962), the men in his art never come in from the cold.[20] In the libidinal economy of the Rauschenberg esthetic, men are everywhere and nowhere simultaneously, locked out of a signifying function in the domestic space but omnipresent as (deceptive) signs of "normal" male specularity, and of male power, in the public realm. In this body of work, vanity is never recognized as a possibility for men – indeed, is *assigned* to women as innate, mythic, eternal – so as to thwart our recognition of the homosexual self-regard which permeates it. The empty *Bed* of 1955 might well accommodate one of his borrowed Venuses (even if she were likely to fall asleep alone), but it will never be occupied, as far as the spectator is concerned, by any of the gymnasts, sprinters, firemen, or football players who bob and weave their way through Rauschenberg's dense and elegant agglomeration of paint and found objects.

In Broad Daylight

It is not until the early 1960s – in the art of David Hockney – that the domestic, the gay, and the modernist are joined in a manner that is neither evasive nor anguished, and that, even in comparison to such a forthrightly gay artist as Paul Cadmus, is notable for its directness.[21] In *Domestic Scene,* 71
Los Angeles, which the artist invented before ever having visited southern California, the American home is the site of a particularly tender kind of

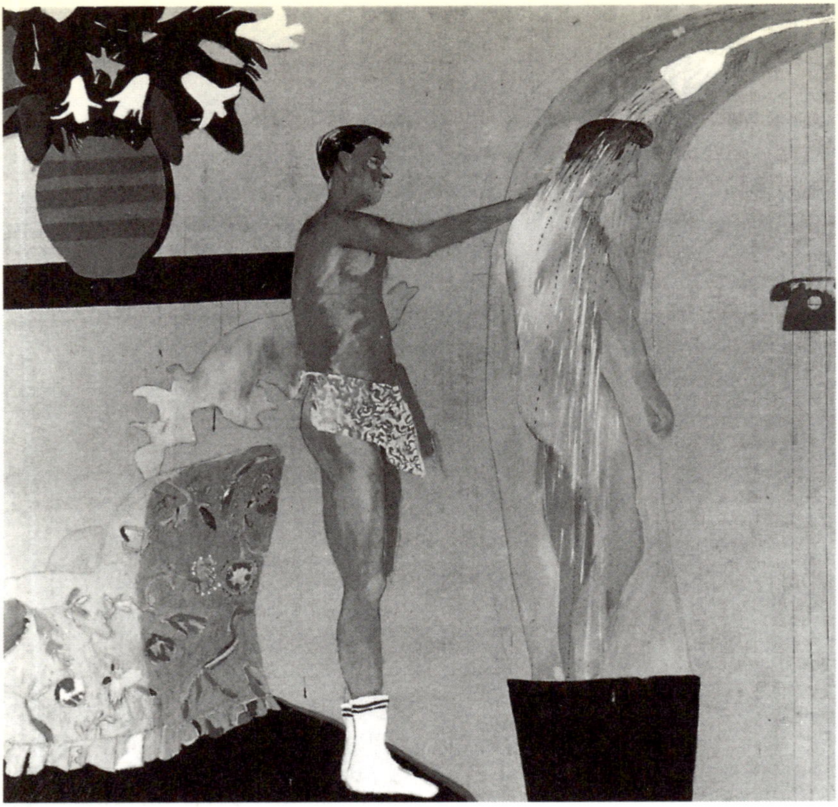

71 *David Hockney,* Domestic Scene, Los Angeles, *1963*

gay domesticity. Hockney's painting is a composite narrative built out of bits and pieces: the slip-covered chair and telephone were modeled after objects in London, the gargantuan vase of flowers was taken from an illustration in a women's magazine, and the protagonists were "poached" from the photograph of a man, with an apron tied around his waist, scrubbing the back of another man, in the American, homo-erotic magazine, *Physique Pictorial.*

Interestingly, the photographs of Eadweard Muybridge again had a crucial role to play in the development of a gay domestic image. Hockney was aware of Bacon's use of the American photographer's motion studies,[22] although his own recycling of one of them points to the humor, as we noted earlier, that might be extracted from the juxtaposition of naked actors and mundane activity: in *Seated Woman Drinking Tea, Being Served by a Standing Companion* (1963), based on a picture in the series of the same title in *Human Figures in Motion*, two nude women engage in the most civilized and quotidian of English rituals. If the image is only marginally a domestic one – Hockney puts the protagonists before a large curtain with a fleur-delys pattern that seems more stage-like than homey – numerous other works of the same year are unequivocally domestic, and they are pictures of men: *Two Men in a Shower*, where, again, the source appears to be Muybridge, if less an appropriation than an adaptation, and where the curtain is now a shower curtain; *Domestic Scene, Broadchalke, Wilts.*, in which two young men sit conversing on a sofa before a large, curtained living-room window; and *Domestic Scene, Notting Hill*, which features one clothed, seated man, before a curtain, and one nude, standing male. In a suite of shower scenes of lone male figures of 1964–65, the gridded backgrounds of Muybridge's photographs seem to have migrated south, and been re-born as ceramic-tile bath enclosures.

No artist before or since has really given us as normalized, or perhaps "normativized," a picture of gay domesticity as David Hockney. Compared to Bacon's distorted and often panic-stricken characters – who perform in a sort of existential arena, equipped with the minimum requirements of home – Hockney's men go about their business in the most unhurried and unselfconscious of ways in domestic spaces that, owing to their utter banality, seem to cool the temperature on the queer lives they encompass. Of course, this is due in large part to the fact that sexual activity per se is not represented in Hockney's work, aside from a group of semi-abstract paintings, of *c.* 1961–63.[23] But even in his *Illustrations for Fourteen Poems from C. P. Cavafy* (1966), in which half of the etchings feature male couples in bed, Hockney's straightforward compositions and *faux-naïf* draftsmanship tend to diminish the exoticism that might accrue to gay representation.

Indeed, as time went on, especially towards the end of the decade, in the gay "marriage" portraits for which Hockney is so well known – *Christopher Isherwood and Don Bachardy* (1968) and *Henry Geldzahler and Christopher Scott* (1969) – and where the details of the domestic settings are so carefully delineated, the sexuality is increasingly toned down, almost but not quite to the point of eradication. In both paintings, the couple is physically separated: Isherwood and Bachardy are sitting in twin chairs, just behind similar stacks of books (although they are linked by way of a bowl of fruit, with a banana suggestively pointed at Bachardy, echoing the direction of Isherwood's gaze, and with a stalk of Indian corn below, repeating this directional emphasis); Geldzahler and Scott are literally across the room from each other. Not that this is so surprising, given a genre whose function is ceremonial rather than descriptive. In Hockney's portraits of Fred and Marcia Weisman (*American Collectors*, 1968), and Gregory Masurovsky and Shirley Goldfarb (1974), and in two others of his own parents, the couples are also separated spatially, rendering their sexuality invisible, and one supposes that to have done otherwise would have been considered tasteless by the sitters. What counts in portraits like these, and what seems to bind together these couples according to Hockney, is not their sexual attraction to each other (which has now been relegated to the private, unseen part of their lives), but their shared living space, and the objects with which they cohabit. We might say that domesticity, in Hockney's art, triumphs over sex, and as the senses give way to the sensible, gay and straight alike take their place in a social order that renders a too-frank sexuality anarchic.

Apprehended

For an artist like Robert Mapplethorpe, who came to maturity in the years after the advent of the Gay Liberation movement, there was no question of relinquishing a sexuality whose representation had been fought for so fiercely. Not only do the homosexual and the domestic assert their respective claims in a portrait like that of *Brian Ridley and Lyle Heeter* (1979), but they do so in such a way that the pungency of each claim is intensified by the juxtaposition. Taken a decade after the Stonewall Riots, this photograph is no less a "social" document than Hockney's portraits of Isherwood/Bachardy and Geldzahler/Scott, and like them, is intended for public delectation. Set in the corner of a living room or study (at any rate, *not* the bedroom), this picture of two specific men in full leather is also a picture of their relationship in the purest, most Platonic (or Hegelian) sense: the Slave, in handcuffs, ankle restraints, and a dog collar, is seated, while the Master, leaning against the chair, brandishes the chain attached to his "boy's" collar in one hand, and a riding crop, which rests on the chair's arm within inches of the Slave, in the other. It is not inappropriate that *Brian Ridley and Lyle Heeter* has acquired the status of a cultural icon, not only because it sums up a historical moment and a particular "corner" of culture so precisely, but also because it is iconic in form: square, frontal, shallow in depth, easily legible. At once a work that is deadly serious and pure burlesque, it is also a work that presents itself as a challenge to normalized gay imagery.

What Mapplethorpe's portrait insists on, for better or worse, is the "queerness" of homosexuality, and what it refuses to forfeit, in the name of normalcy, is sexual lawlessness. Of course, there are myriad ironies here: at the same time that it frankly declares S-and-M love as rebellious, it not only reinscribes, and re-eroticizes, traditional roles of dominance and submission (re-cast for same-sex partners, which makes us think of Arbus's *Two Friends at Home, N.Y.C.*, an obvious precedent for Mapplethorpe's image), but does so in a high-bourgeois, domestic setting. Richard Meyer has said:

> In this image Mapplethorpe exploits a mismatch between the couple's sadomasochistic outfitting and their domestic interior; between their leather, chains, and master/slave hierarchy on the one hand and their wingback chair, oriental rug, grasscloth wallcovering, and white antlers end table on the other.

> This spectacular disjunction not only defuses the leather machismo of Ridley and Heeter, it also asserts that neither their erotic costume nor their domestic context . . . are sufficient metaphors for their identity.[24]

Furthermore, owing to this striking juxtaposition of "outlaw" sexuality and "conventional" home, Mapplethorpe pictures a paradox: at once the impossibility of the social assimilation of Brian Ridley and Lyle Heeter's idiosyncratic love, and at same time the utter ordinariness of all couplings, whatever shape their shackles assume.

Needless to say, the most obvious visual play here is on the "bond of matrimony," or the freely accepted ties that bind us, inextricably, to those we love. In the absence of the usual signifiers of marriage – children, the taking on of a single (family) name – homosexual couples are apt to search for other signifiers of their bond, as Ridley and Heeter have done here, and I am not just referring to the paraphernalia of "leather sex," but to the highly nuanced and elaborated form that interior decorating takes in gay male culture.[25] It seems reasonable that, at the point at which "home" ceases to be the container for a family, and yet still shelters a family that is not granted the name, the symbolic weight of that physical place called home increases exponentially. Indeed, it may be that the "marrage portrait" itself, or any other picture of the homosexual relationship, takes on more importance than it might otherwise, to those who, for whatever reason, are locked out of the dynastic embodiment of their love. The domestic portrait of a gay or lesbian couple – whether it is Francis Bacon's, Diane Arbus's, David Hockney's, or Robert Mapplethorpe's – is the record of a pact that, in most cases, will have no issue; that, even given the most fiery passion and deeply forged devotion, will disappear, like so much smoke up the chimney, upon the death of the partners.

15
Pop at Home

CÉCILE WHITING

In the early 1960s, art collector Leon Kraushar buys Tom Wesselmann's *Bathtub Collage #1* of 1963 and hangs it on the wall of his home. Wesselmann's collage introduces the aura of art into Kraushar's home, distinguishing this space from other interiors, this collector from other individuals. And yet in this photograph, first published in John Rublowsky's *Pop Art* of 1965, the distance between art and the rest of the domestic interior is less pronounced than it might be; indeed, the photograph puns on their similarity. A woman, Mrs Kraushar in fact, strikes a pose next to Wesselmann's work, and like the depicted nude in the picture, she busies herself, at the left side of the image, with her *toilette*. The wife models herself here on the work of art.

In the Kraushar bathroom, and in other similar spaces where art collectors incorporated Pop painting and sculpture into their homes, two standards of taste, on the one hand the aesthetic taste of the collector, and on the other hand the consumer taste of the female homemaker, faced off, but also intermingled. Kraushar's medley, however, depended on an earlier act of cultural appropriation: that by the artist. The pairing of wife in the bathroom and model in the painting, after all, could only take place because Wesselmann, before Kraushar, had taken on the task in his picture of arranging the space of the domestic interior, a task usually performed at the time by the female homemaker, not the modernist painter. Yet while Wesselmann's paintings, and his collectors, brought interior decoration and high art painting into close proximity, in the end, I will argue, Wesselmann's paintings and collectors alike preserved a privileged position for art based on the cultural authority of male vision.[1]

All of Wesselmann's series from the early 1960s – the Great American Nudes and Little American Nudes, the Still Lifes, the Bathtubs – depict interiors of the post-war suburban American home. These interiors transport the viewer to the hearth of an economy of domesticity characterized by an increased number of goods and services marketed to the female consumer and homemaker after World War II. *Still Life #30* of 1963, for instance, includes precisely those appliances and foods that were mass produced and nationally marketed to the American homemaker at compar-

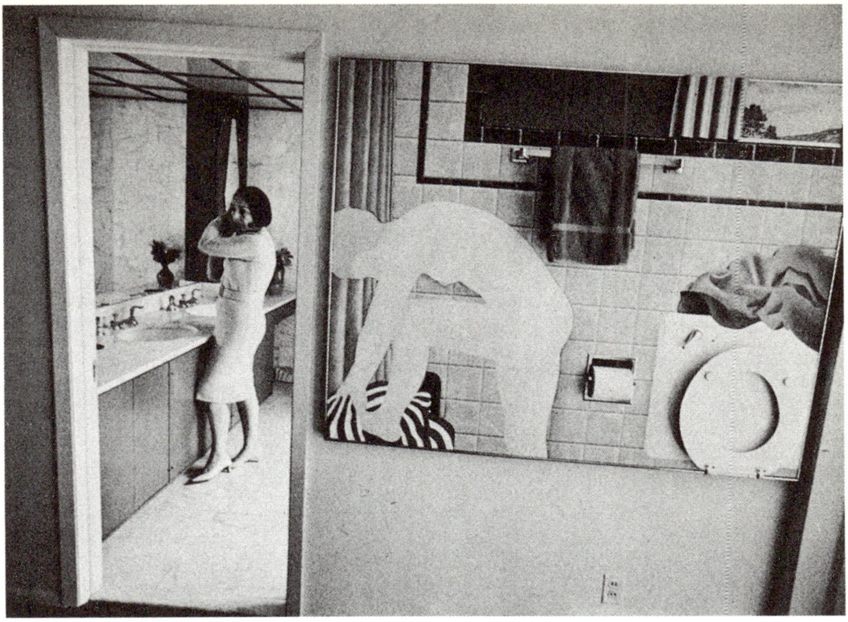

72 *Mrs Kraushar in the Bathroom, New York, 1965*

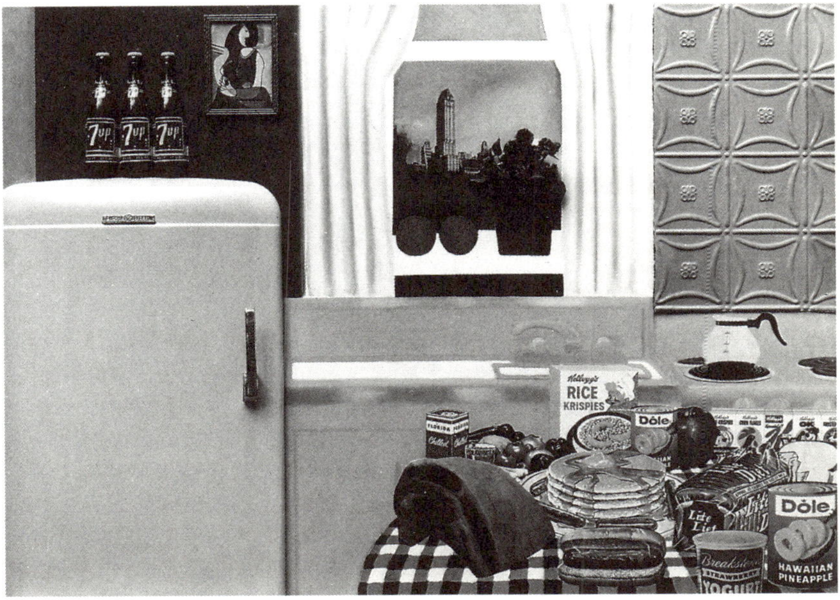

73 *Tom Wesselmann,* Still Life Painting #30, *1963*

atively moderate prices. Modest in scale, the kitchen contains only the most basic units of a range, refrigerator, and sink; these appliances form an orderly backdrop for a rather haphazard display of packaged foods amassed on the kitchen table in the foreground.

The wide availability of the types of foods and appliances contained in Wesselmann's kitchen served as the foundation for the conviction held by many Americans after World War II that the economy and standard of living in the USA outstripped that of all other countries.[2] As the embodiment of American success, the economy of domesticity bolstered public posturing on the advantages of capitalism over the Soviet Union during the Cold War. Elaine May, in a discussion of the famous, "Kitchen Debate" between Vice-President Richard Nixon and Soviet Premier Nikita Khrushchev in 1959, recently highlighted the importance of the domestic sphere in the American government's efforts to demonstrate the superiority of the "American Way of Life" over the communist system.[3] Photographs of this event published in American mass-circulation news magazines portrayed Nixon and Khrushchev leaning over a railing looking into the exhibition space of a model suburban kitchen at the opening of the American National Exhibition in Moscow, while Nixon extolled the benefits of democracy as exemplified by household appliances. Nixon implicitly claimed that the American capitalist system, by surpassing the Soviet system in the provision of consumer goods to all, had created a truly classless society – though, in fact, as Roland Marchand has since documented, only American families with incomes in the top forty per cent could afford such a lifestyle.[4]

The criteria of selection used to arrange the goods and to compose the space of *Still Life #30*, nevertheless, do not seem to manifest any form of ostentatious economic privilege, but conform instead to post-war precepts of moderation and good taste in interior design. The kitchen's fully automated interior appears first and foremost practical: all of the modern, ostensibly functional appliances remain close at hand for maximum efficiency. A coordinated color scheme of bright hues unites the clean lines and sharply defined geometric forms of the appliances. *Still Life #30* thus offers the fantasy of completely up-to-date appliances harmoniously and sensibly organized in a pristine space.

In arranging the various kitchen products of *Still Life #30*, Wesselmann appropriated the visual codes used in women's home and service magazines to display tasteful interiors managed by the efficient middle-class homemaker. Photographs of kitchens in these texts featured a select number of sparkling new appliances orchestrated in tidy spaces according to principles of design and efficiency. In women's magazines good taste, manifested in the felicitous choice and arrangement of goods, functioned in the place of wealth or family name as a sign and reaffirmation of distinction; taste served as the standard for defining a middle-class lifestyle without making explicit the economic basis of that standard.[5]

Wesselmann's pictures – like the post-war American economy of domesticity which they address – thus contain a contradiction between the apparent universal access to goods under a democracy and a standard of good taste and restraint derived from one specific section of that society: the middle class. Neither collages nor domestic culture, however, allow much of that contradiction to come to light: they both seem to pass off the criteria of good taste as universally valid for all Americans.

To the extent that Wesselmann's representations of suburban interiors such as *Still Life #30* embraced the middle-class economy of domesticity and its standard of consumer taste, they would at first appear to be objects easily scorned and rejected by critics committed to preserving the sanctity of high-art modernism. Many critics in the early 1960s did in fact dismiss Wesselmann in the pages of art magazines. These reviewers took for granted that anything that hinted of domesticity and consumer taste was unworthy of treatment in high-art painting. Wesselmann's kitchens, commented one critic, "are curiously inert like some housewife's day-dream."[6] Another critic's quip about Wesselmann's still lifes was that "Everything is intended to look like, and does, some of those double-spread food ads in *Life* that nobody looks at"[7] – nobody, that is, except perhaps female consumers. These reviews formulated pejorative judgments issued from a discourse on taste that assumed a qualitative difference between high-art modernism and consumer culture.

And yet, Wesselmann's interiors could not be dismissed by art critics as easily as could a photograph from the pages of a women's magazine. If Wesselmann's interiors had simply reproduced the products of consumer culture and the visual codes of interior design, they might well have been disregarded by critics as simply unfortunate representations of middlebrow taste. Disturbing perhaps, but only because the housewife's day-dreams and double-spread food ads had left their appropriate place in mass-circulation magazines and ventured into the space of the gallery and art magazine. Were Wesselmann truly beside the point of high-art painting, these critics could have simply ignored him. But they did not. The sharpness of their attacks on Wesselmann may reveal a need to reassert the established cultural hierarchy in the face of a challenge to its authority. Something else about Wesselmann's images, it would seem, provoked these critics.

Perhaps what vexed them was the fact that Wesselmann's interiors are not consistently middlebrow. Over and again, these pictures confuse the difference between the ideal of good taste in interior decoration and the principles of composition in high-art modernism by integrating reproductions of paintings by European modern artists into a decorated ensemble designed according to the precepts of female consumer taste. Often posters and postcards of modernist icons hang on the wall alongside snippets of patterned wallpaper or as backdrops to vases of flowers and bowls of fruit. In *Great American Nude #6* of 1961, for example, a portrait of a young girl by Modigliani appears on the back wall next to a swatch of rose-covered wallpaper and above an intricately patterned oriental carpet. Together these elements, including the painting, formulate a decorative and emphatically feminine interior space.

Sometimes Wesselmann's interiors explicitly mimic the arrangement of motifs in the high-art pictures that ostensibly hang within their walls. Moreover, in the Great American Nude and Little American Nude series from the years before 1965, bodies frequently echo the curves and take the poses of nudes painted by Matisse and Modigliani, yet at the same time appear as modern-day women with blonde hair either left long and loose or cut in a Marilyn Monroe bob.[8] To posit such equivalencies between high art modernism and interior decoration repudiated the privileged hermeticism of the previous generation of Abstract Expressionist artists.

Wesselmann's interiors, it might be argued, only partially disrupted cultural hierarchies, since for the most part they matched interior decoration with modern artists considered, more or less, feminine. The majority of the paintings reproduced in Wesselmann's interiors are by Matisse and Renoir and themselves depict women or fruit and flowers within a bourgeois setting. Matisse and Renoir, with their use of arabesques, Impressionist strokes, and pleasing colors, formed a branch of modernism generally considered feminine and decorative, at least by post-war Americans. Texts published in the USA that analyzed representations of women by these artists consistently employed adjectives associated with the feminine: grace, tranquillity, charm, elegance, delicacy.[9]

Yet even modern artists regarded as unequivocally masculine, such as the hard-edge and rigidly rational Mondrian, were drawn into the compass of Wesselmann's interiors. *Still Life #20* (1962), for instance, imitates the arrangement of rectilinear forms and primary colors of the Mondrian reproduction that hangs on the wall within the depicted kitchen interior. Wesselmann's image thereby elides the essential difference posited by post-war critics between the rigorous and rational control associated with the arrangement of colors and forms in Mondrian's abstract painting and the good taste demonstrated by the 1950s' housewife designing her kitchen decor.

It is not just that works by Matisse, Mondrian and others have to share space with refrigerators and Heinz tomato catsup; Wesselmann's pictures also equate high art and consumer culture by including within his works commercial reproductions of these paintings. Famous paintings appear in Wesselmann's interiors in the guise of posters or postcards, and as reproductions these high-art images lose their status as unique objects above the economic fray. Indeed, posters and postcards blur the line between commerce and art since they transform modernist icons into reproductions disseminated for a profit on a mass scale.[10] Furthermore, reproductions of art works in Wesselmann's collages appear alongside television screens and food labels, and thereby appear to participate in the duplication and dissemination of mass entertainment and consumer goods. Wesselmann's interiors treat the circulation of high-art images as equivalent to various other economic systems that depend on the mass reproduction of images.

Wesselmann's interiors seem to implicate high art in consumer culture, subordinating the high-art aesthetic to consumer taste. Of course, this argument could be turned on its head: rather than suggesting that consumer culture has commandeered high-art modernism, it could be argued that consumer culture in Wesselmann's images aspires to the aesthetic merit of high art. In terms of the maintenance of cultural hierarchies, however, it makes little difference which direction the argument flows: either way, high-art modernism appears to have lost its privileged aesthetic position in opposition to consumer taste. Wesselmann's interiors seem to blur the line between the formal arrangement of a modern painting and the practical arrangement of the modern kitchen, between appreciating the fine arts and managing the suburban household.

Yet even as Wesselmann's images conflate highbrow and middlebrow taste, they maintain a difference between high art and consumer culture by distinguishing between two forms of gendered vision. On the one hand they invite viewers to align their gaze with that of the female consumer. *Bathtub Collage #3* (1963), for instance, displays the material possessions and 74
well-organized household as objects of desire for the middle-class homemaker. The presumed occupant of the bathroom is the home manager who oversees the rational organization and cleanliness of the interior space. On the other hand, the presence of the nude positions the female body as the object of the voyeuristic male gaze.[11] Indeed, critics frequently judged Wesselmann's nudes in terms of the allure of their bodies and evaluated the extent to which the nudes succeeded in arousing desire: as one critic wrote for *Art News*, "the Great American Nude series, each with its curving voluptuous section of rose-pink female arching or lolling across her vivid American environment, is more appealing than any Miss Rheingold poster."[12] Wesselmann's pictures thus treat woman as both subject and object of the gaze; that is, she is both consumer and commodity. The viewer, meanwhile, can oscillate between the two spectatorial positions of female consumer and male voyeur.

Nevertheless, despite this oscillation, Wesselmann's pictures over and again grant priority to the male gaze. The presence of the nude irrevocably transforms *Bathtub Collage #3* from a sanitized middle-class interior seen in

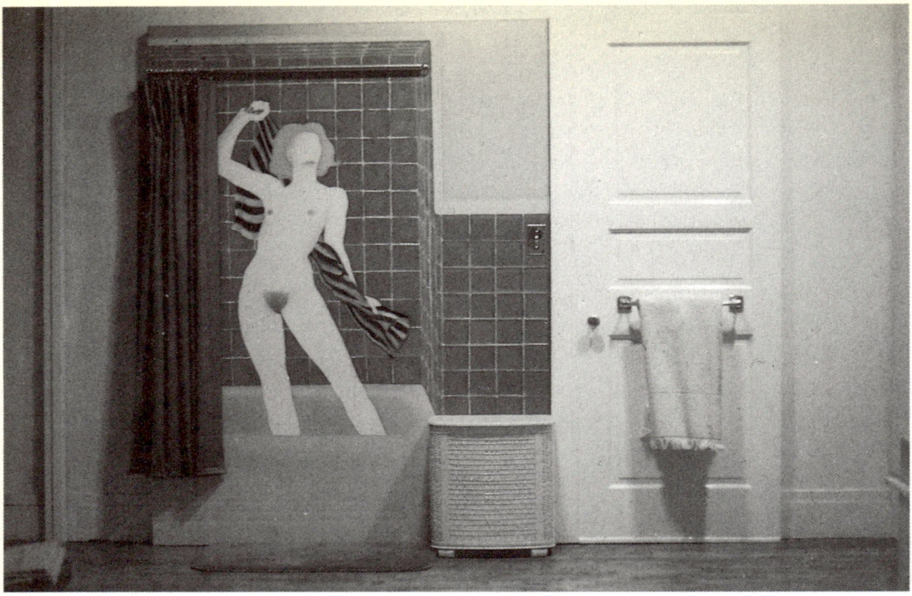

74 *Tom Wesselmann,* Bathtub Collage #3, *1963*

a woman's magazine to a representation of the female body as object of interested male attention. The nude in *Bathtub Collage #3* hardly resembles the well-groomed and efficient looking homemaker of women's magazines with whom the female consumer was often invited to identify. In contemporary advertisements promoting bathroom fittings, the homemaker partakes in such praiseworthy activities as tending to her children or polishing a sparkle into some stylish spout; in no case does she voluptuously strike a pose. The women in Wesselmann's interiors take pleasure in flaunting their bodies rather than in assuming the role of the efficient and rational homemaker and consumer.

Seen against the homemaker of women's magazines, the nudes in Wesselmann's collages function as transgressive signs of sexuality with whom the female viewer can identify only by becoming a body coded to arouse male desire. The young svelte woman in *Bathtub Collage #3*, provocatively posed with thrust-out hip, more likely embodies the post-war fantasy of the sexually available woman of leisure, the imagined playmate awaiting the playboy more than the proper homemaker managing the suburban home of the man in the gray flannel suit.[13] In Wesselmann's pictures from after 1965, which increasingly adopt poses from pornographic magazines, the female becomes even more explicitly the object of the voyeuristic male gaze.

Most important, Wesselmann's pictures hierarchize vision along gender lines by granting only the male gaze control over the very processes of representation. The nudes, objects of male desire, are always painted representations – painted, that is, by Wesselmann himself. These figures appear as two-dimensional forms, typically in solid pink, rendered with a bare minimum of distinguishing features and outlined by thick strokes and arabesques reminiscent of Matisse. Such images hardly try to pass themselves off as real physical women. With their multiple and overt references to art-historical precedents, Wesselmann's nudes invoke instead a long heritage of previous depictions of the nude, most notably those by Matisse and Modigliani. Indeed, critics repeatedly compared Wesselmann's nudes to high art and focused on how they were made – painted in pink, flat, sliced by the frame – rather than treating them as "real" or transparent representations of nudes. The male gaze, it seems, knows the difference between the real and the represented; it can discriminate between the two.

In contrast, the mass-produced goods and household appliances that are objects of the female consumer gaze take a variety of representational forms in Wesselmann's pictures: actual household fixtures, painted representations, and cut-out advertisements that function either as real commercial labels or as representations of actual goods. In *Bathtub Collage #3* an actual shower curtain hangs over the painted image of a bathtub; a real light switch is mounted on painted tiles. Similarly, the still-life tableau of foodstuffs in *Still Life #30* combines items that are both painted by Wesselmann and cut-out from magazines and various other sources[14]; yet it is impossible to tell which is which without close and careful examination. Not coincidentally, this confusion of the real and the represented also happens to be the logic of advertising: advertising depends to a large extent on the interchangeability of a label with its product. The tension between the presence of the image and the absence of the as-yet-unpurchased commodity generates the form of desire known as consumerism. Wesselmann's pictures capitalize on that confusion; his images, in short, attribute the inability to differentiate between the sign and referent to the female consumer.

Thus on one level Wesselmann's pictures conflated icons of the highbrow modernist tradition and middlebrow mass-produced goods within the same pictorial space. Yet, on another level, Wesselmann's pictures preserved the priority of painting over other cultural artifacts by associating it with the power and control of the male gaze over the female body and over processes of representation. Wesselmann's pictures engaged domesticity, but ultimately only for the sake of declaring art's triumph over it.

Viewers would have seen Wesselmann's collages and their reformulation of the prerogative of high art over consumer culture first within the institutional spaces of high art such as the gallery or museum; in such contexts these images affirmed the priority of high art over domesticity, but never really challenged domesticity on its home turf: inside the house. Pop art collectors, however, shifted Wesselmann's pictures, along with other Pop paintings and sculpture, back into the domestic interior. This did not go unnoticed. Beginning in 1964 bold headlines in the popular press directed attention to the way in which various collectors integrated Pop art into their homes: "Life with Pop," "The House that Pop Art Built," or "You Bought It, Now Live With It," they blared.[15] Lavish accompanying photographs exposed the interiors – and frequently the collectors and their families – to the public's scrutiny. These layouts revealed that collectors not only packed their homes with Pop art, but that they also adopted aesthetic principles from Pop art to organize their domestic spaces.

Pop collectors fit their art works into a specific type of domestic space: the high-design modern interior. The living-room in the Manhattan apartment of collectors Robert and Ethel Scull included Mies van der Rohe's famous Barcelona Chair, promoted by the Museum of Modern Art in its publication *Introduction to Twentieth Century Design* of 1959 as "the classic 'monumental' chair of the twentieth century."[16] Collectors Mr and Mrs Kraushar commissoned an architect to design a modern home in Lawrence, New York specifically for their Pop art collection. They explicitly opposed their choice of architecture, complete with soaring ceilings, exposed beams and sliding glass doors, to the predominant style of suburban homes. "They both wanted to get away from the conformist ranch-style look which they felt was dominating suburban architecture," reported *House and Garden*. "Mrs Kraushar, who has a larger margin of nostalgia for tradition than her husband, admits that it took her some months to be reconciled to the uncompromising modernism that her husband had chosen to build in." Although in this anecdote Mrs Kraushar expressed a more cautious taste than her husband, she nevertheless joined him in rejecting the standard conventions of suburban interior decoration: "The decor . . . was left up to interior designer David Barrett, and the decisions, to Mrs Kraushar, who feels that most contemporary houses are too feminine as well as too conformist."[17]

The Kraushars were not alone in their attitudes towards suburban architecture. Many social critics and modern architects in the 1950s and 1960s associated the ranch-style home in the sprawling suburbs with a middle-class ethic of conformity. As Clifford E. Clark Jr explains: "Some social critics, especially sociologists who wrote about suburbia, gleefully lambasted ranch house developments as the tasteless hallmark of a homogenized society."[18] Owing to the link between ranch-style domesticity and conformity, the high-design modern architecture and interiors of Pop art collectors could constitute a distancing mechanism from the middle class.

The arrangement of the interior spaces in the homes of the Pop art collectors repudiated the spare, disciplined aesthetic of the ranch-style home. To violate the homemaker's standard of restraint, Pop art collectors relied on some of the same strategies practiced by the Pop art works they acquired. First and foremost, the collectors appropriated the device of hyperbole from Pop art. Just as countless products spill over the tables and counter tops of Tom Wesselmann's kitchens, so too a disorderly array of art, furniture and people overtakes the homes of Pop art collectors. In the pages of *Life*, for instance, a dizzying display of art works surround Mr and Mrs Kraushar and art dealer Ben Birillo as they engage in animated conversation while seated in the collectors' living-room. Art, according to various news reports, "plastered" the walls and "cluttered" the interior of the Scull apartment in New York City; art aficionados filled the space with gossip. Far from the pristine and empty stage-like spaces reproduced in women's magazines, the library in the Sculls' home, according to Allene Talmey in the pages of *Vogue*, "is not a passive room, built for contemplatives. It is an active one, for active readers, with hi-fi hidden in the far wall. There is jounce and bounce – like the Sculls themselves."[19] The Pop collector's home, teeming with art, music and people, transformed the interior into a site of pleasure, leisure and entertainment. Domestic restraint gave way to unrestrained sociability.

The interiors of Pop art collectors as presented in the print media rejected not only the disciplined order of the female homemaker's interior, but also her self-effacement. The wives of Pop art collectors adopted the role of performers in their domestic spaces rather than receding from sight once they had prepared these spaces for the use of others. In the photograph from Rublowsky's *Pop Art* with which I began this essay, Mrs Kraushar's pose – conventional in its own right – assumes a dramatic flavor once the viewer recognizes that she is playfully emulating the activity of the nude within the Wesselmann collage on the wall near her – much as Wesselmann's interiors themselves often reiterated elements lifted from paintings reproduced within their fictive walls. Likewise, a photograph in Rublowsky's book of Mrs Scull posing before a Warhol multiple portrait of her hanging on a wall in the Scull household has Mrs Scull broadly smiling as she puts her hand to chin, overtly imitating one of the poses used by Warhol within the portrait itself. By confounding the difference between themselves and the women who pose and display themselves in the Pop art images hanging in their homes, Mrs Scull and Mrs Kraushar demand the same visual attention accorded to the works of art.

Similar photographs of male collectors posed in their homes near their Pop art acquisitions had a different effect; these images suggest flirtation, or even sexual trysts, between real men and depicted women, thereby violating the moral propriety of the conventional American home. In yet other photographs published in Rublowsky's book, collector Leon Manuchin leans forward on the edge of his sofa, cigarette in hand, suavely looking over at the female nude by George Segal seated in a chair next to him; while collector Richard Brown Baker sits beside a Roy Lichtenstein scene of romantic despair in such a position that it appears the depicted woman might actually be shedding a tear for him. A few photographs situate such implied encounters within the bathroom and bedroom, enhancing the licentious overtones. In a photograph appearing in *Life*, Mr Kraushar bends over the bathroom sink imitating the pose of the female nude who dries herself in Wesselmann's collage. While the scene almost exactly reiterates the picture of Mrs Kraushar in Rublowsky's book, the opposite sex of the collector in the bathroom – and his lack of clothes – hints strongly at a liaison between the man in boxer shorts and the depicted female nude. In another photograph from *Life*, Mr Kraushar lounges on his bed dressed only in a bathrobe while surrounded by a bevy of women: Andy Warhol's silkscreens of Marilyn Monroe, Elizabeth Taylor and Jackie Kennedy and a nurse painted by Lichtenstein hang on the walls. The Pop art collectors distanced themselves from the homemaker's world of propriety and restraint; these interiors appeared the domain of a set of ribald male collectors seemingly given over to sexual excess.

The sexualization and masculinization of the Pop art collector's interior paralleled another cultural figure of the 1950s and 1960s who rejected the supposed conformity and femininity of conventional domesticity: the Playboy. As Barbara Ehrenreich points out, Hugh Hefner, in *Playboy*'s inaugural editorial in 1953, "announced his intention to reclaim *the indoors for men.*"[20] The Playboy initially procured the urban penthouse as his pad, but by the late 1950s and early 1960s the house joined the apartment as an object of Playboy desire. The magazine emphatically insisted, however, that he not select a home in the suburbs:

> When it comes to buying or building a weekend retreat, his options in design are woefully few: instead of having his choice of country or country houses to complement his city penthouse, he finds himself confronted with Kozy Kottages or split-personality ranch houses or gas-station-modern monstrosities. These, he discovers, are all "oriented." They may be family oriented, kitchen oriented, children oriented, suburb oriented, economy oriented. None seems to have been designed for the man who, perhaps like you, wants his own place away from the city's hurly-burly . . .[21]

The Playboy escaped this morass of homemaker's housing options by living instead in decidedly modern structures, often designed by name architects and located in exotic and unpopulated geographic locations such as "the country," "the oceanside," and "the desert oasis." In 1959, for instance, the pages of *Playboy* offered as a suitable "Weekend Hideaway" a sprawling modern "bachelor's haven" tucked away in the woods.[22] All glass construction – recalling Philip Johnson's famous Glass House of 1949 in New Canaan, Connecticut – allowed dramatic views from the interior onto

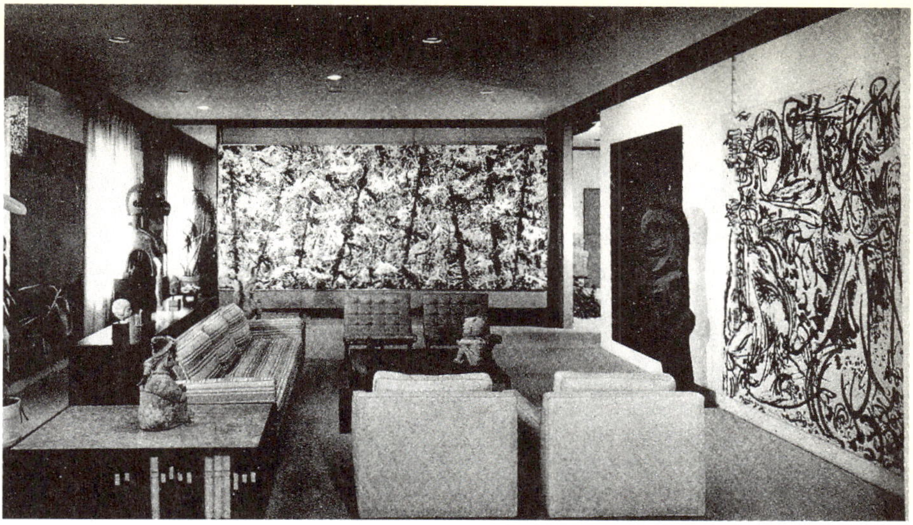

75 *Ben Heller's Living-room with Pollock's* Blue Poles, *1961*

the lake, pool, woods; the living-room had two fixed and six sliding glass panels so that a full twenty feet of floor-to-ceiling glass walls could be opened onto the pool. The Playboy, filling his hideaway with furniture by name designers, selected a Charles Eames lounge chair, a drop-leaf table by Bruno Mathesson, a Jens Risom stacked modular chest, and stools by George Tanier. The Playboy chose both buildings and interior furnishings that were themselves works of modern art and design.

The Playboy's taste encompassed more than just architecture and furniture. The *Playboy* reader, as the magazine imagined and formed him, favored expensive sports cars, fine foods, quality wines, jazz and Abstract Expressionism. The seriousness and individuality of Abstract Expressionism made it the Playboy's art of choice. Hugh Hefner himself hung a painting by Jackson Pollock in the main hall of his mansion, and in his manifesto, "The Playboy Philosophy" (1963) he cited Pollock, Willem de Kooning and Franz Kline as "creators of the most important and most influential work of any artists of our time." Pollock, in particular, exemplified a rebellious independent spirit that the Playboy hoped to claim as his own.[23]

The Playboy's knowledge and appreciation of fine art aligned him with the connoisseur's approach to collecting. Art journals in the late 1950s and early 1960s pointed to Ben Heller, who owned many examples of Abstract Expressionism, as a model art collector; he combined judiciousness with aesthetic appreciation of high quality works of art. He even published an article on "The Roots of Abstract Expressionism" in 1961 in which he adopted the authoritative role of art critic and demonstrated his erudition by explicating the origins of Abstract Expressionism, defining it as an art movement, and quoting from one of the leading critics of the day, Harold Rosenberg.[24] In photographs of Heller's living-room and dining-room spare modern furniture was grouped in the center of the room to leave plenty of space to view the paintings by Pollock, Rothko and Kline on the walls. Heller's interior could function as a silent, evenly-lit stage for the reverential contemplation of art works.

The Pop art collector shared with the Playboy and the art collector such as Heller an appreciation for high-design modern architecture and furniture and, like them, he assumed the role of the collector in charge of both the art and the domestic interior. The articles on Pop art collectors recounted the same tale of adventuresome male collectors whose wives initially expressed skepticism about the art works they selected; the wives in these narratives thus personified conservative taste. "[Mr Scull] goes alone on these expeditions, leaving Mrs Scull, an attractive blonde, with a slight figure and a talent for small talk, with the children," confided *Vogue*. "Sometimes Mrs Scull likes what he buys, sometimes she can not stand it . . . He is the boss, he is the buyer."[25] *Life* reported that Mr Kraushar "was first smitten by pop art two years ago when he came upon a painting forthrightly titled *Hand with Sponge*. His wife was unimpressed."[26] Kraushar implicitly dismissed his wife's preference for Impressionism as too conventional and refined in contrast to his bold taste for Pop: "My wife introduced me to art. About five years ago we began collecting – mostly French post-impressionist and other European works. I was never particularly sympathetic to these paintings. I found the preciousness of the image stale . . . It was when I discovered pop art that I became really involved. Here was a timely and aggressive image that spoke directly to me about things I understood."[27]

And yet in crucial ways, the Pop art collectors repudiated the practices of the Playboy and the connoisseur as surely as they eschewed the standards of the female homemaker. Mr Kraushar, relegating the Playboy's and Heller's taste for Abstract Expressionism to the past, described himself as "strictly a Big Beat Man who consider jazz as passé and as dead as abstract expressionism."[28] Indeed Pop art collectors presented themselves as a brash alternative to the type of taste and erudition exemplified by the Playboy and the connoisseur. Kraushar, who began collecting art in 1961 and quickly amassed one of the largest private collections of Pop art, did not justify his taste by claiming knowledge or aesthetic appreciation when he explained in *House and Garden*: "I decided to get a few paintings. It seemed to be the thing to do; everyone else was doing it . . . Collecting became a big thing in my life. I had never set foot in a museum until four years ago . . . I became addicted, unequivocally hooked by pop art."[29] These collectors relied upon sheer enthusiasm combined with business acumen, rather than the connoisseur's standard of quality and aesthetic distinction to acquire and display Pop art. Mr Scull, described as "a dark-haired man with explosive energies, a neat way with wit, and a garrulous, amusing way of talking,"[30] pronounced in *Time* magazine: "I don't presume to know a great work of art from a so-so effort. I simply buy what I feel I want to own, and I live with these things. I just love them."[31]

Pop art collectors, moreover, refused to maintain the tone of high seriousness about home, furniture and art that characterized the Playboy and the connoisseur. The Playboy might joke about women and sex – indeed the *Playboy* party jokes featured in each issue on the back of the centerfold focused on little else – but art, jazz, architecture and interior decor required earnest attention and the careful exercise of a refined appreciation for honest craftsmanship, quality and beauty. Pop art collectors, in contrast, adopted a humorous stance towards their collection and their homes quite similar to the bawdy humor manifested in Wesselmann's collages. The Sculls, for instance, played around with their art rather than maintaining a reverential distance from it, as *Time* magazine reported: "In the lobby [sits] a life-size plaster cast of one of the Met's curators, Henry Geldzahler, made by Sculptor George Segal. For the Sculls, the plastered Henry has become a household pet. Scull likes to feel Henry's pulse. 'How pale you look,' he murmers."[32] In *Ladies Home Journal* Mr Scull playfully posed next to Segal's sculpture of Henry Geldzahler as if deep in conversation with him. The photograph in the pages of *Life* displaying Mr Kraushar in his boxer shorts manifests a naughtiness on the part of the collector; it would have been unimaginable to see the distinguished Mr Heller in such a pose. Satire sprung as well from the play between real and representation; like Wesselmann punning visually between real refrigerators, fake fruit and painted nudes, Pop art collectors drew a laugh as they knowingly treated sculpted figures as people and posed real people as works of art. Again, Heller's living-room provides a fine counterpoint, where a *cordon sanitaire*, a veritable moat of unencumbered carpet separates the art on the walls from the space for the living. The Pop art collectors' ribald humor came frequently at the expense of women, to be sure, but their humor was directed as well toward the self-importance and solemnity maintained by the Playboy and the connoisseur toward works of art and their own finely crafted interiors.

Most significantly, the Pop art collectors exercised their ribald taste not in some urban pad or isolated hideaway, but rather at the very heart of the domestic interior and the family. Whereas the Playboy retreated from the world of female domesticity by escaping into his private bachelordom, the Pop art collectors, identifying themselves as husbands and fathers, asserted their manner of organizing the home within the space of the family itself. The entire Scull family gathers around the dining-room table for dinner in the pages of Rublowsky's *Pop Art.* In the pages of *Life*, Mr and Mrs Scull enact a scene of domestic partnership in front of Oldenburg's stove. And the scene of Mrs Kraushar posing in the bathroom in emulation of Wesselmann's *Bathtub Collage #1* brings the svelte playmate of the picture into the marital *boudoir* of the long-married couple.

The Pop aesthetic, in essence, had returned home. If Wesselmann's paintings had recast along gendered lines the priority of high art over consumer culture, of male artist over female homemaker, that reassertion of prerogative remained isolated from the American domestic setting – as isolated as the Playboy in his pad or hideaway – as long as Pop art paintings such as Wesselmann's remained confined in the established sancta of high art, the gallery and the museum. Only when the Pop art collectors integrated Wesselmann's paintings back into the family's domestic interior had the cycle been completed. Wesselmann had borrowed and reformulated the visual codes of the post-war domestic economy; his collectors used his standards of taste to re-establish masculine control over the home.

16
Vito Acconci's Bad Dream of Domesticity

CHRISTINE POGGI

> I have a great fear of the notion of home and family.
> *Vito Acconci, 16 February 1992,*
> *Philadelphia Museum of Art*

Vito Acconci entered the art world in the late 1960s, a period marked by social upheaval as well as radical questioning of received assumptions about the meaning and value of works of art and their relation to society. Artists of this generation, inaugurating postmodern challenges to the tenets of modernism, began to critique the definition of the self as autonomous, centered and unique – a definition that sustains a range of private/public dichotomies. Among these is the relegation of privacy largely to the domestic sphere, often equated with the privately owned, comfortably appointed home, which becomes the space of affect, family life, and respite from the competition and pressures of the public sphere. Despite its feminine and sometimes negative associations, within modernism the domestic or private sphere is also the ideal site of artistic production understood as unalienated labor, through which artists are expected to reveal a deeply personal sentiment or idea. By working within the privacy of their studios, which often double as domestic quarters, artists are able to unite their lives and work into a single, coherent whole. When subsequently they exhibit their works in a gallery or museum, this implies the transference of a personal or subjective meaning into a social space. One might even say that the artist delivers something of a hidden, private self into the visible, public domain.

Like many artists of his generation, Acconci refused this model, seeking instead to critique the ideal of personal expression and the home-studio/gallery dyad it implies. His early performances and installations frequently undermine the barrier between private and public life in ways that remain shocking, while exposing the economic relationships that govern notions of privacy and private property. As Acconci's work became more politically explicit in the mid-1970s and 1980s, his critique of the private realm frequently employed architectural structures to articulate and debunk myths of the home. For Acconci the American home symbolizes the private sphere of the autonomous individual, whose world-view is determined by the cultural values it maintains, including ideals of personal property and domestic harmony. Simultaneously, myths of the home define it as a specifically feminine realm, which creative, pioneering males might build, but must then escape. Finally, the home is associated with patriarchal power and authority, and with the sexual repression the nuclear family enforces. These myths function at two levels; they are fully public, a matter of prevalent cultural codes, and yet their true meaning resides largely in individual attitudes and beliefs, which may be unconscious. Acconci's more recent works reveal the individual to be implicated in the construction and perpetuation of these ideological, gendered codes.

Acconci's own works, however, do not fully escape the myths he so clearly exposes as fragile constructs. As his rejection of the private self and the domestic sphere implies, his work remains linked to the modernist ethos of the singular, heroic, transgressive male, whose independence drives him from home. Many of his most notorious works derive their shock value from the artist's explicit assertion of masculine prowess, both as a source of creativity and as sexual privilege, including abusive power over the women in his life; yet Acconci also challenges myths of masculinity, at times mocking or destabilizing his own sexual identity (*Conversions*, 1971; *Trappings*, 1971) as well as cultural assumptions about sexual difference.[1] His position is thus ambivalent; still imbued with a modernist sense of the domestic as a "bad dream" to be rejected, he also exemplifies the postmodernist tendency to demystify the private/public opposition, to critique its gendered meanings, and to reinscribe the individual in the social, public world.

For many of Acconci's contemporaries in the late 1960s and early 1970s seeking to reconsider the relation of the studio/home to the gallery, the exemplary referent was the sculptor Constantin Brancusi. His Parisian studio in the Impasse Ronsin was legendary among artists, collectors and other visitors for its conflation of living, working and exhibition spaces into a harmonious, spiritual, seemingly autonomous world. Brancusi departed from the established model of studio/gallery relations, however, by selling his works only reluctantly, and by stipulating in his will that his works, which he donated to France, must be preserved and exhibited in his studio.[2] Artists of Acconci's generation, among them Daniel Buren, praised Brancusi for keeping his work in the site of its production, understood as the only place in which its meaning could be fully understood. In retrospect, it is surprising to see how romantic a view of the studio Buren held in 1971: "[It] is in the studio and only in the studio that it [the work of art] is closest to its own reality, a reality from which it will continue to distance itself . . . It is therefore only in the studio that the work may be said to belong." For Buren, the work of art was given an impossible mandate: to be made in a specific place to which it must nevertheless *not* refer in order to remain transferable. Since the place of exhibition influences how the observer perceives a work more than its original site, work on view outside the studio is always "out of place." This, according to Buren is "the unspeakable compromise of the portable work."[3]

Most artists, of course, expected their works to be shown in galleries or museums, and once purchased, to be displayed in museums or in private homes. Although created in the studio, ostensibly a private sphere in which artists feel most free to express themselves, the work was destined to find its ultimate "home," and meaning, elsewhere. In this scenario, studio and gallery or museum maintain a symbiotic if often suppressed relationship. For if a work can be successfully transferred and sold, how separate and distinct is the private world of the studio from the public and commercial world of the gallery or museum? To what extent does the demand for expressive unity and formal autonomy both mask and depend upon the fact that most works of art are also commodities, objects of relative exchange value rather than absolute aesthetic value? Brancusi's desire that his works be viewed within the evolving setting of his studio, amid the rough materials they were made from, in relation to each other and to the artist's deliberately "peasant-style" dwelling (complete with handmade violin, coffee pot, dishes, bed and so forth), was idealist and utopian. It implied a necessary connection to the artist's life, and to the entirety of his work still in the process of creation; it also sought to resist the decontextualization that occurs when works of art are viewed as autonomous, moveable commodities. Although departing from a very different impulse – one that sets out to critique the notion of originality rather than to celebrate it, and largely to reject studio-based work – Acconci might be said to share something of Brancusi's utopian impulse: to conceive his art as part of a process or system rather than as a discrete commodity subject to economic exchange.

In 1979 Acconci told Robin White that from the beginning he was reacting against

> The idea of "let's take something from my studio and bring it to a viewing space." . . . Much of that early work seemed to be about this distinction between privacy and publicness. What I was doing was making blatant what it seemed like any artwork does – private person doing work, putting it into a public space. By extension, then, I put my privacy, put myself and my private life, in this public space.[4]

The following year, Acconci elaborated upon his view that "studio art" is

> the convention of work being made in the agent's studio and then transported to showing-space, selling-place; what's being assumed, then, is that, in the

> culture we know, the standard that must be reckoned with is not "space" or "viewer" or "mentality/autobiography," etc., but instead, the exchange between studio and gallery, the exchange between labor and market and consumer.[5]

Acconci's materialist emphasis on the system of exchange operating in the studio/gallery "standard," redefines the artist as an agent/laborer, and the viewer as a consumer. Rendered irrelevant in this market-driven process is "mentality/autobiography" – that is, the assumption that both artist and viewer are individuals constituted as closed monads. This notion of the self as essentially unique and autonomous corresponds to that of the work of art as a unified, self-reflexive object, intended for private contemplation and ownership.

In 1969 Acconci performed *Following Piece*, an early work that exemplifies the artist's obsession with challenging the boundary between private and public domains and with undermining the autonomy of the artist as subject. As this work seeks to demonstrate, these concepts are linked; for only if the individual is understood to have a unique, essential core, do concepts of personal expression and private property make sense. Insofar as *Following Piece* converts the private into the public, it points towards what would emerge in Acconci's later works as a more explicit critique of privacy and of the domestic sphere that this notion entails.

Significantly, *Following Piece* was not an autonomously conceived project, but a contribution to a series of group "shows" called *Street Works*, in which artists executed works on the streets of New York during pre-established periods of time.[6] For his contribution, Acconci selected a random series of individuals, one each day for a period of three weeks, and followed them until they entered a private place: home, office, car and so forth. These episodes ranged from a few minutes to seven or eight hours. Thus, *Following Piece* was performed outside the studio; indeed its very existence depended upon its being executed *only* within a public domain. The work was documented, however, at first by notes and text, and later by (staged) photographs, Acconci believing initially that "a photograph gives too much of the illusion of a thing."[7]

For most people, Acconci's activity was transgressive and potentially violent, any form of surveillance being associated with a threatening intrusion into an individual's privacy. But Acconci has resisted this interpretation, emphasizing instead that this piece gave him an external "reason to move"; forced to relinquish his own freedom by the decision to execute this work, his movements were then dictated by those of an unknown accomplice for an unspecified length of time. Acconci conceived *Following Piece* as a means of inserting his work, and himself, into an existing social system, so that his role as artist was merely "positional": "Fall into position in a system – I can be substituted for – my positional value counts here, not my individual characteristics."[8]

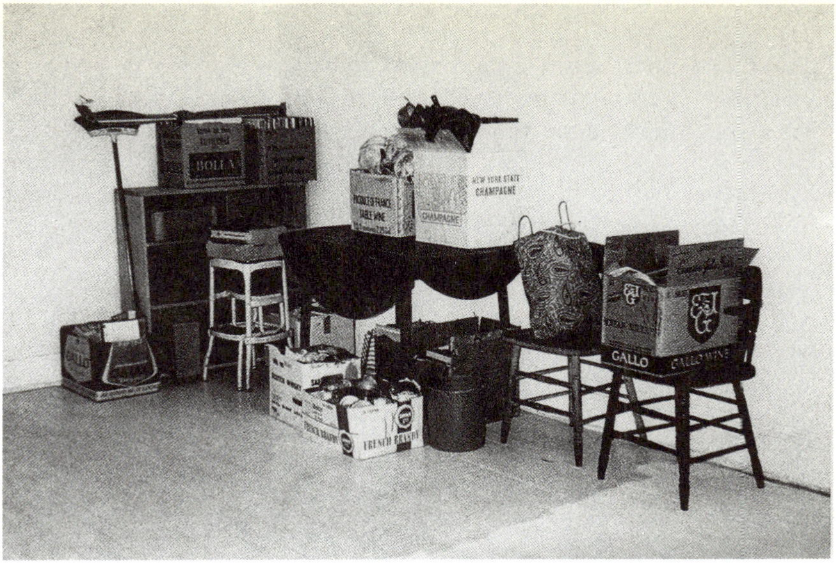

76 *Vito Acconci,* Room Piece, *1970*

Each day for three weeks during the next month, Acconci mailed an FBI-style report detailing the activities of the individual he had followed on that day the previous month, to selected members of the art world. These reports, titled "Private Piece for . . .," parodied the conventional singularity of the work of art, and its presumed revelation of private content. (Insofar as the content was private, it did not originate with Acconci, who merely recorded it in a deadpan, descriptive manner.) The reports also subverted the notion that works of art can be owned by private individuals, since Acconci mailed the same reports, one day at a time the next month, to individuals outside the USA. He also later exhibited and published them, along with "documentary" photographs. Sent through the mail in ever widening circles, the reports further defined art as a system of moving signs, and the art world as a communications network.

Room Piece, performed for the Gain Ground Gallery during three weekends in January 1970, constituted an even more pointed subversion of conventional notions of personal expression and of the home-studio/gallery relationship. Indeed here Acconci first broached the question of private expression as a function of the domestic sphere (equated with the studio), explicitly connecting the two. Rather than allow the gallery director to select a group of works for display and sale, in *Room Piece* Acconci transferred the entire contents of his four room apartment to the gallery. Packed in ordinary wine and liquor boxes, as well as in brown paper bags, Acconci transported his personal possessions via private vehicle and public transportation instead of using the services of trained art handlers.

This difficult, time-consuming process emphasized the physical and economic distance of the uptown gallery from Acconci's Greenwich Village apartment, eighty blocks downtown. Yet the act of moving his belongings into the gallery also revealed the interconnection, even the potential exchangeability of the two spaces, the gallery being temporarily converted into an extension of his apartment. As Acconci put it, in a play on the gallery's name: "My apartment gains a room, eighty blocks away."[9]

Room Piece existed in a state of constant metamorphosis, much like Brancusi's studio while he lived; yet it never achieved the look of a coherent work of art, or even a series of works. Acconci's possessions – a drop-leaf table, several chairs and a stool, a kitchen mop, bookshelf, set of albums, pots and pans, etc. – proved to be utterly banal, suggesting an unremarkable and not especially wealthy owner. Nonetheless, viewers were free to inspect them for what they might reveal about the artist's private life.

Moreover, the belongings on view in *Room Piece* remained in use throughout the exhibition, refusing to assume the status of art. When Acconci needed his toothbrush, for example, he would travel uptown to get it. Thus, while comprising a set of portable commodities, these objects failed to be transformed into saleable works of art, their continuing use value to the artist canceling their potential exchange value. Acconci seems to have wanted to reverse the strategy Marcel Duchamp employed in selecting his readymades, whereby common, mass-produced objects became art by virtue of display in a recognized exhibition space, whether the artist's studio or a museum. Unlike Duchamp's snowshovel, suspended from the museum ceiling and given a new thought by the title *In Advance of the Broken Arm*, Acconci's kitchen mop, leaning against the gallery wall, stubbornly retained its identity without acquiring the aura of fine art. Having learned that it was possible to get along with fewer objects, on the last day Acconci gave some of them away.

Service Area, also of 1970, departed from similar principles. This "performance situation," as Acconci called it, was the artist's contribution to the "Information" exhibition at the Museum of Modern Art. Again Acconci transferred part of his private property into the public domain, this time employing the postal service as his art handler. For the three months of the exhibition, Acconci had his mail forwarded to his space in the museum, so that it functioned as his personal mailbox. Obviously, at any moment the contents would vary and were largely unknown to the artist in advance. Even more than *Room Piece*, this work posed a threat to the artist's privacy, since his mail was open to theft. In his notes on this work, Acconci pointed out that those who stole his mail committed a federal offense. As in *Room Piece*, the contents transferred to the museum retained their instrumental value; when Acconci wanted to read his mail, he was forced to travel to the museum to get it, thereby continually re-enacting the link between himself, his personal property, and the exhibition space. Rather than a static object, *Service Area* exhibited a process that itself was only possible as part of a larger social system. This performance situation was "on the move,"[10] could not be purchased, and seemed out of place within the museum.

As a function of this process, the self revealed by Acconci's mail turned out to be an ad hoc image, formed entirely by others but fully known to none of them. Addressed to Acconci, his mail – including, no doubt, bills, gallery announcements, journals, postcards, and junk advertisements, as well as personal letters – constituted the production of a "you" or a receiver, with whom the artist, as an "I" or subject/agent, would attempt to coincide by travelling towards it. Rather than the autonomous, singular source of artistic meaning, Acconci presents us with a socially constructed, dialogic self, oscillating between the positions "I" and "You."

While performing pieces such as these, which subvert expectations of personal revelation through the medium of art, other of Acconci's early works seemed to test an opposing strategy. What if the artist publicly divulged private obsessions, sexual fantasies and practices, fears and other usually taboo subjects through a disturbingly explicit series of works? These performances would breach social norms by being too embarassingly direct in their exposure of the artist's body, desires, and secrets. Merely by his or her presence, the viewer would be implicated, caught in Acconci's seductive web as in a force field.

Exemplifying this concentration on domestic themes, *Remote Control* and 77
Air Time were performed for video, a new medium that Acconci believed to be inherently intimate. This was due in part to video's boxlike format, which paralleled the boxlike structure of small rooms and the intense psychic effect such enclosures had on their occupants. And in contrast with film, viewed on a larger-than-life screen, video preserved face-to-face scale and contact; the artist might even push himself up close against the screen, "as if to throw myself on the viewer," thereby further decreasing the distance between himself and the viewer. Drawing on the theories of sociologist Edward Hall, Acconci also believed that because of its poorly defined image, video positioned the viewer at an "intimate distance," which demanded greater reliance on sound than on sight. Thus conceived, video seemed an ideal medium with which to explore domestic situations, to view them close-up, as if in a "fishbowl." In this regard, Acconci's videos both resembled and parodied "the living-room situations of TV soap-opera, talk-shows," in which viewers, sitting in their homes near their televisions, avidly consume the private dramas of others.[11]

Remote Control (1971) took place at the Finch College Museum, with Acconci in one room directing his girlfriend Kathy Dillon on how to tie herself up with rope in another. Both performers were seated in open, three-foot-high wooden boxes, and communicated only through the video

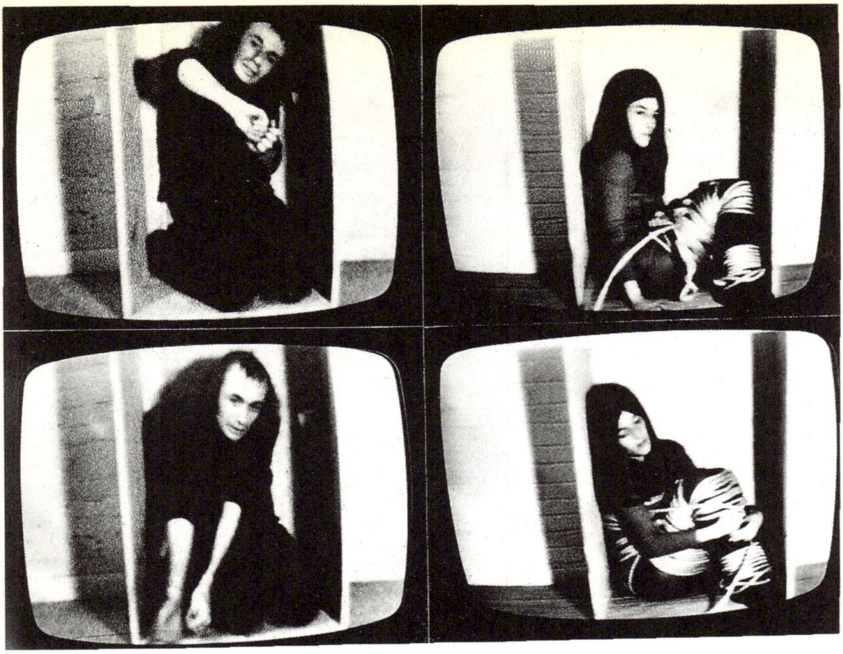

77 *Vito Acconci,* Remote Control, *1971*

monitors. Despite the intent to create an effect of intimacy, Acconci and Dillon's re-enactment of a sexual activity usually carried out in private, failed to proceed smoothly. Dillon, who could not always hear Acconci's voice, found it difficult to stay in tune with his instructions; frequently she got ahead of him or stopped and began to protest. Acconci for his part revealed his frustration at his lack of total control, and his voice grew more insistent as the performance progressed. Although the piece was finally completed, the uncertainty and alienation of the sexual partners, rather than their mutual bond, seems most striking in the video.

Air Time (1973) further dramatizes the splitting or alienation of the subject who is constituted in relation to his desire for, guilt towards, and power over, another. In the forty-minute video, Acconci directs a monologue to his reflection in the monitor, referring to himself sometimes as "I" and sometimes as "You." "You," however, also at times refers to his absent interlocutor, Acconci's girlfriend, or by turns, the viewer in the gallery. The installation of *Air Time* also used continuous audiotapes of this monologue, which were set into small boxes installed throughout the Sonnabend Gallery. The tapes "aired" his personal views on his relationship with a specific woman, in fact using the exhibition to end that relationship in a still shocking conflation of art and life. While the tapes were running, Acconci remained sequestered off to the side of the gallery as if he were in a recording studio, a nearly absent presence, there but not a focal point. As Kate Linker has observed, in this and related pieces Acconci focuses on himself through the medium of a highly charged psychological relation with another: the "You" or "specific person" he addresses in the video, whose identity oscillates with that of the gallery visitor.[12]

Similar concerns had structured three works presented contemporaneously at the Sonnabend Gallery in January 1972, yet they have rarely been analyzed as a group. The more famous of the three was *Seedbed*, in which Acconci withdrew under a low wooden ramp so that he could be present in the gallery yet invisible, *of* the space rather than *in* it. Twice a week from 10 a.m. to 6 p.m., while secluded in this underground space, the artist engaged in "private sexual activity" whose goal was to "cover the floor with sperm, seed the floor." Visitors to the gallery were alerted to Acconci's transgressive behavior by the artist's audible, indeed amplified, sexual fantasies. Although hidden under the ramp, Acconci addressed his visitors personally: "I'm doing this with you now . . . you're on my left . . . you're moving away but I'm pushing my body against you into the corner . . . you're bending your head down, over me . . . I'm pressing my eyes into your hair . . ."[13] Here the I/You structure of the performance parodied a seduction, the viewer positioned as an intimate other, as if the gallery were a bedroom. The ramp, of course, prevented physical and visual contact. Nevertheless the ideality of the gallery space was shattered, the neutral, minimalist appearance of the ramp undermined by the intrusion of forbidden behavior and usually private bodily secretions.

The meaning of *Seedbed* becomes clearer when it is seen in conjunction with *Transference Zone* and *Supply Room*, which Acconci performed on alternate days at the Sonnabend Gallery. For *Transference Zone*, Acconci arranged photographs and other objects including clothing associated with seven "prime people" who had been important in his life, in a small enclosure at one end of the gallery. This room functioned as a domestic space, dominated by fetish objects and an accumulation of memories. In the opposite corner, he created a kind of ante-chamber with chairs, rugs and pillows, where the viewer/participant could wait while considering whether to enter the other room. When performing his piece, Acconci locked himself in the "history room" and attempted to absorb himself into the objects and images associated with the prime people in his life. If a visitor knocked on the door and Acconci was alone, he would let that person in. He would then attempt to transfer his feelings towards a specific prime person to the visitor, putting the latter in a compromising position. Should he or she play along, engage in an intimate dialogue with Acconci? or reject his overtures? *Supply Room* also sought to implicate visitors in an intensely domestic, and certainly embarrassing, situation. Acconci placed himself in one corner of the space blindfolded, behind a green net as if he were a prisoner, while

Kathy Dillon sat in the opposite corner, a prerecorded tape of her voice playing continuously. On the tape, Dillon expressed her feelings of resentment towards the artist and entreated visitors to assist her in liberating herself from Acconci by kidnapping him.[14] Acconci occasionally tried to defend himself against Dillon's accusations, while attempting to sense the approach of visitors, now defined as potential captors. (Crumpled black netting and pillows, presumably materials that might be used to kidnap Acconci, were provided.)

In all three works performed at the Sonnabend Gallery, the character of the space in which the encounter with the visitor took place was significant. *Supply Room* positioned the artist and Dillon at opposite ends of a long narrow space, so that those who wished to avoid the domestic crossfire were forced up against the wall, unable to escape. In *Seedbed* Acconci hid in a low, "underground" space, suggestive of the repressed unconscious; his shocking activity converted a seeming neutral, minimalist space into a domain of private, erotic fantasy. In *Transference Zone* Acconci referred to his private life through the look of the home, although characteristically, it is a home conceived as confining and claustrophic.

Many of the performances of 1973, which were frequently presented in Europe, continued to use domestic themes as material. In pieces such as *Line-Up*, *Reception Room* and *Ballroom*, the artist interrogated his own psychological past, oscillating between admissions of guilt, accusation, denial and uncertainty. These performances seemed to function as a means of forcing Acconci to face up to his past, in particular to explain his dilemma of living with one woman while initiating a relationship with another. In *Line-Up*, performed in the Musée Galliera, Paris, he carried on a monologue, frequently interrupted by pleas to the viewer: "I needed someone to depend on . . . I'm not strong enough . . . she had to be stronger than me . . . someone to cling to . . . please . . . please . . . I'm so small, see? . . . just one more time, please, help me . . . just this once . . ." Viewers were presumably expected to alternate in their reactions as well, between sympathy for Acconci's plight and feelings of rejection if not outrage at his behavior. The images the artist had projected onto his face while he spoke turned him into a target, while the title "Line-Up" suggested that the audience was in a position to finger him as guilty. His fate lay in its hands. Yet much of the time Acconci himself mingled with the viewers while an audiotape of his monologue played and images of himself from prior works were projected onto the screen, so that his role as accuser and judge merged with theirs. He refused to remain in a fixed position or to assume a fixed identity, striving it seemed, to see himself as others saw him.

The question of just how personal these disclosures were remains open, even to the artist. "Was I that interested in revelation of autobiography? I somehow doubt it . . . I wonder about specific incidents of pieces related to specific incidents in life. Were they? I'm not really sure. Am I really not sure, or am I just hiding something in there? I'm not sure about that either." His goal in these works seems to have been less to justify his actions or to divulge the particulars of his domestic situation, than to use this material as a means of establishing a charged relationship with his audience. Beginning in 1972, however, Acconci began to critique his live performances for participating in the cult of personality.[15] Two years later he abandoned performance, coming to believe that

> as long as I was there . . . the work couldn't get beyond my own personality. Whereas in the beginning I could see my stuff as "person meets person," gradually I came to realize it was "art viewer meets art star." I had always been against this notion of cult, or art as religion, or art as sacred object. My shift, then, was from a kind of psychological self to a sociological self.[16]

In subsequent works, the artist's concern with the relation of the private self to the public domain, and with engaging the viewer in dialogue, no longer took the shape of face to face encounters. Nor did his body serve as a ground for marking the boundary between the closed region of the private self and the outside world. Beginning in the mid-1970s, Acconci began to focus more on the production and circulation of cultural signs, especially those dealing with the intersection of ideology, power and sexuality. The early performances had frequently occurred within small, confined spaces, or in underground enclosures, which forced instant intimacy, evoked entrapment, or suggested a "dirty" or repressed content. In the later installations, rooms or houses continue to embody or symbolize psychological or political states. Still seeking to engage a viewer conceived as a participant, and to avoid the creation of static art objects, Acconci's architectural constructions usually contain moveable parts and can be walked through or manipulated. Several must be "erected" through physical exertion, so that the gallery or museum visitor becomes a collaborator, the work achieving visibility only through his or her continuing effort.

Instant House (1980) exemplifies Acconci's use of the house as a meta- 78
phor for private, domestic life as well as for an ideologically constructed world-view. Of course, the two are seen as mutually interdependent, the individual seeing the world only through the language and symbols of culture. *Instant House* consists of a set of walls that lie flat on the ground forming an open cruciform shape. By sitting on the swing in the center of this configuration, the museum or gallery visitor activates an apparatus of cables and pulleys, causing the walls to rise and form a box-like house. On the inside, the walls are emblazoned with American flags, in reverse; on the outside the Russian flag with hammer and sickle appears. It is the visitor's weight and position, in both physical and symbolic terms, that serve to construct the house and bring its signs into view. Ironically, through active

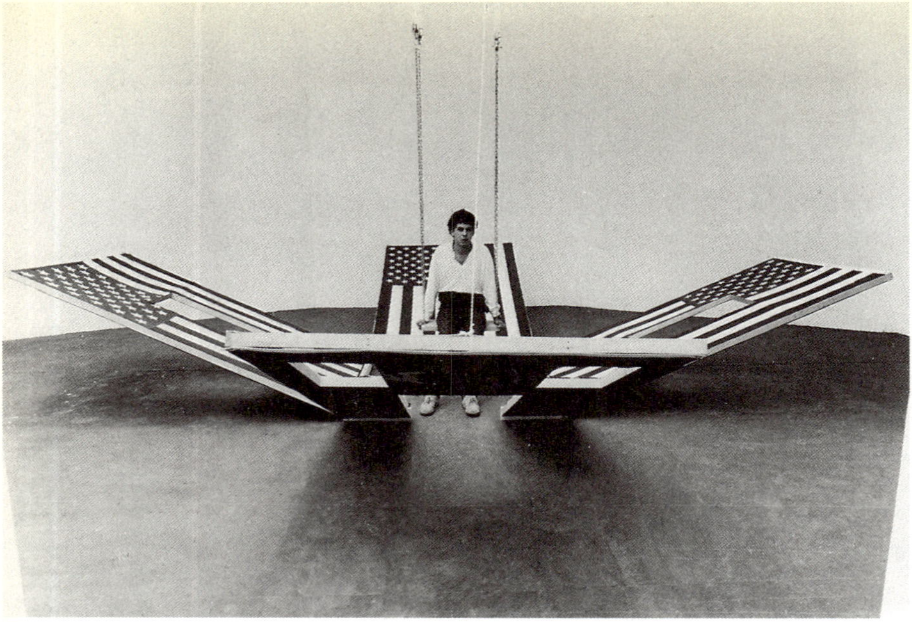

78 *Vito Acconci,* Instant House, *1980*

participation the visitor becomes a dupe of the system he or she props up, an unwitting collaborator in the production of cultural signs. Sitting on the swing (symbolizing innocent play? the playground as a formative ideological site? the principle of oscillation or alternation?), the visitor is caught on the inside, his or her perspective limited by the frame of the individual house. Those on the outside, who have escaped this frame, see the Russian flags as well as fragments of the stars and stripes within. Here Acconci comments on the mutual opposition/definition of two ideological positions, with ownership of a private house implying a necessary rejection of Communism. Yet the Russian flag, signifying an exterior threat, decorates the same walls as the American flag, and is applied in an equally superficial manner to the shed-like building.[17] Neither flag, neither sign system, is inherent to the form of the basic house.

A related work of 1980, *High Rise*, also requires the viewer to erect a house-like structure, although in this case the revealed sign concerns the relation of power to the rhetoric of male sexual prowess. By riding a carnival go-cart, the participant raises a three-story building, whose façade bears a crudely drawn sign of a penis. If the operator of the go-cart is not strong enough, the structure will fail to be fully extended, or may collapse altogether. Again, in this piece Acconci traps the viewer, who by trying to erect the piece, also participates in an absurd (and potentially embarassing) contest that equates strength and masculinity. By implicating the viewer, the

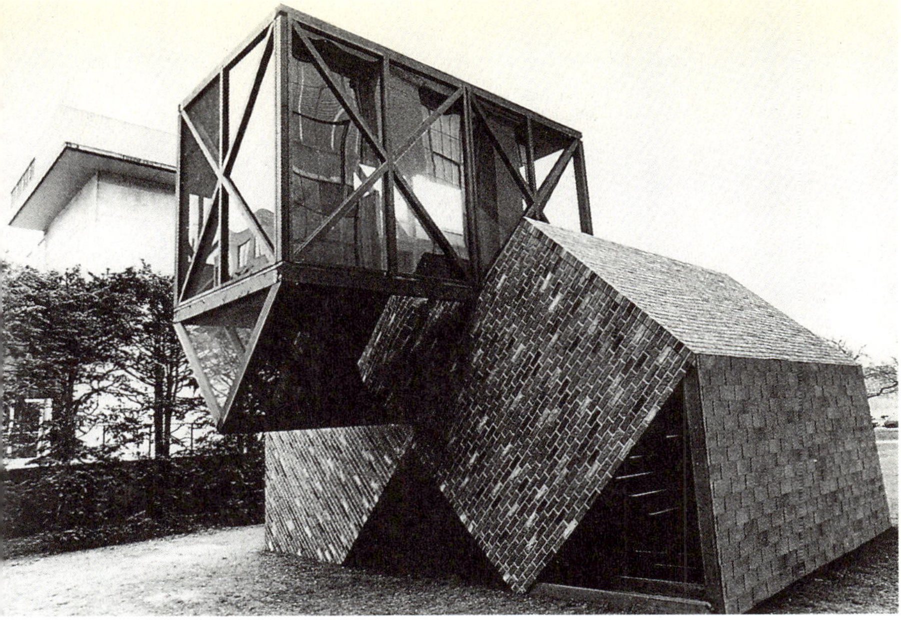

79 *Vito Acconci,* Bad Dream House, *1984*

work reveals both the necessity of individual acquiescence in the production and circulation of sexual signs, and their frailty.

High Rise also alludes to what Acconci calls the "American (male) myth" which "demands the building of the home: but it demands also the outsider who comes and goes as he pleases, who can't (won't) go home again." The male in his role as architect builds the home, but refuses to be trapped within its sphere, which is defined as feminine and prison-like. To play the role of the husband/father, rather than that of architect, is in cultural terms to be seen as a "sissy, a stay-at-home." According to this myth, associated in Acconci's memory with John Wayne films such as *The Searchers*, the American male is "divided in two, and both parts can be defined in relation to that building [the home]."[18]

If building a house or phallic structure masquerades as child's-play in these works, *Bad Dream House* of 1984 evokes a playground, with viewers encouraged to climb through its myriad, disorienting spaces. Like previous works, *Bad Dream House* draws on the language of architecture, employing it as a lexicon of conventional signs that are widely recognized but rarely articulated as such. According to the artist:

> This is a house in the mind: the form and images that make up a piece should be the conventions that everyone, in a particular culture, already knows as a matter of habit (a piece should be something like a poster, something like a billboard).

> But these conventions, that are the building blocks of a piece, are the building blocks of a culture: these conventions are power-signs, that confirm and maintain a dominant class/race/gender.
>
> A piece, then, should take these conventions and subvert them. Take this literally: revise the first sentence – the prototype piece is a house turned upside-down.[19]

Working literally, then, to upend or subvert the architecture of the domestic dwelling, Acconci built a structure supported on two overturned A-frame brick houses, with one side of each shingle-roof resting on the ground. Into these houses he spliced a partly cantilevered, inverted, A-frame plexiglass house with revealed aluminum supports. This collision of divergent architectural languages, traditional (and now postmodernist) brick and shingle-style, forced into co-habitation with modernist pseudo-glass and aluminum, denies the dictum "form follows function" and breaks with notions of stylistic and material unity. Brick no longer signifies simple economy and durability, while the shingle-roofs no longer connote the vernacular; nor, with one side on the ground and the other at a forty-five degree angle to it, can the shingle-roofs provide protection from the rain. Acconci employed plexiglass and aluminum here for a traditional A-frame, rather than International-style flat-roofed structure, although paradoxically, with its floor serving as a ceiling, the glass house does have a flat roof. *Bad Dream House* also shatters the symbolic unity and singularity of the basic A-frame through multiplication, the individual home generating an extended, community dwelling space. Not surprisingly, given Acconci's recurring efforts to subvert the barrier dividing domestic from public spaces, *Bad Dream House* fails to provide privacy or even shelter. With its doubled roof on the ground and lack of floors to take their place, the brick houses are opened up to sky and weather. Similarly, the interior of the plexiglass house, despite some blue-tinted panes, is visible from outside. Once on the inside, visitors find themselves in a disorienting world deprived of right-angles, with stairs that lead nowhere, and with built-in furniture, such as an upsidedown table hanging from the ceiling/floor overhead, which forces the body into unfamiliar and contorted positions.

"This should be the kind of home that makes you a stranger inside it," Acconci declares. Through structures such as *Bad Dream House* he provokes his audience to think critically about the private, traditional dwelling with its associations of order, tranquility and family harmony, and ultimately to reject it. As the artist commented, "If the house makes you cozy, if you can snuggle into it, then you're lost in the past and stabilization; but, if the house makes you itch, if you do a double-take, then you snap out of the present, you can have time to think of the future and change."[20]

Given this commentary, it remains uncertain whether the bad dream of the title refers to Acconci's piece or to the conventional home it seeks to deconstruct. For Acconci, much as for John Wayne, escaping from the home means escaping from the strictures of the family, including its paternal authority and oppressive sexual mores. In *Sub-Urb* (1983), a "usable architectural unit" that explored many of the themes and forms of *Bad Dream House*, Acconci inscribed a series of paired terms on the interior walls: Evolution/Revolution; Private/Public; Liberal/Radical; Sedentary/Nomadic; Soldier/Guerilla; Family/Comrade; Flowers/Weeds; Respect/Analyze; Capital/Commune; Sow/Forage; Father/Patricide; Surplus/Desire; Segment/Flow. It may initially seem surprising to see "patricide" included among the valorized second terms in this suite of oppositions, but Acconci associated the house with paternal domination as an individual manifestation of a larger patriarchal political system. Hence the equation of patricide with revolution and guerilla warfare, weeds and the flow of desire. Acconci also articulated the notion that the cult of the private home subjugates women in a 1986 drawing closely related to *Bad Dream House*.[21] One of the images on a page covered with pitched-roof houses, some upturned, shows a woman's legs emerging from beneath a house. That the house itself is synonymous with her genitalia, and enforces her sexual availability, is made evident by the attachment of gynecological stirrups to either side of the house, producing a horrific image of female sexual domination. By exposing and overturning these conventions of the house, Acconci hopes to decontextualize their gendered meanings and thereby make them available for analysis. Even to take up the house as a theme, he asserts, is "to insert, inside the public realm . . . a region that has been considered by convention to be female."[22]

Although for Acconci the domestic sphere of the home remains a bad dream, something to escape, he recognizes the allure that ownership of private property and a single-family dwelling still holds over most Americans, perhaps including himself. Describing this paradox, Acconci writes: "The American fear is: if you leave the house, the house might disappear. So the American is in a double bind. In order to save the house, the American has to stay at home. But in order to save the self, in order to grow up, the American has to leave home."[23] Since merely staying at home is a clearly unacceptable solution, Acconci has proposed in a work of 1992 a strategy for having it both ways. In *Personal Island*, an aluminum boat is partially 80
embedded in a circular island, whose form and size tell us it has been cut out from the corresponding hole in the shore of a lake. Another boat – sunken into the ground, a tree growing in its bow, its oars laid uselessly on the ground – symbolizes the home-bound, rooted alternative. By rowing the mobile boat and its attached island away from the shore, however, the owner of *Personal Island* is free to escape the home, to be an American pioneer, architect or cowboy, even an artist – while remaining securely on home turf.

Acconci's works and writing provide a cogent critique of the ideology that links American individualism to political and aesthetic myths about the meanings of home and private property, as well as to the division of private and public realms. Yet while undermining these categorical divisions, and the myths that sustain them, he remains caught within their field. The artist's own domestic quarters function as a sign, to be read much as a flag. Within a large loft devoted primarily to the design of his projects and the building of models, Acconci has reduced his living space to the barest minimum while his personal possessions would probably not amount to much more today than they did in *Room Piece*. The private, domestic sphere remains at once a myth to be debunked and a trap to be avoided.

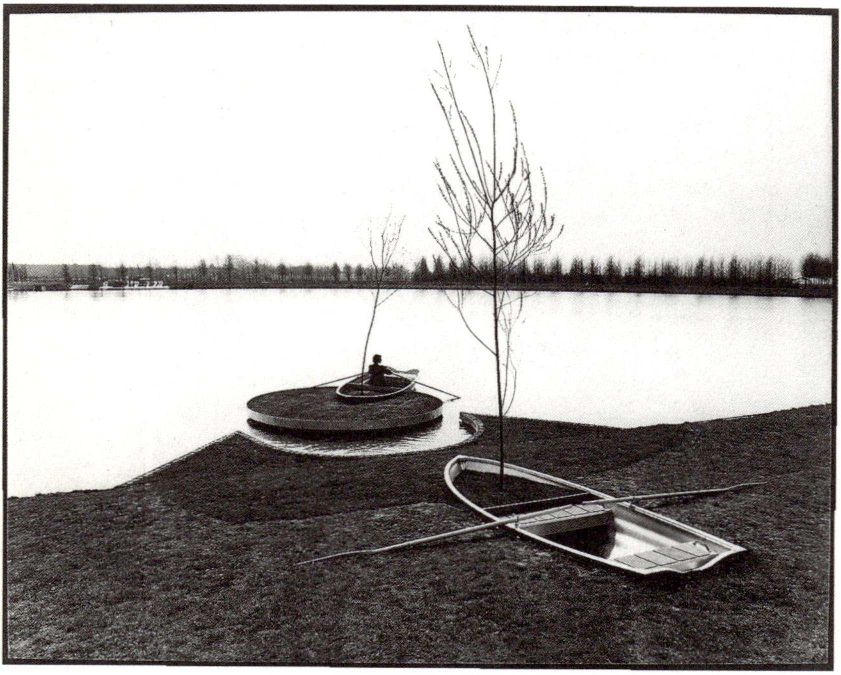

80 *Vito Acconci,* Personal Island, *1992*

17

Coming Home: A Postscript on Postmodernism

SHARON HAAR
AND CHRISTOPHER REED

In contrast to the ambivalent – even antagonistic – relationship between domesticity and modernism, the postmodern era has witnessed a kind of homecoming in high culture, as artists and designers have (re)turned their attention to domesticity. It would be naïve, however, to hail this evolution as a simple solution to the complex problems of modernism. Homes are as often sites of repression and stasis as they are cradles of empowerment and change. This essay charts the place of domesticity in American[1] art and architecture since the 1960s, emphasizing important differences among phenomena often bundled together under the rubric of postmodernism. Specifically, the idea of home today is caught between the stasis of nostalgic historical fantasy and the dynamism of activist engagement with the future; on one hand, the home functions as a potent image or symbol, on the other it exists in all the complexity of daily experience in a three-dimensional world. All history is written with a purpose. Our analysis is frank in its commitment to an idea of the home, not as a symbol of an idealized past, but as a space in which to enact a better future.

The tensions in postmodern invocations of the home may be traced to the 1960s, when two independent movements – Pop and feminism – made domesticity a central element in their defiance of modernism, though with very different motives and effects. The Pop artists' use of domestic imagery (analyzed by Cécile Whiting in this book) finds its architectural counterpart in the work of Robert Venturi, whose 1962 house for his mother deployed, in his words, "the vivid lessons of Pop Art" to challenge "the puritanically moral language of orthodox Modern architecture." Here the anti-functionalist organization of the interior announced an antipathy to modernism reiterated in the exaggerated quotations of exterior elements associated with conventional domesticity. The now famous image of Vanna Venturi sitting on her stoop beneath the oversized split gable roof and gigantic chimney came to exemplify Venturi's goal of "creat[ing] an almost symbolic image of a house."[2]

Along with assaults on International Style architecture, the 1960s saw challenges to modernist urbanism's faith in rational masterplanning.

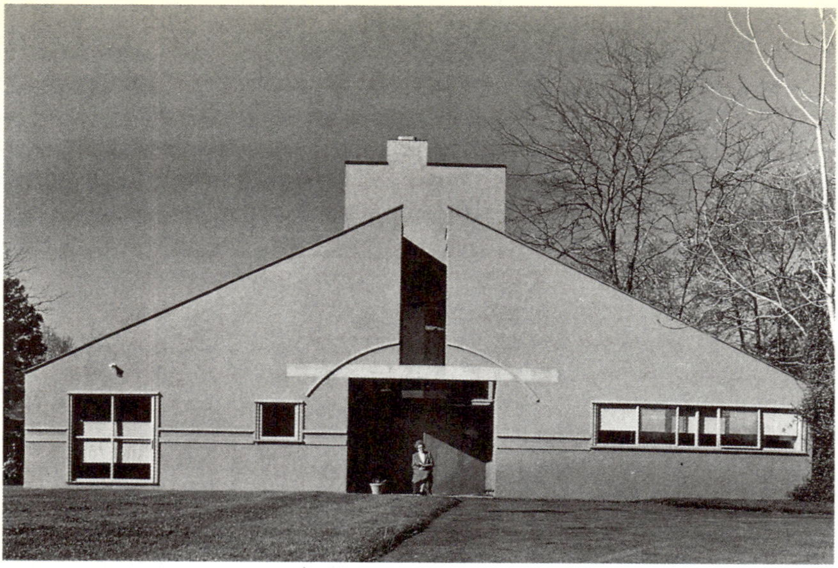

81 *Venturi and Rauch, Venturi House, Chestnut Hill, PA, 1964*

Venturi and his colleagues famously celebrated the everyday chaos of the commercial strip in *Learning from Las Vegas*. Their analogous study of the residential suburb, *Learning from Levittown*, garnered less attention, but is significant for its attempt to counter the modernist emphasis on standardization with an acknowledgement of vernacular self-expression in domestic design and decoration.[3] Especially influential was Jane Jacobs's 1961 book, *The Death and Life of Great American Cities*, which challenged "modern, orthodox city planning" based on separate residential, office, and industrial areas connected by super-highways. Jacobs's defense of the pedestrian-scale urban neighborhoods confronted modernist master planning with a standard rooted in common experience. "I shall be writing about common, ordinary things," her introduction explains.[4] Though not domestic per se, her method, like Pop, used the daily and specific to debunk the abstract and universal. Unlike the men identified with Pop, however, Jacobs's promotion of the pedestrian (in both senses of the term) was not ironic or self-consciously avant-garde. On the contrary, the anger, the earnestness, and ultimately the optimism behind Jacobs's study anticipate the character of the feminist challenges to modernism that emerged around 1970.

For feminists, rebellion was not an avant-garde strategy. They aimed to undo the conventions that neglected or disparaged categories of culture associated with women – prime among these, the home. The link between feminism and domesticity was explicit in the catalog for the landmark 1977 exhibition, *Women in American Architecture*, curated by Susana Torre. The show began from the premise, "the dominant element in women's relationship to architecture has been, since the obscure beginnings of humankind, the relationship to the domestic, including everyday caretaking and maintenance labor."[5] *Women in American Architecture* showcased a range of feminist approaches to architecture, offering a rich overview of histories of women reformers and builders, theoretical propositions about the relationship of gender to design, and current work by women architects. At the same time, it disputed the ideologies that confined women to a domestic sphere conceived as subordinate or marginal to the public realm. Just as the feminist dictum "the personal is political" propelled women's issues into public discourse, so for feminists in architecture, the domestic was not a retreat from the world but the arena where social forces interact with daily life.

By the early 1980s, feminist studies in architecture had produced an important body of literature. Pioneering books by Gwendolyn Wright and Dolores Hayden – original contributors to *Women in American Architecture* – chronicled the history of American domestic architecture, charting connections between the design of the home and the changing image of the American dream; exploring turn-of-the-century efforts by women activists to link home, labor, and urban design; and advocating the restructuring of family and community life through a redesign of housing and cities. Leslie Kanes Weisman's later book reviewed and expanded her contributions to early feminist discussions of architecture. In 1974, Weisman co-founded the Women's School of Planning and Architecture, a summer program and professional association whose members contributed to the important special architectural issue of the feminist magazine *Heresies* in 1981. The journal documented recent work by feminist designers and collectives, and expanded the scope of historical inquiry to include pioneering European women architects, such as Eileen Gray and Lilly Reich. Linking the historical and current projects was a rejection of the modernist stress on standardization, efficiency, and style; in its place, feminists emphasized flexibility, individuality, and the social and physical organization of living space. These emphases reflect two currents in this generation of feminist thought: a widespread fascination with tactility and interiority as "women's ways of knowing" (in contrast to supposedly masculine reliance on vision and projection), and an activist commitment to social change. Both tendencies are present in the work that epitomizes early feminist engagement with domesticity: *Womanhouse*.

Womanhouse was the project of twenty-three women in Judy Chicago and Miriam Schapiro's Feminist Art Program at the California Institute of the Arts in the winter of 1971–72. According to Schapiro, their question was, "What would art look like if made in the image of domesticity by a group of women artists?" Their answer turned an abandoned mansion into a walk-in rumination on the condition of women's lives. Included were elaborate doll houses; a "Womb Room" encased in a web of crochet; a nursery where giant furniture reduced adults to the scale of toddlers; a dining-room with a sumptuous meal displayed as art, the food rendered in fabrics, vinyl and petrified bread dough; a pantry with a numbingly repetitious array of breakfasts, lunches, and dinners; and a "Nurturant Kitchen" where fleshly-pink cabinets and appliances stood out against walls studded with breasts that echoed the forms of fried eggs stuck on the ceiling. Two "woman-nequins" enacted a deeply ambivalent relationship to the home: one, nude, was embedded in the tidy linen closet, surrounded by stacks of clean sheets, her body sliced through by the shelves; the other was a beautifully arrayed bride on the staircase with her white train trailing into the kitchen as it turned gradually gray. The most private of domestic spaces became in *Womanhouse* powerful public statements as visitors encountered a "Lipstick Bathroom" painted entirely in red; a "Fear Bathroom" where a bathing female figure made of sand dissolved in a tub; and a "Menstruation Bathroom" set up like a shrine where viewers peered through a veil of gauze to see that, in its maker's words, "under a shelf full of all the paraphernalia with which this culture 'cleans up' menstruation was a garbage can filled with the unmistakable marks of our animality." In addition to these installations, a program of performances during the month *Womanhouse* was open to the public choreographed such domestic rituals as scrubbing floors, ironing sheets, applying and removing make-up, or simply waiting.[6]

Like the uncanny domestic architecture proposed by the Surrealists (described in this volume by Anthony Vidler), *Womanhouse* aimed to disrupt conventions that rendered the home familiar and banal. The feminists' motive, however, was practical and political. As it was summed up by Arlene Raven, "*Womanhouse* turned the house inside out. The isolation and anger that many women felt in the single-nuclear-family dwelling in every suburb of America were flung out at the public who came to see the environment and performances . . . exposing a sadness which had been covered by the roofs of many in their own private homes."[7]

Although *Womanhouse* was created in just six weeks and open to the public for only four, it was seen by almost 10,000 visitors. Paradoxically, however, *Womanhouse* has gone unexamined – and barely acknowledged – by art historians, despite its anticipation of the themes and strategies for much subsequent feminist art. Both Chicago and Schapiro sustained its domestic focus through well-known later work. Chicago's *Dinner Party* installation involved over 400 craftspeople in setting a banquet table for women excluded from history. Schapiro's paintings, collaged with swatches of fabric in a technique she called "femmage", brought quilting and the domestic arts into galleries and museums.[8] Nor was *Womanhouse* the only manifestation of feminist artists' domestic orientation. Indeed, it was just the first example cited in an article on women artists working with domestic themes that Lucy Lippard published in *Ms.* in 1973. By the early 1980s, museums across America were mounting exhibitions on domesticity and art in recognition of the substantial body of recent work challenging the modernist indifference to the home.[9] For Donna Dennis, whose giant doll houses (or are they miniature buildings?) were featured in a number of these exhibitions around 1980, "Focusing on these humble structures is for me very much like the feminist movement focusing on the lives of women and discovering there a whole world that was previously overlooked." And twenty years after *Womanhouse*, Portia Munson's massive displays of scavenged pink plastic objects – everything from toilet brushes, shower caps, and curlers to Barbie dolls and sex toys – sustained the half-furious, half-exultant energy of early feminist explorations of the domestic.[10]

During the 1980s, however, in both art and architecture, the feminist focus on the domestic faced competing trends that turned the home from an arena for reform to a symbol of nostalgia. Although both tendencies can be construed as postmodernist in their challenge to the modernist aversion to the home, this does not obscure their significant differences. The art critic Hal Foster has usefully distinguished between what he characterizes as "a postmodernism of resistance and a postmodernism of reaction." The first, he says, seeks to "resist the status quo." The second – which he describes as "far better known" because of its high profile in architecture – presents itself "as a necessary turn toward 'tradition.'"[11] This dynamic is clear in the resurgence of domesticity in the art and architecture of the 1980s: both the feminists, ambitious to invent a new world, and the traditionalists, anxious to realize nostalgic fantasies of the past, gave the home a central role in postmodern culture.

The equation of domesticity with tradition or convention is a cliché of Western culture. The movie *The Wizard of Oz* famously reflects the conviction that the attractions of adventure and change – especially for little girls – pale before the pleasures of stasis registered in Dorothy's fervent mantra, "There's no place like home!" Less entertainingly, perhaps, the influential writings of phenomenologist philosophers Emmanuel Levinas and Gaston Bachelard extrapolated from "the pabulum of Heideggerian nostalgia" (the phrase is Vidler's) to authorize the conflation of domesticity and convention through their arguments that the home is constituted through childhood memories. "Only from this recollection does the building take on the signification of being a dwelling," says Levinas, echoing Bachelard's claim that "after we are in a new house, when memories of other places we have lived in come back to us," . . . "an entire past comes to dwell in a new house."

For both Levinas and Bachelard, domesticity is equated with visions of a safe childhood that, evoked through memory or fantasy, enable existence and action in a world outside the home: for Bachelard the "inhabited space" is "the non-I that protects the I"; for Levinas, "dwelling" makes "labor" possible. This perspective is the prerogative of men, positioned as the beneficiaries of domestic nurturance, a logical induction confirmed by Bachelard's casual linkage of domestic love with motherlove "in the bosom of the house," and by Levinas's assertion, "The woman is the condition for recollection, the interiority of the Home, and inhabitation."[12] For women – historically confined within and responsible for creating the conditions of domesticity – the lure of nostalgia is accompanied by a more critical realization that the house is very much of the world, that domesticity is as much an activity oriented toward the future as it is a state of mind rooted in the past. In the art and architecture that dominated the markets for "postmodernism" in the 1980s, however, feminist campaigns for the critique and reform of the home were overwhelmed by nostalgic formations of domesticity.

In the 1980s, widespread disillusionment with modernism's promises of a utopian future was expressed as nostalgic fascination with an idealized past, especially with the years around mid-century that comprised the childhood of most adults.[13] Ronald Reagan's politics of nostalgia and the renewed popularity of television comedies from the 1950s and 1960s (particularly those featuring children) attest to a yearning for the imagined simplicity of an idealized childhood, while panic over child kidnapping and satanistic day-care workers, along with pop-psychology schemes for unhappy adults to reconstitute their "inner child," register concomitant anxieties over the inevitable corruption of impossibly nostalgic fantasies. Whether footnoted to phenomenology or absorbed from popular culture, the perspective of the grown-up child pervades the art and exhibitions that, during the 1980s, focused on the home. A good deal of popular recent art uses conventional – and even archaic – media to create nostalgic visions of the home. A related phenomenon is the rise in art dealing with the inevitably broken promises of this simplistic domestic ideal.

One of the most prominent young artists of the 1980s was Eric Fischl, whose stylistically conservative paintings of unhappy suburban families deal with the theme of domestic corruption. For Fischl, "privacy" – a cardinal component of domesticity – is "what you do when you're not supposed to do something . . . Privacy is – you're playing with yourself, you're stealing, you're having sex with your neighbor, whatever, you're not supposed to be doing it." Similar associations between domesticity and secrecy animated the much publicized 1991 photography exhibition at the Museum of Modern Art, *Pleasures and Terrors of Domestic Comfort*, which documented the focus of recent photography on what it called "the *terra incognita* of the domestic scene."[14]

Despite their superficially similar evocations of the domestic uncanny, significant differences separate this perspective of disappointed nostalgia from feminist projects like *Womanhouse*. Though both defamiliarize the home, feminist work is informed by political analysis and oriented toward the possibility of change. In contrast, Fischl acknowledges, "There's no specific doctrine I am pushing to change things. There is criticism and a kind of analysis, but no proposal for an alternative. I don't know any." Likewise, the MoMA show – both the selection of images and the catalog essay – depoliticizes domestic imagery, allying it all with Fischl's celebrated "psycho-theater of domestic drama." Reasserting the modernist myth of the isolated figure of the artist-hero, the catalog disavows the kind of solidarity that brought women together under the banner of feminism, insisting that "the photographers represented here have worked not as . . . [a] team but as independent artists, most of them unaware of most of the others." The strong political commitment of photographers like Carrie Mae Weems and Nan Goldin was neutralized by a selection of work based on the principle that "less explicit" is "more compelling," and viewers were admonished in the catalog that, though "one may be tempted to approach these works of art as if they were illustrations to a sociological report[,] the temptation should be resisted"; for example, "to read [Goldin]'s work as social criticism is to read only its surface."[15] This drive to replace politics with aesthetics encapsulates the "postmodernism of reaction," in which nostalgic celebrations of the home and nihilistic ruminations on its corruption – flip sides of the same phenomenon – counter the feminist commitment to reform in the future with a passive fixation on the beauties of the past.

This dynamic of discouraged nostalgia was registered, not just in the thriving art market of the 1980s, but also in the decade's real-estate boom. Exemplary of the architects who came to prominence in the 1980s were Robert Stern, Witold Rybczynski, and the team of Andres Duany and Elizabeth Plater-Zyberk, all of whom looked to the past for the house of the future. Stern's writings promoting a return to the "bourgeois virtues" enshrined in turn-of-the-century suburbs and "shingle style" houses made him a leading designer of the revival-style suburban house and condominium developments built during the 1980s. His self-styled "modern traditionalist" practice is epitomized by his "Dream House," created for a *Life* magazine cover story in June of 1994. This relatively large (2100 square feet) and expensive ($150,000 at Midwestern prices, not counting the land) house, available in a variety of tacked-on styles and centered on a large family room, reiterates the forms of conventional up-scale suburban development, inscribing them as the appropriate "dream" solution to the needs of *Life*'s middle-class readers.[16]

More imaginative among the beneficiaries of the building boom of the 1980s were those who shared with earlier feminists a recognition that domesticity as lived experience is more complicated – both historically and socially – than an expensive image. Rybczynski's 1986 best-seller, *Home: A Short History of an Idea*, chronicled the development of the concept of domestic comfort in order to challenge both the modernist "machine for living" and grandiose postmodern reincarnations of historical styles. As an alternative, Rybczynski attempted to isolate the quality of domesticity – defined as "a feeling of privacy," "an atmosphere of coziness," and a manifestation of "bourgeois traditions" – which his later designs aim to recreate on a small scale. Rybczynski's "Grow Home" answers the need for new housing with a return to the modest nineteenth-century row house, just 14 feet wide, 1100 square feet, at a construction cost of $36,386. Behind its "elegant" façade, "designed in a traditional manner," the owners grow into the home through the gradual addition of partitions, storage areas, and remodeling.[17] Responding to the loss of community in suburbs scaled for cars, the "Traditional Neighborhood Development" projects of Duany and Plater-Zyberk revitalized turn-of-the-century town planning codes – pedestrian scale business districts, city parks, and civic monuments – in the belief that the restoration of historical architectural and land-use prototypes can restore old ways of life. While their best-known work is in expensive suburbs and resorts, the most interesting projects of Duany and Plater-Zyberk seek to create or restore an old-fashioned municipal infrastructure in such unhospitable settings as burnt-out urban neighborhoods (Cleveland and Trenton) and run-down shopping malls.[18]

Despite their successes, however, what these back-to-the-future solutions illuminate most clearly is the failure of the modern home and suburb. Yet simply to return to the turn of the century for viable models of domesticity ignores what has changed in our ways of life since then. On a practical level, the interests of ethnic and religious minorities and dual-career couples, for instance, go unacknowledged in a nostalgic return to villages clustered around one or two places of worship and a single business district. Likewise, rebuilding Victorian houses reinscribes Victorian notions of family structure and divisions of public/private without taking into account widespread changes in the family or the impact of communication technologies that permeate the home with twenty-four-hour access to and from the outside world. On a more symbolic level, Gwendolyn Wright's analysis of the xenophobia encoded in the self-consciously old-fashioned turn-of-the-century residential developments held up as a model for "Traditional Neighborhood Development"[19] may be extended to similar anxieties over racial and ethnic difference that animate postmodern returns to the same symbols of tradition and consensus. While these projects undoubtedly offer real improvements in the physical configuration of daily life, their "reactionary" (to use Foster's term) appeal misses the opportunity to engage more "resistant" forms of postmodern culture.

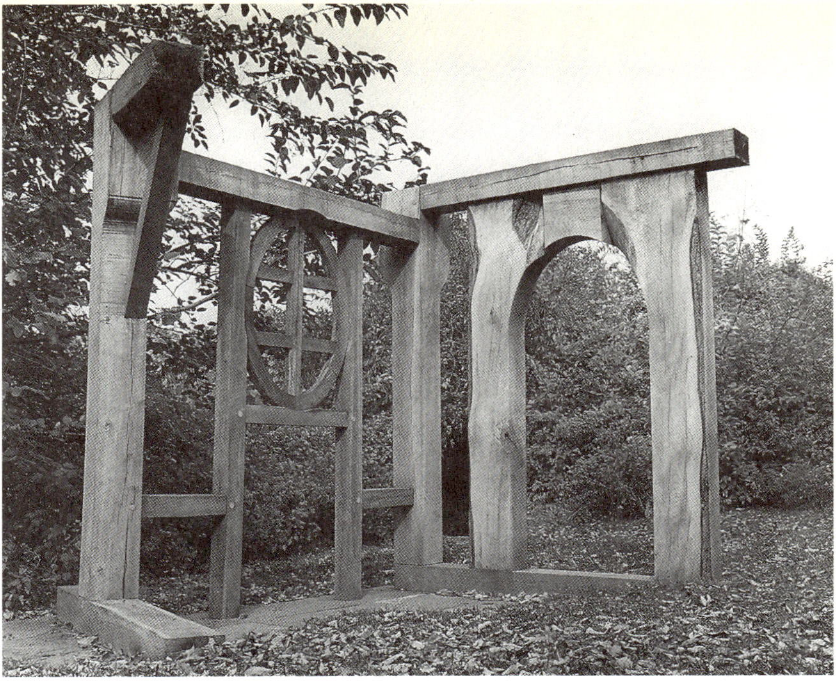

82 *Alice Adams,* The Lost House, *1979*

In contrast to such nostalgic visions, it has been widely argued that a defining characteristic of "resistant" postmodernism is its acknowledgement of difference, often phrased in terms of "multiculturalism," "diversity," and "identity."[20] Applied to domesticity, this argument implies a different reading of Dorothy's famous cry. It's true: there is no (single) place *like* home. There are multiple places that *are* home for different kinds of people. So domestic typologies founded on myths of a universal childhood experience set in an ideal past necessarily offer only partial solutions to the housing needs of the increasingly diverse populations of the present and future. In its activist orientation, "resistant" postmodernism is very much the heir to earlier feminist engagement with the home, though its focus has expanded beyond the articulation of gender differences to include perspectives differentiated by race, ethnicity, sexuality, and other forms of identity.

Two strategies characterize the domestically focused art associated with this "resistant" form of postmodernism. The first seeks to problematize the nostalgia surrounding the home; the second articulates varieties of identity by exploring the differences in the ways different communities live. Exemplary of the first strategy is Alice Adams, a painter and weaver who, self-taught as a carpenter, during the 1970s produced a series of sculptures dealing with the materials of home construction: first latex casts of plaster walls, then more complicated intersections of walls and vaults and constructions of lathing. From the beginning, Adams confessed her nostalgia, not just for her childhood home in the suburbs, but also for her father's print shop in a Manhattan factory loft, a space she describes as "in a way homier, closer than a house." Despite their nostalgic impulse, however, Adams's work does not so much idealize the house as demystify it, revealing its physical framework and making explicit what is taken for granted. "When you come into a room you *expect* to see a wall," she says, explaining how her wall sculptures force viewers into an awareness of their environment, since "you're forced to compare them to the real walls."

Adams's investigation of domesticity culminated in a series of massive outdoor sculptures: *Adams' House* of 1977, *Three Structures on a Slope* of 1978,
82 and *Lost House* of 1979. The first evoked the house she grew up in, and Adams presented it as an attempt "to possess in my art some part of my past that is really gone," though its skewed proportions and permanently unfinished status questioned the practicality of such memories of childhood perspective. *Three Structures* is even less coherent as a domestic space: just a ramp, a porch, and a flat platform are uneasily juxtaposed on a hill. Comparing the first and last of these works, Adams said the "*Adams' House* was the container of my childhood and gave me the chance to go home again," while *The Lost House* "is all about NOT being able to go home again."[21] As a series and individually, Adams's domestic pieces confront the inevitable gap between the ideal and the specific, between fantasy and practice, between memory of the past and practical engagement with the here and now.

A second strategy of artists challenging the homogenizing nostalgia of mainstream approaches to the domestic is to insist on the diversity of domestic experience. Some of this work addresses – with a specificity and a commitment absent from Fischl's or MoMA's vague invocations of domestic "terror" – social issues such as domestic violence, divorce, child abuse, and homelessness. A number of exhibitions in the late 1980s collected work dealing with social problems associated with the home, including Peggy Diggs's powerful sculptures dealing with domestic violence, such as her 1991 *Objects of Abuse*, an assemblage of apparently innocuous domestic objects (a boot, a pillow, a coffee pot, a candle stick) that turn out to be weapons in domestic abuse cases. Diggs may be best known for her imaginative efforts to use art to interrupt cycles of domestic violence by designing posters and, most imaginatively, milk cartons that carry anti-violence information into the daily lives of people who may never visit a museum or gallery. Diggs's "domestication of activist art" has been interestingly analyzed as a reflection of the collapse of the boundaries between public and private at a time when the electronic media bring formerly public institutions – the theatre, for instance, or the legislature – into the home.[22]

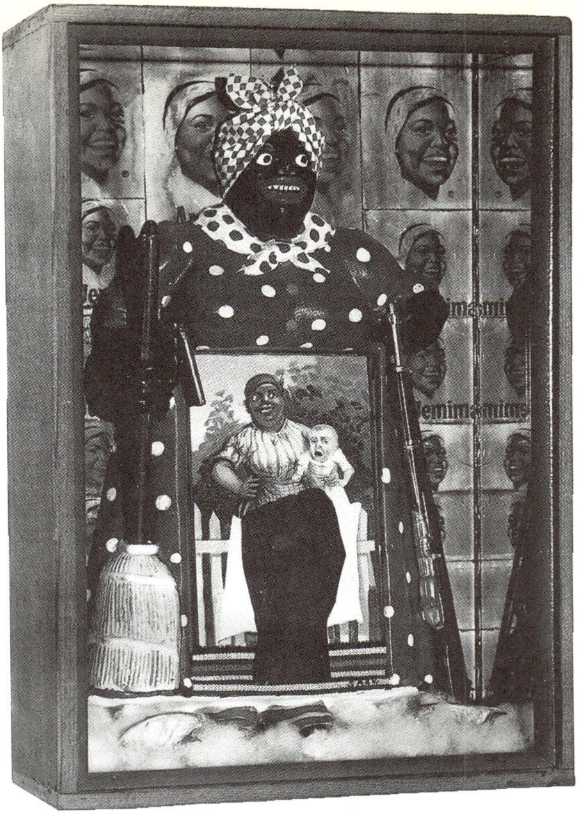

83 *Betye Saar,* The Liberation of Aunt Jemima, *1972*

While the public penetrates the private realm, for many Americans homelessness brings the private into the streets. Addressing this issue, Martha Rosler's 1989 *Home Front* installation used a domestic setting to document the causes and consequences of homelessness, and Krzysztof Wodiczko invented a "Homeless Vehicle" that distills the essential requirements for urban life into a compact, mobile unit that makes a powerful political point in the gallery or on the streets.[23]

For other artists, invoking the domestic is a way of foregrounding issues of "difference," an abstraction concretely embodied in variations of everyday life. Throughout long careers, Betye Saar and Faith Ringgold have used the bric-à-brac of daily life – dolls, quilts, and cookie jars – to describe the experience of black American women. Both, for instance, have invoked the ambivalent legacy of Aunt Jemima, the stereotypical "mammy" whose image is embedded in the fabric of American domestic life through the packaging of a popular brand of breakfast food. Throughout the 1970s, Saar collaged sculptures juxtaposing this familiar icon of domesticity with records of more obvious forms of racism. Ringgold's 1983 story-quilt,

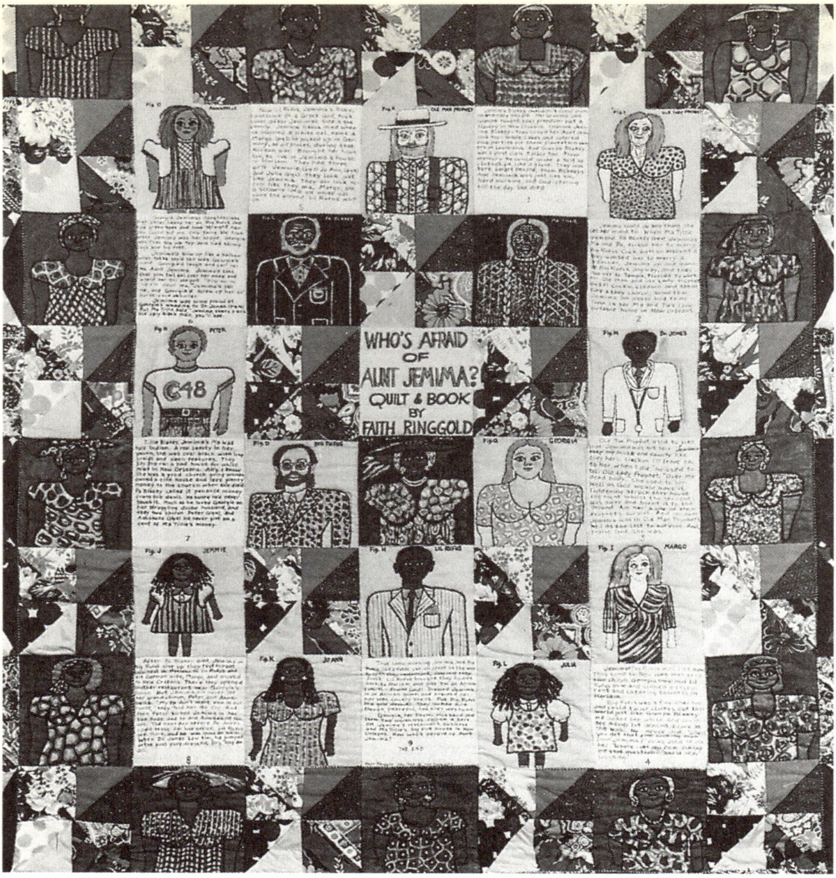

84 *Faith Ringgold,* Who's Afraid of Aunt Jemima?, *1983*

Who's Afraid of Aunt Jemima, like her other quilt pieces, exploits old techniques to weave myths appropriate for black women today; in this version of the story, Aunt Jemima comes north and gets rich running a restaurant in New York. Appropriating craft techniques and domestic objects, the work of both artists brings home issues of race.[24]

For younger black artists, too, images of home are central to the enunciation of identity. Beverly Buchanan's colorful, fragile doll-house-scale models of shacks invoke the living conditions of rural blacks who built their houses from scrap materials. Carrie Mae Weems's photographs with texts document black family life, stage racial stereotypes in domestic settings, or suggest the daily dramas that go on around the kitchen table in a black home. Both Pat Ward Williams and Clarissa Sligh collage old family photographs into their work, insisting on a specifically black domesticity. Explaining her alienation from mainstream images of the home, Sligh says,

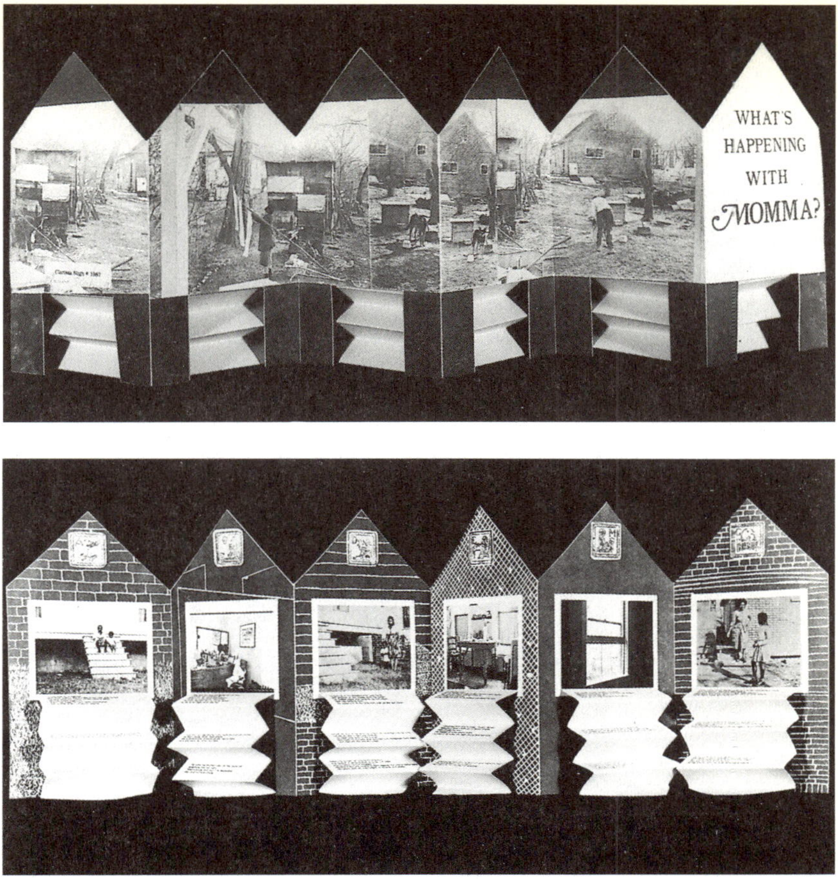

85 *Clarissa Sligh,* What's Happening with Momma?*, inside and outside, 1987*

"In New York City people live in apartment buildings, they don't live in little houses with picket fences. And here I was living in the country in the South, and I didn't have picket fences either."[25]

Artists exploring other ethnic and racial identities have also turned to images of domesticity. Angelica Pozo thematizes her identity as a black Cuban émigrée in her installations of furniture and dishes decorated with images and statistics about her homeland. The Korean-American artist Yong Soon Min often blends domestic imagery with traditional Korean clothing: in a 1991 piece, a poem entitled "Home" is painted on a diaphanous robe in English on one side and in Korean on the other; in the 1994 version of *Dwelling*, a similar dress becomes a container for personal memorabilia and is suspended over a stack of books topped with a volume open to mutilated pages on history and capped with a tiny house – in a later version of this piece, the house disappeared and the books were charred.

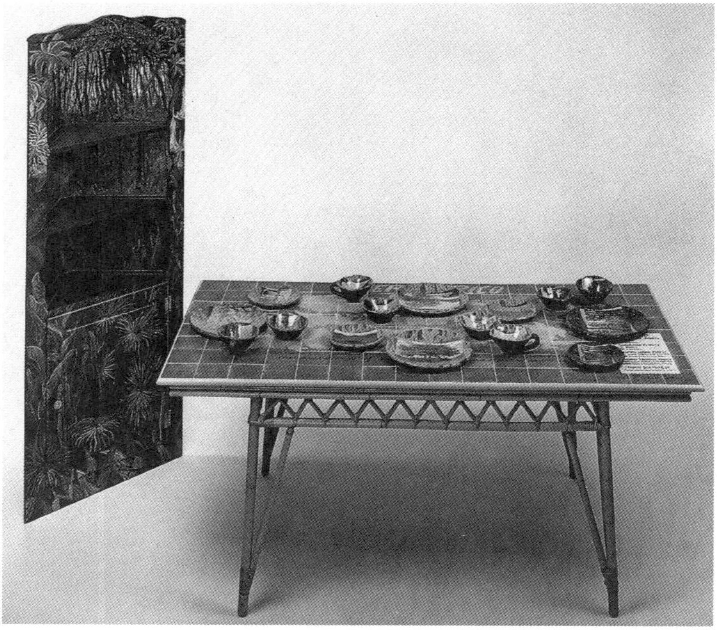

86 *Angelica Pozo,* Puerto Rico . . . . Five Differing Areas of Natural Vegetation, *1991*

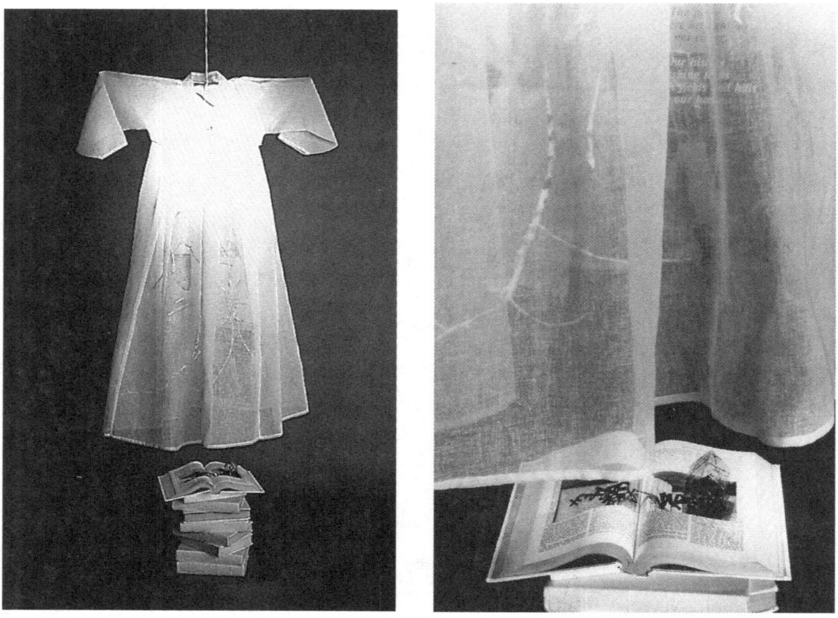

87 *Yong Soon Min,* Dwelling, *1994. Right, detail.*

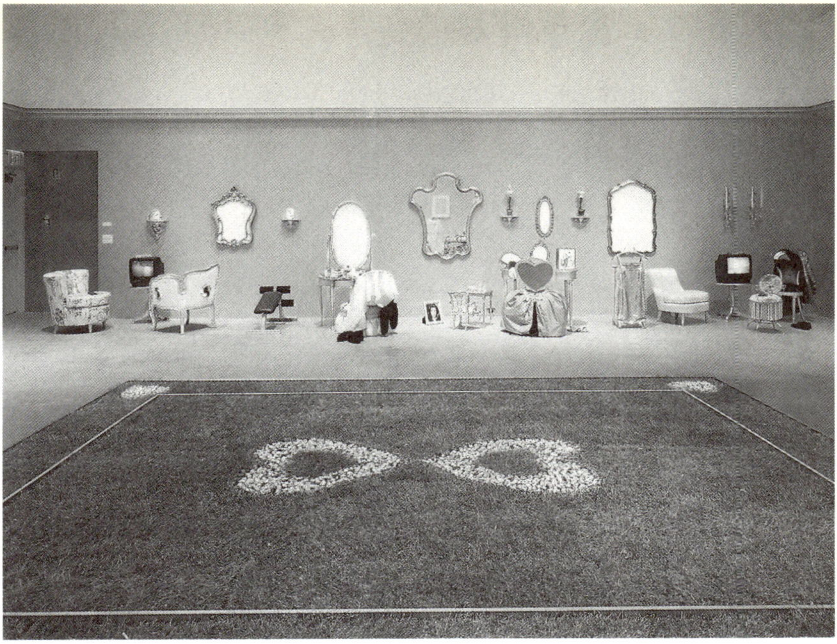

88 *Stuart Netsky,* Time Flies, *1993*

Meyer Vaisman's 1993 *Verde por fuera, rojo por dentro* (*Green Outside, Red Inside* – a reference to watermelon), his first work to engage the specificity of his Venezuelan upbringing, took the form of a brick-and-cinderblock slum shanty with tiny peep-holes framed by pelvis bones that allowed viewers to spy the neat bedroom of his prosperous youth within.[26] And it would be possible to go on enumerating powerful examples of art bearing testament to the importance of the home in preserving and transmitting racial or ethnic identity.

Nor are race and ethnicity the only forms of difference enacted in the realm of the domestic. In an era when "lifestyle" became a euphemism for sexual orientation, images of daily life were often used by artists interested in alternatives to the conventional nuclear family. Kenneth Silver, in this book, describes the range of gay domestic spaces from David Hockney's "normativized" idylls of gay couples at home to Robert Mapplethorpe's insistence on "the 'queerness' of homosexuality" as it is lived out in the daily experience of (some) men. Silver's analysis of the challenge to modernist machismo posed by a gay domestic sensibility is paralleled by the art of Stuart Netsky. Reworking Impressionist paintings in sequins and geometric Abstract Expressionist compositions in textiles, Netsky blurs the contentious boundaries between art and decoration, gallery and home,

88 masculine and feminine. In the 1993 installation, *Time Flies*, Netsky creates a corner of gay domesticity very different from Mapplethorpe's S-and-M theatrics, but nevertheless unmistakably gay. Around a carpet of grass and rose petals are strewn the fabulous accoutrements of drag: gilt furniture, an embarrassment of shoes and accessories, televisions constantly screening old "camp" movies and more recent (but equally campy) celebrity exercise programs. At one point, an elaborate vanity strewn with toiletries faces a chair displaying a cushion embroidered, in place of any conventional aphorisms of homey virtue or heterosexual bliss, with a quotation of a famous (or notorious) queen: "When Quentin Crisp was asked how he was going to spend his day he replied, 'I believe I'll try a new eye shadow.'"[27]

A wide range of sexual and gender identities is explored in the photographs of Nan Goldin, most famously her *Ballad of Sexual Dependency*, a constantly evolving slide show scored for musical accompaniment. Goldin describes her visual "diary" as a "history of a re-created family, without the traditional roles." Accreting images of companions, lovers, and acquaintances from her circle of urban adventurers, Goldin documents lives far – even outrageously – beyond the domestic norm. And yet, in their attention to the iconography of daily life – wallpaper, telephones, laundry and dirty dishes – Goldin's images describe an existence that is not so much anti-

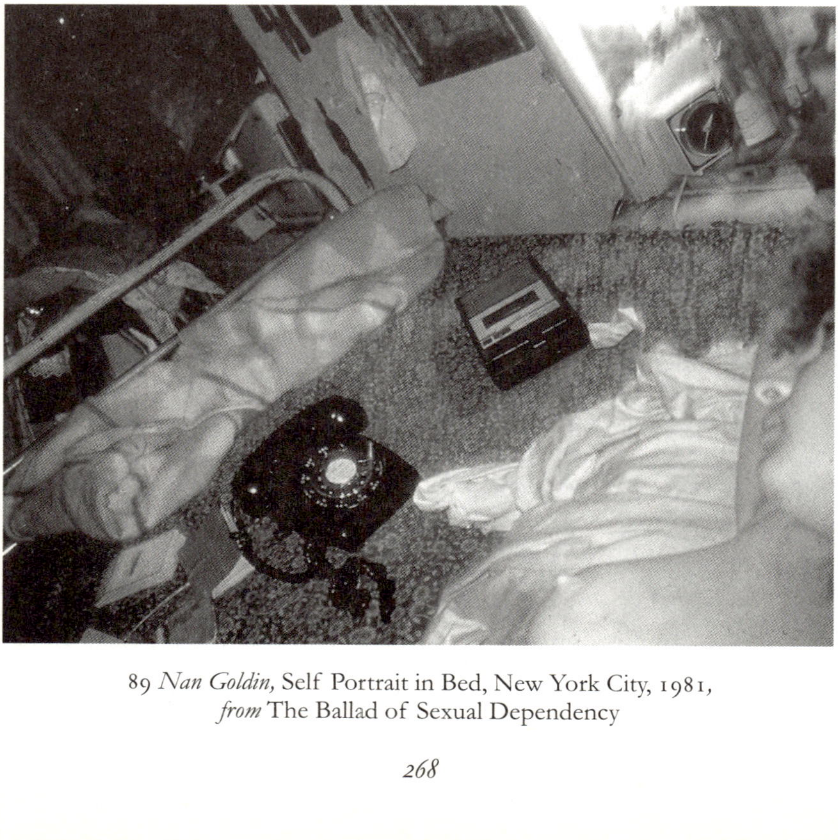

89 *Nan Goldin,* Self Portrait in Bed, New York City, 1981, *from* The Ballad of Sexual Dependency

domestic as an alternative form of domesticity. Countering clichés about how an undifferentiated "we" live, Goldin insists on the specificity of her experience: "I don't ever want to be susceptible to anyone else's version of my history."[28]

Architecture – far more reliant on patronage and subject to legislative surveillance than the visual arts – is among the most conservative and homogeneous cultural fields. Nevertheless, the 1980s witnessed a substantial rise in architectural awareness of the diversity of domestic experience, especially as expressed in building function and program. This shift was registered in the mid-1980s by a number of competitions soliciting, as alternatives to the highly standardized housing projects of the previous three decades, domestic designs that acknowledged, rather than suppressed, differences in ways of living.

Entrants to the 1984 "New American Home" competition in Minneapolis, for example, were asked to design small urban houses that combined work and domestic space for households of "single-parent families, two-income families, unrelated young adults sharing a single residence, adults without children at home, and retired, active adults . . . which are emerging to replace the traditional nuclear family." The winning entry by Jacqueline Leavitt and Troy West was a "kit of parts" that included in each residence a work area that could be converted to a rental unit.[29]

The 1987 *Vacant Lots* project, sponsored by the Architectural League of New York, focused on small city-owned lots that "could be developed by small-scale contractors or community-based development groups, [and] could be the basis of a new strategy for reweaving the fabric of neighborhoods." Emerging from this series of public programs and exhibitions were a number of projects addressing the needs of non-nuclear families, day-care and vocational training facilities, and constituencies such as people with AIDS.[30] Competitions for affordable housing sponsored by the New York State Council for the Arts (1985–86) and by the Los Angeles Museum of Contemporary Art (1988) exemplify the growing determination of cultural institutions in the 1980s to spark new thinking about the physical environment of the home.[31] At the same time, the magazine *Progressive Architecture* augmented its coverage of domestic commissions by prominent architects with issues devoted to homelessness, affordable housing, and the needs of "a diverse population."[32]

Less common – and more complicated – than this acknowledgment of functional diversity were projects that engaged more conceptual forms of
diversity. The 1987 exhibition, *Room in the City*, documented a project in 90
which nine teams of architects remodeled apartments in a small New York tenement as a way of "[using] architectural form as a critical instrument for the scrutiny of lifestyle."[33] The aim was to challenge the usual notion of an apartment as a ranch-style house, simply cramped and stacked. Instead, the

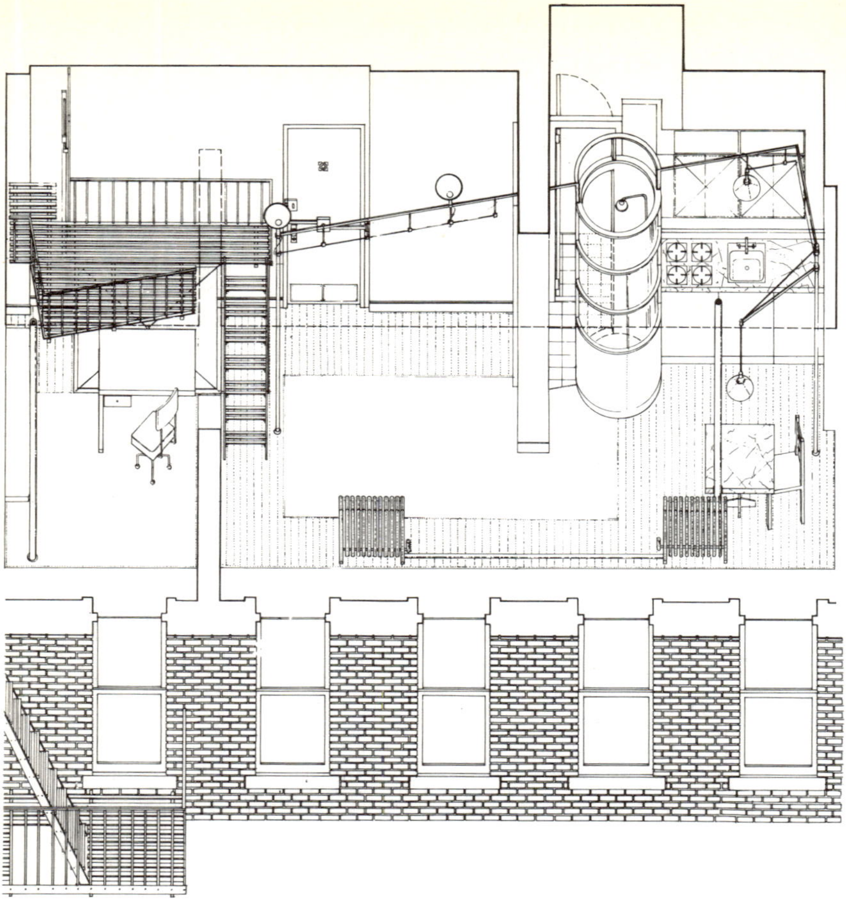

90 *Brian McGrath, Proposal for the renovation of a New York tenement building,* Room in the City, *1987*

architects grappled with the specific physical and conceptual conditions of urban domesticity. Brian McGrath, for instance, brought the urban fabric indoors, extrapolating the pattern of neighborhood streets into the layout of his tiny apartment where the sleeping loft took the form of an indoor fire escape and the shower was modeled on the water towers visible through the window. Other projects worked from the inside out, emphasizing the adaptability of spaces that serve multiple functions throughout the day. These projects celebrate specifically urban spaces and habits.

It is symptomatic of the conservatism of the architectural profession that not until the mid-1990s did architects begin to engage the issues of identity that were central to postmodernism in the broader culture. High-profile architectural theorists reinvigorated discussions of domesticity through their use of feminist psychoanalytic and critical theory, though without engaging the more politically oriented work of 1970s' feminists.[34] The 1994 *House Rules* exhibition, curated by Mark Robbins at the Wexner Center, attempted to incorporate highly theoretical forms of analysis with political forms of identity, exploring the implications of both for "the design of a single-family home in a suburban setting." Ten "theorists" – many representing a marginalized racial, ethnic, gendered and/or sexual identity – were paired with architects to design suburban homes on individual lots, questioning the implications of conventional building codes, materials, floor plans, and marketing.

In some of the *House Rules* projects, unconventional attacks on the spatial configuration of the house symbolized challenges to conventional family structures. In other projects, the emphasis was on the diversity already present in American housing. Architectural historian Margaret Crawford, for instance, teamed up with ADOBE LA, a collaborative group of Hispanic artists and architects, to document the distinctive decoration

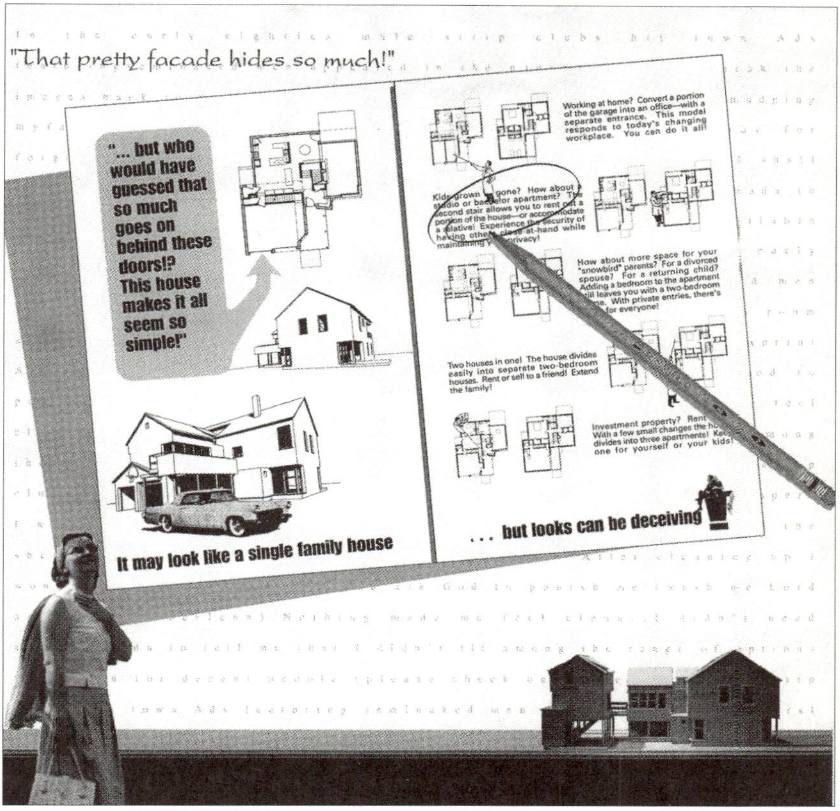

91 *Benjamin Gianni and Scott Weir, presentation drawing for "Queers in (Single-Family) Space",* House Rules, *1994*

of yards and walls in Latino neighborhoods of East Los Angeles. In contrast to this ebullient architectural expression of identity, the project "Queers in (Single-Family) Space" explored the extent to which conventional houses already both contain and mask diverse living arrangements. Emphasizing that "queerness" – a term understood to incorporate a broad range of departures from the nuclear family norm – will be defined and lived by the inhabitants rather than "staged by the architect," designers Benjamin Gianni and Scott Weir proposed what looked like a typical suburban house that "can be easily altered to accommodate a range of living situations . . . without breaching the social contract of community consensus." An example of "playing it straight" – "the suburban strategy par excellence" – the designers use careful room layout, sound-baffling walls, and multiple entrances to ensure maximum flexibility for the various inhabitants over the life of the house.[35] This project follows Robbins and Gianni's proposal for the *Queer Space* show in New York earlier that year. There they displayed a matrix of captioned snapshots of gay households solicited through ads in gay papers that asked readers to send pictures of the inside and outside of their homes. In answer to the questions, "Who are we? Where are we? How do we live?" Gianni and Robbins answered, "In gay ghettos, it is apparent, but the majority of gay people live among their heterosexual neighbors. Some of us react against normative symbols of domesticity, others of us embrace them."[36] This imbeddedness of identity within normative structures of home and community is at the core of the later proposal for *House Rules*.

On one level, these projects are comparable to Hockney's art in their interest in "normativized" gay domesticity, far removed from "gay ghettos" where emblems of sexual identity (such as flags and posters) combine with carefully renovated houses, high-style boutiques, and gay/lesbian bookstores and bars to mark the varieties of identity explored by artists like Mapplethorpe and Netsky. Such environments – gay equivalents to the Latino spaces documented by ADOBE LA – have not been the concern of architects to date. But should they be? Gianni argues that identity is more a product of living than of design; in this view, good houses are those that encourage a variety of domestic configurations that change over time. Unlike the modernists' faith in standardization – and even unlike the nostalgic counter-norms of "Traditional Neighborhood Development" – such architecture accepts Nan Goldin's determination to refuse "anyone else's version of my history."

This approach is not without its costs, however. Design that refrains from imposing a patriarchal family structure on its inhabitants is not the same thing as architecture that articulates specific alternatives. Lost in this vision of the house as a neutral vessel for any family group is the earlier feminists' insistence on change, whether within families or in the relation of individuals to communities and houses to neighborhoods. The activist legacy of feminism was neglected in the 1980s, however. The era's nostalgia did not extend to the turn-of-the-century feminist housing projects documented by Dolores Hayden, nor was the work of feminists in the 1970s incorporated into the postmodern architectural theory that informed the participants in *House Rules*, where the acceptance of a suburban setting predicated on the single family home discouraged considerations of community. Describing the cycles of oblivion and re-invention that characterize feminist art in general, *Womanhouse* co-creator Miriam Schapiro says, "Each generation opens the wounds, which close in the night behind them."[37]

Breaking this cycle is the challenge of future efforts to re-imagine domesticity. Postmodernism has returned our culture's attention to the home, challenging the modernist antagonism toward the domestic with a new interest in the history and variety of home life. For those of us unwilling simply to fall back on nostalgic formations of domesticity, the effort now is to bring the legacy of feminism – the activist commitment to specific social change, the anger that eschews the innocuous and safe – into productive combination with current concerns for critical theory and multiculturalism. We offer the history sketched in this essay as a foundation for that work.

Notes

Introduction

1. Walter Benjamin, "Louis-Philippe or the Interior," *Charles Baudelaire: A Lyric Poet in the Era of High Capitalism*, trans. Harry Zohn (London: Verso, 1973), 167.
2. Classic works on the avant-garde include Renato Poggioli, *The Theory of the Avant-Garde*, trans. Gerald Fitzgerald (Cambridge: Harvard University Press, 1962); and Peter Bürger, *The Theory of the Avant-Garde*, 1974, trans. Michael Shaw (Minneapolis: University of Minnesota Press, 1984). An excellent introduction is Linda Nochlin's "The Invention of the Avant-Garde, France, 1830–80," in T. B. Hess and John Ashbery, eds., *Avant-garde Art* (London: Collier, 1968), 1–24.
3. Charles Baudelaire, *"The Painter of Modern Life" and Other Essays*, trans. Jonathan Mayne (London: 1964), 1–18. On the *flâneur* see Rémy G. Saisselin, *The Bourgeois and the Bibliot* (New Brunswick: Rutgers University Press, 1984), 19–30; and Robert L. Herbert, *Impressionism: Art, Leisure, and Parisian Society* (New Haven: Yale University Press, 1988), 33–37.
4. Griselda Pollock, "Modernity and the Spaces of Femininity," *Vision and Difference: Femininity, Feminism and the Histories of Art* (London: Routledge, 1988), 50–90. A careful analysis of Impressionist techniques casts doubt on the extent to which these paintings were actually made out of doors, as demonstrated by Robert Herbert, "Method and Meaning in Monet," *Art in America* (September 1979), 90–108.
5. Glenna Mathews challenges Rybczynski's celebration of the late-nineteenth-century "domestic engineers," whom she assesses more critically as unwittingly inaugurating attacks on domesticity in the name of modernism. Whether one dates this development closer to 1850 or to 1900, the antagonism between domesticity and modernism remains a defining feature of twentieth-century culture.
6. Adolph Loos, "Ornament and Crime," in Ulrich Conrads, ed., *Programmes and Manifestoes on 20th-Century Architecture*, trans. Michael Bullock (London: Lund Humphries, 1970), 19–24. Other quotations and analysis from Beatriz Colomina, "The Split Wall: Domestic Voyeurism," *Sexuality and Space* (Princeton: Princeton University Press, 1992), 73–128.
7. Le Corbusier, *Towards a New Architecture*, trans. Frederick Etchells (London: Architectural Press, 1927), 18–23, 210.
8. Walter Benjamin, "Erfahrung and Armut" ["Experience and Poverty"], *Gesammelte Schriften*, vol. 2, part 1, Rolf Tiedemann and Hermann Schweppenhäuser, eds. (Frankfurt am Main: Suhrkamp Verlag, 1977), 217–18.
9. Henry Russell Hitchcock and Philip Johnson, *The International Style* (1932, repr. New York: W. W. Norton, 1966), 93.
10. Julius Meier-Graefe, *Modern Art: Being a Contribution to a New System of Aesthetics*, trans. Florence Simmonds and George W. Chrystal (1908, repr. New York: Arno Press, 1968), 2–3, 9–10. My thanks to Lisa Wainwright for drawing my attention to this text.
11. Wyndham Lewis, quoted in M.M.B., "Rebel Art in Modern Life," *Daily News and Leader* [London], 7 April 1914.
12. Max Kozloff, "An Interview with Robert Motherwell," *Artforum* (September 1965), 37. Adolph Gottlieb and Mark Rothko, letter to *The New York Times*, 1943, in Ellen H. Johnson, ed., *American Artists on Art from 1940 to 1980* (New York: Harper and Row, 1982), 10–14.
13. Clement Greenberg, "Milton Avery," 1957, in *Art and Culture* (Boston: Beacon, 1961), 197–202; repr. *Clement Greenberg: The Collected Essays and Criticism*, vol. 4, John O'Brian, ed. (Chicago: University of Chicago Press, 1993), 39–44. Maurice Denis, "From Gauguin and Van Gogh to Classicism," (1909), repr. Francis Frascina and Charles Harrison, *Modern Art and Modernism* (London: Harper and Row, 1982), 53–54.
14. John Ruskin, *Stones of Venice*, vol. 2, chap. 6, section 13; *Mornings in Florence*, chap. 2, section 36; *Two Paths*, lecture 3, section 95.
15. Wilde's American lectures were published in his *Miscellanies*, Robert Ross, ed. (1908, repr. London: Dawsons, 1969), 243–308.
16. William Morris, "Making the Best of It," 1879, in *The Collected Works of William Morris*, vol. 22 (London: Longmans Green, 1914), 86.
17. On Art Nouveau, see citations of Ruskin and Morris in Debora Silverman, *Art Nouveau in Fin-de-Siècle France: Politics, Psychology, and Style* (Berkeley: University of California Press, 1989). On Belgium, see Klaus-Jürgen Sembach, *Henry van de Velde*, trans. Michael Robinson (New York: Rizzoli, 1989). On Austria, see Kirk Varnedoe, *Vienna 1900: Art, Architecture, and Design* (New York: Museum of Modern Art, 1986). On Germany, see John Heskett, *German Design, 1870–1918* (New York: Tapling, 1986); Peg Weiss, *Kandinsky in Munich: The Formative Jugendstil Years* (Princeton: Princeton University Press, 1979).
18. *The Journal of Henry D. Thoreau*, Bradford Torrey and Francis Allen, eds. (Boston: Houghton Mifflin, 1906), 182–83. Ralph Waldo Emerson, "Art," *Essays* (Boston: Houghton Mifflin, 1883), 336. See also Eileen Boris, *Art and Labor: Ruskin, Morris, and the Craftsman Ideal in America* (Philadelphia: Temple University Press, 1986); Wendy Kaplan, *"The Art That is Life": The Arts and Crafts Movement in America, 1875–1920* (Boston: Museum of Fine Arts, 1987).

19. Norma Broude, "Miriam Schapiro and 'Femmage': Reflections on the Conflict Between Decoration and Abstraction in Twentieth-Century Art," 1980, repr. in Norma Broude and Mary Garrard, eds., *Feminism and Art History* (New York: Harper and Row, 1982), 315–29.
20. See Wright's late *The Living City* (New York: Horizon, 1958).
21. A pre-eminent example is Nikolaus Pevsner's highly influential *Pioneers of the Modern Movement from William Morris to Walter Gropius* (London: Faber and Faber, 1936), which canonized Morris as "the true prophet of the twentieth century, the father of the Modern Movement" (24).
22. Clement Greenberg, "Feeling is All," 1952, *Collected Essays*, vol. 3, 99–106. A somewhat altered version of this essay appeared in Greenberg's *Art and Culture*, 146–53.
23. Clement Greenberg, "The Avant-Garde and Kitsch," 1939, *Art and Culture*, 3–21; "Art," 1948; "Art," 1947; "The Crisis of the Easel Picture," 1948, *Art and Culture*, 154–57, all repr. *Collected Essays* vol. 1, 5–22; vol. 3, 240–42; vol. 2, 134–37; vol. 3, 221–25. On Greenberg and the decorative, see Donald B. Kuspit, *Clement Greenberg: Art Critic* (Madison: University of Wisconsin Press, 1979). Harold Rosenberg, "The American Action Painters," *The Tradition of the New* (Chicago: University of Chicago Press, 1960), 32–35.
24. Clement Greenberg, "Cézanne," 1951, *Art and Culture*, 50–58; for the somewhat different original version of this essay, see *Collected Essays*, vol. 3, 82–91.
25. Michel Foucault, *The History of Sexuality, Volume I: An Introduction*, trans. Robert Hurley (New York: Random House, 1978), 95.

1. The Chic Interior and the Feminine Modern

The research and writing of this essay were supported by a postdoctoral grant from the Getty Center for the History of Art and the Humanities. Perry Friedman's critical comments on both the writing and arguments of this essay were invaluable. I am also grateful to Christopher Reed, David Farber, Ingmar Nyman, and Martin Tiersten for their judicious comments and encouragement.

1. Etincelle, *Carnet d'un mondain* (Paris: Rouveyre, 1881–82), vol. 1, 19.
2. Emile Bayard, *L'art de bon goût* (Paris: Garnier Frères, 1908), 227.
3. M. Fresson, *Enseignement professionel* (Paris: Capiomont, 1887), Lecture of 27 March 1886, 51–52; Marius Vachon, *La belle maison: Principes et lois de l'esthétique pour aménager, meubler, et orner sa demeure* (Lyon: J. Deprelle et M. Camus, 1925), 20. The book was based on a course he gave in 1913. See Adeline Daumard, "Conditions de logement," in *Le Parisien chez lui au XIX siècle* (Paris: Archives Nationales, 1977) for confirmation that nineteenth-century French bourgeois families tended to move and to refurnish their homes several times in a lifetime.
4. Henri de Noussane, *Le goût dans l'ameublement* (Paris: Firmin-Didot et Cie, 1896), 8.
5. *Vachon, *La belle maison*, 88; Octave Uzanne, *L'Art et les artifices de la beauté* (Paris: F. Juven. 1902), 171.
6. Vachon, *La belle maison*, 14–15; Jules Claretie, "La femme," *L'Art de la mode*, vol. 1, no. 4 (November 1880), 91; Etincelle, *Carnet d'un mondain*, vol. 1, 15.
7. Francis de Miomandre, "Promenade à travers les styles," in *L'Ameublement au Palais de la Nouveauté: Palais du Mobilier*," Grands Magasins Dufayel publicity (n.d.), n. pag. Archives de la Seine: D 39Z (carton 2); "Qu'est-ce que le Chic?" *Femina*, no. 235 (1 November 1910), 557–78.
8. *Exposition des soieries*, Pygmalion publicity (1904), n. pag. Bibliothèque Historique de la Ville de Paris. Actualités: 120 Pygmalion; G. de Landemer, *Le carnet de fiançailles* (Paris, 1890), n. pag.
9. Henri Duvernois, *Pour vous, Madame*, Galeries Lafayette publicity (n.d. [early twentieth century]), n. pag. Archives de la Seine: D 39Z (carton 2); Octave Uzanne, "Notes sur le goût intime et la décoration personnelle," *L'Art et l'idée* (20 November 1892), 259–60.
10. Noussane, *Le goût dans l'ameublement*, 150–51; La Direction, "Aux Lecteurs," *L'Intérieur* (November 1911), 3; Etincelle, *Carnet d'un mondain*, vol. 1, 27.
11. L. Roger-Milès, "Le goût et la mode," *Le figaro-modes*, no. 1 (January 1903), 16.
12. Etincelle, *Carnet d'un mondain*, vol. 1, 27; Blanche de Regnault, "Le confort et l'élégance chez soi," *Le salon de la mode* (1 March 1890), 70; (10 May 1890), 151.
13. Regnault, "Le confort," *Le salon de la mode* (10 May 1885), 150; Fresson, *Enseignement professionel*, 53; 43.
14. Vachon, *La belle maison*, 12–13.
15. Emile Cardon, *L'Art au foyer domestique* (Paris: Renouard, 1884), 29.
16. Frisette, "La femme chez elle," *Femina*, no. 149 (1 April 1907), 166; Louise de Salles, "A propos de l'ameublement de style," *Paris-mode* (20 January 1892), 1; Marcelle Tinayre, "L'Art de parer son foyer," *Femina*, no. 221 (1 April 1910), 189.
17. Noussane, *Le goût dans l'ameublement*, 19; Salles, "A propos de la Parisienne," *Paris-mode* (20 March 1892), 1.

2. The Chromo and the Art Museum

My thanks to Amelia Rauser and Christine Bell and especially to Michael Leja for their comments on various articulations of the material discussed here. Thanks also to Christopher Reed for his exceptional dedication and helpfulness. I am grateful for grants from the Winterthur Museum and Library and from the American Antiquarian Society, which provided financial support and research resources early on.

1. *Bulletin of the American Art-Union* (1850), inside front cover.
2. For a brief history of the American Art-Union, see Lillian Miller, *Patrons and Patriotism: the Encouragement of the Fine Arts in the United States, 1790–1860* (Chicago: University of Chicago Press, 1966), 160–72. For further details and documents, see Mary Bartlett Cowdrey et al., *American Academy of Fine Arts and American Art-Union* (New York: The New York Historical Society, 1953).
3. *The Crayon*, vol. 1, no. 1 (3 January 1855), 1. Janice Simon, *"The Crayon", 1855–1861: The Voice of Nature in Criticism, Poetry and the Fine Arts* (Ph.D. dissertation, University of Michigan, 1990).
4. *Prang's Chromo*, vol. 1, no. 1 (January 1868), 1, reprinted an article from the *Boston Daily Advertiser* which stated that 19,000 copies of the chromo *Chickens* had already been sold. The print had

been on the market for only two years, and such chromos could remain in catalogues for decades. Some caution is advisable in considering such sales figures, since the likely source of the information was the chromo publisher himself.

5. "Color Printing From Wood and From Stone," *The Nation* (10 January 1867), 36–37. "Art in the House," *New York Times* (9 February 1879).

6. Mary Kelley has proposed that the writers and readers of sentimental fiction "deplored society's materialism and called for reimmersion in the spiritual." This proposal applies to the visual arts as well. See "The Sentimentalists: Promise and Betrayal in the Home," *Signs* (Spring 1979), 437.

7. Catharine Beecher and Harriet Beecher Stowe, *The American Woman's Home* (New York: J. B. Ford, 1869), 84. The Beecher sisters considered statues and engravings, but focused their attention on chromos. They recommended four particular examples (91), three of them made by Prang, one of which was the Bierstadt *Sunset* (fig. 2).

8. *Boston Daily Advertiser* as quoted in *Prang's Chromo*, vol. 1, no. 1 (January 1868), 1.

9. "Autotypes and Oleographs," *The Nation* (10 November 1870), 317–18. "Color Printing," 36–37. *Art Amateur*, vol. 5, no. 4 (September 1881), 68. "Chromolithographs, American, English, and French," *The Nation* (31 October 1867), 359.

10. "Color Printing," 36.

11. "Autotypes," 318.

12. *New York Daily Tribune* (20 November 1866), 6. For some more appreciative responses to Prang's efforts, see Cook's columns of 27 April 1866, 7, and 14 March 1867, 2.

13. "Autotypes," 318. Clement Greenberg, "Avant-Garde and Kitsch," 1939, in *Clement Greenberg: The Collected Essays and Criticism*, vol. 1, John O'Brian, ed. (Chicago: University of Chicago Press, 1986), 5–22.

14. Reprint from the *Boston Commercial Bulletin* in *The Aldine* (May 1869), 39; quoted in Peter C. Marzio, *The Democratic Art; Pictures for a 19th-Century America* (Boston: David R. Godine, 1979), 96.

15. "Chromo-Civilization," *The Nation*, vol. 5 (24 September 1874), 201–2.

16. Alan Trachtenberg, *The Incorporation of America: Culture and Society in the Gilded Age* (New York: Hill and Wang, 1982).

17. Charles C. Perkins, *American Art Museums* (Boston: Fields, Osgood, & Co., 1870), 7, reprinting an article from the *North American Review*.

18. Walter Smith, *Art Education, Scholastic and Industrial* (Boston: James R. Osgood and Company, 1873), v.

19. Ibid., 22.

20. Margaret Henderson Floyd, "A Terra-Cotta Cornerstone for Copley Square: Museum of Fine Arts, Boston, 1870–1876, by Sturgis and Brigham," *Journal of the Society of Architectural Historians*, vol. 33, no. 2 (May 1973), 83–103. Neil Harris, "The Gilded Age Revisited: Boston and the Museum Movement," *American Quarterly*, vol. 14, no. 4 (Winter 1962), 545–66.

21. Figure 4 was the cover image for the issue of the Museum's *Bulletin* that profiled the newly opened building, and thus served the Museum as an official self-presentation. The dramatic profile, the vertical format, the low point of view, and the selection of a distinctly classical portion of the building all suggest the impression of reverential awe the building was meant to convey.

22. See Carol Duncan and Alan Wallach, "The Museum of Modern Art As Late Capitalist Ritual," *Marxist Perspectives* (Winter 1978), 28–51, and Duncan and Wallach, "The Universal Survey Museum," *Art History*, vol. 3, no. 4 (December 1980), 448–74.

23. See Kathleen D. McCarthy, *Women's Culture: American Philanthropy and Art, 1830–1930* (Chicago: University of Chicago Press, 1991), 150ff.

3. Model-Families

1. A preliminary version of this essay was presented at a Metropolitan Museum of Art symposium organized in conjunction with the exhibition *American Impressionism and Realism: The Painting of Modern Life*. I would like to thank H. Barbara Weinberg, Curator of American Paintings and Sculpture at the Metropolitan, for inviting me to participate in this event. I am also grateful to Julia Vicinus, who provided imaginative research assistance, to Janet Marstine, who offered insightful criticism of a first draft, and to Christopher Reed, who contributed invaluable conceptual commentary and editorial suggestions.

2. Quoted in Celia Betsky, "In the Artist's Studio," *Portfolio*, vol. 4 (January–February 1982), 34.

3. On the cultural significance of the artist's studio, see Sarah Burns's important essay, "The Price of Beauty: Art, Commerce, and the Late Nineteenth-Century American Studio Interior," in David C. Miller, ed., *American Iconology: New Approaches to Nineteenth-Century Art and Literature* (New Haven: Yale University Press, 1993), 209–38.

4. Chase admired Whistler's art, and when the two men met in London in the summer of 1885, they formed an instant and, from Chase's point of view, increasingly challenging friendship. At Whistler's suggestion, they undertook to paint portraits of one another. Whistler's work was never finished, but Chase's picture (Metropolitan Museum of Art) so outraged the subject that it precipitated the rapid disintegration of their relationship. On Chase and Whistler, see Ronald G. Pisano, *A Leading Spirit in American Art: William Merritt Chase* (Seattle: Henry Art Gallery, University of Washington, 1983), 77–82; and Doreen Bolger Burke, *American Paintings in the Metropolitan Museum of Art*, vol. 3 (New York: Metropolitan Museum of Art, 1980), 81–85. *The Open-Air Breakfast*, which may have been a private response to Whistler's anger, remained in Chase's possession throughout his lifetime and was first exhibited publicly the year before his death.

5. Mary Sullivan was the daughter of a Charlestown contractor. As a young convent school student, she modeled briefly for Tarbell's art classes but left the studio after only a week. When Mary was sixteen her father died, and she returned to modeling to finance her education as a professional nurse. She worked at Massachusetts General Hospital until 1905, when she married Boston Brahmin Stephen Codman, Jr. A newspaper account of the Codman/Sullivan wedding notes, "In early childhood [the bride's] exceptional beauty attracted much attention. Tall, slender, and graceful, with a fine complexion, deep blue eyes and a wealth of golden hair, she was admired by all who saw her." Although many Boston artists invited Sullivan to pose for them, she refused all but Tarbell and a few members of his circle. The Codmans owned several paintings by the artist. Edmund C. Tarbell Papers, Archives of American Art, Smithsonian Institution, microfilm roll 4701.

6. Frederick W. Coburn, "Edmund C. Tarbell," *International Studio*, vol. 32 (September 1907), 82.

7. Daphne Spain, *Gendered Spaces* (Chapel Hill: University of North Carolina Press, 1992), 112–14.

8. Griselda Pollock, "Modernity and the Spaces of Femininity," *Vision and Difference: Femininity, Feminism and the Histories of Art* (London: Routledge, 1988), 78.

9. On the pictorial representation and social history of the American home and city in this period, see H. Barbara Weinberg, Doreen Bolger, and David Park Curry, *American Realism and Impressionism: The Painting of Modern Life, 1885–1915*, exh. cat. (New York: Metropolitan Museum of Art, 1994), 135–309.

10. Warren I. Susman, *Culture as History: The Transformation of American Society in the Twentieth Century* (New York: Pantheon Books, 1984), 271–85.

11. On women and the American aesthetic movement, see Roger B. Stein, "Artifact as Ideology: The Aesthetic Movement in Its American Cultural Context," in *In Pursuit of Beauty: Americans and the Aesthetic Movement*, exh. cat. (New York: Metropolitan Museum of Art, 1986), 23–51.

12. On this subject, see Martha Banta, *Imaging American Women: Idea and Ideals in Cultural History* (New York: Columbia University Press, 1987), 143–78, 288–374, and *passim*; Bernice Kramer Leader, "The Boston School and Vermeer," *Arts Magazine*, vol. 55 (November 1980), 172–76; and by the same author, "Antifeminism in the Paintings of the Boston School," *Arts Magazine*, vol. 56 (January 1982), 112–19; and Bailey van Hook, "Decorative Images of American Women: The Aristocratic Aesthetic of the Late Nineteenth Century," *Smithsonian Studies in American Art*, vol. 4 (Winter 1990), 45–69.

13. *Daily Graphic* [New York] (17 February 1887). Quoted in Pisano, 1979, 40.

14. Katharine Metcalf Roof, *The Life and Art of William Merritt Chase* (New York: Charles Scribner's Sons, 1917), 150.

15. On Chase's Tenth Street Studio, see Nicolai Cikovsky, Jr, "William Merritt Chase's Tenth Street Studio," *Archives of American Art Journal*, vol. 16 (1976), 2–14. See also Mary Sayre Haverstock, "The Tenth Street Studio," *Art in America*, vol. 54 (September–October 1966), 54–55; Betsky, "In the Artist's Studio," 34–36; and Burns, *passim*.

16. Kenyon Cox, "William M. Chase, Painter," *Harper's New Monthly Magazine*, vol. 78 (March 1889), 549–57.

17. On Chase at Shinnecock, see D. Scott Atkinson and Nicolai Cikovsky, Jr, *William Merritt Chase: Summers at Shinnecock, 1891–1902*, exh. cat. (Washington, DC: National Gallery of Art, 1987).

18. John Gilmer Speed, "An Artist's Summer Vacation," *Harper's New Monthly Magazine*, vol. 87 (June 1893), 3–14.

19. The "living hall" was a characteristic feature of Victorian summer houses. Derived from the Elizabethan great hall, this large open room functioned as "entry and stair hall, reception room, family gathering place, and circulation center of the house." See Karen Halttunen, "From Parlor to Living Room: Domestic Space, Interior Decoration, and the Culture of Personality," in Simon J. Bronner, ed., *Consuming Visions: Accumulation and Display of Goods in America, 1880–1920* (New York: W. W. Norton, 1989), 165–67. A photograph of the Shinnecock hall, made from the same angle as Chase's painting, appeared in Speed's article, in which the picture itself is referred to as a "pastel study."

20. Chase was a founding member of the Society of Painters in Pastel, which held its first exhibition in 1884. On the artist's admiration for Velázquez, see Atkinson and Cikovsky, 60–61.

21. Royal Cortissoz, "Spring Art Exhibitions. The Society of American Artists," *Harper's Weekly*, vol. 39 (6 April 1895), 316.

22. William Howe Downes, "William Merritt Chase, A Typical American Artist," *The International Studio*, vol. 39 (December 1909), 29–30.

23. See Atkinson and Cikovsky, 34–36.

24. William Merritt Chase Papers, Archives of American Art, Smithsonian Institution, microfilm roll N69–137.

25. Roof, v–vi.

26. John Higham, "The Reorientation of American Culture in the 1890s," in *Writing American History: Essays on Modern Scholarship* (Bloomington: Indiana University Press, 1970), 73–102. For a corrective to Higham's definition of masculinity in this period, see Margaret Marsh, "Suburban Men and Masculine Domesticity, 1870–1915," *American Quarterly*, vol. 40 (June 1988), 165–86. Marsh's analysis of "companionate marriages," in which suburban men participated in selection of household furnishings and nurturing of children, provides an intellectual and historical context for artists like Chase and Tarbell who straddled the border between male and female spheres.

27. Bethany Tarbell, "Edmund C. Tarbell in Private: A New England Painter and the Family that Inspired Him," *Art and Antiques* (January 1993), 48.

28. Edmund C. Tarbell Papers, Archives of American Art, Smithsonian Institution, microfilm reel 4701.

29. Patricia Jobe Pierce, *Edmund C. Tarbell and the Boston School of Painting, 1889–1980* (Hingham, MA: Pierce Galleries, 1980), 36.

30. The sister on the far left appears twice in this painting.

31. Edmund C. Tarbell Papers, Archives of American Art, Smithsonian Institution, microfilm roll 4701.

32. Trevor J. Fairbrother, "Edmund C. Tarbell's Paintings of Interiors," *Antiques*, vol. 131 (January 1987), 224.

33. John E. D. Trask, "About Tarbell," *American Magazine of Art*, vol. 9 (April 1918), 226.

34. See Harrison Rhodes, "Why Is a Bostonian?" *Harper's Magazine*, vol. 132 (January 1916), 169–70.

35. Burns, 237.

36. Kenyon Cox, "The Recent Work of Edmund C. Tarbell," *Burlington Magazine*, vol. 14 (January 1909), 258. The identity of the model in *Girl Crocheting* has yet to be firmly established. For information on this picture, see *Ten American Painters* (New York: Spanierman Gallery, 1990), 163–65.

37. Charles H. Caffin, "The Art of Edmund C. Tarbell," *Harper's New*

Monthly Magazine, vol. 117 (June 1908), 72.

38. Francis Hamilton, "Artists' Homes as They Paint Them," *International Studio*, vol. 81 (September 1925), 417–18.

39. Edmund C. Tarbell Papers, Archives of American Art, Smithsonian Institution, microfilm roll 4701.

40. Josephine's intellectual energy in *Girls Reading* stands in marked contrast to the melancholy passivity of Berthe Morisot's pregnant sister in the *Portrait of Edma Morisot Pontillon and Cornélie Thomas Morisot* (National Gallery of Art, Washington, DC), which probably provided inspiration for Tarbell's composition. On Morisot's painting, see Anne Higgonet, *Berthe Morisot's Images of Women* (Cambridge: Harvard University Press, 1992), 67–68; and by the same author, *Berthe Morisot* (New York: Harper & Row, 1990), 62–63.

41. Tarbell, 48.

42. Charlotte Barton succeeded Mary Sullivan as Tarbell's favorite model. She worked for him and for his friend the sculptor Bela Pratt until 1909 when she married and moved to Portland, Oregon. Barton posed for Tarbell's *Girl Reading* (Museum of Fine Arts, Boston), which, according to Patricia Jobe Pierce, she commissioned from the artist for $4500. See Charlotte Barton West Papers, Archives of American Art, Smithsonian Institution, microfilm roll 75; and Pierce, 195.

43. Josephine's pose in *New England Interior* is similar to that of the figure in *Girl Mending* of 1905.

44. See Fairbrother, 232; and Tarbell, 49.

45. Celia Betsky, "Inside the Past: The Interior and the Colonial Revival in American Art and Literature, 1860–1914," in Alan Axelrod, ed., *The Colonial Revival in America* (New York: W. W. Norton, 1985), 266.

46. Edmund C. Tarbell Papers, Archives of American Art, Smithsonian Institution, microfilm roll 4701.

47. Ibid.

48. Ibid.

49. Ibid.

4. Psyche and Sympathy

1. Walter Benjamin, "Louis Philippe or the Interior", *Charles Baudelaire: A Lyric Poet in the Era of High Capitalism*, trans. Harry Zohn (London: Verso, 1973), 167–68.

2. This is part of a larger ongoing study on interiority in ninteenth-century visual culture, which is based on my dissertation: Susan Sidlauskas, "A 'Perspective of Feeling': The Expressive Interior in Nineteenth-Century Realist Painting" (Ph.D. dissertation, University of Pennsylvania, 1989).

3. Benjamin, 168.

4. Susan Stewart, *On Longing. Narratives of the Miniature, the Gigantic, the Souvenir, the Collection* (Durham and London: Duke University Press, 1993), 104.

5. For an early link between asymmetry and modernity, see Louis-Emile Edmund Duranty, *La Nouvelle Peinture*, 1876, trans. and repr. in Charles Moffett, *The New Painting. Impressionism 1874–1886*, exh. cat. (Fine Arts Museums of San Francisco, 1986).

6. César Daly was the founding editor of the journal *Révue Générale de l'Architecture et des Travaux Publics*. See Ann van Zanten, "Form and Society: César Daly and the *Révue Générale de l'Architecture*," *Oppositions*, vol. 8 (Spring 1977), 137–45, 140.

7. These quotes are taken from Heinrich Wölfflin, "Prolegomena to a Psychology of Architecture," in *Empathy, Form and Space. Problems in German Aesthetics 1873–1893*, intro. and trans. Harry Francis Mallgrave and Eleftherios Ikonomou (Getty Center Publication Programs, 1994), 157–58; from Anthony Vidler, *The Architectural Uncanny. Essays in the Modern Unhomely* (Cambridge, MA, and London: MIT Press, 1992), 73; and from Wölfflin, 1994, 173.

8. One of César Daly's most influential works was *Architecture privée aux XIXe siècle* (Paris, 1877). On the relation of Art Nouveau to contemporary theories of the psyche, see Debora Silverman, *Art Nouveau in Fin-de-Siècle France: Politics, Psychology, Style* (Berkeley: University of California Press, 1989).

9. For a recent analysis of this painting, see Linda Nochlin, "A House is not a Home. Degas and the Subversion of the Family," in Richard Kendall and Griselda Pollack, eds., *Dealing with Degas* (New York: Universe, 1991).

10. Paul Bourget, *Nouveaux Essais de Psychologie Contemporaine* (Paris: Lemeure, 1886), 152.

11. On the social and political contexts for this exposition, see Silverman, 1989, as in note 8, 186–206.

12. For Vuillard's involvement in the theater see Belinda Thomson, *Vuillard* (Oxford: Phaidon Press, 1988), 77–103.

13. A wood engraving of the painting is illustrated in *The Chefs d'Oeuvres d'Art of the International Exhibition* (London, 1878), 131.

14. John McCoubrey, *American Tradition in Painting* (New York: George Braziller, 1963), 39.

15. For a different interpretation of this painting, see David Lubin, *The Act of Portrayal* (New Haven: Yale University Press, 1990).

16. Henry James, *American Scene* (orig. 1907, repr. Bloomington: Indiana University Press, 1968), 15–16.

17. Eugène Minkowski, "Toward a Pathology of Lived Space," in *Lived Time. Phenomenological and Psychopathological Studies*, trans. and intro. by Nancy Metzel (Evanston, IL: Northwestern University Press, 1970), 429.

18. On Sargent's childhood, see Stanley Olson, *John Singer Sargent. His Portrait* (New York: St Martin's Presss, 1986), 6.

19. Henry James, *What Maisie Knew* (orig. 1897, repr. Harmondsworth: Penguin Books, 1966), 9–10.

20. Quoted in Cynthia Griffin Wolff, *A Feast of Words. The Triumph of Edith Wharton* (Oxford, London: Oxford University Press, 1977).

21. Virginia Woolf, "Tuesday, September 12, 1935," from *A Writer's Diary*, Leonard Woolf, ed. (New York, Harcourt Brace, 1953), 246.

22. Virginia Woolf, *To the Lighthouse* (orig. 1927, repr. New York: Harcourt Brace, 1955), 79.

23. See Jane Becket, "The Abstract Interior," in *Towards a New Art* (London: Tate Gallery, 1980), 90–124.

24. Anthony Vidler quotes Benjamin in "Homes for Cyborgs," orig. in *The Architectural Uncanny: Essays in the Modern Unhomely* (Cambridge, MA, and London: MIT Press, 1992), 147. Tzara and Echaurren are discussed on 151–53.

5. The Ideal Swedish Home

I am indebted to the Fulbright Commission for funding the leave during which this essay was written; to Marianne Sandels and her staff at the Nationalmuseum Library,

Stockholm and to Marianne Nilsson, curator of Carl Larsson-gården, Sundborn for facilitating my research; to Kirk Varnedoe for first giving me the opportunity to write about Lilla Hyttnäs; to Peter Brix Sondergaard for his stimulating insights into turn-of-the-century interiors; and to Gustaf Francis for his editorial expertise.

1. Ellen Key, *Skönhet för alla* (Stockholm: Albert Bonniers förlag, 1913) and *Individidualism och socialism* (Stockholm: Albert Bonniers förlag, 1901). For an analysis of the articles by Gosse, see Larry E. Scott, *Pre-Raphaelitism and the Swedish 1890s* (dissertation, University of Washington), 62–71.

2. William Morris, "The Lesser Arts," *Hopes and Fears for Art* (New York: Longmans, Green and Co., 1917), 36.

3. See the essay published by Strindberg in the 7 March 1877 issue of *Dagens Nyheter*, repr. in Torsten Eklund, ed., *Före Röda Rummet. Strindbergs ungdomsjournalistik* (Stockholm: Albert Bonniers förlag, 1946), 264.

4. John Kruse, "Föreningen för svensk hemslöjd," *Ord och Bild*, vol. 14 (1905), 239–41.

5. August Brunius, "Carl Larsson som hembyggare," *Idun* (25 May 1913), 330.

6. Carl Larsson, *Ett hem* (Albert Bonniers förlag, 1899), 1.

7. Theodor W. Adorno, *Kierkegaard. Construction of the Aesthetic*, ed. and trans. Robert Hullot-Kentor (Minneapolis: University of Minnesota Press, 1989), 47.

8. See Walter Benjamin, "Louis-Philippe or the Interior," *Charles Baudelaire: A Lyric Poet in the Era of High Capitalism*, trans. Harry Zohn (London: Verso, 1973), 167–69.

9. Gustaf af Geijerstam, "Hur tankarna kommer och går," *Ord och Bild* (1892), 19.

10. Arne Naess, *Ecology, Community and Lifestyle*, trans. David Rothenberg (Cambridge: Cambridge University Press, 1989), 178.

11. Pierre Bourdieu, *Distinction. A Social Critique of the Judgement of Taste*, trans. Richard Nice (Cambridge, MA: Harvard University Press, 1984), 281.

12. Ernst Bloch, "Hieroglyphs of the Nineteenth Century," *Heritage of Our Times* (Berkeley-Los Angeles: University of California Press, 1990), 347.

13. *A Home*, 5.

14. Anonymous, "Carl Larsson," *Svenska morgonbladet* (24 January 1919), n. pag.

15. *Ett hem*, 8–9.

16. Charles de Secondat, Baron de Montesquieu, *The Spirit of Laws* (London: George Bell and Sons, 1878), vol. 1, 241.

17. *Ett hem*, 4.

18. For an analysis of folkish thought and its consequences in Germany, see George Mosse, *The Crisis of German Ideology. Intellectual Origins of the Third Reich* (New York: Schocken Books, 1964), 13–51.

19. Quoted in Ingemar Lindberg and Per Holmberg, *En bok om rättvisa* (Stockholm: Utbildningsförlaget Brevskolan, 1993), 22. Sweden had Social Democratic prime ministers from 1932 until 1991, and the party's ideology had a decisive influence on policy decisions both before and since.

20. Brunius.

6. Frank Lloyd Wright's Kindergarten

1. See also, Robert C. Twombley, *Frank Lloyd Wright, his Life and Architecture* (New York: John Wiley & Sons, 1979), esp. ch. 2, and Brendan Gill, *Many Masks: A Life of Frank Lloyd Wright* (New York: G. P. Putnam's Sons, 1987). Lisa Schrenk, a graduate student at the University of Texas, has completed a manuscript on the members of the Oak Park Studio.

2. Harriet Monroe, *John Wellborn Root: A Study of his Life and Work* (New York: Houghton Mifflin, 1896), esp. 121–24; Charles Moore, *Daniel Burnham: Architect; Planner of Cities* (New York: Houghton Mifflin, 1921), vol. II, ch. 26. Also, my essay, "The Projecting of Chicago as a Commercial City and the Rationalization of Design and Construction," in *Chicago and New York: Architectural Interactions* (Chicago: Art Institute of Chicago, 1984).

3. Perkins, Hunt, and Tallmadge were prominent residents of Evanston and built extensively there, yet none ever maintained an office in Evanston or listed himself in the professional section of the city business directories. On the situation in Oak Park, see Paul E. Sprague, *Guide to Frank Lloyd Wright and Prairie School Architecture in Oak Park* (Oak Park: Oak Park Landmarks Commission, 1976). The celebrated precedent for Wright's move was Henry Hobson Richardson who, during the 1870s and 1880s, maintained his office attached to his house in Brookline, MA. The structure itself, however, had no architectural pretense.

4. Alfred Granger, "An Architect's Studio," *House Beautiful* (December 1899); Robert C. Spencer, "The Work of Frank Lloyd Wright," *Architectural Review* (April 1900), 61–72. Contemporaneously it was published in the 1900 *Chicago Architectural Club Catalogue* with a similar short explanation.

5. *Architectural Record*, vol. 23 (March 1908), 155–65, esp. 164.

6. Wright mentions this in a letter to the Australian government in response to their inquiry about his former draftsman, Walter Burley Griffin (specifically, about Griffin's contribution to the Wright office), after Griffin won the competition in 1912 to design the Australian capital of Canberra. See Donald Leslie Johnson, *The Architecture of Walter Burley Griffin* (Melbourne: Macmillan, 1977), 22.

7. I treat this at length in the essay "Schooling the Prairie School: Frank Lloyd Wright's Prairie Style as a Communicable System," in Carol Bolen, Robert Nelson and Linda Seidel, eds., *The Nature of Frank Lloyd Wright* (Chicago: University of Chicago Press, 1988), 70–84.

8. Spencer, "The Work of Frank Lloyd Wright." Also, Grant Carpenter Manson, *Frank Lloyd Wright to 1910: The First Golden Age* (New York: Reinhold, 1958), 6–10; Stuart Wilson, "The Gifts of Friedrich Froebel," *Journal of the Society of Architectural Historians*, vol. 26 (December 1967), 238–41; Edgar Kaufmann, Jr, "Form Become Feeling, A New View of Froebel and Wright," *Journal of the Society of Architectural Historians*, vol. 40 (May 1981), 130–37.

9. On the Hillside Home School, see Mary Ellen Chase, *A Goodly Fellowship* (New York: Macmillan, 1940), ch. 4.

10. "In the Cause of Architecture (Second Paper)," *Architectural Record*, vol. 35 (May 1914), 405–14, esp. 407.

11. The transformation of the architectural profession in the 1890s is a large topic. See, on Richardson's office, James O'Gorman, *H. H. Richardson and His Office*

(Cambridge: Harvard University Library, 1974). Also: Andrew Saint, *The Image of the Architect* (New Haven: Yale University Press, 1983).
12. The distinction between the downtown and the suburb, viewed censorially, appears as early as Friedrich Engels's *Condition of the Working-Class in England* (first English edition, London: 1892). On social marks and zones, see also: Mary Douglas, *The World of Goods* (New York: Basic Books, 1979) and Paul Fussell, *Abroad: British Literary Travelling Between the Wars* (New York: Oxford University Press, 1980).

7. "Hi Honey, I'm Home"

The author wishes to acknowledge Christopher M. S. Johns and Paul Barolsky for their thoughtful and faithful readings of early drafts of this essay. Unless otherwise noted, translations are the author's. My thanks to Mort Guiney for his assistance with the French passages.
1. English translation from *The Complete Works of Horace*, trans. Charles E. Passage (New York: F. Ungar, 1983), 99–101.
2. Renato Poggioli, *The Oaten Flute: Essays on Pastoral Poetry and the Pastoral Ideal* (Cambridge: Harvard University Press, 1975), 4.
3. Henri Matisse, "Notes d'un peintre," *La Grande Revue*, vol. LII, no. 24 (25 December 1908), 731–45. Repr. in translation in Jack Flam, *Matisse on Art* (New York: Phaidon, 1973), 35–40.
4. Joseph Masheck, "Embalmed Objects; Design at the Modern," *Artforum*, vol. 13, no. 6 (February 1975), 49–55, especially the appendix "Art as Rest and Rehabilitation;" and *idem*, "The Carpet Paradigm: Critical Prolegomena to a Theory of Flatness," *Arts Magazine*, vol. 51, no. 1 (September 1976), 82–109.
5. Any study of Matisse and the "decorative" is indebted to John H. Neff's pioneering work. See especially his essay "Matisse and Decoration: An Introduction," *Arts Magazine*, vol. 49, no. 9 (May 1975), 59–61.
6. Tom Lutz, *American Nervousness, 1903: An Anecdotal History* (Ithaca: Cornell University Press, 1991), 6.
7. George Frederick Drinka, *The Birth of Neurosis: Myth, Malady, and the Victorians* (New York: Simon and Schuster, 1984), 208.
8. Anson Rabinbach, *The Human Motor: Energy, Fatigue, and the Origins of Modernity* (New York: Basic Books, 1990), 153.
9. Drinka notes that a number of European doctors ran elaborate experiments on humans and animals hoping to discover the true physiological basis of neurasthenia. Charles Féré, a disciple of Jean-Martin Charcot, subjected patients to a variety of sensory stimulations and measured, among other things, muscle strength and blood pressure aided by several specially designed instruments. As Drinka notes, Féré discovered that "intellectual work is accompanied equally by an exaggeration of the circulatory tendency [blood pressure], in the frequency and amplitude of respiration, a greater abundance of secretion, and an increase in the dynametric force." See Drinka, 214–16. See Rabinbach, chapter six, for a discussion of "fatigue research" undertaken in the 1880s and 1890s. For a related study see *idem*, "The Body without Fatigue: A Nineteenth-Century Utopia," in S. Drescher, D. Sabean, and A. Sharlin, *Political Symbolism in Modern Europe* (New Brunswick: Transaction Books, 1982), 42–62.
10. Rabinbach, 157.
11. Fernand Levillain, *La Neurasthénie, Maladie de Beard* (Paris: Maloine, 1891), 38–39.
12. Drinka, 216. Drinka cites a case study undertaken by the neuropsychiatrist Georges Gilles de la Tourette in the 1890s in which a 45-year-old businessman was chosen as the exemplary "shock" neurasthenic.
13. Ibid., 220.
14. Included among the causes of neurasthenia in females were "the abuse of societal pleasures, sexual excess, the loss of one or more children . . . and neuropathic heredity." See Léon Bouveret, *La Neurasthénie* (Paris: Baillière, 1890), 31. Increased intellectual activity on the part of women was also often cited as a primary cause of nervous exhaustion.
15. Elaine Showalter, *The Female Malady: Women, Madness, and English Culture, 1830–1980* (New York: Pantheon Books, 1985), 138. A well-known account of the debilitating (and maddening) effects of the "rest cure" is Charlotte Perkins Gilman's "The Yellow Wallpaper," which Showalter labels "a powerful polemic against Mitchell's methods" (141). See also Ellen L. Bassuk, "The Rest Cure: Repetition or Resolution of Victorian Women's Conflicts?" in Susan Rubin Suleiman, ed., *The Female Body in Western Culture* (Cambridge: Harvard University Press, 1985).
16. Bouveret, 12.
17. For a discussion of the increased interest in exercise and the rise of the sports movement in conjunction with the perceived spread of neurasthenia, see Robert A. Nye, "Degeneration, Neurasthenia and the Culture of Sport in *Belle Epoque* France," *Journal of Contemporary History*, vol. 17, no. 1 (January 1982), 51–68.
18. Émile Laurent, *La Neurasthénie et son traitement* (Paris: Maloine, 1895), 52.
19. Ibid., 53.
20. For a discussion of the doctrine of the *femme au foyer* and the ideology of separate spheres in late nineteenth-century France, see James C. McMillan, *Housewife or Harlot: The Place of Women in French Society, 1870–1940* (New York: St Martin's Press, 1981).
21. Jules Simon, *La Femme du Vingtième Siècle* (Paris: Calmann Levy, 1892), 67.
22. In "Of Queens' Gardens" (1865), Ruskin championed women as keepers of the home and hearth and praised their ability for "ordering, arrangement and decision." Consequently, the domestic interior served as a protective place of refuge for the male dweller after "his rough work in open world." For Ruskin, the home's true function was to provide shelter and a "place of Peace" amidst the chaos of modern life. See John Ruskin, "Of Queens' Gardens," in *Sesame and Lilies* (New York: J. Wiley and Sons, 1887), 99–100.
23. Jacob von Falke, *Art in the House: Historical, Critical, and Aesthetical Studies on the Decoration and Furnishing of the Dwelling* (Boston: Prang and Company, 1879), 315–16.
24. Gustave Soulier, "Une Installation de Château," *L'Art décoratif*, vol. 4 (May 1902), 84.
25. O. Gerdeil, "L'Intérieur," *L'Art décoratif*, vol. 3 (June 1901), 126.
26. M. H. Baillie Scott, *Houses and Gardens* (London: G. Newnes, 1906), 53.
27. Vincent Van Gogh to Theo Van Gogh, October 1888. Excerpted in translation in Herschel

B. Chipp, *Theories of Modern Art* (Berkeley: University of California Press, 1968), 40–41.

28. Alphonse Germain, *Le Sentiment de l'art et sa formation par l'étude des oeuvres* (Paris: Bloud and Cie, 1902), 145–46. This text is a reprint with some modifications of "Pour le beau", which appeared originally in *Essais d'art libre*, vol. 3 (February–March 1893) and was published in book form as *Pour le beau. Essai de kallistique* (Paris: E. Girard, 1893).

29. For an extensive discussion of the critical formulation of the decorative landscape, see Joyce Henri Robinson, "A 'Nouvelle Arcadie': Puvis de Chavannes and the Decorative Landscape in Fin-de-Siècle France," (Ph.D. dissertation, The University of Virginia, 1993). See also Roger Benjamin, "The Decorative Landscape, Fauvism, and the Arabesque of Observation," *The Art Bulletin*, vol. 75, no. 2 (June 1993), 295–316.

30. Alphonse Germain, "Le paysage décoratif, *L'Ermitage*, vol. 3 (November 1891), 645. "Quel meilleur moyen de transformer nos cases maussades en oasis où puisse halter l'esprit retour des soucis vulgaires! . . . Oh! oublier la laideur des rues devant le paysage idéalisé . . ."

31. Alphonse Germain, "Théorie des déformateurs: exposé et réfutation," *La Plume*, vol. 3 (September 1891), 289–90. On Germain's early career as a Symbolist critic, see Michael Marlais, *Conservative Echoes in Fin-de-Siècle Parisian Art Criticism* (University Park: Pennsylvania State University Press, 1992), 171–80.

32. Germain, *Le Sentiment de l'art*, 151–52.

33. Robert Herbert, *Neo-Impressionism* (New York: Solomon R. Guggenheim Foundation, 1968), 21.

34. Louis Vauxcelles, "Francis Auburtin," *Art et décoration* (September 1912), 78. For a discussion of Auburtin within the context of late ninteenth-century pastoral painting, see Joyce Henri Robinson, "La représentation de l'Age d' or," in Christian Briend, et al., *Jean-Francis Auburtin, 1866–1930* (Paris: Délégation à l'Action Artistique de la Ville de Paris, 1990), 65–81.

35. Debora L. Silverman, *Art Nouveau in Fin-de-Siècle France: Politics, Psychology, and Style* (Berkeley: University of California Press, 1989), 77.

36. Joris-Karl Huysmans, *Against Nature*, trans. Robert Baldick (New York: Penguin Books, 1959), 63.

37. Silverman, 79.

38. René Boylesve, "Les Arts: Salon de l'Art Nouveau, Galerie Bing," *L'Ermitage* (1896), 116. Camille Pissarro, Letter to Lucien Pissarro, 27 December 1895, as quoted in Nancy J. Troy, *Modernism and the Decorative Arts in France: Art Nouveau to Le Corbusier* (New Haven and London: Yale University Press, 1991), 25.

39. Arsène Alexandre, "L'Art nouveau," *Le Figaro* (28 December 1895), 1, as quoted in translation in Silverman, 278.

40. Ibid., as quoted in Silverman, 278; and Boylesve, 116.

41. André Hallays, "Au jour le jour," *Le Journal des Débats* (12 January 1896), 1, as quoted in Gabriel P. Weisberg, *Art Nouveau Bing: Paris Style 1900* (New York: Abrams, 1986), 77.

42. Marius Vachon, *Puvis de Chavannes* (Paris: Braun, Clement, 1895), 1–2.

43. Roger-Ballu, *Exposition de Tableaux, Pastels, Dessins par M. Puvis de Chavannes* (Paris: Galerie Durand-Ruel, 1887), 7.

44. Julius Meier-Graefe, *Modern Art*, vols. 1 and 2, trans. Florence Simmonds and George W. Chrystal (London: W. Heinemann, 1908), 48.

45. Roger Marx, "Cartons d'Artistes: Puvis de Chavannes," *L'Image* (July 1897), 242.

46. *La Plume*, vol. 6 (15 January 1895), 50. Bonnat's comments were read aloud in his absence at the 1895 banquet held in Puvis's honor. Quoted in translation in Louise d'Argencourt et al., *Puvis de Chavannes, 1824–1898*, exh. cat. (Ottawa: National Gallery of Canada, 1977), 172.

47. Marx, 242.

48. Victor Joze, "Le Féminisme et le bon sens," *La Plume*, vol. 6 (15 September 1895), 392.

49. Poggioli, 22.

50. Horace, *Epodes* 2.7.

8. Domesticity, Decoration and Consumer Culture

1. Martha Ward, "Impressionist Installations and Private Exhibitions," *The Art Bulletin*, vol. 73 (December 1991), 599–622.

2. Ibid., 618–21.

3. Albert Gleizes and Jean Metzinger, *Du "cubisme"* (1912), trans. in Robert L. Herbert, ed., *Modern Artists on Art: Ten Unabridged Essays* (Englewood Cliffs, NJ: Prentice-Hall, 1964), 5.

4. Rioux de Maillou, "Les Arts décoratifs et les machines," *Revue des Arts Décoratifs*, vol. 15 (February–March 1895), 225.

5. Debora L. Silverman, *Art Nouveau in Fin-de-Siècle France: Politics, Psychology, and Style* (Berkeley: University of California Press, 1989), 71.

6. Ibid., 71.

7. "Impotence" is their term: ". . . we ought to regard a preoccupation for decoration, if we find it in a painter, as an anachronistic artifice, useful only to conceal impotence." Gleizes and Metzinger (as in note 3), 5.

8. Albert Aurier, "Le Symbolisme en peinture: Paul Gauguin," *Mercure de France*, vol. 2 (March 1891), 163.

9. See Lisa Tierston's essay in this volume.

10. Bloemenwerf, the home Van de Velde built in Uccle, near Brussels, in 1895–96, exemplified his commitment to the domestic environment as an artistic and morally sound setting for the family. "My wife and I felt duty bound to shield our children from the sight of ugly things," Van de Velde later recalled. "I refused to allow the presence of any object in my home which was not as basically honest, genuinely straightforward and altogether above suspicion as the character of the friends we received there." Henry van de Velde, "Extracts from his Memoirs, 1891–1901," intro. P. Morton Shand, *Architectural Review*, vol. 112 (September 1952), 153.

11. André Mare, Letter to Maurice Marinot (20 February 1912), André Mare Archive, Paris.

12. Ibid.

13. See the discussion of the Maison Cubiste in my *Modernism and the Decorative Arts in France: Art Nouveau to Le Corbusier* (New Haven and London: Yale University Press, 1991), ch. 2.

14. Daniel Robbins, "From Symbolism to Cubism: The Abbaye of Créteil," *The Art Journal*, vol. 23 (Winter 1963–64), 113.

15. For the formulation of ideas set out in this paragraph, I am indebted to an unpublished seminar paper written in 1988 by a former student, Nancy Ring.

16. Malcolm Gee, *Dealers, Critics,*

and Collectors of Modern Painting: Aspects of the Parisian Art Market Between 1910 and 1930 (New York and London: Garland Publishing, 1981), 214.
17. Daniel-Henry Kahnweiler with Francis Crémieux, *My Galleries and Painters*, trans. Helen Weaver (London: Thames and Hudson, 1971), 36.
18. Ibid., 41.
19. Kahnweiler, quoted in Gee, 21, n. 2.
20. *La Collection particulière de M. Paul Poiret* (Paris: [Galerie] Barbazanges, 26 April–23 May 1923), preface by André Salmon; *Catalogue des Tableaux Modernes, Pastels, Aquarelles et Dessins . . . de la Collection de M. Paul Poiret*, sale catalogue (Paris, Hôtel Drouot, 18 November 1925). Brancusi is not listed in either of these publications, but Poiret acquired a sculpture by him in 1912. See Billy Klüver and Julie Martin, "Man Ray, Paris," in Merry Foresta, et al., *Perpetual Motif: The Art of Man Ray* (New York: The Abbeville Press, and Washington, DC: National Museum of American Art, 1988), 98, fig. 81.
21. "Poiret's New Kingdom," *Vogue*, vol. 40 (1 July 1912), 16.
22. Gustave Babin, "Une Leçon d'élégance dans un parc," *L'Illustration*, no. 3515 (9 July 1910), 21.
23. See Paul Cornu, "L'Art de la robe," *Art et Décoration*, vol. 29 (April 1911), 101–118.
24. Ibid., 112.
25. Paul Poiret, *My First Fifty Years*, trans. Stephen Haden Guest (London: Victor Gollancz, 1931), 185ff.
26. Ibid., 188.
27. Peter Wollen, "Fashion/Orientalism/The Body," *New Formations*, vol. 1 (Spring 1987), 12.
28. See the ad Poiret published as a "Warning Against False Labels," in *Women's Wear* (13 October 1913), 3; and "Poiret's Label," in *Women's Wear* (17 October 1913), 3. On fake labels, see Samuel Hopkins Adams, "The Dishonest Paris Label: How American Women are Being Fooled by a Country-Wide Swindle," *Ladies Home Journal* (March 1913); repr. in *Dress: The Journal of the Costume Society of America*, vol. 4 (1978), 17–23.
29. Ad for R. H. Macy & Co., *New York Times* (24 September 1913), 5.
30. Ad for Gimbel Brothers, *New York Times* (19 October 1913), 16.
31. Ad for Kurzman, *New York Times* (24 September 1913), 5.
32. Poiret ad, "Warning Against False Labels," (as in n. 28).
33. On the Syndicat, see: "To Stop Pirating of Dress Fashions," *New York Times* (29 May 1914), 4; "Projet d'organisation de la copie et de la reproduction des modèles des grands couturiers," *Les Elégances Parisiennes* (August 1916), 70; "First News of French Fashion Syndicate's Official Plans," and "Statutes of French Fashion Syndicate, now Published for the First Time," *New York Times* (23 January 1916), 2. On the Fête Parisienne, see: "$100,000 in Gowns Arrive from Paris," *New York Times* (3 November 1915), 15; "Pet Animals Figure in Winter Styles," *New York Times* (23 November 1915), 5; Roger Boutet de Monvel, "Fashioning our First Fashion Fête," *Vogue*, vol. 45 (15 December 1915), 34–35.

9. Forgotten Ties

1. E. H. Gombrich, *The Sense of Order: A Study in the Psychology of Decorative Art* (Ithaca: Cornell University Press, 1979), 62.
2. Franz Glück reports that it is unclear where "Ornament and Crime" was first published; see Adolf Loos, *Sämtliche Schriften*, vol. 1 (Vienna: Herold, 1962), 457. Two important venues were Karl Kraus's Viennese journal *Die Fackel* in 1908 and Herwarth Walden's *Der Sturm* (Berlin) in 1912. It is reproduced in the *Sämtliche Schriften*, 276–88. Unless otherwise noted, translations are mine.
3. Ibid., 161. Under the title "Damenmode," Loos editor Glück notes the date 21 August 1898, but he reports that the article is first known to have been published in *Dokumente der Frau*, a Viennese journal (1 March 1902).
4. Naomi Schor, *Reading in Detail: Aesthetics and the Feminine* (New York: Methuen, 1987), 4, 50–58.
5. Wassily Kandinsky, *Über das Geistige in der Kunst* (Munich: Piper, 1912), 82. The traditional English translations shift the outcome Kandinsky predicts: ". . . we shall produce works which are mere decoration, which are suited to neckties or carpets," trans. M. T. H. Sadler, 1914 (New York: Dover, 1977), 47; or ". . . we shall produce works which are mere geometric decoration, resembling something like a necktie or carpet," trans. Francis Golffing, et al. (New York: Wittenborn, 1947), 68. Kandinsky's implicit denigration – "grob gesagt, to put it crudely" – is thus reified into "*mere* decoration." In addition, "geometrische Ornamentik, geometric ornamentation" slides into "(geometric) decoration," pointing not only to the difficulty of translating decorative arts terms but also to the fluidity of those terms – about which, see below.
6. Norma Broude, "Miriam Schapiro and 'Femmage': Reflections on the Conflict between Decoration and Abstraction in Twentieth-Century Art," 1980, repr. in Broude and Mary D. Garrard, eds., *Feminism and Art History: Questioning the Litany* (New York: Harper, 1982), 315–29.
7. Mark A. Cheetham, *The Rhetoric of Purity: Essentialist Theory and the Advent of Abstract Painting* (Cambridge: Cambridge University Press, 1991).
8. Karl Scheffler, "Meditationen über das Ornament," *Die Kunst*, vol. 4, no. 10 (1901), 401.
9. At the beginning of the chapter, "The Language of Form and Color," Kandinsky claims music's ability to act directly on the soul, quotes Eugène Delacroix on emotional correspondences of colors, and then in a footnote directs the reader to compare this "interesting article by K. Scheffler." Kandinsky, 44, n. 1. Peg Weiss discusses the reference in *Kandinsky in Munich: The Formative Jugendstil Years* (Princeton: Princeton University Press, 1979), 107, 110–11.
10. Scheffler, "Dekorationsmalerei," *Dekorative Kunst*, vol. 2, no. 8 (1898), 70.
11. Scheffler, "Korrespondenzen: Berlin," *Dekorative Kunst*, vol. 1, no. 2 (1898), 87, 89.
12. Scheffler, "Korrespondenzen: Berlin," *Dekorative Kunst*, vol. 1, no. 4 (1898), 187.
13. Otto Weininger, *Geschlecht und Charakter. Eine prinzipielle Untersuchung* (Vienna: Braumüller, 1903).
14. Scheffler, *Die Frau und die Kunst. Eine Studie* (Berlin: Bard, 1908), 38, 49, 17, 59–63, 105–9.
15. Scheffler, "Volkskunst," *Die Kunst*, vol. 4, no. 4 (1901), 142.
16. Scheffler, "Neue Eckmann-Teppiche," *Die Kunst*, vol. 4, no. 6 (1901), 226.
17. Scheffler, "Unterricht im Kunstgewerbe," *Die Kunst*, vol. 6, no. 10 (1902), 367–68, 370, 372, 376, 377, 380.
18. Renate Berger's history of the

conditions of female artistic production in Germany demonstrates the paucity of artistic training available to women before the turn of the century, countered by women's influx into decorative arts programs – and the establishment of some of these programs for women only – especially in the first decade of the twentieth century, *Malerinnen auf dem Weg ins 20. Jahrhundert. Kunstgeschichte als Sozialgeschichte* (Cologne: DuMont, 1986), esp. 90–91. Berger claims that this influx "alarmed" Scheffler, thereby provoking him to write *Woman and Art*, ibid., 66. See Amy Kathleen Hackett, "Toward the Rights of Association and Assembly: The Transitional Phase, 1902–1908," in "Politics of Feminism in Wilhelmine Germany, 1890–1918" (Ph.D. dissertation, Columbia University, New York, 1976), 547–680.

19. Nancy Troy, *Modernism and the Decorative Arts in France: Art Nouveau to Le Corbusier* (New Haven: Yale University Press, 1991), 31–46.

20. Julius Meier-Graefe, *Entwickelungsgeschichte der modernen Kunst. Vergleichende Betrachtung der bildenden Künste, als Beitrag zu einer neuen Aesthetik*, vol. 1 (Stuttgart: Hoffmann, 1904), 12–13. This translation from Florence Simmonds and George W. Chrystal, trans., *Modern Art: Being a Contribution to a New System of Aesthetics*, vol. 1 (New York: Putnam's, 1908), 6. Many of the allusions to the commercial (and most to the decorative) drop out of the later major editions of the text (1915, 1920), repeating yet again the elision that concerns me here. For an analysis of Meier-Graefe's aesthetics as at least partially constituted by commercial interest, see Robert Jensen, "Der Fall Meier-Graefe," in *Marketing Modernism in Fin-de-Siècle France* (Princeton: Princeton University Press, 1994), 235–63.

21. See esp. Theodor Adorno and Max Horkheimer, "The Culture Industry: Enlightenment as Mass Deception," in *Dialectic of Enlightenment*, 1944, trans. John Cumming (New York: Continuum, 1972), 120–67; Clement Greenberg, "Avant-Garde and Kitsch," 1939, in *Art and Culture: Critical Essays* (Boston: Beacon, 1961), 3–21; Peter Bürger, *Theory of the Avant-Garde*, 1974, trans. Michael Shaw (Minneapolis: University of Minnesota Press, 1984); and Andreas Huyssen, "Mass Culture as Woman: Modernism's Other," in *Across the Great Divide: Modernism, Mass Culture, Postmodernism* (Bloomington: Indiana University Press, 1986), 44–62.

22. Leo Colze, *Berliner Warenhäuser*, 1908 (Berlin: Fannei, 1989), 11.

23. Michel Foucault, *The Order of Things: An Archaeology of the Human Sciences* (New York: Vintage, 1973), 251, 239, 242.

24. See esp. Charles Baudelaire, "The Painter of Modern Life," in *The Painter of Modern Life and Other Essays*, trans. and ed. Jonathan Mayne (London: Da Capo, 1964), 1–40; Clive Bell, *Art* (New York: Stokes, 1913); Roger Fry, *Vision and Design* (New York: Brentano's, 1924); and Greenberg, *Art and Culture.*

25. Foucault, p. 239.

26. The first German edition came out already in 1883 as *Zum Glück der Damen*, trans. Armin Schwartz (Budapest: Grimm), then as *Zum Paradies der Damen*, trans. Paul Heichen (Berlin: Neufeld, *c.* 1890). According to Hans Fromm, there were at least six German versions each running into several editions by 1900; *Bibliographie deutscher Übersetzungen aus dem Französischen, 1700–1948* (Baden-Baden: Verlag für Kunst und Wissenschaft, 1953). Two reviews after the one devoted to the Wertheim façade, Scheffler invokes the novel specifically, referring to the Wertheim's newly completed interior as the "Paradies der Damen"; "Korrespondenzen: Berlin," *Dekorative Kunst*, vol. 1, no. 6 (1898), 266.

27. Doody wrote the preface for a small edition of the novel published by Management Horizons in 1976, quoted in Émile Zola, *The Ladies' Paradise*, Kristin Ross, ed. (Berkeley: University of California Press, 1992), xxii.

28. Ibid., 16–17.

29. Ibid., 7.

30. Julius Posener, *Berlin auf dem Wege zu einer neuen Architektur. Das Zeitalter Wilhelms II* (Munich: Prestel, 1979), 473.

31. Immanuel Kant, *Kritik der Urteilskraft*, Karl Vorländer, ed. (Hamburg: Meiner, 1990), 65, §14.

32. Jacques Derrida, *The Truth in Painting*, trans. Geoff Bennington and Ian McLeod (Chicago: University of Chicago Press, 1987), 53ff.

33. Kant, 40, §2.

34. Ibid., 66, §15. "Zweckmässigkeit ohne Zweck" is translated variously as "purposefulness/finality without end/concept." "Objective purposefulness" can also be "inner," that is, in the "completeness of the object [*die Vollkommenheit des Gegenstandes*]." Kant establishes, however, that the latter is not to be confused with beauty, which is judged purely subjectively, without concept.

35. Ibid., 69, §16.

36. Ibid., 70, §16.

37. Will Grohmann, *Paul Klee* (New York: Abrams, 1954), 213. For a cogent analysis of Grohmann's circle metaphors see Christine Hopfengart, *Klee: Vom Sonderfall zum Publikumsliebling; Stationen seiner öffentlichen Resonanz in Deutschland 1905–1960* (Mainz: von Zabern, 1989), 190–93.

38. Jean-Joseph Goux, *Symbolic Economies: After Marx and Freud*, trans. Jennifer Curtiss Gage (Ithaca: Cornell University Press, 1990), 1–4.

10. "A Room of One's Own"

1. Lytton Strachey to Duncan Grant, 25 August 1909, British Library.

2. E. M. Forster, *Marianne Thornton* (London: Edward Arnold, 1956), 188; unpublished memoir, in John Colmer, *E. M. Forster: The Personal Voice* (London: Routledge & Kegan Paul, 1975), 3.

3. Critics hostile to Bloomsbury have long focused on the group's clubbiness, an attitude now echoed by some feminists, who see the group as a drain on its female members. See Bridget Elliott and Jo-Ann Wallace, "Modernist Anomalies: Bloomsbury and Gender," *Feminist Arts News*, vol. 3, no. 4, 21–24, which argues that Vanessa Bell and Virginia Woolf were isolated within Bloomsbury from contact with other women modernists, a provocative argument that, however, overlooks the question of these women's agency in identifying with the group. Elsewhere I have illuminated the element of homophobia in attacks – feminist and otherwise – on Bloomsbury's cohesiveness; see my "Bloomsbury Bashing: Homophobia and the Politics of Criticism in the Eighties," *Genders*, no. 11 (Fall 1991), 58–80.

4. Leslie Stephen, quoted in Frances Spalding, *Vanessa Bell* (London: Weidenfeld and Nicolson,

1983), 23. Woolf, *Moments of Being*, Jeanne Schulkind, ed. (New York: Harvest/HBJ, 1985), 184. Vanessa Bell, unpublished memoir, quoted in Spalding, 49.

5. Vanessa Bell to Virginia Woolf, 1 November 1904, New York Public Library.

6. Virginia Woolf, "Phyllis and Rosamond," *Complete Shorter Fiction*, Susan Dick, ed. (London: Triad Grafton, 1985), 27–43; *Freshwater: A Comedy* (New York: Harvest/HBJ, 1985). Clive Bell to Vanessa Bell, 9 August 1916, Tate Gallery Archives.

7. Roger Fry, catalog essay for the Second Post-Impressionist Exhibition, 1912, repr. as "The French Post-Impressionists," *Vision and Design* (London: Chatto and Windus, 1920), 238. Virginia Woolf, *Roger Fry: A Biography* (London: Hogarth Press, 1940), 214–15.

8. On Symonds, Browning, and Dickinson, see Jeffrey Weeks, *Coming Out: Homosexual Politics in Britain from the Nineteenth Century to the Present* (London: Quartet, 1977), which quotes Noel Annan, 253; and Ian Anstruther, *Oscar Browning: A Biography* (London: John Murray, 1980). Grant's letter of 16 June 1907 is at the British Library.

9. Robert Skidelsky, *John Maynard Keynes: Hopes Betrayed 1883–1920* (New York: Viking, 1983), 108–110, 235. Grant discusses the evolving decoration in his letters to Keynes of 1910, now at the British Library.

10. The photographs are mentioned in several letters of 1910 from Grant to Keynes now at the British Library. These images or similar ones are reproduced in Douglas Turnbaugh, *Duncan Grant and the Bloomsbury Group* (Secaucus, NJ: Lyle Stuart, 1987), ills. 3, 4. For a broad study of the homoeroticism northern Europeans saw in Mediterranean culture, see Robert Aldrich, *The Seduction of the Mediterranean: Writing, Art and Homosexual Fantasy* (London: Routledge, 1993).

11. On Bloomsbury's relationship to the forms of homosexual identity proposed by the Aesthetes, see my "Making History: The Bloomsbury Group's Construction of Aesthetic and Sexual Identity," *Journal of Homosexuality*, vol. 27, no. 1/2 (1994), 189–247. Grant saw Piero's murals in Arezzo in 1907, and the Keynes Collection at King's College includes one of his copies from Piero, tentatively dated to 1906. Grant's letters to Keynes of October 1910 document his project to copy the mural-scale *Entombment* attributed to Michelangelo in the National Gallery. Grant's quotation is from Ian Dunlop, *The Shock of the New: Seven Historic Exhibitions of Modern Art* (New York: American Heritage Press, 1972), 158. Bell's is from an unpublished memoir, in Spalding, *Bell*, 92. Grafton Gallery, "The Post-Impressionists," preface to *Manet and the Post-Impressionists* [authored by Desmond MacCarthy from notes by Roger Fry] (London, 1910).

12. Roger Fry, "The Grafton Gallery – I," *The Nation* [London] (19 November 1910), 331–32; "The Post-Impressionists – II," *The Nation* (3 December 1910), 331–32; "Post-Impressionism," *Fortnightly Review* (1 May 1911), 865. Only three Matisse paintings were in the exhibition: a Fauve portrait, *La Femme aux yeux verts* (now at the San Francisco Museum of Modern Art), and two early landscapes, *Trees Near Melon* (now in the Belgrade Museum of Art and Archeology) and another unidentified from Leo Stein's collection. Eight sculptures by Matisse, including *Le Serf*, along with some unidentified drawings were also on display. Fry had studied with Bernard Berenson and his first book was *Giovanni Bellini* (London; 1899).

13. Fry, "Grafton Gallery – I."

14. On Matisse's vase, see Museum of Modern Art, *Four Americans in Paris: The Collections of Gertrude Stein and her Family* (New York: 1970), cat. no. 11. Grant's extant preliminary sketches for the Keynes mural are in private collections; one is illustrated in Richard Cork, *Art Beyond the Gallery in Early 20th Century England* (New Haven: Yale University Press, 1985), 121. On Grant's vases see Watney, 29.

15. Spared destruction, these projects are the earliest of Bloomsbury's domestic decorations still extant. Fry's Guildford house remains privately owned. On its design, see "A Possible Domestic Architecture," *Vision and Design*, 272–78.

16. Abigail Frost, "Omega Anonymous," *Crafts*, vol. 66 (January–February 1984), 40–44. Woolf, *Roger Fry*, 190–99. Roger Fry, Omega circular (11 December 1912), copy in George Bernard Shaw's papers, British Library; Fry quoted in M.M.B., "Post-Impressionist Furniture," *Daily News and Leader* (7 August 1913), 10, which illustrated Grant's design. For a thorough history of the Omega, see Judith Collins, *The Omega Workshops* (Chicago: University of Chicago Press, 1984).

17. Collins 60; see ills. 35, 37, 46. Cork, ill. 190. *Pots et Citrons* was owned by the Bells, and is illustrated in Clive Bell's *Art* (London; Chatto and Windus, 1914).

18. Vanessa Bell to Clive Bell, 27 December 1912, Tate Gallery Archives. Roger Fry, "Post-Impressionist Furniture." See Collins, ill. 21; Cork, ill. 182.

19. "Post Impressionist Furniture," cited above. "A Post-Impressionist Flat," *The Daily Mirror* (8 November 1913), in Cork, 154. P. G. Konody, "Post-Impressionism in the Home," *The Observer* (14 December 1913), in Collins, 66–68. S. K. Tillyard's study of the journalistic reactions to Post-Impressionism, *The Impact of Modernism 1900–1920* (London: Routledge, 1988), characterizes the editorial stance of *The Observer*'s publisher as "preoccupied with threats to the British Empire and constitution" (96).

20. Cork, 158–59. Waldemar Januszczak, "Fry's French delights," *The Guardian* [Manchester] (18 January 1984), 9. Januszczak's attitude is cogently criticized by Simon Watney, "Critics and Cults," *Charleston Newsletter*, no. 17 (December 1986), 25–29.

21. Christopher Nevinson and Filippo Marinetti, "Futurist Manifesto," *The Observer* (7 June 1914). *Blast I*, quoted in Richard Cork, *Vorticism and Abstract Art in the First Machine Age*, vol. 1 (London: Gordon Fraser, 1975), 285, which also supplies the gloss. Lewis's 1913 open letter is quoted in Quentin Bell and Stephen Chaplin, "The Ideal Home Rumpus," *Apollo* (October 1964), 285.

22. Hilton Kramer, "Bloomsbury Idols," *The New Criterion* (January 1984), 1–9; "The Essential Cubism in London," *The New Criterion* (June 1983), repr. in *Revenge of the Philistines* (New York: Free Press, 1985), 77.

23. Virginia Woolf, *Collected Essays*, vol. 2 (London: Hogarth Press, 1967), 146.

24. Vanessa Bell, memoir, in S. P. Rosenbaum, ed., *The Bloomsbury*

Group: A Collection of Memoirs, Commentary and Criticism (Toronto: University of Toronto Press, 1975), 83. Woolf, *Fry*, 238.

25. *The Letters of Roger Fry*, 385. Woolf's first letter is from Nigel Nicolson and Joanne Trautmann, eds., *The Letters of Virginia Woolf*, vol. 2 (New York: Harcourt Brace Jovanovich, 1976), 147; the second is quoted in Diane Filby Gillespie, *The Sisters' Arts: The Writing and Painting of Virginia Woolf and Vanessa Bell* (Syracuse: Syracuse University Press, 1988), 47.

11. Homes for Cyborgs

1. Walter Benjamin, *Das Passagen-Werk*, in *Gasammelte Schriften*, vol. 5 (Frankfurt: Suhrkamp, 1982), 513.

2. Donna Haraway, "A Manifesto for Cyborgs: Science, Technology, and Socialist Feminism in the 1980s," in Elizabeth Weed, *Coming to Terms: Feminism, Theory, Politics*, New York: Routledge, 1989), 174, 176. (First published in *Socialist Review*, no. 80, 1985).

3. See Alice Jardine, "Of Bodies and Technologies," in *Discussions in Contemporary Culture*, no. 1, Hal Foster, ed. (Seattle: The Bay Press for The Dia Art Foundation, 1987), 151–58.

4. Haraway, 176.

5. Leonora Carrington, *The House of Fear: Notes from Down Below*, introduction to the English edition by Marina Warner (New York: E. P. Dutton, 1988), 2.

6. Carrington, 72.

7. Carrington, 42, 134, 135.

8. Le Corbusier, "Louis Soutter. L'inconnu de la soixantaine," *Minotaure*, vol. 9 (October 1936), 62.

9. Benjamin, 573.

10. Tristan Tzara, "D'un certain automatisme du Goût," *Minotaure*, vol. 3–4 (December 1933), 84.

11. Ibid., 84.

12. Freud's interpretation of the uncanny desire for intrauterine existence was evolved from his analysis of the "Wolf Man," written down in winter 1914–15 and published in 1918 under the title "From the History of an Infantile Neurosis" (*Collected Papers*, vol. 3, trans. Alix and James Strachey [New York, 1959]). The Wolf Man's complaint, noted Freud, "was that for him the world was hidden by a veil," a veil that could only be torn through the action of the bowels. But this veil was also a kind of mysterious generator of the uncanny: "nor did he keep to the veil. It evaporated into a sense of twilight, into *ténèbres*, and into other impalpable things." During the treatment it became clear that this veil was the response to the circumstances of his birth "with a caul" (*Glückshaube*, or "lucky hood") that, until the onset of castration fears, made him feel he "was a child of fortune":

> Thus the caul was the veil which hid him from the world and hid the world from him. The complaint that he made was in reality a fulfilled wish-fantasy: it exhibited him as back once more in the womb, and was, in fact, a wish-fantasy of flight from the world. It can be translated as follows: "Life makes me so unhappy! I must get back into the womb!" (*Collected Papers*, vol. 3, 580–81)

In this way Freud was able to explain the peculiar functions of intestinal movements that, tearing the veil, precipitated a sort of "rebirth," which was in turn connected to the primal scene of his parents' coitus, imaged in the vision of the wolves in the tree. The tearing of the veil corresponded to the opening of his eyes, and thence the opening of the window; the womb fantasy itself was linked to his attachment to his father, an indication of his desire to be inside the mother's womb in order to replace her during coitus, to take her place with regard to the father. Thus, concluded Freud triumphantly, "two incestuous wishes were united." Here, as Ned Lukacher remarks, Freud "wants to tell a story about what is prior to presence and what has always already been forgotten." (Ned Lukacher, *Primal Scenes; Literature, Philosophy, Psychoanalysis* [Ithaca: Cornell University Press, 1986], 36–37.)

13. Matta Echaurren, "Mathématique sensible – Architecture du temps" (adaptation by Georges Hugnet), *Minotaure*, vol. 11 (1938), 43.

14. Cited by Dalibor Veseley in "Surrealism and Architecture," *Architectural Design*, vol. 48, nos. 2–3 (1978), 94.

15. Salvador Dalí, "De la beauté terrifiante et comestible, de l'architecture modern'style," *Minotaure*, vol. 3–4 (December 1933), 72.

16. Ibid., 73.

17. Le Corbusier, *The Decorative Art of Today*, trans. and intro. James I. Dunnett (Cambridge, MA: MIT Press, 1987), 72.

18. Benjamin, *Passagen-Werk*, 680, citing Salvador Dalí, "L'Âne pourri,' in *Surréalisme au service de la Révolution*, vol. 1 (Paris, 1930), 12. The first attempt to "take the measure of technique" was that of realism; the second, Art Nouveau.

19. Benjamin, *Passagen-Werk*, 694.

20. Ibid., 693, 118.

21. See the evocative passages on Max Ernst and "mechanized adornment" in Giedion's *Mechanization Takes Command* (New York: Oxford University Press, 1948), 360–61, 387–88.

22. Ibid., 388. The illustration discussed (fig. 199, p. 341) is Ernst's "Night Shrieks in Her Lair . . .," from *La Femme 100 têtes* (Paris, 1929).

23. Le Corbusier, 77.

24. See Jean-François Lyotard, *Les TRANSformateurs DUchamp* (Paris: Galilée, 1977), 46–47.

25. Jardine, 157.

26. Michel de Certeau, *The Practice of Everyday Life*, trans. Steven Rendall (Berkeley and Los Angeles: University of California Press, 1984), 147.

27. Le Corbusier, *L'Art décoratif d'aujourd'hui* (Paris, 1925), 76, 79.

28. Jardine, 155.

29. Alfred Jarry, *Les Jours et les nuits* (Paris, 1897), cited in de Certeau, *The Practice of Everyday Life*, 151.

30. Haraway, 194.

31. See Michel de Certeau's description of the "cybernetic system," as it "moves forward on its own; it is becoming self-moving and technocratic; it transforms the subjects that controlled it into operators of the writing machine that orders and uses them. A cybernetic society." (*The Practice of Everyday Life*, 136.)

32. Ibid., 146.

33. William Gibson, *Neuromancer* (New York: The Berkeley Publishing Group, 1984), 11.

34. William Gibson, "Johnny Mnemonic," in *Burning Chrome* (New York: The Berkeley Publishing Group, 1986), 13–14.

35. See Mahmoud Sami-Ali, *Le banal* (Paris, 1980).

36. Theodor Adorno, *Stadien auf dem Lebensweq*, vol. 1 (Jena, 1914), 289: "Homesickness results from distancing. The art would be to experience it at the same time as staying at home, which requires illusionistic virtuosity."

37. Jardine, 171. Jardine lists four possible responses to the "cyborg orgy" depicted by Haraway. The first would be an antitechnological position, which in its back-to-nature guise would be politically to the left and in its antiabortion guise firmly on the right; the second would be a protechnological stance that would to all intents and purposes say "go ahead and be a cyborg, it's great"; the third would consider technology as a way of liberating men from real women, investing reproductive technologies with the role of finally draining the female body of the feminine; and the fourth, a kind of paranoid version of the third, would imagine machine as woman. In these last two versions, technology appears as a male phantasm of the maternal body, mythicized and accessible through psychoanalysis. None of these versions, by itself, seems to accept Haraway's attempt at a politically ironic stance, embodied in the very notion of the cyborg itself.
38. Haraway, 173.
39. In one of Haraway's more utopian moments, cyborg "sex" is depicted (in a vision that recalls Charles Fourier's dream of a third sexuality) as restoring "some of the lovely replicative baroque of ferns and invertebrates," "organic prophylactics against heterosexism" ("Manifesto for Cyborgs," 174).

12. Domestic Differences

I am grateful to the Newberry Library for providing me with a research fellowship, to the National Endowment for the Humanities for a Travel to Collections Grant which enabled me to consult the Mies van der Rohe Archives at the Museum of Modern Art and in the Library of Congress, and to the Bunting Institute, Radcliffe College. My visit to the Farnsworth House was made possible by the Society of Architectural Historians and its former Director, David Bahlman. An expanded version of this essay will appear in my forthcoming book about houses designed for women in the twentieth century (New York: Harry N. Abrams).
1. Edith Farnsworth, *Memoirs*, unpublished ms. in three notebooks. Farnsworth Collection, Newberry Library, Chicago, ch. 3.
2. For Mies's biography, see Franz Schulze, *Mies van der Rohe: A Critical Biography* (Chicago: University of Chicago Press, 1985). The suggestion in Schulze, 252, that Farnsworth chose Mies from a list of architects supplied by the Museum of Modern Art is echoed in the transcript of an interview (1 June 1973) with Myron Goldsmith, the project architect for the Farnsworth house, but this is contradicted by Farnsworth's own recollection.
3. For a fuller discussion of this point see Wini Breines, *Young White and Miserable: Growing up Female in the Fifties* (Boston: Beacon Press, 1992). See also Elaine Tyler May, *Homeward Bound: American Families in the Cold War Era* (New York: Basic Books, 1988) and Rochelle Gatlin, *American Women Since 1945* (Jackson, MS: University Press of Mississippi, 1987). Gerald Gurin et al., *Americans View Their Mental Health* (New York: Basic Books, 1960), 117. The survey also found that single women were happier but worried more than single men, and that they "experienced an approaching nervous breakdown less often than other women", 233–35. Farnsworth's nephew, Fairbank Carpenter, remembers her "regaling the family with tales" at holiday dinners: "She was a spellbinding story teller and totally wrapped up in her own experiences. No one minded her selfishness as she was so entertaining." Personal letter, Fairbank Carpenter to Alice Friedman, 22 October 1991.
4. See Breines, "Alone in the 1950s: Anne Parsons and the Feminine Mystique," *Theory and Society*, vol. 15 (1986), 805–43.
5. *Memoirs*, ch. 3.
6. Ibid., ch. 11.
7. E. A. Duckett and J. Fujikawa, *Impressions of Mies: An Interview on Mies van der Rohe* (Knoxville: University of Tennessee Press, 1988), 26.
8. *Memoirs*, 11.
9. Ibid.
10. *The Listener* (15 October 1959), 620–22.
11. Fritz Neumeyer, *The Artless Word: Mies van der Rohe on the Building Art*, trans. Mark Jarzombek (Cambridge, MA: MIT Press, 1991) [German edition, 1986].
12. Neumeyer, 317.
13. *Memoirs*, ch. 11.
14. See Wolf Tegethoff, *Mies van der Rohe: The Villas and Country Houses* trans. Russell M. Stockman (Cambridge, MA: MIT Press, 1985), 99–104, 110–19 and 121–22 (projects 12, 14, 15 and 17).
15. Mies van der Rohe, "Haus. H., Magdeburg," *Die Schildgenossen*, vol. 14, no. 6 (1935), 514–15. Repr. in English trans. in Neumeyer, 121.
16. *The Listener* (15 October 1959), 621.
17. Christian Norberg-Schulz, "A Talk with Mies van der Rohe," published in *Baukunst and Werkform*, vol. 11, no. 11 (1958), 615–18. Repr. in Neumeyer, 338–39 (quote on 339).
18. Farnsworth Folders, nos. 11, 28, Mies van der Rohe Archives, Museum of Modern Art, New York. See also *Memoirs*, ch. 13.
19. The story is told in detail in Schulze, 252–59.
20. *Memoirs*, ch. 13. For costs of Levitt houses see Kenneth T. Jackson, *Crabgrass Frontier: The Suburbanization of the United States* (New York: Oxford University Press, 1985), 234–38.
21. "Defendant's brief," December 1952, Farnsworth Folder, no. 31, MoMA.
22. For Mies's office notes on the house, assembled in preparation for the trial, see Farnsworth Folder, no. 31, MoMA. The issue of the fee is discussed in an interview with Myron Goldsmith on 1 June 1973; transcript in the Mies van der Rohe Archives, MoMA. The case was heard in the Circuit Court of Kendall County in Yorkville, Illinois; the information about the suits comes from a summary of the proceedings. The matter is discussed in *Memoirs*, 13.
23. "Charges famed architect with fraud, deceit," *Chicago Daily Tribune*, 30 October 1951 (Farnsworth Clipping File, MoMA).
24. *Memoirs*, ch. 13.
25. Elizabeth Gordon, "The Threat to the Next America," *House Beautiful*, vol. 95 (April 1953), 126–30; 250–51 (quote on 250).
26. Joseph A. Barry in *House Beautiful*, vol. 95 (May 1953), 172–73; 266–72 (quote on 270).
27. "Glass House Stones," *Newsweek* (8 June 1953), 90.
28. Lynn Spigel, *Make Room for TV: Television and the Family Ideal in Postwar America* (Chicago: University of Chicago Press, 1992), esp. ch. 3 ("Women's Work") and 4 ("The Home Theater").
29. *Memoirs*, ch. 12.
30. As reported by Myron Goldsmith in conversation with the

author in April 1988. I am grateful to Robert Baldwin for his insights on this point.

31. See Paulette Singley, "Living in a Glass Prism: The Female Figure in Mies van der Rohe's Domestic Architecture," *Critical Matrix*, vol 6, no. 2 (1992), 47–76. For the role of domestic objects, see Miriam Gusevich, "Decoration and Decorum: Adolf Loos's Critique of Kitsch," *New German Critique*, no. 43 (Winter 1988), 97–123 and Remy G. Saisselin, *The Bourgeois and the Bibelot* (New Brunswick, New Jersey: Rutgers University Press, 1988). See also Emily Apter and William Pietz, *Fetishism as Cultural Discourse* (Ithaca, NY: Cornell University Press, 1993).

32. *Memoirs*, ch. 13.

33. Grete Tugendhat, "Die Bewohner des Hauses Tugendhats aussern sich," *Die Form*, no. 7 (November 1931), 437–38; repr. in English trans. in Tegethoff, 97–98. See also Richard Padovan, "Machines à Mediter," in Rolf Achilles et al., *Mies van der Rohe: Architect as Educator* (Chicago: University of Chicago Press, 1986), 17–26.

34. *Memoirs*, ch. 14.

13. Robert Rauschenberg's Fabrics

1. Since first postulated in Harold Rosenberg's well-known essay, "The American Action Painters," the rhetoric surrounding Abstract Expressionism has continued to highlight a kind of heroic struggle seemingly implicit in the process of gestural or action painting. See Harold Rosenberg, "The American Action Painters," *Art News* (December 1952), 22–23, 48–50.

2. Quoted in Dore Ashton, ed., *Twentieth-Century Artists on Art* (Pantheon: New York, 1985), 243. On collage and intellectual relativism, see Donald Kuspit, "Collage: The Organizing Principle of Art," *The New Subjectivisim: Art in the 1980s* (New York: Da Capo Press, 1993), 503–20.

3. Alan Solomon, *Robert Rauschenberg*, exh. cat. (New York: The Jewish Museum, 1963), n. pag.; quoted in Dean Swanson, *Robert Rauschenberg: Paintings 1953–1964*, exh. cat. (Minneapolis: Walker Art Center, 1965), 2; quoted in Lawrence Alloway, *Robert Rauschenberg*, exh. cat. Washington DC: National Collection of Fine Arts, Smithsonian Institution, 1976), 7.

4. Solomon, n. pag.; Andrew Forge, *Robert Rauschenberg* (New York: Harry N. Abrams, 1969), 18–19; Brian O'Doherty, *American Masters*, (New York: Random House, 1973), 202; and "The Emperor's Combine," *Time* (18 April 1960), 92.

5. Walter Hopps, *Robert Rauschenberg: The Early 1950s*, exh. cat. (Houston: The Menil Collection, 1991), 166.

6. James Leggio makes the same assertion in describing the context for Rauschenberg's construction of *Bed*: "Its making occurs at a time of reorientation – after the birth of his son, after his divorce from Susan Weil and his recognition of his own sexual identity, but still early in his family history with Johns . . . and . . . at the start of the radical new phase in his work signaled by the combines." James Leggio, "Robert Rauschenberg's *Bed* and the Symbolism of the Body," in John Elderfield, ed., *Studies in Modern Art, no. 2: Essays on Assemblage* (New York: Harry N. Abrams, 1992), 104.

7. Quoted in Mary Lynn Kotz, *Rauschenberg: Art and Life* (New York: Harry N. Abrams, 1990), 90.

8. Interview with Paul Brach and Miriam Schapiro, New York City, 18 April 1989.

9. Hopps, 14.

10. Judith Bernstock also reads a nostalgic mother figure in this work, which she relates to a sentimental longing implicit in Rauschenberg's use of certain Impressionist and Post-Impressionist reproductions. See Judith Bernstock, "A New Interpretation of Rauschenberg's Imagery," *Pantheon*, vol. 46 (1988), 152.

11. Forge, 19.

12. Irving Sandler, *The New York School, the Painters and Sculptors of the Fifties* (New York: Harper and Row, 1978), 100.

13. Rauschenberg's interest in appropriating from mass culture might also be read as a proto-feminist strategy, much in the same way that Schapiro accessed his use of fabric above. See Andreas Huyssen, "Mass Culture as Woman: Modernism's Other," in Tania Modleski, ed., *Studies in Entertainment: Critical Approaches to Mass Culture* (Bloomington: Indiana University Press, 1986), 188–207.

14. Jeanne Siegel, *Artwords: Discourse on the 60s and 70s* (Ann Arbor: UMI Research Press, 1985), 151.

15. Barbara Rose, *An Interview with Robert Rauschenberg* (New York: Vintage Books, 1987), 62.

16. Leggio, 103.

17. Solomon, n. pag.

18. "The Boy from Port Arthur: Robert Rauschenberg reflects on his Texas Roots," *Art and Antiques* (February 1986), 58–61.

19. Robert Rauschenberg in conversation with Walter Hopps; told to the author in an interview with Hopps, 13 February 1992; Jill Johnston, "The World Outside his Window," *Art in America*, vol. 80 (April 1992), 118; and Mary Lynn Kotz reporting how Rauschenberg "hated the hunting, even though the hunting dogs, Queenie and Rex, were his pets. He could not understand how anyone could kill animals for sport, when in his own backyard he had a number of pets – ducks, rabbits, frogs, a goat. And he was terrified of his father, a strict disciplinarian who did not spare the rod." Kotz, 50.

20. Roni Feinstein similarly noted *Satellite*'s nostalgic edge oddly coupled with the work's sexual motifs. See Roni Feinstein, "Robert Rauschenberg's *Satellite*, 1955," *Bulletin of the Whitney Museum of American Art*, vol. 9 (1987), 24.

21. Hopps interview.

22. Bob Jones productions, *Preview Video # 290*, 120 min., n.d.

23. Susan Stewart, *On Longing: Narratives of the Miniature, the Gigantic, the Souvenir, the Collection* (Durham: Duke University Press, 1993), 150.

24. Ibid., 152.

25. Kotz, 87.

26. Hopps interview.

27. Kotz writes, "Near the white shoes is a portrait of a pensive young man in his twenties, in what Rauschenberg called "a gorgeous photograph. It is Jasper Johns." Kotz, 87.

28. Stewart, 135.

29. In her book on gay codes from the 1960s, Judy Grahn explained that "in the urban Gay underground culture participants have developed elaborate methods of signaling each other . . . a handkerchief of a certain color in the back pocket tells watchful, in-the-know strangers what type of sex the bearer desires." See Judy Grahn, *Another Mother Tongue: Gay Words,*

Gay Worlds (Boston: Beacon, 1984), 212.

30. Frank O'Hara, "Reviews and Preview: Bob Rauschenberg," *Art News*, vol. 53 (January 1955), 47.

31. Jonathan Katz, "The Art of Code: Jasper Johns and Robert Rauschenberg," in Whitney Chadwick and Isabelle de Courtivron, eds., *Significant Others: Creativity and Intimate Partnership* (London: Thames and Hudson, 1993), 189–207; see also Kenneth Silver, "Modes of Disclosure: The Construction of Gay Identity and the Rise of Pop Art," in Russell Ferguson, ed., *Hand-Painted Pop: American Art in Transition 1955–1962*, exh. cat. (Los Angeles: The Museum of Contemporary Art, 1992).

14. Master Bedrooms, Master Narratives

This article is dedicated to members of the Benefits Committee of the "Association of Lesbian and Gay Faculty, Administration, and Staff" of New York University, who successfully campaigned for "domestic partner" benefits at the University. I would also like to acknowledge the friends and colleagues who have discussed with me the issues raised in this article, for which I am most grateful: Susan Aberth, Donna DeSalvo, Ariella Budick, Tim Donehoo, John Goodman, Ed LaMance, Carol Ockman, Ed Stein, and Bill Valerio.

1. Although he does not discuss Muybridge's photographs, Whitney Davis has a good deal to say about Thomas Eakins' more-or-less contemporaneous photographs of his nude students in relationship to the American "physical culture" movement of the late nineteenth-century in "Erotic Revision in Thomas Eakins's Narratives of Male Nudity," *Art History* (September 1994), 301–41.

2. For Bacon's interest in and use of Muybridge in relationship to *Two Figures* see John Russell, *Francis Bacon* (Greenwich, Conn.: New York Graphic Society, 1971), 146, 155; Hugh M. Davies, *Francis Bacon: The Early and Middle Years, 1928–1958* (New York and London: Garland Publishing, 1978), 119–53; and Dawn Ades, "Web of Images," in *Francis Bacon*, exh. cat. (London: Tate Gallery, with Thames and Hudson, 1985), 22.

3. I am indebted to Molly Nesbit's fine and innovative work on Atget's photographs and their status (and work) as "documents." See Molly Nesbit, *Atget's Seven Albums* (New Haven and London: Yale University Press, 1992).

4. Mark Roskill, "Francis Bacon as a Mannerist," *Art International* (25 September 1963), 44.

5. It was not until 1967 that "homosexual acts between consenting adults in private" was legalized in England. Bacon painted *Two Figures* the year before the appointment of the Wolfenden Committee, convened in order to consider the standing anti-homosexual laws. In fact, autumn 1953 and winter 1954 marks a particularly intensive moment of the government pursuit of homosexuals, involving arrests for homosexual offenses throughout England. See H. Montgomery Hyde, *The Love that Dared Not Speak Its Name: A Candid History of Homosexuality in Britain* (Boston: Little, Brown and Company, 1970).

6. Although none of them deal directly with my concerns here, related aspects of Arbus's aesthetic are taken up in Shelley Rice, "Essential Differences: A Comparison of the Portraits of Lisette Model and Diane Arbus," *Artforum*, vol. 18 (May 1980), 66–71; Catherine Lord, "What Becomes a Legend Most: The Short, Sad Career of Diane Arbus," in Richard Bolton, *The Contest of Meaning: Critical Histories of Photography* (Cambridge, MA: MIT Press, 1989), 111–23; and Carol Armstrong, "Biology, Destiny, Photography: Difference According to Diane Arbus," *October*, vol. 66 (Fall 1993), 29–54.

7. Kenneth E. Silver, "Modes of Disclosure: The Construction of Gay Identity and the Rise of Pop Art," *Hand-Painted Pop: American Art in Transition, 1955–62*, exh. cat. (Los Angeles: The Museum of Contemporary Art, with Rizzoli Publishers, 1993), esp. 201–2.

8. Andreas Huyssen, "Mass Culture as Woman: Modernism's Other," in Tania Modelski, ed., *Studies in Entertainment: Critical Approaches to Mass Culture* (Bloomington, IN: University of Indiana Press, 1986).

9. Harold Rosenberg, "The American Action Painters," *Art News* (December 1952), 22. All quotes below are from this original publication, 22–23 and 48–50.

10. Barbara Rose, "Hans Namuth's Photographs and the Jackson Pollock Myth, Part One: Media Impact and the Failure of Criticism," *Arts Magazine* (March 1979), 113.

11. Ibid., 116.

12. The photograph is reproduced in Ellen G. Landau, *Jackson Pollock* (New York: Abrams, 1989), 17. Another photograph, probably from the same series, which shows Krasner sitting by herself in Pollock's studio space has been published in Anne M. Wagner, "Lee Krasner as L. K., " *Representations*, vol. 25 (Winter 1989), 45.

13. The Art Director's Club awarded a Certificate of Merit to "Andy Warhol's Mother" on 1 April 1958. See Donna De Salvo, ed., *Success is a Job in New York: the Early Art and Business of Andy Warhol*, exh. cat. (New York: Grey Art Gallery, N.Y.U. and Pittsburgh: The Carnegie Museum of Art, 1989), 32, 78 (no. 67).

14. Andy Warhol and Pat Hackett, *POPism: The Warhol 60s* (New York and London: Harcourt, Brace, Jovanovich, 1980), 12–13.

15. See Cécile Whiting's work on Pop, gender, and class including "Pop Art Domesticated: Class and Taste in Tom Wesselmann's Collages," *Genders*, vol. 13 (Spring 1992), 43–72, and "Borrowed Spots: The Gendering of Comic Books, Lichtenstein's Paintings, and Dishwasher Detergent," *American Art* (Spring 1992), 9–35.

16. Interestingly, Warhol's name for his work space, the Factory, was the antithesis of domestic (although people like Billy Name in fact lived there) and, we might say, highly masculine in association. For an interesting approach to this subject see Caroline A. Jones, "Andy Warhol's 'Factory': The Production Site, Its Context, and Its Impact on the Work of Art," *Science in Context*, vol. 4, no. 1 (1991), 101–31.

17. Allan Kaprow, "The Legend of Jackson Pollock," *Art News* (October 1958), 56.

18. Dorothy Miller, ed., *Sixteen Americans*, exh. cat. (New York: Museum of Modern Art, 1959), 58.

19. Daniel Wheeler, *Art Since Mid-Century: 1945 to the Present* (Englewood Cliffs, NJ: Prentice-Hall, 1991), 131. Wheeler in fact reproduces (fig. 139) Bacon's *Two*

Figures, amongst other works by the artist, in his book. Rauschenberg himself, on the other hand, has called *Bed* his "friendliest" picture (131).

20. See my discussion of the homosexual aspect of Johns' art in "Modes of Disclosure," op. cit. See also Jonathan Katz, "The Art of Code: Jasper Johns and Robert Rauschenberg" in Whitney Chadwick and Isabelle de Courtivron, eds., *Significant Others: Creativity and Intimate Partnership*, (London: Thames and Hudson, 1993).

21. Paul Cadmus painted male domestic scenes such as *The Bath* (*c.* 1950–51). See Jonathan Weinberg, "Cruising with Paul Cadmus" *Art in America* (November 1992), 102–9.

22. David Hockney, *David Hockney by David Hockney*, Nikos Stangos, ed. (New York: Harry N. Abrams, 1976), 90–91.

23. I'm thinking of works like *Hotel* (1962); *Berlin: A Souvenir* (1962–63). See *David Hockney: Paintings of the Early 1960s*, exh. cat. (New York: Andre Emmerich Gallery, 1985).

24. Richard Meyer, "Robert Mapplethorpe and the Discipline of Photography," in Abelove, Barale, and Halperin, *The Lesbian and Gay Studies Reader*, (New York and London: Routledge, 1993), 370.

25. See Henry Urbach's interesting analysis of gay and lesbian partners portrayed in interior design magazines, "Peeking at Gay Interiors," *Design Book Review*, vol. 25 (Summer 1992), 38–40.

15. Pop at Home

I am grateful to Jim Herbert, Chris Reed and Sarah Whiting, who read this text with care and offered many helpful suggestions. My thanks as well to the U.C.L.A. Academic Senate and the Center for the Study of Women at U.C.L.A. for grants which funded the research for this project, and to my research assistants Katie Hauser and Bill Begert.

1. Although I will examine in this article both Wesselmann's appropriation of the codes of interior decoration and the incorporation of Pop art into the homes of collectors, I will concentrate here on the collectors, since I have already analyzed in detail the association between Wesselmann's collages and interior decoration in my article, "Pop Art Domesticated: Class and Taste in Tom Wesselmann's Collages," *Genders*, vol. 13 (Spring 1992), 43–72. The fully developed version of my argument about both Wesselmann and Pop art collectors is forthcoming in my book, *A Taste for Pop: Pop Art, Gender, and Consumer Culture* (Cambridge University Press).

2. See, for instance, David M. Potter, *People of Plenty: Economic Abundance and the American Character* (Chicago: University of Chicago Press, 1954).

3. Elaine Tyler May, *Homeward Bound: American Families in the Cold War Era* (New York: Basic Books, 1988), 163.

4. Roland Marchand, "Visions of Classlessness, Quests for Dominion: American Popular Culture, 1945–1960," in Robert H. Bremner and Gary W. Reichard, eds., *Reshaping America: Society and Institutions 1945–1960* (Columbus: Ohio State University Press, 1982), 168–170.

5. Pierre Bourdieu makes the point that taste functions as a marker of class in his book *Distinction: A Social Critique of the Judgment of Taste* (Cambridge, MA: Harvard University Press, 1984).

6. Suzi Gablik, "Tom Wesselmann," *Art News*, vol. 64 (March 1965), 17.

7. Vivien Raynor, "Tom Wesselmann," *Arts*, vol. 37 (January 1963), 45.

8. For example, *Great American Nude #8* of 1961 reverses Matisse's *Pink Nude* of 1935, as pointed out by Sidra Stich in *Made in U.S.A.* (Berkeley: University of California Press, 1987), 30.

9. Probably the most important book on Matisse to appear in English after World War II was Alfred Barr, *Matisse: His Art and His Public* (New York: Museum of Modern Art, 1951). Jean Renoir's memoir about his father generated many articles in both art magazines and the popular press linking Renoir's paintings devoted to the "charms" of the feminine world to the romantic exploits of Renoir's personal life. Jean Renoir, *Renoir, My Father* (London: Collins, 1962).

10. At the same time such reproductions reaffirm the uniqueness of the original upon which they are based. As Richard Shiff has argued: "In one sense at least, the most theocentric one, abundance and repetition reinforce the original: if one returns to the 'original' or 'classic' meaning of *original* – having existed from the first – originality can only be enhanced by recreative replication." Richard Shiff, "Mastercopy," *IRIS: Revue de théorie et du son*, vol. 1 (1983), 126.

11. I am relying here on terminology that various feminist film theorists have appropriated from psychoanalysis to describe masculine spectatorship. Laura Mulvey offers the classic formulation of masculine spectatorship in Freudian terms in "Visual Pleasure and Narrative Cinema," *Screen*, vol. 16 (Autumn 1975), 6–18. See also Mary Ann Doane, *The Desire to Desire: The Woman's Film of the 1940s* (Bloomington: Indiana University Press, 1987), 13–22.

12. Jill Johnston, "Tom Wesselmann," *Art News*, vol. 61 (November 1962), 15. Many critics found Wesselmann's nudes appealing, sensual and erotic; even negative criticisms of Wesselmann's nudes were articulated in terms of the desirability of the bodies.

13. One good example of a text heralding the sexual revolution is Lawrence Lipton, *The Erotic Revolution: An Affirmative View of the New Morality* (Los Angeles: Shelbourne Press, 1965).

14. Wesselmann, writing under the pseudonym of Slim Stealingworth, stated his preference for product brochures over magazine advertisements as a source for his cut-outs, because magazines were printed with bad inks on inferior quality paper. Slim Stealingworth, *Tom Wesselmann* (New York: Abbeville Press, 1980), 24.

15. "Un Appartement Pop," *L'Oeil*, vol. 106 (October 1963), 12–19; "At Home With Henry," *Time*, vol. 83 (21 February 1964), 68–71; Emily Genauer, "Can This Be Art?" *Ladies Home Journal*, vol. 81 (March 1964), 151–55; Francine du Plessix Gray, "The House that Pop Art Built," *House and Garden*, vol. 107 (May 1965); 158–63; John Rublowsky, "Collectors and Galleries," in *Pop Art* (New York: Basic Books, 1965); Elizabeth Sverbeyeff, "Life with Pop," *New York Times Magazine* (2 May 1965), 98–99; Allene Talmey, "Art is the Core," *Vogue*, vol. 144 (July 1964), 116–23, 125; Sidney Tillim, "Further Observations on the Pop Phenomenon," *Artforum*, vol. 4 (November 1965), 17–19; and "You Bought It, Now Live With It," *Life*, vol. 59 (16 July 1965), 56–61.

16. Arthur Drexler and Greta

Daniel, *Introduction to Twentieth Century Design from the Collection of The Museum of Modern Art New York* (Garden City, New York: Doubleday, 1959), 43.
17. Gray, 158.
18. Clifford E. Clark, *The American Family Home, 1800–1960* (Chapel Hill: University of North Carolina Press, 1986), 217.
19. Talmey, 118, 119.
20. Barbara Ehrenreich, *Hearts of Men: American Dreams and the Flight from Commitment* (Garden City: Anchor Books, 1983), 44.
21. "Playboy's Weekend Hideaway," *Playboy*, vol. 6 (April 1959), 51.
22. "Playboy's Weekend Hideaway," 49–56. See also "Modern Living: A Playboy's Pad," *Playboy*, vol. 10 (May 1964), 71–76; "Playboy Pad," *Playboy*, vol. 12 (October 1965), 97; "The Playboy Mansion," *Playboy*, vol. 13 (1966), 116; "A Playboy Pad: Palm Springs Oasis," *Playboy*, vol. 13 (April 1966), 119; "A Playboy Pad: Texas Retreat," *Playboy*, vol. 13 (October 1966), 105.
23. "The Playboy Mansion," 112; and Hugh Hefner, "The Playboy Philosophy," *Playboy*, vol. 10 (February 1963), 44. Several cartoons poking fun at Pop art were published in the pages of *Playboy*. See *Playboy*, vol. 12 (July 1965), 144; and *Playboy* vol. 12 (August 1965), 162.
24. Ben Heller, "The Roots of Abstract Expressionism," *Art in America*, vol. 49 (1961), 40–49.
25. Talmey, 118, 123. Referring to his purchase of *The Stove* by Claes Oldenburg, Mr Scull stated: "Ethel thought I was crazy when the stove arrived. But now she calls it my emerald and she won't let anyone else touch it." "You Bought It, Now Live with It," 57. Emily Genauer reported: "Mrs Scull was less receptive. Several purchases had to be kept in storage because she refused to allow them in the house." Genauer, 153.
26. "You Bought It, Now Live With It," 58.
27. Rublowsky, 157.
28. Gray, 158.
29. Ibid., 162.
30. Talmey, 118.
31. "At Home with Henry," 68.
32. Ibid.

16. Vito Acconci's Bad Dream of Domesticity

1. For recent discussions of the nexus of male subjectivity and power as they function in Acconci's art, see Amelia Jones, "Dis/Playing the Phallus: Male Artists Perform their Masculinities," *Art History*, vol. 17, no. 4 (December 1994), 546–84 and Kate Linker, *Vito Acconci* (New York: Rizzoli, 1994).
2. To comply with Brancusi's will, a replica of his studio was built in the plaza in front of the Centre Georges Pompidou, Paris. Recently, however, the difficulty of maintaining this structure caused it to be closed and Brancusi's works are now integrated into the collection of the Centre Georges Pompidou where they have indeed lost all connection to their site of production.
3. Daniel Buren, "The Function of the Studio," 1971, *October*, vol. 10 (Fall 1979), 53–56.
4. Vito Acconci, "Interview by Robin White at Crown Point Press," *View*, vol. 2, nos. 5/6 (Oakland, CA: Point Press, 1979), 19–20.
5. Vito Acconci, "Towards a Theory of Image/Instrument/Decoration," *Cover*, vol. 2, no. 1 (January 1980), 23.
6. The series *Street Works*, comprising five group shows, was initially organized by John Perreault, Marjorie Strider and Hannah Weiner. *Following Piece*, performed for *Street Works IV*, was sponsored by the Architectural League of New York and was city-wide. For more information on the individual shows and their participants, see John Perreault, "Critique: Street Works," *Arts Magazine*, vol. 44, no. 3 (January 1970), 18.
7. Vito Acconci, "On Art and Artists [Interview with Kate Horsfield]," *Profile*, vol. 4, nos. 3/4 (Summer 1984), 9. Acconci has since said that he regrets having had the photographs taken. Interview with the author, 5 October 1991.
8. Vito Acconci, "Following Piece," *Avalanche*, vol. 6 (Fall 1972), 31.
9. Vito Acconci, "Room Piece," *Avalanche*, vol. 6 (Fall 1972), 16.
10. See: Acconci, "Service Area," *Avalanche*, vol. 6 (Fall 1972), 17 and Acconci, "Interview with Robin White," 15.
11. For Acconci's views on the characteristics of video, see Vito Acconci, "10-Point Plan for Video," in Ira Schneider and Beryl Korot, eds., *Video Art: An Anthology* (New York: Harcourt, Brace and Jovanovich, 1976), 8–9, and "Some Notes on my Use of Video," *Art-rite*, vol. 7 (Autumn 1974), 2–3. His understanding of "intimate distance" is based on Edward Hall's analysis of the spatial and interpersonal aspects of intimate, personal and social distance. See: *The Hidden Dimension* (New York: Doubleday & Co., 1966).
12. Linker, 55.
13. Vito Acconci, "Power Field – Exchange Points – Transformations," *Avalanche*, vol. 6 (Fall 1972), 62.
14. Vito Acconci, "Supply Room," *Avalanche*, vol. 6 (Fall 1972), 60.
15. Acconci, "On Art and Artists [Interview with Kate Horsfield]," 27–28.
16. Quoted in Schwartz, 97.
17. Kate Linker has discussed the relevance of Robert Venturi's idea of the decorated shed to Acconci's use of architectural structures in: *Vito Acconci*, 112–17. Acconci began reading Venturi in 1978 or 1979.
18. Acconci, "Projections of Home," *Artforum*, vol. 26, no. 7 (March 1988), 126.
19. Vito Acconci, "Home-Bodies (An Introduction to My Work, 1984–85)," in *Vito Acconci: The House and Furnishings as Social Metaphor*, exh. cat. (Tampa, FL: USF Art Galleries, University of South Florida, 1986), 8.
20. Ibid.
21. For a reproduction of this drawing, see Linker, 146.
22. Acconci, "Projections of Home," 128.
23. Ibid., 126.

17. Coming Home

1. In the interests of (relative) brevity, we have confined our discussion of domesticity and postmodernism to North America, although we believe the issues we raise are applicable to other contexts. For interested readers, a provocative overview of the history of domesticity was offered by the exhibition associated with the 17th Milan Triennale, curated by Georges Teyssot: *Il progetto domestico: La casa dell'uomo, archetipi e prototipi* (Milan: Palazzo della Triennake, 1986), and the installation exhibitions *Chambres d'Amis* (Ghent, 1986) and *Chambre 763* (Paris, 1994) showcased a wide range of contemporary artists' responses to the interior. In England, debates over the relationship of art and domesticity crystalized around the sculptor Rachel Whiteread, who won the 1993 Turner Prize at the same time as her controversial *House* sculpture was slated for destruction. Challenges to modernist architecture and planning similar to those described in this essay have been articulated since the early 1950s by English designers Alison and Peter Smithson, and by the Italian architect, Aldo Rossi (see his *The Architecture of the City*, 1966, trans. Diane Ghirardo and Joan Ockman, Cambridge: MIT Press, 1982). In England, the more nostalgic version of postmodernism is associated with Rob and Leon Krier (see especially Demetri Porphyrios, ed., *Leon Krier: Houses, Palaces, Cities*, London: Architectural Design, 1984), though it found its most prominent spokesman in the Prince of Wales.

2. Robert Venturi, *Complexity and Contradiction in Architecture* 1966 (repr. New York: Museum of Modern Art, 1977), 104, 16, 118. See also Venturi's *Mother's House: The Evolution of Vanna Venturi's House in Chestnut Hill* (New York: Rizzoli, 1992).

3. Robert Venturi, Denise Scott Brown, and Steven Izenour, *Learning from Las Vegas* (Cambridge, MA: MIT Press, 1972); this work was based on a studio taught at Yale University in 1968; *Learning from Levittown*, another teaching studio, was packaged as an exhibition, *Signs of Life: Symbols and the American City* (Washington, DC: Renwick Gallery, 1976), and explicated in Denise Scott Brown, "Suburban Space, Scale, and Symbols," *VIA*, no. 3 (1977), 41–47.

4. Jane Jacobs, *The Death and Life of Great American Cities* (New York: Vintage, 1961), 3. For later feminist critiques of American urbanism, see "Women and the American City," special issue of *Signs: Journal of Women in Culture and Society*, vol. 5, no. 5, (Spring 1980).

5. Susana Torre, ed., *Women in American Architecture: A Historic and Contemporary Perspective* (New York: Whitney Library of Design, 1977), 11.

6. Miriam Schapiro, *Femmages 1971–1985* (St Louis: Brentwood Gallery, 1985), n.pag.; and in *Womanhouse* catalog (Valencia, CA: California Institute of the Arts, 1972), n.pag. Judy Chicago, *Through the Flower: My Struggle as a Woman Artist* (Garden City, NY: Doubleday, 1975), 103–32. On *Womanhouse* and related projects, see Faith Wilding, *By Our Own Hands: The Women Artist's Movement, Southern California, 1970–76* (Santa Monica, CA: Double X, 1977); see also Faith Wilding, "The Feminist Art Programs at Fresno and CalArts," and Arlene Raven, "Womanhouse," both in Norma Broude and Mary D. Garrard, eds., *The Power of Feminist Art: The American Movement of the 1970s, History and Impact* (New York: Abrams, 1994), 32–65. Portions of *Womanhouse* were recreated for the exhibition, *Division of Labor: "Women's Work" in Contemporary Art*, (New York: Bronx Museum of the Arts, 1995).

7. Arlene Raven, *At Home* (Long Beach, CA: Long Beach Museum of Art, 1983), 5.

8. Judy Chicago, *Embroidering Our Heritage: The Dinner Party Needlework* (Garden City, NY: Anchor/Doubleday, 1980). Norma Broude, "Miriam Schapiro and "Femmage": Reflections on the Conflict Between Decoration and Abstraction in Twentieth Century Art," *Arts* (February 1980), 83–87.

9. In 1978, the Institute of Contemporary Art in Philadelphia mounted *Dwellings* and the downtown branch of New York's Whitney Museum showed *Out of the House*. These were followed in 1981 by *The Image of the House in Contemporary Art* in Houston and by *Home Work*, curated by the sculptor Harmony Hammond for the National Women's Hall of Fame in Seneca, New York. Two 1983 exhibitions continued the trend: *The House that Art Built* and *At Home*, curated by Arlene Raven. The following year in Massachusetts, *Domestic Tales* presented a selection of recent women's art dealing with the home.

10. Donna Dennis, in *The House that Art Built* (Fullerton, CA: California State University Main Art Gallery, 1983), 43. See Munson's work in The New Museum of Contemporary Art, *Bad Girls* (Cambridge, MA: MIT Press, 1994), 86–87.

11. Hal Foster, ed., *The Anti-Aesthetic: Essays on Postmodern Culture* (Seattle: Bay Press, 1983), xi–xii.

12. Gaston Bachelard, *The Poetics of Space*, 1958, trans. Maria Jolas (Boston: Beacon Press, 1964), 5–7. Emmanuel Levinas, *Totality and Infinity: An Essay on Exteriority*, 1961, trans. Alphonso Lingis (Pittsburgh: Duquesne University Press, 1969), 154–62. Although phenomenologist philosophy presents itself as absolute, it in fact describes very specifically the conditions of consciousness of middle-class men under capitalism. No effort is made to consider the nature of dwelling in cultures without a highly developed system of private property.

13. Our analysis is paralleled by the discussion of the "nostalgia film" in Frederic Jameson, "Postmodernism and Consumer Society," 1982, repr. Foster, 111–25; see especially his discussion of the small-town setting of *Body Heat*.

14. Eric Fischl in Nancy Grimes, "Eric Fischl's Naked Truths," *Art News* (September 1986), 70. Peter Galassi, *Pleasures and Terrors of Domestic Comfort* (New York: Museum of Modern Art, 1991), 7.

15. Eric Fischl in *Fischl: An Interview with Donald Kuspit* (New York: Random House, 1987), 42. Galassi, 11, 12, 20.

16. Robert A. M. Stern and John M. Massengale, *The Anglo-American Suburb* (London: Academy Editions, 1981); Luis F. Rueda, ed., *Robert A. M. Stern: Buildings and Projects 1981–1985* (New York: Rizzoli 1986), 86–93, 120–23, 156–59, 170–73, 174–83, 234, 235, 258–61, 276–79, 280–83; Stephen Petranek and Jennifer Allen, "A House For All America," *Life* (June 1994), 82–92.

17. Witold Rybczynski, *Home: A Short History of An Idea* (New York: Viking Penguin, 1986), 221; *Looking Around: A Journey Through Architecture* (New York: Viking Penguin, 1992), 71–98.

18. Andres Duany and Elizabeth Plater-Zyberk, *Towns and Town-Making Principles* (New York: Rizzoli, 1991).

19. Gwendolyn Wright, "Domestic Architecture and the Cultures of Domesticity," in *House and Home*, special issue of *Design Quarterly*, vol. 138 (1987), 17–18.

20. See Christopher Reed, "Postmodernism and the Art of Identity," in Nikos Stangos, ed., *Concepts of Modern Art*, 3rd ed. (London: Thames and Hudson, 1994), 271–93. See also Abigail Solomon-Godeau and Constance Lewallen, *Mistaken Identities* (Seattle: University of Washington Press, 1993).

21. Alice Adams, quoted in Lucy Lippard, "The Abstract Realism of Alice Adams," *Art in America* (September 1976), 72–76; and in *The House the Art Built*, 25.
22. In addition to the 1992 exhibition, *Good-bye to Apple Pie*, a number of exhibits on social issues associated with the home are described in Phyllis Rosser, "There's No Place Like Home," in Joanna Frueh, Cassandra Langer, Arlene Raven, eds., *New Feminist Criticism* (New York: Harper Collins, 1994), 73–76. On Diggs, see Patricia C. Phillips, "Peggy Diggs: Private Acts and Public Art" in Nina Felshin, ed., *But Is It Art?: The Spirit of Art as Activism* (Seattle: Bay Press, 1995), 283–308.
23. Rosler's *Home Front*, along with related installations and programming, is documented in Brian Wallis, ed., *If You Lived Here: The City in Art, Theory, and Social Activism, A Project by Martha Rosler* (Seattle: Bay Press, 1991). See also *Public Address: Krzysztof Wodiczko* (Minneapolis: Walker Arts Center, 1992).
24. On the Aunt Jemima image, see Lucy Lippard, *Mixed Blessings: New Art in a Multicultural America* (New York: Pantheon, 1990), 234–36. On Saar, see Elizabeth Shepherd, ed., *Secrets, Dialogues, Revelations: The Art of Betye and Alison Saar* (Los Angeles: Wight Art Gallery, University of California, 1990). On Ringgold, see Eleanor Flomenhaft, *Faith Ringgold: A 25 Year Survey* (Hempstead, NY: Fine Arts Museum of Long Island, 1990).
25. See Jock Reynolds, *House and Home: Spirits of the South, Max Belcher, Beverly Buchanan, and William Christenberry* (Seattle: University of Washington Press, 1994). On Weems, see Andrea Kirsh and Susan Fisher Sterling, *Carrie Mae Weems* (Washington, DC: National Museum of Women in the Arts, 1993). Clarissa Sligh, in Laura U. Marks, "Reinscribing the Self: An Interview with Clarissa Sligh," *Afterimage* (December 1989), 8.
26. On Pozo, see New Orleans Museum of Art, *Emigrés* (n.p.: National Council on Education for the Ceramic Arts, 1994). On Min and other Asian-American artists, see Margo Machida, *Asia/America: Identities in Contemporary Asian American Art* (New York: Asia Society Galleries, 1994); see also *Mistaken Identities*, 57–59. On Vaisman, see Kurt Hollander, "The Caracas Connection," *Art in America* (July 1994), 82–83.
27. On Netsky, see Judith Tannenbaum, *Time Flies: Stuart Netsky* (Philsdelphia: Institute of Contemporary Art, 1994). Other photographers dealing with lesbian and gay domesticity include Deborah Coitto and Doug Ischar, both featured in *Disclosing the Myth of Family* (exh. flyer, Betty Rymer Gallery at the School of the Art Institute of Chicago, 1991).
28. Nan Goldin, *The Ballad of Sexual Dependency*, Marvin Heiferman, Mark Holborn, and Suzanne Fletcher, eds. (New York: Aperture, 1989). See also her *The Other Side*, David Armstrong and Walter Keller, eds. (New York: Scalo, 1993). As an example of the extremely common tendency to homogenize domestic experience, see Galassi.
29. Competition brief quoted in Jacqueline Leavitt, "Two Prototypical Designs for Single Parents: The Congregate House and the New American House," in Karen A. Franck and Sherry Ahrentzen, eds., *New Households New Housing* (New York: Van Nostrand Reinhold, 1991), 161–86. This book includes several projects addressing similar concerns.
30. Carol Willis and Rosalie Genevro, eds., *Vacant Lots* (New York: Princeton Architectural Press and the Architectural League of New York, 1989), 7.
31. Ghislaine Hermanuz, ed., *Reweaving the Urban Fabric: Approaches to Infill Housing* (New York: New York State Council on the Arts, 1988). Elizabeth A. T. Smith, "Extending the Case Study Concept," *Blueprints for Modern Living: History and Legacy of the Case Study Houses* (Cambridge, MA: MIT Press, 1989), 213–25.
32. Special issues of *Progressive Architecture* included, "Solving the Housing Crisis" (October 1988); "Affordable Housing: An American Birthright?" (June 1991); and "Housing a Diverse Population" (August 1992).
33. Susana Torre, introduction, *Room In the City* (New York: City Gallery, 1987), 6.
34. See essays by Beatriz Colomina, Mark Wigley, and Elizabeth Grosz in Beatriz Colomina, ed., *Sexuality & Space* (New York: Princeton Architectural Press, 1992). See also Anthony Vidler, *The Architectural Uncanny: Essays in the Modern Unhomely* (Cambridge, MA: MIT Press, 1992), including "Homes for Cyborgs," reprinted in this volume.
35. Michael Moon, Eve Kosofsky Sedgwick, Benjamin Gianni, and Scott Weir, "Queers in (Single-Family) Space," *House Rules*, exh. cat. published as special issue of *Assemblage*, no. 24 (August 1994), 30–37. Additional quotations from Benjamin Gianni, "Queering (Single-Family) Space," *Sites*, no. 26 (1995), 69–77.
36. Mark Robbins and Benjamin Gianni, exhibition leaflet from *Queer Space* (New York: Storefront for Art and Architecture, 1994).
37. Miriam Schapiro, in *The Power of Feminist Art*, 83. A similar critique of the neglect of feminist forerunners in discussions of women artists and gender in the 1980s is offered in Mira Schor, "Patrilineage," in *New Feminist Criticism* (cited above), 42–59. For examples of contemporary architectural theory see note 31 above. Especially troubling is *Architecture and the Feminine: Mop-up Work*, conference proceedings published in *ANY*, vol. 4 (January–February 1994), which is an analysis of the "feminine" in architecture without any acknowledgment of the feminist.

Bibliography

Introduction

ARIÈS, Philippe, *Centuries of Childhood: A Social History of Family Life*, trans. R. Baldick. New York: Vintage, 1962.

CAMP, Wesley Douglas, *Marriage and the Family in France Since the Revolution*. New York: Bookman, 1961.

COTT, Nancy, *The Bonds of Womanhood: "Women's Sphere" in New England, 1780–1835*. New Haven: Yale University Press, 1977.

DEGLER, Carl, *At Odds: Women and the Family in America from the Revolution to the Present*. New York: Oxford University Press, 1980.

FLAHERTY, David, *Privacy in Colonial America*. Charlottesville: University of Virginia Press, 1972.

GOWANS, Alan, *The Comfortable House: North American Suburban Architecture, 1890–1930*. Cambridge, MA: MIT Press, 1986.

GOODE, William, *World Revolutions and Family Patterns*. New York: Free Press, 1963.

LASLETT, Peter, ed., *Family Life and Illicit Love in Former Generations*. Cambridge: Cambridge University Press, 1977.

MATHEWS, Glenna, *"Just a Housewife": The Rise and Fall of Domesticity in America*. New York: Oxford University Press, 1987.

PERROT, Michelle, ed., *A History of Private Life: From the Fires of the Revolution to the Great War*, trans. Arthur Goldhammer. Cambridge, MA: Harvard University Press, 1990.

RYBCZYNSKI, Witold, *Home: A Short History of an Idea*. New York: Viking Penguin, 1986.

STONE, Lawrence, *The Family, Sex and Marriage in England, 1500–1800*. New York: Harper and Row, 1977.

1. The Chic Interior and the Feminine Modern

AUSLANDER, Leora, "After the Revolution: Recycling Ancien Régime Style in the 19th century," in Bryant T. Ragan, Jr. and Elizabeth A. Williams, eds., *Re-creating Authority in Revolutionary France*. New Brunswick: Rutgers University Press, 1992.

BERMINGHAM, Ann, "The Aesthetics of Ignorance: The Accomplished Woman in the Culture of Connoisseurship." *The Oxford Art Journal*, vol. 16, no. 2 (1993), 3–20.

DAUMARD, Adeline, "Conditions de logement et position sociale," in *Le Parisien chez lui au XIX siècle*. Paris: Archives Nationales, 1977.

SILVERMAN, Debora, "The 'New Woman,' Feminism, and the Decorative Arts in Fin-de-Siècle France," in Lynn Hunt, ed., *Eroticism and the Body Politic*. Baltimore: Johns Hopkins University Press, 1991.

Art Nouveau in Fin-de-Siècle France: Politics, Psychology, and Style. Berkeley: University of California Press, 1989.

WALTON, Whitney, *France at the Crystal Palace: Bourgeois Taste and Artisan Manufacture in the 19th Century*. Berkeley: University of California Press, 1992.

VICKERY, Amanda, "Women and the World of Goods: A Lancashire Consumer and Her Possessions, 1751–81," in John Brewer and Roy Porter, eds., *Consumption and the World of Goods*. New York: Routledge, 1993.

HALTTUNEN, Karen, "From Living-Room to Parlor: Domestic Space, Interior Decoration, and the Culture of Personality," in Simon Bronner, ed., *Consuming Visions: Accumulation and Display of Goods in America, 1880–1920*. New York: Norton, 1989.

WILLIAMS, Rosalind, *Dream Worlds: Mass Consumption in Late Nineteenth Century France*. Berkeley: University of California Press, 1982.

CSIKSZENTMIHALYI, Mihaly, and Eugene Rochberg-Halton, *The Meaning of Things: Domestic Symbols and the Self*. Cambridge: Cambridge University Press, 1981.

2. The Chromo and the Art Museum

DIMAGGIO, Paul, "Cultural Entrepreneurship in 19th-Century Boston." *Media, Culture, and Society*, vol. 4 (1982), 33–50, 303–22.

DUNCAN, Carol, and Alan Wallach, "The Museum of Modern Art As Late Capitalist Ritual." *Marxist Perspectives* (Winter 1978), 28–51.

"The Universal Survey Museum." *Art History*, vol. 3, no. 4 (December 1980), 448–74.

HARRIS, Neil, "The Gilded Age Revisited: Boston and the Museum Movement." *American Quarterly*, vol. 14, no. 4 (Winter 1962), 545–66.

LEVINE, Lawrence W., *Highbrow/Lowbrow: The Emergence of Cultural Hierarchy in America*. Cambridge, MA: Harvard University Press, 1988.

MARZIO, Peter C., *The Democratic Art; Pictures for a 19th-Century America*. Boston: David R. Godine, 1979.

MCCARTHY, Kathleen D., *Women's Culture: American Philanthropy and Art, 1830–1930*. Chicago: University of Chicago Press, 1991.

MILLER, Lillian B., *Patron and Patriotism; the Encouragement of the Fine Arts in the United States, 1790–1860*. Chicago: University of Chicago Press, 1966.

PERKINS, Charles C., *American Art Museums*. Boston: Fields, Osgood, and Co., 1870.

STOWE, Harriet Beecher, and Catharine Beecher Stowe, *The American Woman's Home*. New York: J. B. Ford, 1869.

TRACHTENBERG, Alan, *The Incorporation of America: Culture and Society in the Gilded Age*. New York: Hill and Wang, 1982.

4. Psyche and Sympathy

BECKET, Jane, "The Abstract Interior," *Towards a New Art*. London: Tate Gallery, 1980, 90–124.

BENJAMIN, Walter, "Louis-Philippe or the Interior," *Charles Baudelaire: A Lyric Poet in the Era of High Capitalism*, trans. Harry Zohn. London: Verso, 1973.

BOURGET, Paul, *Nouveaux Essais de Psychologie Contemporaine*. Paris: Lemeure, 1886, 152.

DALY, César, *Architecture privée aux XIXe siècle*. Paris, 1877.

DURANTY, Louis-Émile Edmund, *La Nouvelle Peinture*, 1876, trans. and repr. in Charles Moffett, *The New Painting. Impressionism 1874–1886*. Exh. cat., Fine Arts Museums of San Francisco, 1986.

JAMES, Henry, *American Scene*. Orig. 1907, repr. Bloomington: Indiana University Press, 1968.

MINKOWSKI, Eugène, "Toward a Pathology of Lived Space," in *Lived Time. Phenomenological and Psychopathological Studies*, trans. and intro. Nancy Metzel. Evanston, IL: Northwestern University Press, 1970.

NOCHLIN, Linda, "A House is not a Home. Degas and the Subversion of the Family," in Richard Kendall and Griselda Pollack, eds., *Dealing with Degas*. New York: Universe, 1991.

OLSON, Stanley, *John Singer Sargent. His Portrait*. New York: St Martin's Press, 1986.

SILVERMAN, Debora, *Art Nouveau in Fin-de-Siècle France. Politics, Psychology, Style*. Berkeley: University of California Press, 1989.

THOMSON, Belinda, *Vuillard*. Oxford: Phaidon Press, 1988.

VIDLER, Anthony, *The Architectural Uncanny. Essays in the Modern Unhomely*. Cambridge, MA, and London: MIT Press, 1992.

WÖLFFLIN, Heinrich, "Prolegomena to a Psychology of Architecture," in *Empathy, Form and Space. Problems in German Aesthetics 1873–1893*, trans. and intro. Harry Francis Mallgrave and Eleftherios Ikonomou. Santa Monica: Getty Center Publication Programs, 1994.

WOOLF, Virginia, *To the Lighthouse*. Orig. 1927, repr. New York: Harcourt Brace, 1955.

ZANTEN, Ann Lorenz van, "Form and Society: César Daly and the *Révue Générale de l'Architecture*." *Oppositions*, vol. 8 (Spring 1977), 137–45.

6. Frank Lloyd Wright's Kindergarten

ALOFSIN, Anthony, *Frank Lloyd Wright: The Lost Years, 1910–1922*. Chicago: University of Chicago Press, 1993.

BOLEN, Carol, Robert Nelson, Linda Seidel, eds., *The Nature of Frank Lloyd Wright*. Chicago: University of Chicago Press, 1988.

COTT, Nancy F., *The Bonds of Womanhood: "Woman's Sphere in New England, 1780–1835*. New Haven: Yale University Press, 1977.

EATON, Leonard, *Two Chicago Architects and their Clients: Frank Lloyd Wright and Howard Van Doren Shaw*. Cambridge, MA: MIT Press, 1969.

FRANK LLOYD WRIGHT HOME AND STUDIO FOUNDATION, *The Plan for Restoration and Adaptive Use of the Frank Lloyd Wright Home and Studio*. Chicago: University of Chicago Press, 1977.

SAINT, Andrew, *The Image of the Architect*. New Haven: Yale University Press, 1983.

SMITH, Norris Kelly, *Frank Lloyd Wright: A Study in Architectural Content*. Englewood Cliffs, NJ: Prentice Hall, 1966.

WRIGHT, Gwendolyn, *Moralism and the Modern Home: Domestic Architecture and Cultural Conflict in Chicago, 1873–1913*. Chicago: University of Chicago Press, 1980.

7. "Hi Honey, I'm Home"

GERMAIN, Alphonse, "Le paysage décoratif," *L'Ermitage*, vol. 3 (November 1891).

BOUVERET, Léon, *La Neurasthénie*. Paris: Ballière, 1890.

LAURENT, Émile, *La Neurasthénie et son traitement*. Paris: Maloine, 1895.

LEVILLAIN, Fernand, *La Neurasthénie, Maladie de Beard*. Paris: Maloine, 1891.

MARX, Roger, "Cartons d'Artistes: Puvis de Chavannes," *L'Image* (July 1897).

MASHECK, Joseph, "Art as Rest and Rehabilitation," *Artforum*, vol. 13, no. 6 (February 1975).

NEFF, John H., "Matisse and Decoration: An Introduction," *Arts Magazine*, vol. 49, no. 9 (May 1975).

ROBINSON, Joyce Henri. "A 'Nouvelle Arcadie': Puvis de Chavannes and the Decorative Landscape in Fin-de-Siècle France." Ph.D. dissertation, The University of Virginia, 1993.

SILVERMAN, Debora L., *Art Nouveau in Fin-de-Siècle France: Politics, Psychology, and Style*. Berkeley: University of California Press, 1989.

8. Domesticity, Decoration and Consumer Culture

GEE, Malcolm, *Dealers, Critics, and Collectors of Modern Painting: Aspects of the Parisian Art Market Between 1910 and 1930*. New York and London: Garland Publishing, 1981.

Paul Poiret et Nicole Groult: Maîtres de la mode art déco. Exh. cat., Paris: Musée de la Mode et du Costume, 5 July–12 October 1986.

SILVERMAN, Debora L., *Art Nouveau in Fin-de-Siècle France: Politics, Psychology, and Style*. Berkeley: University of California Press, 1989.

SPIES, Werner, "Vendre des tableau – donner à lire," *Daniel-Henry Kahnweiler: marchand, éditeur, écrivain*. Exh. cat., Paris: Centre Georges Pompidou. Musée national d'art moderne, 22 November 1984–28 January 1985.

TROY, Nancy J., *Modernism and the Decorative Arts in France: Art Nouveau to Le Corbusier*. New Haven and London: Yale University Press, 1991.

9. Forgotten Ties

FOUCAULT, Michel, *The Order of Things: An Archaeology of the Human Sciences*. New York: Vintage, 1973.

GOMBRICH, E. H., *The Sense of Order: A Study in the Psychology of Decorative Art*. Ithaca: Cornell University Press, 1979.

GOUX, Jean-Joseph, *Symbolic Economies: After Marx and Freud*, trans. Jennifer Curtiss Gage. Ithaca: Cornell University Press, 1990.

KANDINSKY, Wassily, *Über das Geistige in der Kunst*. Munich: Piper, 1912 [*Concerning the*

Decorative in Art, trans. M. T. H. Sadler. New York: Dover, 1977].
KANT, Immanuel, *Kritik der Urteilskraft*, Karl Vorländer, ed. Hamburg: Meiner, 1990 [*The Critique of Judgement*, trans. James Creed Meredith. Oxford: Clarendon, 1952].
LOOS, Adolf, *Sämtliche Schriften*, Franz Glück, ed. 2 vols. Vienna: Herold, 1962.
"Ornament and Crime," in Ludwig Münz and Gustav Künstler, *Adolf Loos, Pioneer of Modern Architecture*. New York: Praeger, 1966.
MEIER-GRAEFE, Julius, *Entwickelungsgeschichte der modernen Kunst. Vergleichende Betrachtung der bildenden Künste, als Beitrag zu einer neuen Aesthetik*. 3 vols. Stuttgart: Hoffmann, 1904 [*Modern Art: Being a Contribution to a New System of Aesthetics*, trans. Florence Simmonds and George W. Chrystal. New York: Putnam's, 1908].
SCHEFFLER, Karl, "Dekorationsmalerei," *Dekorative Kunst*, vol. 2, no. 8 (1898).
Die Frau und die Kunst. Eine Studie. Berlin: Bard, 1908.
"Korrespondenzen: Berlin," *Dekorative Kunst*, vol. 1, no. 2 (1898).
"Korrespondenzen: Berlin," *Dekorative Kunst*, vol. 1, no. 4 (1898).
"Korrespondenzen: Berlin," *Dekorative Kunst*, vol. 1, no. 6 (1898).
"Meditationen über das Ornament," *Die Kunst*, vol. 4, no. 10 (1901).
"Neue Eckmann-Teppiche," *Die Kunst*, vol. 4, no. 6 (1901).
"Notizen über die Farbe," *Die Kunst*, vol. 4, no. 5 (1901).
"Unterricht im Kunstgewerbe," *Die Kunst*, vol. 6, no. 10 (1902).
"Volkskunst," *Die Kunst*, vol. 4, no. 4 (1901).
SCHOR, Naomi, *Reading in Detail: Aesthetics and the Feminine*. New York: Methuen, 1987.
ZOLA, Émile, *The Ladies' Paradise*, Kristin Ross, ed. Berkeley: University of California Press, 1992.

10. "A Room of One's Own"

ANSCOMBE, Isabelle, *Omega and After*. London: Thames and Hudson, 1981.
BELL, Clive, *Art*. London: Chatto and Windus, 1914.
COLLINS, Judith, *The Omega Workshops*. Chicago: University of Chicago Press, 1984.
CRAFTS COUNCIL, *The Omega Workshops*. Exh. cat., London: 1984.
FRY, Roger, *Vision and Design*. London: Chatto and Windus, 1920.
NAYLOR, Gillian, ed., *Bloomsbury: Its Artists, Authors and Designers*. Boston: Little Brown, 1990.
ROSENBAUM, S. P., ed., *The Bloomsbury Group: A Collection of Memoirs, Commentary and Criticism*. Toronto: University of Toronto Press, 1975.
SPALDING, Frances, *Roger Fry: Art and Life*. New York: Granada, 1980.
Vanessa Bell. London: Weidenfield and Nicolson, 1983.
SUTTON, Denys, ed., *Letters of Roger Fry*. 2 vols. London: Chatto and Windus, 1972.
TURNBAUGH, Douglas, *Duncan Grant and the Bloomsbury Group*. Secaucas, NJ: Lyle Stuart, 1987.
WATNEY, Simon, *The Art of Duncan Grant*. London: John Murrary, 1990.
WOOLF, Virginia, *Roger Fry: A Biography*. London: Hogarth Press, 1940.

11. Homes for Cyborgs

BANHAM, Reyner, *Theory and Design in the First Machine Age*. London: Architectural Press, 1960.
COLOMINA, Beatriz, "The Split Wall: Domestic Voyeurism," *Sexuality and Space*. New York: Princeton Architectural Press, 1992.
PETER COOK, ed., *Archigram*. London: Studio Vista, 1972.
LE CORBUSIER, *The Decorative Art of Today*, trans. James I. Dunnett. Cambridge, MA: MIT Press, 1987.
The Modulor: A Harmonious Measure to the Human Scale Universally Applicable to Architecture and Mechanics, trans. Peter de Francia and Anna Bostock. Cambridge, MA: Harvard University Press, 1954.
Towards a New Architecture, trans. Frederick Etchells, 1927. New York: Prager, 1960.
DILLER, Elizabeth, and Ricardo Scofidio, *Flesh: Architectural Probes*. New York: Princeton Architectural Press, 1994.
"The WithDrawing Room: A Probe Into the Conventions of Private Rite," *AA Files*, vol. 17 [published by Architectural Association] (Spring 1989), 15–23.
"A Delay in Glass," *Assemblage*, vol. 6 (June 1988), 63–71.
GIBSON, William, *Burning Chrome*. New York, Berkeley, 1986.
Neuromancer. New York: Berkeley, 1984.
GIEDION, Sigfried, *Mechanization Takes Command*. New York: Oxford University Press, 1948.
HARAWAY, Donna, "Homes for Cyborgs," 1985, repr. in Elizabeth Weed, ed., *Coming to Terms: Feminism, Theory, Politics*. New York: Routledge, 1989.
HAYS, K. Michael, "Tessenow's Architecture as National Allegory: Critique of Capitalism or Protofascism?" *Assemblage*, vol. 8 (February 1989), 105–23.
HEIDEGGER, Martin, "Building, Dwelling, Thi, *Poetry, Language, Thought*, trans. Albert Hofstadter. New York: Harper and Row, 1971.
JARDINE, Alice, "Of Bodies and Technologies," in *Discussions in Contemporary Culture*, no. 1, Hal Foster, ed. Seattle: Bay Press, 1987.
PHILLIPS, Lisa, *Frederick Kiesler*. Exh. cat., New York: Whitney Museum of American Art, 1989.
WIGLEY, Mark W., "Heidegger's House: The Violence of the Domestic," *Colombia Documents of Architecture and Theory*, vol. 1 (1992), 91–121.

12. Domestic Differences

NEUMEYER, Fritz, *The Artless Word: Mies van der Rohe on the Building Art*, trans. Mark Jarzombek (original German ed. 1986). Cambridge, MA: MIT Press, 1991.
"Space for Reflection: Block versus Pavilion," in F. Schulze, ed., *Mies van der Rohe: Critical Essays*. Cambridge, MA: MIT Press, 1989, 148–71.
PADOVAN, Richard, "Machines à mediter," in Rolf Achilles et al., *Mies van der Rohe: Architect as Educator*. Chicago: University of Chicago Press, 1986, 17–26.
POMMER, Richard, "Mies van der Rohe and the Political Ideology of the Modern Movement," in F. Schulze, ed., *Mies van der Rohe: Critical Essays*. Cambridge, MA: MIT Press, 1989, 96–146.

SCHULZE, Franz, *Mies van der Rohe: A Critical Biography*. Chicago: University of Chicago Press, 1985.
SINGLEY, Paulette, "Living in a Glass Prism: The Female Figure in Mies van der Rohe's Domestic Architecture." *Critical Matrix: The Princeton Journal of Women, Gender and Culture*, vol. 6, no. 2 (1992), 47–76.
TEGETHOFF, Wolf, *Mies van der Rohe: The Villas and Country Houses*, trans. Russell M. Stockman (original German ed. 1981). Cambridge, MA: MIT Press, 1985.

13. Robert Rauschenberg's Fabrics

FEINSTEIN, Roni, "Random Order: The First Fifteen Years of Robert Rauschenberg's Art, 1949–1964". Ph.D. Dissertation, New York University, 1990.
HOPPS, Walter, *Robert Rauschenberg: The Early 1950's*. Houston, TX: Houston Fine Art Press, 1991.
JOHNSTON, Jill, "The World Outside His Window." *Art in America*, vol. 80 (April 1992).
KATZ, Jonathan, "The Art of Code: Jasper Johns and Robert Rauschenberg," in Whitney Chadwick and Isabelle de Courtivron, eds., *Significant Others: Creativity and Intimate Partnership*. London: Thames and Hudson, 1993.
KOTZ, Mary Lynn, *Rauschenberg/Art and Life*. New York: Abrams, 1990.
LEGGIO, James, "Robert Rauschenberg's *Bed* and the Symbolism of the Body," in John Elderfield, ed., *Studies in Modern Art, no. 2: Essays on Assemblage*. New York: Abrams, 1992.
Robert Rauschenberg. Exh. cat., Washington DC: National Collection of Fine Arts, Smithsonian, 1977.
ROSE, Barbara, *Rauschenberg*. New York: Vintage Books, 1987.

14. Master Bedrooms, Master Narratives

HUYSSEN, Andreas, "Mass Culture as Woman: Modernism's Other," in Tania Modleski, ed., *Studies in Entertainment: Critical Approaches to Mass Culture*. Bloomington, IN: University of Indiana Press, 1986.
MEYER, Richard, "Robert Mapplethorpe and the Discipline of Photography," in Abelove, Barale, and Halperin, eds., *The Lesbian and Gay Studies Reader*. London and New York: Routledge, 1993.
POLLOCK, Griselda, "Modernity and the Spaces of Femininity," *Vision and Difference: Femininity, Feminism, and Histories of Art*. London and New York: Routledge, 1988.
ROSE, Barbara, "Hans Namuth's Photographs and the Jackson Pollock Myth, Part One: Media Impact and the Failure of Criticism." *Arts Magazine* (March 1979).
SILVER, Kenneth E., "Modes of Disclosure: The Construction of Gay Identity and the Rise of Pop Art," *Hand-Painted Pop: American Art in Transition, 1955–62*. Exh. cat., Los Angeles: The Museum of Contemporary Art, with Rizzoli Publishers, 1993.
WOLF, Reva, "Portrait as Gossip: Andy Warhol's 1963 Cover Design for *C: A Journal of Poetry*." *Harvard Library Bulletin*, New Series, vol. 5, no. 2 (Summer 1994).

15. Pop at Home

BOURDIEU, Pierre, *Distinction: A Social Critique of the Judgment of Taste*. Cambridge: Harvard University Press, 1984.
CLARK, Clifford, *The American Family Home, 1800–1960*. Chapel Hill: University of North Carolina Press, 1986.
DOANE, Mary Ann, *The Desire to Desire: The Woman's Film of the 1940s*. Bloomington: Indiana University Press, 1987.
EHRENREICH, Barbara. *The Hearts of Men: American Dreams and the Flight from Commitment*. Garden City: Anchor Books, 1983.
MARCHAND, Roland, "Visions of Classlessness, Quests for Dominion: American Popular Culture, 1945–1960," in Robert H. Bremner and Gary W. Reichard, eds., *Reshaping America: Society and Institutions 1945–1960*. Columbus: Ohio State University Press, 1982.
MAY, Elaine Tyler, *Homeward Bound: American Families in the Cold War Era*. New York: Basic Books, 1988.
MULVEY, Laura, "Visual Pleasure and Narrative Cinema," *Screen*, vol. 16 (Autumn 1975).

16. Vito Acconci's Bad Dream of Domesticity

ACCONCI, Vito. Special issue on the artist. *Avalanche*, vol. 6 (Fall 1972).
"Transference Room," "Security Zone," "Conversions," "Remote Control," "Seedbed," "Claim," "Directions," "Openings," "Trappings," "Broadjump." *Interfunktionen*, vol. 10 (1972), 39–53.
"Towards a Theory of Image/Instrument/ Decoration." *Cover*, vol. 2, no. 1 (January 1980), 22–25.
"Some Notes on my Use of Video." *Art-rite*, vol. 7 (Autumn 1974), 2–3.
"10-Point Plan for Video," in Ira Schneider and Beryl Korot, eds., *Video Art: An Anthology*, New York: Harcourt, Brace and Jovanovich, 1976, 8–9.
"High Rise," "Instant House," "Mobile Home," and "Vito Acconci," (edited interview) in "The Exuviae of Time: Architecture as Subject for Art." *Perspecta 18: Yale Architectural Journal* (1982), 100–107.
"Projections of Home." *Artforum*, vol. 26, no. 7 (March 1988), pp. 126–28.
Vito Acconci: The House and Furnishings as Social Metaphor. Exh. cat., Tampa, FL: USF Art Galleries, University of South Florida, 1986.
HORSFIELD, Kate, "On Art and Artists: Vito Acconci [Interview]." *Profile*, vol. 4, nos. 3/4 (Summer 1984), 2–47.
KIRSHNER, Judith Russi, *Vito Acconci: A Retrospective, 1969–1980*. Exh. cat., Chicago: Museum of Contemporary Art, 1980.
KRAUSS, Rosalind, "Video: The Aesthetics of Narcissism." *October*, vol. 1 (Spring 1976), 50–64.
LINKER, Kate, *Vito Acconci*. New York: Rizzoli, 1994.
ONORATO, Ronald, J., *Vito Acconci: Domestic Trappings*. Exh. cat., La Jolla, CA: La Jolla Museum of Contemporary Art, 1987.
SCHWARTZ, Ellen, "Vito Acconci: 'I Want to Put the Viewer on Shaky Ground.'" *Art News*, vol. 80, no. 6 (June 1981), 93–94.
WHITE, Robin, "Interview with Vito Acconci at Crown Point Press." *View*, vol. 2, nos. 5/6. Oakland, CA: Point Press, 1979.

List of Illustrations

Notes on the Contributors

JENNY ANGER is David E. Finley Fellow 1994–97 at the Center for Advanced Study in the Visual Arts, National Gallery of Art, Washington, DC. She is completing her dissertation, "Modernism and the Gendering of Paul Klee," at Brown University. She recently published a review of the current Klee literature, "How Many Klees Today?" in *Revue d'art canadienne/Canadian Art Review (RACAR)*.

MICHAEL CLAPPER is a Ph.D. candidate in the Department of Art History at Northwestern University, Evanston, Illinois. His dissertation, "Popularizing Art in Boston," examines the Prang chromolithograph company and the Museum of Fine Arts, Boston as examples of late nineteenth-century institutions seeking to make art more widely available.

LINDA J. DOCHERTY is Associate Professor and Chair of the Art Department at Bowdoin College. A specialist in American art, she has published articles on Winslow Homer and on colonial and federal portraiture and is currently completing a book on late nineteenth-century American art criticism and American identity.

MICHELLE FACOS teaches Art History at Indiana University. She has written and lectured extensively on Scandinavian painting, and is completing a book on nationalism and cultural identity in turn-of-the-century Sweden.

ALICE T. FRIEDMAN is Professor of Art and Co-Director of the Architecture Program at Wellesley College. She is the author of *House and Household in Elizabethan England: Wollaton Hall and the Willoughby Family* (Chicago: 1989) and of numerous articles on architectural and cultural history. She is currently writing a book about the role of women in the design and patronage of twentieth-century houses, which will be published by Harry N. Abrams, Inc. in 1996.

SHARON HAAR is an architect and Assistant Professor of Architecture at the University of Illinois at Chicago where she is Director of the B.A. in Architectural Studies program. In addition to built projects, her recent writing includes: "Urban Design on the Edge," "Mapping the Modern Landscape" (essays and lectures published by the Association of Collegiate Schools of Architecture) and "The AIDS Holocaust Memorial," published in *Sites 24* (Lumen Books). She is currently working on a book on housing prototypes and the contemporary city based on housing studios in the Lower East Side of New York, a subject she taught while she was Director of the Master of Architecture program at Parsons School of Design.

CHRISTINE POGGI is Associate Professor of the History of Art at the University of Pennsylvania. She is the author of *In Defiance of Painting: Cubism, Futurism, and the Invention of Collage* (New Haven: Yale University Press, 1992).

JOYCE HENRI ROBINSON, a specialist in late nineteenth-century French art, has taught at the University of Virginia, Kenyon College, Davidson College and the American University in Paris. She has written on *fin-de-siècle* French art, Thomas Jefferson and Monticello, and African-American art, and has authored numerous reviews of contemporary art. Her recent and forthcoming publications appear in *Winterthur Portfolio*, *Studies in the Decorative Arts*, and *New Art Examiner.* Presently, she is an independent scholar and curator in State College, Pennsylvania.

SUSAN SIDLAUSKAS is Assistant Professor in the Department of the History of Art at the University of Pennsylvania. She has published on Edgar Degas, J. M. W. Turner and John Soane, and is completing a book called *The Body in the House: Imagining Interiority in Nineteenth-Century Culture.*

KENNETH E. SILVER is Associate Professor of Fine Arts at New York University and Contributing Editor of *Art in America.* He is the author of *Esprit de Corps: The Art of the Parisian Avant-Garde and the First World War* (Princeton University Press, 1989) and is currently working on a book about modern artists on the French Riviera.

LISA TIERSTEN is Assistant Professor of History at Barnard College, Columbia University. Since completing her Ph.D. at Yale University in 1991, she also has taught at Wellesley College and has been a Postdoctoral Fellow at the Getty Center for the History of Art and the Humanities. Her writings have appeared in *Radical History Review.* She is currently completing a book on consumer culture in *fin-de-siècle* France.

NANCY J. TROY is Professor of Art History at the University of Southern California and Editor-in-Chief of *The Art Bulletin.* She is the author of *The De Stijl Environment* (Cambridge, MA: MIT Press, 1983) and *Modernism and the Decorative Arts in France: Art Nouveau to Le Corbusier* (Yale University Press, 1991). She is currently writing a book entitled, *Couture and Culture: Fashion and the Marketing of Modernism.*

ANTHONY VIDLER is Professor of Art History and Architecture and Chair of the Department of Art History at the University of California at Los Angeles. He is an historian and architect whose writings include *The Writing of the Walls* (Princeton Architectural Press, 1986), *Claude Nicolas Ledoux* (Cambridge, MA: MIT Press, 1990) and *The Architectural Uncanny: Essays in the Modern Unhomely* (Cambridge, MA: MIT Press, 1992).

LISA WAINWRIGHT is an Associate Professor in the Art History, Theory, and Criticism Department at The School of the Art Institute of Chicago. She has lectured widely on the art of Robert Rauschenberg and the history of found object art and has published several exhibition catalogues, as well as contributed articles to *The New Art Examiner* and *Art International.*

CÉCILE WHITING is Associate Professor of Art History at the University of California at Los Angeles. She has published *Antifascism in American Art* (New Haven: Yale University Press, 1989) and numerous articles in *American Art, Art Criticism, Genders, Oxford Art Journal, Prospects* and *RACAR.* Her book *A Taste for Pop: Pop Art, Gender and Consumer Culture* is forthcoming from Cambridge University Press.

DAVID VAN ZANTEN is Professor of Art History at Northwestern University. He is a scholar of modern architecture whose publications include *Designing Paris: The Architecture of Duban, Labrouste, Duc and Vaudoyer* (Cambridge, MA: MIT Press, 1987), which won the Alice Davies Hitchcock Award from the Society of Architectural Historians, and *Building Paris: Architectural Institutions and the Transformation of the French Capital, 1830–1870* (Cambridge University Press: 1994).

Index

Page numbers in *italics* refer to illustrations